"To read this book by Leanne Payne is a privilege. It is, and will surely come to be widely recognized as, a major work in spiritual autobiography. This account of her life has been written and prayed through with great sensitivity and care. It is written in the light of Holy Scripture, and is pervaded with the voices of the great classical Christian tradition. These voices have illuminated the depths and meaning of her life and thereby cast their light on us, the reader. While reading, the reader is led, nay practically compelled, to pause and reflect on his or her own life in the light that comes from God in Christ. We begin to share something of the 'steep ascent' of which Leanne speaks.

"This book is a gift that cannot be read quickly; it is far too rich, too penetrating, and too provocative for that. In her preface Leanne expresses the hope that in reflecting upon her story and undertaking the difficult work of writing it down, she will help us, the readers, to discern the calling from God and to God that pervades our story as well. In this she surely succeeds.

"By all means buy this book, and take the time to meditate your way through it."

Rt. Rev. John H. Rodgers Jr., dean/president, Trinity Episcopal School for Ministry, and bishop, Anglican Mission in America, Province of Rwanda

"In this book a great soldier for Christ, wearing the armor of the ages, allows us to see God's faithful dealings with a soul given to Him, and her tender and intelligent responses to heaven's call. How it all works out is a thing of beauty and alarm. You'll need to linger over it, and return again and again, for it to grow you in the power of resurrection life for the spiritual battle which is our age—the battle in which, know it or not, you are now submerged. You'll need to know who the players are and what the available resources are, and here you can get a good view."

Dallas Willard, author, *The Divine Conspiracy*

"A provocative and moving spiritual autobiography that vividly portrays the ongoing struggle of a person of faith toward wholeness and healing. It poignantly shows how the author has been mightily used by the spirit of God to spearhead a ministry of renewal and celebration."

Dr. Donald G. Bloesch, author, *Essentials of Evangelical Theology*

"I am delighted to recommend this fascinating account of an unusually interesting life. This is more than an autobiography, however. Indeed, the details of the author's life—told with great color and conviction—serve as the opportunities to insert deeper reflections on the significance of God's blessing on her life and ministry. I am very glad Leanne Payne did us all the kindness of writing this book. It reveals some otherwise concealed personal dimensions of her other writings. Long associated with the religious movements chronicled in this book, I particularly appreciate Leanne's keen, critical discernment concerning their history. The richness and variety of her interests and reading is simply bewildering. For example, how many 'renewal' Christians have studied the works of Josef Pieper? Leanne has!"

Fr. Patrick Henry Reardon, editor, *Touchstone*, and author, *Christ in the Psalms*

"What we have here is the courageous, candid, and intense witness of a woman whose experience of God has asked, quite simply, everything from her. In chapter after chapter, readers will see what wholehearted obedience to God may cost His servant. It is an extraordinary tale."

Thomas Howard, author and retired English professor

"Each path to heaven is unique. Leanne Payne's account of her journey to date relates a steep and often lonely path, full of rare terrors and beauties. Reading this rich, eye-opening memoir of pilgrimage, one cannot but be grateful for the bravery and frankness of the walker, not to mention the faithful persistence of her Guide. A story of dead ends, rabbit trails, giddy ridges, and spectacular summits, *Heaven's Calling* quickens and encourages one's own steps along the way."

Michael Ward, author, *Planet Narnia*, and chaplain, Peterhouse, Cambridge

"The light from the many sides of this gem lights up social history, family dynamics, church life, the gospel, contemporary worldviews, discipleship, the stark realities of the human condition, and the riches of a living encounter with God. Yet through it all shines the life of Christ incarnate in the life of one who has found Him to be the Pearl of Great Price.

"An amazing story full of great insights, and glorious interplay of theology, philosophy, psychology, pastoral skills, and costly personal journey. Christ-centred, faith-inspiring, life-giving, lived truth."

Canon Robert Warren, author, *The Practice of Prayer*

"What joy to once again read a book written by Leanne Payne! As a Christian friend for over thirty years, I never cease to be amazed—and awed—that she is such a clear channel for the Lord so that her words, whether written or spoken, drive me deeper into the awareness of Jesus within me, His forgiveness, His love, and His healing power, as well as driving me higher to more clearly envision His purpose in my life and to be a more obedient and faithful servant of His.

"Leanne's gifts and ministry have brought wholeness to thousands throughout the world, and I pray that through this deeply personal, soul-searching, and soul-healing book, she will touch many new hearts with a love for Jesus and an assurance He is in every breath we draw. I never leave her presence or finish reading one of her books without being deeply touched—and changed. I pray all will share that life-changing experience."

Joan Francis, past and present trustee for Trinity Episcopal School for Ministry, Episcopal Renewal Ministries, and the American Anglican Council

HEAVEN'S CALLING

A Memoir of One Soul's Steep Ascent

Leanne Payne

BakerBooks

a division of Baker Publishing Group
Grand Rapids, Michigan

© 2008 by Leanne Payne

Published by Baker Books
a division of Baker Publishing Group
P.O. Box 6287, Grand Rapids, MI 49516-6287
www.bakerbooks.com

Printed in the United States of America

Library of Congress Cataloging-in-Publication Data
Payne, Leanne.
    Heaven's calling : a memoir of one soul's steep ascent / Leanne Payne.
        p. cm.
    Includes bibliographical references and index.
    ISBN 978-0-8010-1312-6 (cloth)
    ISBN 978-0-8010-7199-7 (intl. pbk.)
    1. Payne, Leanne. 2. Spiritual life—Christianity. 3. Spiritual healing. I. Title.
BR1725.P325A3 2008
277.3′082092—dc22
[B]   2008017083

To the memory of Mother
and to those generations of family members
who have gone before me,
carrying forth and sowing the golden seeds of the Gospel

Brothers who are dedicated to God, you who are sharers
in heaven's calling, because of all this you must fix your
attention on Him whom our creed holds to be the apostle
and the high priest of God, I mean Jesus.

Hebrews 3:1
William Barclay translation

For the one who runs toward the Lord, there is no lack of
space. The one who ascends never stops, going from beginning to beginning, by beginnings that never cease.

Gregory of Nyssa

Contents

Preface   9

Part 1 1932–1958

1. Hard Times   13
2. God, Our Source and Being   19
3. My All-Time Heroine, Mother   25
4. A Home Brings Us Together Again   31
5. Grandma   35
6. The Influence of My Extended Family   43
7. The Fateful Move   57
8. The Remedial Path   69

Part 2 1958–1965

9. Home to the Father   79
10. The Lighted Path: "The Spirit and the Gifts Are Ours"   91
11. Learning Lessons through Spiritual Battle   99
12. Foundational Lessons   109
13. The Unthinkable Looms: Time to Leave Home?   125
14. Life at Wheaton Academy   133
15. The Birthplace of Renewal   143

Part 3 1965–1976

16. Choosing a Goal   159
17. The Joy of Academe   171
18. Modern Myth with Professor Kilby   189
19. Revival!   199
20. "In the Night My Heart Instructs Me"   211

Part 4 1976–

21. The Search for Home   223
22. Beauty and Truth in the Midst of Spiritual Battle   237
23. An Abundance of Seeds to Sow   249
24. The Year at Yale   263
25. Interlude—Henri Nouwen   273
26. Joy in the Midst of Incorporation   279
27. "For Such a Time as This"   291
28. Jubilation!   299

Acknowledgments   313
Notes   315
Index   325

Preface

Whether you turn to the right or to the left, your ears will hear a voice behind you, saying, "This is the way; walk in it."

Isaiah 30:21 NIV

To hearken to the call of the Lord is, as Gregory of Nyssa said centuries ago, to go "from beginning to beginning, by beginnings that never cease." Born to adversity, we are born as well to listen, to hear God calling us back to Himself, calling us to climb the steep ascent back to heaven, our home. This book is about one soul's arduous battle to overcome her deafness, and then the learning how, through prayer, to help others overcome theirs. Though supernatural and miraculous, this is merely the living out of our baptism into Christ.

Writing the story of my life and ministry has not been easy. There have been many levels to it: the outer and the inner story, the physical, the emotional, and the spiritual all coming into play. In addition, and almost as significant, is the way the multifaceted lives of others have impacted my own.

But more than facing a complex task, I have never wanted to write this book. I've long known it was required of me, for I have seen how women (and especially single women) who have founded Christian ministries have needed to keep the record straight by writing their own accounts. But I feared it would be an overly subjective exercise of looking at my life and experiences, a consistent focusing on myself that would get most unpleasant before the long work of writing a book was finished. Instead, as I have written this book, one surprise after another has greeted me. Before starting, I received prayer that I could focus on Christ in such a way as to be able to tell my story with true-to-reality memory. After this prayer, I felt as if the eyes of my heart were as large as my chest and utterly fixed on Christ. The effect of this has been both wonderful and terrible as we review my life together! It is surely a humbling foretaste of that final day when we will once again meet all our words and deeds.

And, rather than the writing involving simply a focusing on my life at different stages or a searching to recall the past, it has turned out to be a surprising experience of descending, so to speak, back into and through the childhood years. I've been awed at the depth of the remembering and the vividness of emotions, feelings, and seeings that are there in this reliving—and all the more grateful for the perspective and maturity the years have brought.

There have been other surprises as well. Early in the book, I had to take myself very firmly in hand lest I write a book about Mother's life rather than my own because it is so wonderful to "rise up and call her blessed" (Prov. 31:28). She indeed was the shining star of my early life, and my story apart from something of hers could never truly be told or understood. This is true, in lesser degrees, of others, for in John Donne's immortal words, "no man is an island": we live not unto ourselves alone. Like everyone, my story has been uniquely impinged upon and impacted by others.

Other things I have simply hesitated to write, those which are pertinent to the story but which I have found hard to say because of family or other loyalties. We cannot, however, be understood apart from our extended (including ancestral) families: those whose very genes are passed down to us, and whose lives, for good or ill, have so impacted us that we find their expressions in our mirrors, their patterns of living showing up in our own. I've been surprised at the strength of my resistance to writing some few things, and am reminded again why negative patterns remain so long in families—we tend to stay in denial about them because they have never come to light through being spoken aloud, even if only to ourselves.

It is my prayer that sharing my story will open others more fully to their own, if need be, and that most especially it will strengthen many in the understanding of God's call, His ongoing faithfulness to call us into relationship and wholeness in Himself and thereby into His service.

I close this preface with the profound words of William Barclay, the twentieth-century Scottish theologian:

> The call that comes to a Christian has a double direction. It is a calling *from* heaven and it is a calling *to* heaven. It is a voice which comes *from* God and calls us *to* God. It is a call which demands concentrated attention because of both its origin and its destination. A man cannot afford to give a disinterested glance to an invitation *to* God *from* God.[1]

PART 1

1932–1958

Shades of the prison-house begin to close
Upon the growing Boy
But he
Beholds the light, and whence it flows,
He sees it in his joy. . . .

William Wordsworth
"Ode: Intimations of Immortality
from Recollections
of Early Childhood"

1

Hard Times

All the days ordained for me were written in your book before one of them came to be.

Psalm 139:16 NIV

Tragedy struck early in the life of my little family. My most vivid memory, when I was just eight weeks past my third birthday, is that of my young father, age twenty-nine, lying in his casket. Mother, not yet twenty-five, held me in her arms as we looked down on my father's face and upper body (the lower body being covered, as with most caskets). I clearly recall asking, "Where are Daddy's feet?" My mother then turned and fainted as someone lifted me out of her arms.

Life was never the same for our family after August 22, 1935, the day my father died of a sudden onset of encephalitis. The municipal swimming pool in Omaha, Nebraska, carried the deadly germ that killed not only my father but several others who had sought respite from a baking August summer. I remember "swimming" on his back that fateful day, and throughout her life Mother kept the tiny swimsuit I had worn.

In overwhelming sorrow my mother moved to Little Rock, Arkansas, the home from which my parents had fled during the Great Depression. Like many in the southern regions of the United States, they had gone north to try to eke out a living. Thus I was born on June 26, 1932, to my father,

Robert Hugh Mabrey, and mother, Forrest Mabrey (born Forrest Irene Williamson) in Omaha, Nebraska, where my father took two part-time jobs—as an apothecary and as a chef.

I was not an easy infant to nurture nor child to raise. Early on, I was an astonishment to my parents, and later, to my entire family. I had an odd kind of precociousness that outran natural caution at each stage of my development, and it was with me from the very beginning. When only a few months old, I could not be placed on a bed without bars because I would fall off—something unaccountable for in so young a baby. One day, thinking his wife simply had not learned to care for an infant as yet, my father placed me on their bed and said, "Forrest, the only thing you have to do is to take care of this baby." At that very moment I flipped out from under his hand and onto the floor, whereupon we made a quick trip—one of several to come—to the hospital. He never again reprimanded my mother for what neither she nor he could very well handle.

Before I was nine months old, my father was forced to build a screen over the top of the baby bed to keep me from climbing out, even though it had the usual high sides. At eighteen months I managed to escape from an office manager who was in charge of me while my mother paid our insurance. I immediately climbed out a seventh-story window and onto a fire-escape ladder. This had all happened so quickly that no one knew where I was until calls came from an adjacent office building, crying out, "For heaven's sake, get the baby off the fire escape!" It took several squads of Omaha firemen and policemen to do just that, and in the meantime, my mother had to be revived—mere days before giving birth to my sister, Nancy.

Even before this incident, and certainly from then on, I was haltered and reined. That however did not prove to be enough, and so my father decided (at great financial sacrifice, this being the heart of the Depression) to put me in a nursery with real nurses. Oddly and amazingly, I can remember this place. I can see even now in my mind's eye the large room and the other adults and babies—all as a sort of conglomerate to which I distinctly remember having absolutely no attachment. And I can still see the spacious playground outside where I wanted to be. I was utterly focused on two things in that yard; one was a playhouse (like a large doghouse) with a pitched roof that I managed to climb, being in no way interested in going into the small space inside. The other was the big swings, those without bars that the older children used. I recall the strong desire to climb up into them, and the struggle to do so once the last white-coated nurse went inside. Immediately, when my goal was reached, I fell out on my head. My father came and hastily took me back home to a safer environment.

Apparently I could shinny up just about anything and I remember climbing to the top of a kitchen cabinet at an aunt's home. Mother had come down by train from Omaha to St. Louis where her eldest sister and family now lived. She was anxious to present her two infants to this branch of her family and was likely hoping for more insight on how to manage me. It must have taken some time for Mother's sisters to realize the extent of the "problem" with me, but this visit drove it squarely home to all of them. For instance, my Aunt Ellie tried to keep chocolate milk out of my reach by putting it high atop an old-fashioned tall cabinet, one with upper shelves and a built-in flour sifter. I remember managing to get all the way to the top and the milk spilling down to the floor—into a packed and open suitcase.

My father had some of this physical precociousness in his infancy but apparently it did not cause the trouble mine did. Later on, the stories in the family about me were rather hushed—none of them understood such a thing. But all agreed with Mother when she said, "Leanne will never pay for her rearing," meaning, of course, I would surely never reproduce and have to manage such a child.

There seemed to be only one thing I was fearful of, and that was feathers. Beginning with this visit to St. Louis, downy goose feathers were soon pasted in windows and in every high place I might be tempted to climb. I recall one uncle holding me up very high so I could see the places I wanted to climb and be duly warned by seeing feathers pasted there. The warning of course did not sink in. Instead, I reached for the ceiling. Ceilings were high in those days, but my handprints were on ceilings in Aunt Ellie's home—there to be seen for years.

Later on, I was haunted by a truly significant fear. Throughout my childhood I recall seeing Mother faint during illnesses, and the chief fear of my youth was that my fragile mother would also die. The eighth and last child of her parents, she had been born in 1910 before the advent of incubators, weighing less than three pounds. My maternal grandmother told the heart-stopping story of how she had barely managed, with the help of the heat of an old oven, to keep Mother alive. She would cup her hands and say, "Your mother was so small, she could fit into these hands, and into only one of your grandfather's!"

With such an unpromising beginning, it is not surprising that Mother had a difficult time with childhood diseases. After a severe case of rheumatic fever, she remained physically delicate and at times very ill throughout her life. But she was our sole support. The fact that as a widow in the South during the Great Depression she raised two daughters is remarkable.

Throughout the years we tended my father's grave, taking flowers on special occasions. For the first several years after his death, Mother and I would make the long and tiring trek to the cemetery together. I was very young to walk that far and can remember pleading with her to take me, declaring I would not complain when I grew tired of walking. And I did not. The desire to be with Mother, to know she was okay and never to be left at home with Grandma, was strong enough to stave off complaints.

We would sit quietly and rest near the grave, Mother not speaking a word except to answer one of my questions about my father. The response I would often know by heart. She would pray, talking not only to God but, as widows are wont to do, mutely crying out to my father as well. Bereft of his loving strength and wisdom, she earnestly sought help and guidance in the very difficult circumstances we faced. This, I now realize, was one of the ways Mother was working through her intense grief. Because she never cried or spoke of it, she did not know that I was feeling her sorrow very deeply and was internalizing it along with my own. Once I asked her why she never cried. "Some things," she said in her brief, quiet way, "are too deep for tears."

My love for Mother, my need to protect and shield her, was from early on an integral part of my childhood consciousness. I was quick to sense any slight or danger coming her direction and tried to intercept it. It took years to relax my vigil, but it was unnecessary, as my father's death was the very tragedy that turned her toward an extraordinary trust in God. This loss, implacable in its scope and intensity (as only the finality of death can make it), made Mother spiritually strong. From the human standpoint, my father's death was the senseless loss of a promising young life. For Mother, it was the tragic circumstance that moved her toward a remarkable walk with Christ, one that blessed many.

Though by any standard my early childhood days were hard times for the United States and its citizens, and immeasurably more so for us who were so wounded and stunned by loss, my mother and sister and I were not without consolation. We had the comfort and the hope that only Christians can have. Mother's deeper conversion had been underlaid by the faithful prayers and lives of wholly committed Christian ancestors, devout men and women of strong faith. My ancestors, principally Scots and English, came to these shores seeking release from political and religious oppression, and they came preaching and living out their freedom in Christ. Some, in fact, were circuit riders and preached the gospel across the frontiers of our growing country as the immigrants pushed westward. Through our great need, we sensed God's blessing that accrued to us through these devout men and women.

In addition, we had the consolation of a large, jovial, and mostly congenial maternal family surrounding us, themselves the benefactors of this same Christian inheritance. Though Mother's siblings, with one exception, were yet in need of the profound spiritual awakening she had experienced, they and their families were richly drawing on the moral capital of our ancestors. Mother had five sisters and two brothers, and they, together with their children, maintained close family ties, thinking of themselves as a Scots clan. In large part we were. The impress by our MacFarlane and Campbell ancestors on our genes and our character traits seems to have run deep. We loved getting together to feast on good, Southern-prepared fish and game when my uncles had been successful at hunting or fishing, or in leaner times simply with hot coffee, steaming cinnamon rolls, and lots of good talk and uproarious laughter.

Once the talk turned serious, politics and religion were the main subjects. The first was fairly safe since all generally agreed on political matters, but conversations invariably got hot and tense when religious subjects came up—which they nearly always did. These discussions had a deep effect upon me, and not all salutary. Even so, happily for us, especially since we had no means of transportation and would have been isolated otherwise, our house was the meeting place for these lively family get-togethers. This was because Grandma,[1] the doting mother of this clan, came to live with us after my father's death and our return to the South.

It was only many years later that I understood the depth of the emotional wound my father's death had wrought in me. It would combine with, and perhaps even contribute to, my Achilles' heel (impulsiveness), which would result in life-altering, destructive choices. But that is getting ahead of my story.

2

God, Our Source and Being

"Why hast Thou made me thus?" the clay pot is apt to ask the Potter. Why was I such a difficult infant and child to rear? As I have pondered these and other questions in the writing of this book, I have earnestly petitioned God to shine a spotlight on my early years. In so doing I have been deeply struck by several profound truths. The first concerns God, our source.

Why this early physical precocity? The thing underlying these traits surely was a compelling desire to experience the wide, wonderful world outside myself, a part of that strong need to know and to understand that exists to some extent in every healthy, growing soul. But why did I respond to this need so early and so strongly?

A number of reasons could be posited. The first, which I mentioned in the last chapter, is the genetic one. My father had these strong early traits, and I saw them in at least two others in his family as they showed up later in me as a teenager and young adult. Another explanation could be that I was born with food and environmental allergies, which can induce hyperactivity.

One explanation that accords with what I know about myself is that, besides any one of these inheritable tendencies, I must have felt terribly restricted in the womb. Mother, weighing less than a hundred pounds when she conceived, gave birth to a full-term baby weighing almost eight pounds, and it was as though I came out of the womb extraordinarily intent on throwing off these physical restrictions. Later on, these strong, premature impulses manifested in other ways as well.

I believe that all the above had something to do with my early, strong responses, but only since beginning this autobiography do I wonder if something yet more fundamental—and profound—underlies this matter. If so, it is common to all of us, no matter what our genetic and physical circumstances. I have long known that God is truly our Source: "the dust returns to the ground it came from, and the spirit returns to God who gave it" (Eccles. 12:7 NIV).[1] But it was only after I spread out my earliest years before the Lord in earnest prayer that I understood this in a profounder and more literal way: that my genesis, so to speak, was not necessarily at the moment of conception, and that before the foundation of the world, I might have been perhaps more than a thought in the Creator's mind.

These inspirations immediately caused me to wonder if the more basic thing behind my early strong reactions might not have been something deeper than, say, feeling cramped in my mother's womb. Simply put: *it has to be hampering to take on the limitations of time, space, and mortality.*

Could I have remembered a time when I was not so hampered? Speculation—only speculation—but that we come from God we know for sure. On the physical plane, the uniting of sperm and egg is the biological reason for our existence, but as living souls we come down from God (see John 6:38). Much of our maturing comes in learning to balance two competing facts—that we live in a house of clay not only physically but intellectually and psychologically ("For you are dust, and to dust you shall return" [Gen. 3:19]), while at the same time we know that as spirits/souls we are not finite but eternal. We arrive stamped with the *Imago Dei*, the image of our Source, and we know there are shackles to throw off[2] and obstacles to overcome. Although born to adversity, we are born as well to listen, to hear God calling us to climb the steep ascent back to heaven our home.

I find it extremely interesting that as William Wordsworth was recollecting his early childhood, this same literalness stood out for him, as seen in these well-loved lines:

> Our birth is but a sleep and a forgetting:
> The Soul that rises with us, our life's Star
> Hath had elsewhere its setting,
> And cometh from afar:
> Not in entire forgetfulness,
> And not in utter nakedness,
> But trailing clouds of glory do we come

From God, who is our home:
Heaven lies about us in our infancy![3]

While these profound truths have been occupying my thoughts, I am discovering the great mind and heart of Josef Pieper, a Christian philosopher whose works are translated into English from his native German.[4] Here he speaks to this very matter:

> The primordial condition [i.e., before conception], being at the same time the true goal and end of human existence, constitutes the object of man's remembrance as well as his longing. However, both remembrance and longing can unfold only if man, be it ever so briefly, leaves behind the busyness and steps outside the concerns of his workaday world.[5]

Pastor A. W. Tozer speaks of this same knowing in this way: "Deep calleth unto deep, and though polluted and landlocked by the mighty disaster theologians call the Fall, the soul senses its origin and longs to return to its Source."[6]

As I think about these matters on a human level, I find it mind-boggling when applying them to Jesus. I simply cannot imagine how hampering it was for the Creator to descend into His own creation via the womb of Mary and there take on and be limited by human form. Surely the Incarnation is the greatest miracle we can contemplate. Here, as in all things, Jesus is our model and pattern, and we, His created brothers and sisters, do in some lesser way also come "trailing clouds of glory." On finding ourselves in this vast universe, we are at once intensely interested in exploring it while simultaneously hampered and at risk in doing so.

> Therefore, my brothers, marked out for a holy life, who have been made partakers of a call from heaven, fix your minds on Jesus, on Him who was sent forth to make known the faith which we profess and to be its high priest.
>
> Hebrews 3:1 Cassirer

Thinking about our genesis in and through God, our source, has led me to ponder the other matter that, with the starting of these memoirs, has made such an impact on me. I spoke of it in the preface; it is the utter reality of God's call to us. Truly He continually calls us up and out of any state that restricts our *becoming* in Him, or as Pieper puts it, our "orientation toward fulfillment."[7]

Only the greatest of the Christian philosopher-theologians can rightly express our struggle between nothingness on the one hand (that dreadful place of estrangement from God and therefore from our eternal selves in Him) and with eternally being and becoming on the other. From nothing we were created and to nothing we will return if we do not respond to the loving God who is always calling us back to Himself.

And when we do respond to Him, we find ourselves and not only realize our darkened, fallen state, but also know how utterly dependent we are on our Source. The healing, saving virtue of humility is born in those who are moment by moment finding themselves—their reality—in their union with God who is the Real. The summons is heavenward, a steep ascent attainable only by and through grace.

Throughout our lives and at every stage of our becoming, though we see as through a glass darkly, if we consistently love and honor truth, we will have the Spirit-given capacity to know it in all its fullness. By this I mean those things that St. Paul desired would be firmly set into the lives of the Ephesians when he prayed for them:

> that, being rooted and grounded in love, you may, along with all those who are dedicated to God, *have the power to fathom the breadth, the length, the height, the depth of whatever there is,* and to come to know that which surpasses all knowledge, the love of Christ, so as to be filled with all the fullness of God.
>
> Ephesians 3:17–19 Cassirer (italics mine)

That this power to fathom the unfathomable is available to us is especially difficult for moderns to accept, but it is nevertheless true. As we answer God's call, we are led into that goodness and reality that transcends and yet fills all nature as we know it.

God's individual call to me, to my becoming in Him, included overcoming my besetting character defect and sin, which I began to understand was impulsiveness. As I shared in my book *Listening Prayer*,[8] some of the strongest petitioning in my early prayer journals was for wisdom, for I came to see my *impetuous* responses to the need to know and to explore the outer world of my existence as sin. It is one thing to be cramped and limited; it is quite another to respond amiss.

Mother, with not an impulsive bone in her body, often had to say to me from infancy onward: "Child, you must learn to look before you leap." But in my impatience to live I often reversed those two things and had to learn the hard way. I remember almost despairing over this character flaw, it being such a deeply unconscious thing, wondering if God could or would remove my blind spot. Much of it simply had to be outgrown before I could be mature enough to wait before God for full deliverance.

In many ways we all are the product of the biological and genetic strains that have gone into our making, but we have a heavenly Father whose imprint is upon our souls. Made in His image, we have the capacity to hear and follow Him, up and out of any determinism, biological or otherwise. Here is precisely where God's calling comes in: as we obediently listen, He brings us up and out of that which has held us in an immature place or wrongly determined us. This has certainly been true for me.

In respect to my capacity or urge to climb, as an older child between the ages of five and twelve, perhaps in response to strong discipline, at least some natural caution had kicked in and I was more or less normal in this area. I was also most anxious to obey my mother. But I had great difficulty keeping one of her commandments in particular, and it concerned climbing "my tree," as I called it.

It was great for climbing, a huge and beautiful old tree in the midst of the woods next to our home. High up in its branches was the perfect place to lie down and look to the sky. I did some of my best thinking and praying there, guilty conscience or no. Something in me had to climb up there ever so often, had to look up into the heavens and somehow find myself or *be me*, and then pray big prayers to God.

In retrospect it is easy to see what was going on—I was climbing up to a place where I could think my own thoughts, dream my own dreams, fling off or rise up and above the family ethos—something we all have to do to find ourselves. I was differentiating myself from my mother, sister, grandma, and extended family, and God was calling me to do this very thing.

This is not at all odd when one thinks about it. Often in this ministry God has called me to, I find myself calling people forward into the presence of God. For it is here that the *real I* comes forward, as we've learned to express it. As the Scottish theologian P. T. Forsyth puts it, "By prayer we acquire our true selves,"[9] and as a child, perplexed and hemmed in by many things, I had to climb high from time to time to get a new perspective, to pray "big prayers."

To this day, I avoid close quarters. This avoidance does not amount to compulsive behavior or to anything neurotic so far as I can see; I simply love roominess and light and go for it whenever I can. One of the first things I notice when going into a new place is whether or not I can expand my lungs and breathe deeply, and whether or not there is good natural light flooding in. I even modified my house to let the skies in, taking the ceiling out of my first-floor living room and cutting eleven large windows into my roof. Downstairs I also removed a wall to make the space a combination library-living room that is open to the sky. In this way most of the downstairs and all of the upstairs are expansive and fully open to light.

In thinking about my early years, I am reminded of the story of the cowbird, who lays its huge eggs in smaller birds' nests. These tiny parents, then, face the perilous situation of raising what must be to them a monstrous kind of offspring. I was confounded by this story the first time I heard it—thinking how awful that nature has given us such a creature as the cowbird's natural mother, and the resulting situation facing the tiny adoptive birds. My sympathy is all with these latter and their natural offspring.

But truth to tell, it is the baby cowbird with which I identify. Mother, being so different from me, must surely have wondered where such a foundling as I came from. But raise me, she did, and I wouldn't trade her (or the circumstances into which I was born) for any other in the world. I never once in my life wished I were someone else. Indeed, I have never understood how anyone could want to be someone else. Surely we are all so unique, all born with the need to respond to the truth of who we are, where we have come from, and with what we are born to do and become. Many refuse to grapple with this. Perhaps our greatest challenge, and one we ignore to our peril, is that of finding the very large gift that often resides within our very weaknesses or liabilities. And so it was in my case, as I would later discover.

3

My All-Time Heroine, Mother

Everything of a secure or protected nature vanished from our lives with my father's death. C. S. Lewis, who lost his mother at an early age, wrote: "With my mother's death all settled happiness, all that was tranquil and reliable, disappeared from my life. There was to be much fun, many pleasures, many stabs of Joy, but no more of the old security. It was sea and islands now; the great continent had sunk like Atlantis."[1] With the loss of my father, our world slipped from beneath us, and at first we came near to sinking with it too. If there were even any islands left, Mother could not see them.

Our small family, which had barely made ends meet in our adopted city, Omaha, was suddenly back in the South in the worst of this country's Depression with no home, no income—nothing at all. My uncles were often out of work, and what they could find paid the barest subsistence wages. In those days, even with so large an extended family as we had, there were scarcely the means for helping others. We entered into a time when often the basic necessities were missing, and at first we were not even able to stay together. Mother and I were crowded into the home of one relative, while my sister was in the care of our maternal grandmother in another.

It was during this desperate time that Mother, brought to the utter end of herself, was reborn in Christ. And in being found of Him, she found herself as well. It was truly extraordinary to grow up watching this frail little mother overcome the worst of adversities. To my sister and me,

Mother was simply our all-time hero and heroine combined. But before she became this honored person, she passed through an exceedingly dark year or two.

Prostrate with grief, unable to keep her children together, and thinking that they would be better off without her, Mother came very close to suicide. This is not something she would have ever told me, but years later Aunt Maude, her next-to-eldest sister, did. Maude was the one person in the family who had experienced profound renewal in her relationship to Christ. Therefore she was able to hold on to God with one hand, as it were, and Mother, until she emerged from her despair, with the other. Aunt Maude became as a lifeline thrown out to Mom. Once the tempest was past, she became Mother's discipler in the faith, as well as her closest friend and prayer partner.

Mother's despair had been of the deepest kind. It brought her to the utter end of herself and dispelled any illusion that she could make it on her own. She could not have a shallow faith; only a real and present Jesus could save her. All material comfort, all reliance on husband, on earthly support, on help with raising her children were gone. The continent on which she had stood had vanished forever. But in sinking with it, at least insofar as she touched to the bottom of her own grief and despair, she found her feet standing on solid rock. She found firm beneath her the "ground of being" philosophers and theologians are wont to speak of, and holding her, it rose with her standing tall into the light of a new day. She was resurrected in Christ and emerged a new person, one in possession of her soul—a *real* self. She came out of her darkest hour having died to her old self and will, even to all her old hopes and dreams, and found herself immediately as one "separated unto the gospel" (Rom. 1:1 KJV). Jesus was as present and real to her as ever He had been to the blind, the lame, the deaf, the hurting when He walked this earth. Ever afterward she proclaimed Him and His truth to others.

From her new beginning she quickly grew in maturity and walked from that time forth, uprightly and strongly, as the new woman she was. Her reliance would now be fully on God, and there was nothing abstract about her trust. It was moment by moment and day by day, and it brought wondrous results. Nothing could possibly have more greatly impacted my life for the good than Mother's profound conversion into Christ.

I write in some detail about my mother not only because she was both hero and heroine in my young world, and my life's story cannot be told apart from hers, but also because so many people, when I write or speak about Mother, are hungry to hear more. Many today have no idea of what a godly mother is, and they hang onto and remember every word I share about mine.

As C. S. Lewis would have expressed it, Mother was a *mere* Christian, but then we live in a time when the real thing needs description. She was, first of all, a woman of prayer. "Prayer," says P. T. Forsyth in his profound book *The Soul of Prayer*, is "the means for appropriating . . . things as they are."[2] Mother, in touch with the *real*, was immediately aware of its substitutes. When falsehood, cant, or sentimentality intruded into a conversation or a situation, she knew it, and when appropriate, in a brief and surprisingly objective manner, she spoke truth in the face of it.

She was never one to waste words, and when she deemed it not right to speak, I was quick to know this and would ask her why later. She always honored my questions and used these opportunities to teach me. That she was not a "talker" also contributed to her giftedness as a disciplinarian—usually only a word from her sufficed. We knew that all her words carried weight; they counted.

Indeed, I was formed by the Word of God as it came through my mother. She took in the Word of Truth thoroughly, lived it before me, and was expert in passing it on. She modeled the way of prudence and godly wisdom and inspired in me love of truth, because she herself radiated it. Thus in this way I was formed in the faith and given a voracious appetite for the lessons of all of my great teachers since then who have, like Mother, loved Christ and walked in Him as the unique Way, Truth, and Life. I can't remember learning much of great moment in theological studies that I did not learn the basics of first and better at my own mother's knee.

Her special gifting was that of teacher, and this gift was put to good effect both inside and outside the home. Daily as we grew up, she taught my sister and me from the Bible and led us in prayers of thanksgiving, praise, and petition to God. And when she taught, whether my sister and I, the children in Sunday school, or her adult Bible class, the Word of Truth was creative and *did* things.[3] The message she brought was never muddied or hampered in any way by superfluous words. There was nothing dour or stringent in it or anything that lacked joy. Nor was there anything legalistic about it, and so far as I know, she was unconscious of its winsomeness and power. It is my sense that others were unconscious of this characteristic of Mother as well, and simply saw her as quiet or retiring. The fact is, she unaffectedly loved truth, especially as it comes to us in and through the Scriptures, and she reverenced the spoken or written word that embodied and conveyed it. In such a soul, words that at once picture and convey truth do indeed come alive, walking up and down in the hearts of those with eyes to see and ears to hear.

Mother had a keen, discerning mind, and read continually from the great Bible commentators. The full set of Adam Clarke commentaries was a remarkable treasure in our humble home, and through his and other great Christian minds and hearts, Mother gained a liberating knowledge of other times, places, and peoples.

She taught the good, the beautiful, the true—that which is just and prudent, that which is brave and temperate, that which participates in faith, hope, and love. And yet at the same time she merely named evil as we confronted it. She knew it was important to rightly name the vices, and this she did while showing what the counteracting virtue in a soul looks like.

No subject, then, seemed too great or too high for Mother to teach her young ones about, and so she passed on to us the profound things—early. In simple and down-to-earth ways, the hope of heaven, the understanding of the eternal (ontological) dimensions of being, the fact that we are created in God's image and eternal likeness: all these things were passed on to us in words and images we could retain. She had herself done as St. Paul had admonished Timothy: "Take hold of the eternal life to which you were called" (1 Tim. 6:12), and therefore could pass on the knowledge of this in story form, along with the real thing itself. She was a sacramental channel of the presence of God and of a most precious faith and hope.

No account of Mother's life would be complete apart from a description of intercessory prayer as she practiced it, or of her great love of singing. An old rabbinic insight is that "He who prays within his house surrounds it with a wall that is stronger than iron," and her prayer and songs most surely mounted a divine wall of protection about our extremely vulnerable little cottage and lives.

Except when she was ill, Mother sang every day, and we loved it. It was not that she had a great voice—she didn't—but that her heart was chock-full of thanksgiving and praise, which she expressed in song. "One bird in the woodlands singing at dawn will wake the whole forest glade to music."[4] That is the way it was with Mother; her thankful heart assured a light-filled atmosphere. She exuded Christian *hope*, and no matter what the circumstances were, she had joy.

Once her praise and thanksgivings were sung, Mother majored on hymns that celebrated the cross and the hope of heaven. Though she had to be away from the house earning a living the greater part of the day, when she was at home, the house would ring with the songs of Christ's atonement for our sins and of His gracious and loving invitation to sinners: "When I see the blood . . . I will pass over you"; "There is a fountain filled with blood drawn from Immanuel's veins"; "The Old Rugged Cross"; "Jesus paid it all, all to Him I owe." Her voice climbed to its highest untrained reaches when she sang the old favorite, "When we all get to heaven, what a day of rejoicing that will be!" As she sang, the transcendent world became a little more present, and Sis and I often joined in.

Prayer was regular too; Mother closeted herself away to pray. On Saturday mornings she interceded on behalf of the church services the next day and for the Sunday school class she taught. As Mother immersed herself more and more in intercession for others, she would forget herself, and her voice would slowly rise. Then there would be strong crying out to God for the concerns of the church and the nation.

There was not the least hint that her praying was either a legalistic thing or an excessively grueling work. More times than not there was a special sense of God's presence in the home as Mother's intercessions mounted up, and as a child my spirit too would be infused with a spirit of prayer. Though not with her in the prayer closet, I would enter into prayer with her. On a few occasions, visiting playmates did the same—a thing not altogether understood by their parents.

Mother treasured the writings of Andrew Murray on prayer. What he wrote, she lived out before me. Like any working mother who toils relentlessly both outside and in the home, she had little or no leisure time. If anyone had an excuse for not praying, due to fatigue or lack of time, Mother did. But for these very reasons, Mother knew it would be sheer folly to neglect prayer. And real prayer is hard work because it is creative—through it we give birth, as it were, to the will of God, the works of God.

Besides the fact that Mother did not deem intercessory prayer a peripheral matter, she knew what a gift it was—even to herself. Her full trust, even for the most basic necessities of life, was in God alone. She knew and experienced the fact that, in Forsyth's words: "Prayer brings with it, as food does, a new sense of power and health," that it makes real persons of us. Though Mother could not have expressed the following with the finality and authority that Forsyth has, she would have immediately put a firm amen to his words:

> All progress in prayer is an answer to prayer—our own or another's. And all true prayer promotes its own progress and increases our power to pray. The worst sin is prayerlessness. Overt sin, or crime, or the glaring inconsistencies which often surprise us in Christian people are the effect of this, or its

punishment. We are left by God for lack of seeking Him. Not to want to pray, then, is the sin behind the sin. And it ends in not being able to pray. That is its punishment—spiritual dumbness, or at least aphasia, and starvation.[5]

In her intercessions for others, Mother learned something about what love really is and the awesomeness of God's true and even terrible love for His people. She never confused love for others, the church, or the nation, with *feelings* of love for them; she did not turn from the object of her prayers to examine her feelings. She was singularly lacking in such a vice. Nor was she involved with sentimentalism, a dark and dangerous vice that riddles the organized church today and successfully passes itself off as love.

As my mother entered into the ministry of intercession, loving others in this way, she found that the floodgates of heaven opened on her as well. Besides experiencing the most amazing answers to her prayers for others, from time to time she received gifts of pure grace. For example, Mother received a prayer language without petitioning for it—indeed, without knowing anyone else who had the gift. She didn't even tell my sister and me about it until after we too had received gifts of the Holy Spirit. Needless to say, she found her prayer language a great aid in intercessory prayer.

And it was during prayer for others that she experienced the love of God in such a way as to be forever changed and strengthened. She referred to this as a "baptism of God's love." She described it as liquid love that came upon her, wave after wave. Each wave came in vivid colors beyond her power to describe. Love, in its very essence, seemed to wash over and into her, as the Shekinah glory, she said, and it was almost more than she could bear and still live. To the end of her life she wisely shared this with very few people. Such *joy* as this, especially when not at all understood by one's hearers, can dissipate when shared indiscriminately. But it multiplies in its healing effects for oneself and others when rightly garnered and stewarded. All these things she knew because she was a woman of prayer, one who received wisdom from above.

Mother, with little or no protection or security other than that found through Christian hope and faith, was surely a model for what a godly single mother can be. She was, of course, human, and as such had limitations and weaknesses. But in being "*merely*" but thoroughly Christian, she never stopped learning and growing. She did indeed, with and in Christ, "overcome the world" (John 16:33).

Mom's year or so that began in black despair ended in the full light of spiritual progress and hope. She seems to have walked very quickly into the mature stage just outlined. I have no memories of Mother when she was anything less than the woman she was in reality all the while becoming.

4

A Home Brings Us Together Again

About a year after our return to Little Rock, my family came together again when we were established in a house that belonged to Mother's eldest sister and her husband. Aunt Ellie, in hopes of moving her family back to Little Rock from St. Louis once the Depression years lifted, had clung tenaciously to ownership of the home where her children had been born and raised. Once its tenants had left, we, together with Grandma, moved into this house that held within it warm memories and past family history.

Only one neighboring home was close to ours; it lay to the west of us, with a full country-sized yard in between. To the east stood several wooded acres through which a fine creek ran, replete with crawfish and swarms of tadpoles. The back of our house faced south and received the bright sunshine, where we had a good-sized garden. This was cared for by a gentle giant, an elderly African-American man whom we liked very much. His name was John, but he was respectfully known as "Ole John." He would share with us the delectable vegetables he grew in our garden.

My sister and I looked forward to the rare occasions when he would bring along his grandchildren. We would have loved to play with them, but Grandma held us back, so we enjoyed looking at one another instead. I can still see them, peeping from behind a great old tree and smiling at us with wide grins. Firmly held behind Grandma's skirts, my sister and I would smile back at them from ear to ear.

There was little or no noise pollution in and around our home. Only two or three times can I remember hearing our squeaky old radio being played—surely one of the first ever made. These had to do with world-shaking events, the one I most clearly recall being December 7, 1941, when the Japanese bombed Pearl Harbor. Television was yet to be invented, and had it been available, we would not have had a set for the same reason we did not attend movies. Even if we could have afforded to go, on principle Mother would not have taken us because of the immoral and antifamily influences coming out of Hollywood. Therefore our days were quiet, and we were able to hear the birds sing, the bees hum, the frogs croak, and all the other wonderful sounds of woods, creek, and garden. Thus we lived out our lives in this tranquil setting throughout my grade-school years.

The fact that we were three generations of feminine souls under one roof, and to a great extent isolated, forms no small part of my childhood story. Grandma shielded us from Ole John's grandchildren not just because of racial differences but because among them there were little boys. To her, being responsible for our care meant that we were to be fenced in, restricted to porch and yard—most often denied even the wooded lot and creek—and by what she gently but firmly thought little girls should be allowed to do.

I can hardly imagine how different our lives would have been had Mother birthed a son. Grandma would have honored his wishes, for in her world and time, the masculine voice had only to command, and the fence would have come down at least in part for my sister and me as well. From early on, I would have become accustomed to being on the same planet as the male of the species and later would not have been so confounded by gender differences and such things as the masculine "drive toward power." Of course I might never have labored to get to the bottom of such matters or written about them either.[1]

So it was only when the extended family gathered that we heard the voices of men in our little home, and truth be told, their booming qualities could easily intimidate. Men could be unpredictable where the affairs of little children were concerned, so we would often stand back and watch while Grandmother proudly catered to them. Once in a while I'd be asked to go to the piano and play a piece for them, or sent to fetch some drawing or bit of schoolwork for their approval. But for many years men remained to me as foreign and inscrutable as creatures from another planet.[2]

Saturdays were especially wonderful because Mother would be home for a nice, long stretch of time, and together we would sail through the cleaning of the house so she could get to her prayers and preparations for teaching her Sunday school class the next day. With windows wide open, sunshine streaming in, we would be shaking out bed covers, dusting and sweeping, all the while singing and celebrating the story of salvation and eternal life. Later on, in what could only be a miraculous answer to her prayers, we acquired an old player piano with a fine tone, and to Mother's delight I quickly learned to accompany her as she sang the great hymns of the church.

On Sundays, if we were fortunate, we wouldn't have to walk the several miles to church but could ride in a most exciting fashion in "Sister" Orah's old Model-T Ford. It had only a front seat and in place of a trunk, a rumble seat. Of course small children could not be entrusted to a rumble seat that opened up on the outside of a car, so my sister and I would be tucked in on the shelf between the car seat and the rearview window. This was a great spot behind and almost around Mother's neck and that of her friend and prayer partner, the driver of this marvelous contraption. It was a wonderful way to break out of the isolation of our little bungalow and yard.

From our place of comparative quiet and seclusion, we could glimpse another world beyond our front yard. Just across the road from our house was a fenced-in pinewoods that lay at the foot of a baseball field and stadium that was owned and operated by the Little Rock Boys Club. The sport of baseball was alien to us, of course, but those spacious grounds boasted what was for those days a superbly well-equipped playground. Until my sister and I finally gained at least a limited entry into it, we put up quite a hue and cry. We begged, coaxed, and pleaded with Grandma to take us there, but so far as I know, she never once set foot on those grounds. That for her was a man's world.

Eventually a wonderful thing happened. As the Depression wore on, the government began to create jobs for people who had been long out of work. Out of this program came a certain Mrs. Jones, who for about two years took up daily residence in the stadium offices of the baseball field. Her sole concern was to make a place for girls in this sports arena. In due time, Mother paid a visit to Mrs. Jones and liked and trusted her. So to our great excitement we were permitted to go to a place where attention and care were given to feminine delights and concerns.

Besides teaching all manner of arts and crafts, Mrs. Jones also taught games. Mother had taught Nancy and me to play jacks, but at the field we participated in exciting tournaments in which we both excelled. We even learned how to build a safe fire and to cook outdoors in those same woods that fronted our house, using pine needles as fuel and large lard cans as tiny stoves.

While Mrs. Jones became a most welcome and felicitous avenue to the outside world, she was also the teacher who helped me spend happier leisure hours at home. Thanks to her, I soon had crocheting, embroidering, knitting, and other little projects going on when Mother was away. And Mrs. Jones gave me the needed opportunity and direction for play with other children. Grandmother, necessarily in charge of our leisure time, was oddly remiss in all these areas. This was not because of physical limitation, for she had unusual stamina for her age; in fact she had extraordinarily good health. Had she been twenty years younger, things would have been much the same.

Since Mrs. Jones was connected to the Boys Club, she knew all about the annual Christmas program that, besides featuring Santa Claus and gifts of fruit and nuts for the children, sponsored a talent contest. This latter proved most exciting for me because I played the piano in it. I can clearly recall the thrill of winning the honor of accompanying the gathered assembly in Christmas carols. The two years we attended, the already exciting programs were topped off by what dazzled me beyond belief: the movie *Shirley Temple and the Blue Bird* the first year, and *Lassie Come Home* the second. Mother approved of such films as these, and the one movie a year, in concert with the other equally thrilling activities, provided the keenest delight for my sister and me.

All the spiritual and moral blessings of my childhood have borne sturdy and lasting fruit throughout my life. Many of the just plain human needs, however, went unmet. For example, our isolation was for me both blessing and curse. It came with undue restrictions that worked unnecessary mischief where my Achilles' heel—impulsiveness—was concerned.

5

Grandma

Your life is smooth and flowing, or broken over stones of sorrow, or headlong in its impetuosity.

F. B. Meyer

My Achilles' heel consisted in the fact that I was hardly born before I went leaping into life, always ten steps ahead of where I was capable of standing or ought to be. That pattern, changing only in terms of the ways it manifested itself, remained with me. My early life therefore was all of a piece.

Underlying my impulsiveness, and perhaps basic to it, was an even stronger and more constant trait: an optimism that permeated my entire being—spirit, soul, and body. Throughout the years it has never wavered and has long outlasted the impulsiveness. No doubt a great deal of it is rooted in supernatural grace: the Christian virtue of hope. In the natural, however, I was born with a bent toward laughter and joy. The great Austrian psychologist Viktor Frankl writes of one of the last human freedoms we enjoy when all other freedoms have been taken from us—the ability to "choose one's attitude in a given set of circumstances."[1] This freedom was put to good use, for in terms of attitude, I always chose the high road, one full of hope and determination to transcend whatever troubled me.

Meandering through this state of being, however, like a deep underground river in my soul, was the grief and fear of loss connected with the

35

death of my father. It carried with it a sense of the tragic side of life, a knowledge that calamity can and often does occur. This subterranean current of grief also carried with it fears of rejection and even an anticipation of loss, a common reaction of children to the loss of a parent, whether through divorce, death, or personal rejection. The fear that Mother too would die often came painfully to my conscious mind, while in contrast the other losses and fears operated at a subconscious or even deliberately unacknowledged level. It took a long time to admit and come to terms with these fears, none of which I ever shared with Mother or another soul.

Experiencing the death of my father and its effects on Mother, me, and our little family unit left me in need of an understanding and healing that I would not find before adulthood. Of course my father's death brought about not only these underlying fears, but also the outward deprivation of the love, guidance, and protection that only a father can provide. A good father affirms the very existence of a child, the child's *being*, as it were, and that affirmation forms the foundation and context of his or her destiny. As I grew older, the lack of this affirmation would show up increasingly, for if ever a young girl needed a father to stabilize her and lead the way into the greater world, thereby directing her mental, spiritual, and physical energies into the proper channels, I did. Without my father's guidance, the flow of my considerable energies had neither the affirmation nor the proper direction in which to go.

In prayerfully descending back into and through the years of my childhood, I see clearly the exterior events that either helped or exacerbated the inner, hidden current of grief. Two other ongoing circumstances strongly impacted my childhood as well, namely the extended family's reaction to Mother's conversion (which I will explore more fully in the next chapter) and Grandma's odd quirk (which I will explore later in this chapter). These things taken together shaped my early years and, in my coming to terms with them, the person I am today.

I can see that in the writing of an autobiography, the difficulties one either overcomes or forever is stymied by usually stand out and demand top billing, while the more mundane, joyous, and pleasurable things of life get short shrift. It's clear that my story will be no different. It's difficult to include all my little pleasures and triumphs because that which caused me to be stretched to the limit gets full coverage.

In this writing I've been struck anew by how little I missed of what was going on around me as a child, and of how intense I was about much of it. As the author Willa Cather would say, I was one of those "born interested." In my eagerness to learn, I was always drawn toward adults and their conversations, finding negligible so much that held the attention of children my age. This keen awareness alone would militate against a carefree childhood.

Catherine Marshall, in *Meeting God at Every Turn*, said that her childhood "was a crazy mixture of exuberant joy interspersed with moments of fear" and it was a mystery to her why this should be so and "certainly must have been to those around me." She was, she said, "so shy and fearful . . . yet as soon as my father was near, my world was invulnerable."[2] In contrast, my world was at all times vulnerable; the underground river in my soul made it so. Catherine's shyness and fear were named and visible, whereas my grief and fear were not. The crazy mixture that was me must surely have mystified my elders, and no one more so than Grandma.

My maternal grandmother was one of the most sedentary individuals I've ever known, and at her age must have felt the affliction of having such a child as myself in her care. The strongest and most abiding memory I have of her is of her sitting in her rocker or on our front-porch swing with her hands folded in her lap. At times she would have the Bible open, her magnifying glass over the passage for the day, but usually she wouldn't be reading. She would be pleasantly looking off into the distance. Grandma could be happy and full of contentment doing almost nothing.

Outside her family, Grandma had no friends or interests. She had acquaintances whom she greeted pleasantly, but from the distance of porch or yard. She did not take walks, and I cannot recall her going to the neighborhood grocery or even once taking her two young charges onto a bus or streetcar to town or anywhere else. She even retired early from attending church. Yet she was not a recluse. Simply, she cared for nothing so much as being within the circumference of our home and yard, and unless her children took her for a short visit to their homes, here she stayed.

Unlike her daughters, Grandma never had the knack of housekeeping. For her, cleaning was a matter of sweeping a path through the clutter, so, from the first, she was relieved of that duty. Since her cooking mostly consisted in southern frying whatever meat was available, creaming potatoes, making cream gravy with canned milk to go over the lot, and endlessly stewing something green (usually from a can), we were in trouble there as well. My sister relished Grandma's cooking and clamored for it, but after the school nurse informed Mother I was underweight and undernourished, Grandma was also relieved of her cooking chores. With her sedentary life and diet, her lifelong good health is a mystery, but my sister and I cannot ever remember her complaining of so much as a headache or stomach upset!

As I write, I have before me a small, framed photo of her, one so like her that she could step right out of it. It captures the pleasant, even beatific expression that shone from her face and reflects a soul invariably placid and gentle in all its ways. I do not recall even one instance of her raising her voice in anger, and in light of the fact that my sister and I must have tried her to the limit, this surely reveals goodness. Complaining and murmuring were foreign to her; there was not an ounce of gossip in her being.

She did, however, have what every member of her family called an "odd quirk." It caused us all, Mother and me in particular, a great deal of pain and frustration. But aside from this oddity, she simply was more or less passive and dependent on others as though retired from active participation in life.

Anyone who has read L. M. Montgomery's book *Anne of Green Gables* and remembers Anne's early years with Marilla will instantly have a picture of the ethos under which Grandma operated. Like Marilla, Grandma was blind and deaf to the imaginative and opposed to any affirming word coming my direction. Unlike Marilla, this was not simply lest I become vain but, and here we begin to touch on her strange quirk, because she feared I would somehow outperform my younger sister.

Grandma's odd quirk consisted in the irrational way she centered on the baby of the family. All of her children had experienced this oddity. Every time a new infant arrived, the others were more or less dropped and asked not only to serve the baby but to put up with almost anything the child fancied. Mother, being the last of eight, was the only child who had not gone through something similar, but she did not recall her favored position with pleasure or even with her usual sense of humor. This position had had its own problems, one being that it made her a nuisance from time to time. For example, she loved to sing even as a child and she was an early riser. Therefore early in the morning, her singing filled the house. Her older siblings, however, were working hard to support the family after my grandfather had died and they needed their sleep. Nonetheless, Grandma encouraged Mother to do as she liked, and apparently the siblings were so habituated to the family system that they suffered it in silence.

This strange trait of Grandma's, of course, accompanied her into our midst. The particular problem in Nancy's and my situation was that the perspective of additional brothers and sisters coming along was lacking, and so we didn't see this anomaly in Grandmother's character duplicated. As we grew a little older, Grandmother simply set us at loggerheads with one another, no small difficulty either for us or for Mother. Mother, all too aware of the quirkiness of the problem, and the added difficulty it posed for two children alone, attempted to stand against it.

Grandma's trait then morphed into something even more complicated for Mother to try to deal with, something that was not present in Mother's and her siblings' experiences. The fact that Grandma felt it necessary to put me down in order to put my younger sister forward worked mischief in Nancy's direction in that it ignored her own gifts (which were certainly considerable yet very different from mine) and insisted she either have mine or denigrate my gifts.

In response to me, therefore, and apparently seeing my giftings as "putting on airs," Grandma nearly always said and thought all the wrong things. The most hurtful was when she assigned wrong motives to me, for I internalized some of the accusations, fearing they might be true. All Mother's efforts to right this situation were utterly frustrated, and this difficulty with Grandma continued to display itself in a variety of ways.

Years later, in coming to terms with a writer's block, I began to understand what it means to be cut off from parts of one's authentic self, that is, the bents and giftings that are natural to a person but are unaffirmed or perhaps even disaffirmed. The need, of course, is to recognize and validate these gifts and then gratefully accept them. As I did, I gained more insight into Grandma as well and into my reactions to her particular weaknesses.

Needless to say, all these early mishaps God has wonderfully used, for in my own struggle for understanding, I learned how to pray for others who were cut off from valid parts of themselves. Whether those parts concern giftings or even such things as mental capacity or gender identity, I knew that truly in Christ there is restoration and affirmation.[3]

In my grammar school we were blessed with teachers who knew how to impart the basics of reading, writing, arithmetic, history, geography, and so on. Throughout those first six school years, I was seldom if ever restless or bored in class and was at the head of the class when interested or challenged. Consistently I won awards in music and art as well. This circumstance, however, set the scene for what ended in sheer trauma for me, and an ongoing situation with the one teacher in the school in whose presence I was several times literally sick.

The mother of a classmate seems to have been the storm center behind several episodes. This mother apparently saw her daughter as being in competition with me for awards and for good grades, as we scored the highest in the class. My classmate also played piano but in a rote sort of way. Her mother was president of the PTA—the meetings of which my working mother was unable to attend—and for whatever reason, she was almost daily at school. I remember becoming increasingly timid and fearful of her as she questioned me from time to time, leaving me very uneasy.

She was often with "Ms. C," the music teacher who was pretty in a small, pink, fluffy sort of way. Appearances to the contrary, however, she was the one teacher I instinctively distrusted. She related to some of the children in a lilting, saccharine-sweet voice, but to others—including me—hardly at all. She was in remarkable contrast to Miss Polk, the geography-history teacher, who was tall, square-bodied, authoritative, and stern of speech, but whose intelligence and teaching skills made her subjects come alive. She I greatly admired.

Together, Ms. C and Miss Polk were in charge of the daily convocation. This was a time when all six grades met to pledge allegiance to the flag, sing "My Country 'Tis of Thee," hear announcements, and so forth. The horror of World War II was breaking upon us at this time, so we also sang with greatest fervor our national anthem and the patriotic songs of the armed forces. I accompanied at the piano.

One day Ms. C announced that I would no longer accompany the students but that my classmate would, and she asked me to come up front to see her at the end of the class. As I tremulously went forward, Miss Polk, straightening up into her tallest, primmest posture, marched up as well. Casting my quivering presence behind her, Miss Polk mightily accosted Ms. C. Apparently there had been some politicking between the classmate's mother and the music teacher, and Miss Polk would have none of it. She loudly asserted that I would continue to play, and there was no doubt whose will would prevail.

Although I continued to play, I never again felt even remotely safe in Ms. C's presence; instead, I felt a sense of shame and somehow at fault. Oddly and ironically, this situation mirrored the difficulty I had at home with Grandma, though there was nothing alarming about Grandma. I wish I could report that the difficulties with this teacher stopped after this appalling incident, but they didn't. Thus the protracted school situation contributed to the feeling that I was a bit much for some people, and that succeeding too well can get one into a great deal of trouble.

I continued to do well in school, now fully conscious that to do so was to be in competition where certain adults had taken sides, but the greater part of my thoughts and heart were involved with the difficulties the adults in my world at home were experiencing. My home was where history was made and the most important battles won or lost; above all, this was where death and loss could occur when least expected.

These circumstances no doubt helped shape the child that I was, one who thought deeply about things and struggled to express them in words, through art, music, and poetry—all ways guaranteed to get me further crosswise with Grandma as a child suffering with "notions," or even worse, "putting on airs." A child overly concerned with the adult world, who from early on needed to make sense of death, sorrow, and even the world's problems, was simply not a child Grandma could come alongside in a meaningful way.

Though Mother taught and affirmed in us the invaluable spiritual and moral dimensions of life, she did not have the stamina or perhaps even the know-how to introduce us to the outer world we were to enter. What could help us toward firm aims and purposes in education, for example, was missing, as were the more homely, human pleasures, such as social occasions with other families, drives in the countryside, visits to museums and libraries, family picnics, and recreation. Pleasurable pursuits that are conduits for understanding and joy on a purely human plane are the things that most often go begging when mothers work, fathers are absent, and when the twin specters of ill-health and poverty remain as shadows over lives. One of the reasons the hour or so a week with Mrs. Jones looms so large in my memory is that her time was exclusively given to those things for which mothers such as mine had not the means, time, or energy.

For a child such as I not to be challenged in well-rounded ways was to invite trouble. I had an intensely inquiring mind; from early on I needed great books and projects that could properly fill in and balance the training I had in the moral and spiritual. Without these things, I went through my ordeals, small and large, thinking of them mostly in spiritual terms. For instance, when I ran into problems, I believed that *something must be wrong with me and I must try to be a better Christian.* What was needed, of course, was help to understand and react to the difficulties of life in grounded, down-to-earth ways. The matters I struggled with needed to be considered and worked out as the thoroughly human ones they were.

Through my father's death and the ensuing hardships, I learned to so fend for myself that I could not share my emotional problems and needs. I could tell no one about the grief, which showed up in recurring dreams, or my fear for Mother's safety and welfare. Partly due to my need to protect Mother but also to my inability to verbalize these matters even to myself, I never once expressed the grief and insecurity I felt. Mother, of course, did not openly share sorrows or troubles with me, but since I fully intuited them, perhaps I modeled after her in this regard. But the fact is I could not *ask* for help in these matters, and this inability extended to being unable to ask even for necessary things. Thus I was a child locked in with my difficulties from early on. I could talk with Mother about the great external and eternal realities, but I could not talk to her about my gravest inner concerns and fears.

This dilemma could only get worse as I entered the teen years, and it did. Would school counselors have been able to help me? No. Only Mother could have broken through, and she had no understanding of the need or what to do about it. If we could have talked through all these things, it would have made all the difference. As it was, I had to grow up, experience more of life, mature, read, study, and find understanding, affirmation, and healing through prayer. I had to find the proper bridge to the outer world that on the human level my father would have been.

But I've gotten ahead of my story here. First of all, I must tell of my extended family, both Mother's and Father's.

6

The Influence of My Extended Family

We wake up from the unconsciousness of infancy to find ourselves in a world of revolt, and learn that so far as the memory of man reaches back into the past, this conflict has been recognized as existing between man and himself, man and his fellow, man and God.

F. B. Meyer

"Human life is uncomfortable, and it demands to be transcended," I've heard someone say. In prayerfully reentering the experiences of my early youth, I have been amazed at the depth of my remembering and at the vivid emotions that came up. A major surprise for me was that nothing brought more feelings of indignation and consternation than when revisiting the family's reaction to Mother's conversion. Their reactions no doubt reflected a legitimate concern that Mother might become "fanatical"; they found it alarming, for example, that she did not use lipstick or go to movies. Those concerns were not the main thing, however, for my family's reactions reflected a deeper trend in the nation, namely the prevailing winds blowing us in the direction of materialism. This preoccupation with the material would really take over in the late forties as the war drew to a close and we headed into unprecedented affluence—a situation still with us in the twenty-first century.

One would think that in seeing Mother's profound experience of God's love and life and the transformation it wrought in her, her family would be delighted. With few exceptions, Aunt Maude being the chief one, they were not. Watching Mother stand and prevail in the midst of major, ongoing pressure to conform to, in effect, the "christian" world of her family, prepared me for just about every ill the church in the twentieth century suffered.

I learned that to live with any measure of integrity one must enter into mortal conflict with the cultural winds that blow against what is real and true. The family confabs on religious subjects were for me a troubling lesson in contrasts between *living* the Christian life and merely *arguing* about it. These heated discussions, from which Mother stood back (she never argued) and was herself most often the object of criticism, were for me a window flung wide open. I saw not only the thoughts and passions of those who took part, but where these ideas (mostly mixtures of denominational pride and self-serving theological notions that opposed the work of the Holy Spirit), when unrepented, eventually led. As these ideas worked for ill in individual lives, so they did in their churches.

These larger family gatherings occurred only a few times a year, often during holidays. Then our tranquil feminine abode filled with the booming sounds of men's voices and the noise of dearly loved cousins. My sister and I looked forward to these get-togethers with great anticipation. But once the adults settled down to talk, my sister and cousins scattered out to play far away from the adults. Not me. I took great care to be there and remain as invisible as possible lest I be sent away. So I watched as Mother stood alone. Well, not quite alone—everything in me stood hard with her.

In memory I see that loyal and loving clan, replete with an archetypical Scots character or two, in agreement over many things but not religious matters. When all were there, the group included eight brothers and sisters along with their spouses and children. By this time, Mother's siblings attended four different Protestant churches, and the pride and the ignorance that go along with denominationalism would invariably surface. When their father (my grandpa) lived, all had attended his church. Its legalism had perfectly suited his religious views, but eventually all but the eldest daughter left it.

Grandmother's preference was for the "old-time Methodists," and she reverted to them after her husband's death. Things had begun to happen within that denomination, however, that eventually turned Grandmother,

Mother, and Aunt Maude to a group that came together to preserve the holiness tradition. Their particular church, First Nazarene, became a center for renewal and revival in the 1930s, led by the remarkable pastor, Agnes White Diffee. Both as a theologian and a leader, she commanded the respect of even those pastors most adamant against such a strange phenomenon for that time and place—a woman preacher.

Three of Mother's sisters had married men active in the Masonic Lodge, and two of these were Southern Baptists. From their talk and interests, it was fairly clear that the men gathered on Sunday mornings more as a fellowship of Masons than as Christian disciples. Their spirituality, therefore, was at this point in their lives either missing or gravely weakened. And in fact among them was a spirit of unbelief that strongly militated against the work of the Holy Spirit and also affected their wives and children. These families were the most voluble in their opposition to what was occurring in Mother's life.

Though Mother attended First Nazarene and taught there throughout her life, she was never denominational in spirit. She numbered among her prayer partners those from the sacramental as well as the holiness tradition. Had the renewal of her day been in the High Church, she would have been with them. This is not to say that she fully understood the implications of the loss of the sacramental dimensions of worship in the church she attended, but she regretted the lack of a more balanced liturgy, worship, and order. She knew the more objective opportunities this balance provides for looking steadily up to an awesome sovereign God, the Creator of all, which in turn causes us to acknowledge our own creatureliness. She had an intense distaste for the wrong kind of subjectivity, for "the flesh" getting into things; that is, excess and ungoverned emotion standing in the way of the solid content of truth that brings with it authentic feelings and the capacity to forget oneself in the worship of God.

The aunt I was closest to, Rhoda, and her husband, Gus, were Lutheran, and as a young adult, I attended the Lutheran church with them. Though I shall be forever grateful for the holiness tradition and much of the preaching I heard as a child in the Nazarene church, I hungered for protection against the subjectivism (and the resulting legalism) into which renewal movements in informal churches are apt to degenerate. From early on, I was starved for beauty and for symbol in worship, for a fully sacramental understanding of Christian reality that can only come with the right order of a full liturgy.

This then is something of the mix of people who would gather around an old potbellied stove where a pot of steaming coffee sat alongside homemade cinnamon or pecan rolls, a rare extravagance in those hard times. Religious topics never came up first, but once they did, the most voluble of my aunts and uncles would boisterously proclaim their beliefs, mainly those reflecting negatively on Mother's. In their view, she was the baby sister to be straightened out. Although the contested denominational issues were the thing enthusiastically and loudly expounded, all this was done with genuine civility and wholesomeness. Nothing even approaching the hint of evil or of coarse speaking entered the discussion. Nor was there any judging or gossiping about individuals. However, typical regional prejudices not only entered in but had free play.

Though Mother seldom entered the fray, when she did speak, it was effective. Any statement she made came with a finality difficult for even the most argumentative to withstand. So far as I could see, she would not be in the least discomfited by all the talk, even though she was the one whose practices and beliefs were nonconforming. With a smile or an appropriate gesture, all that was said would simply roll off her like water off a duck's back. It didn't quite roll off mine, however, for I lacked the realization then that she won every debate simply by standing, by *being,* in the truth.

Though I perceived these arguments as an attack on Mother, I had respect and love for even the most vociferous of these family members. Perhaps this is because Mother loved and respected them, never once speaking ill of them. I especially admired her sisters, who were conservative and yet laughter-loving and gregarious. I believe that my grandmother's lack of an inquiring mind or strong personal interests gave unusual scope to her daughters, who, unlike her, were full of initiative and free to develop. Superbly endowed with Scots practicality and good common sense, they were souls completely comfortable with themselves. Self-acceptance for them, either as persons or as women, was not an issue. They were remarkably whole individuals.

My uncles, however, were much more of a mystery. I knew Mother's brothers and brothers-in-law were faithful, hardworking husbands and fathers. Only a generation removed from the farm, they were blue-collar workers. Not a single one expressed aspirations toward higher learning; they even seemed prejudiced against it. This, in light of the family history, came apparently through two ways. Their long experience of poverty was one, for it seemed to have removed even the possibility of university training from the realm of their imaginations. But I do not believe that was the chief cause. Our progenitors who settled this country had known famine and hardships, but from copies of their last wills and testaments, along with what I know of their Christian vision and accomplishments, I am assured that they were not afflicted with this prejudice against higher education. The deeper reason lay in a lack of vision for personal participation in the country's educational, civil, and social institutions, which had rendered my family more or less isolationist. I believe this frame of mind, together with regional racial prejudice, was one of the dread effects of the Civil War and its aftermath upon many in the South. The racial prejudice contrasted with our forebears' attitudes and marked a degeneration of Christian thought and practice.

Mother was three years old when her father died, and she had no memories of him. Whenever James Monroe Williamson's children spoke of him, they usually told of his strictness with himself and with them. Yet they revered their father's memory. Though Grandfather was stern, legalistic in his faith, and strongly authoritarian with his children, his love for God and his children seemed to have compensated in part. His father, also a godly man, had been taken captive in the Civil War. Likely this experience contributed both to his father's early death and to his own sober and rigid response to life.

When she was a young girl, Grandmother and her family moved to Arkansas from Missouri. They were descendants of the Townsends, MacFarlanes, Campbells, and Arnolds and passed on a rich store of ancestral tales about family and land connections in England and Scotland, though they had long since lost touch with relatives there.

My grandparents met and married in Scott County, Arkansas, where Grandfather farmed, but he soon turned to operating a wood mill in Perry County. Shortly before he died, he brought his large family to Little Rock. As a widow with dependent children, my grandmother was supported by her older children, particularly the eldest son, and later my mother after my father died.

The struggle to survive and raise a large family was no small one for my maternal grandparents, and their faith sustained them through all of life. They passed on many tales of the Civil War, being only a generation removed from those who fought in it. They, of course, experienced the worst of its aftermath and were consequently affected by it, as were their immediate descendants, all my aunts and uncles.

With so many years of counseling others in distress, I know how few modern children can grow up with the vital moral certainties I had as a child. That Mother would speak the truth, even under threat of death, I knew; also

I knew that I could depend upon the veracity of every word—if not every interpretation—coming from Grandma and the family around me. That Mother and Maude had that extra something called divine wisdom and discernment I also knew, and therefore I treasured and sought their insights. These came as precious gems to be stored away in my heart, and their wisdom illumined all of life for me. They understood life's vagaries and ambiguities, the fact that at bottom life is tragic, though it holds great joys in the present and even greater hopes for eternity. They knew that good is objectively real and can in no way be reconciled with evil. They knew that with the help of God we can line up our lives with the way things really are. They understood the many ways good and evil impact the soul, and therefore the prime necessity of disciplining and guarding oneself in spirit, soul, and body.

Besides the fact that I was growing up with, in effect, a thoroughgoing Christian anthropology, I also could count on the fact that, except under the rarest circumstances, marriages stay together, that one would walk a weary mile to pay back a penny owed to another, and that those around me would act with courage, justice, and temperance. All these things I took for granted. They were part of the great Judeo-Christian moral inheritance accruing to us from our ancestors.

Yet fissures were beginning to appear in this foundation as the spiritual base underlying the moral good was slipping out from under some family members. In my family's reaction to Mother's conversion, I saw what would show as cracks in the next generation, and greater rents in yet another. Materialism had crept into our families on the back of a long and terrible Depression that had itself come on the heels of years of deprivation and hardship following the Civil War. There was yet, of course, the crying need to somehow survive the Great Depression—simply to stave off starvation. Even so, the highest aspiration of the men was no longer spiritual, not even noble. Though honest and manly, it was just to bring in the highest salary.

As the Depression eased and with the start of World War II, they attained their goals. To finish high school was a privilege denied the older siblings, but Mother and three of her sisters did. However, not one in the generation of all my mother's family (cousins to seconds and thirds included) aspired to the ministry or to the mission field or even to something altruistic. Here we were, descendants of families whose first allegiance was to serve God, but except for Mother and Maude, the family no longer had the vision. This condition was at the heart of what was going on in these religious confabs where Mother was called to stand her ground.

Since all were churchgoers, the materialistic values that crept in had taken on a "theological" overlay of sorts and thereby seemed sanctioned.

The bogus mostly showed up as a decadent Calvinism that was often wont to shout "once saved, always saved," while comfortably accommodating itself to the values and prejudices of the culture. This illusion of cheap grace was easily maintained because their churchgoing was safe from any exposure to an actual move of God. Under a new and truly terrible teaching that had filtered in, the work of the Holy Spirit was steadfastly and even angrily denied. This teaching maintained that the gifts of the Holy Spirit are not available to this age, to this "dispensation." Such a teaching conveniently enabled its adherents to conform to materialism. For them there simply was no Christian supernatural by which to be interrupted or embarrassed.

In contrast, Mother's allegiance was to a God who, when rightly worshiped and invoked, quite regularly and drastically interrupts lives. She knew the glory of God, His manifest presence, and that He is still active in the world today, redeeming people, healing them, ennobling them. So she refused to come under their "theological" overlay; such a place was far from the country and the air where she now lived and breathed.

As Mother and Maude wholly gave themselves to Christ, they threatened the secularization that was taking root in the family, even as in the nation. Though they were women (which prompted family theological debates as well), they were their generation's teachers of the Word and missionaries to the lost. What they had received from God, they freely and sacrificially passed on to others, whether in the prisons, the asylum for the insane, or the unwed mothers' home.

From my earliest years, then, I've had my eyes wide-open to what it means to be in a church, proud and comfortable with one's moral goodness, believing in a "God" from whom not much was expected and whose manifest presence would be welcome only if it came in a predictable way. What had happened to Mother of course flew in the face of all this. From the time I was five or six years old, I saw the shallow and false religious sentiment for what it truly was, because year after year it was set forth in full relief by one small, frail woman whose light shone all around me. This ended years and years later with deeper conversions for most of the family members, and with even her most formidable opponents referring to her as "a spiritual giant." And that she was—a very humble but gifted one. I stand on her shoulders.

While interacting closely with my mother's family, I had on the edge of my awareness the existence of my father's family in the same city, one that we visited several times a year. From time to time these visits included our other set of young cousins along with the extended paternal family, always a special treat. For me the most compelling thing was the hope that our half-sister from my father's previous marriage, Dorothy Alice, would be there as well. That happened only once or twice. When as usual she was not there, Grandmother Mabrey or Aunt Willa would whisper a word or two of news and show us the latest picture of her. Alas, I was grown before I really got to know her, and then we had only a few years, for like my father she died at age twenty-nine. Had our father lived, we would have known this side of the family more intimately, and as a child I sensed the ineffectiveness of the adults' attempts to bridge this gap. However, I saw myself in them and they in me, and even then knew something of their contribution to who I am.

Father's family, like Mother's, were of Scots and English extraction, but on my father's side the English blood and traits heavily prevailed. Both father's grandfathers were ministers, as were a good number of their sires before them. Uncles and cousins in this family were men of the cloth as well. It is a blessing to meet relatives descended from them and to recognize in them the vital, stalwart faith of our ancestors. This family had before the Civil War been people of means. Grandmother was college-educated—an exceedingly rare thing for her time and place—and had taught school before she married.

Life had been difficult for Mother and her family, but they were familiar figures to me and were by nature self-revealing. My maternal grandmother was an uncomplicated countrywoman who asked nothing more than to have her children about and the family Bible within reach. She was by no means a tragic or mysterious figure to my mind or imagination. But Grandmother Rose Fulton Mabrey was. So were her surroundings. It is hard to say which inspired the most awe in me, she herself or the home she inhabited.

In my memory she stands out as prim and proper, with modest, sensible attire. I especially remember her as dressed for church in a dark dress with a dainty lace collar. In the summertime she donned immaculate white gloves and hat as well. To me, she was not so much the Southern lady as a proper English one. Though she was invariably gentle and loving, an austerity about her always put my sister and me on our best behavior.

Part of the reserve my sister and I felt was due to the more formal atmosphere surrounding this grandmother, something our paternal cousins were used to. Mother's sister Grace never tired of describing my father, always drawing a contrast between his family's "Englishness" and our "Scotsness." Aunt Grace thought Father was especially handsome and admirable and on several occasions mentioned that he had an infectious laugh, a well-modulated and even a musical voice, and a delightful chuckle. She hinted that my voice and laughter might take after his, so her words came not only as a welcome glimpse of my father, but as a thrilling hope that I might be like him. He was, she said, "a man's man—what another man would consider a man, *but* . . ." and this word she emphasized in order to draw out the necessary contrast with "our" family, "*he did not laugh uproariously.*" He also, as she told me, would reprove Mother for going at a fast clip, saying to her, "Forrest, ladies walk; they never run"—not a notion that ever fettered Mother or her sisters. Unlike the clan gatherings surrounding Grandma Williamson then, any time the Mabrey/Fulton family gathered, whether for dinner or tea, there was a lovely bit of ceremony to go with it, along with the full complement of Grandmother's exquisite heirloom china, silver, and linen.

But Grandmother's more formal and reserved nature was not what I sensed as tragic about her; indeed, this reserve was deeply authentic to the person she was. Rather it seemed to me that things had gone terribly wrong for her, and that somehow, unlike my mother, she had been unable to set them right. The elegant but impoverished old mansion she lived in seemed to reflect all this.

The house was never owned by the family; the family home and much else had been lost and left behind when she and Grandfather Mabrey moved their young family to Little Rock from Missouri. This old manse had been her home, however, since long before I was born, and my father had grown to manhood there. Remarkably, Grandmother's family heirlooms, from life-sized portraits to plantation silver, fit as though original to this house. The manse stood, as the crow flies, no more than a mile from the Arkansas state capitol in Little Rock. Before the Civil War, it was the heart of a plantation, and some of its grounds yet remained when I was a child.[1] French in architecture, it was three stories high, counting the mammoth attic that topped the two high-ceilinged floors beneath it, four if one counted the underlying netherworld of the basement.

Simply to walk through Grandmother's front door was to enter the past, a bygone era that was at home with oversized oak furniture and even a large spinning wheel. Once in the front door I would automatically gaze down the great hall that originally ran the full length of the house. The wonderful thing about this hall was that its walls were actually oak panel doors and could be pushed back, thereby opening up the drawing room-living room on the one side and the library-dining room on the other. That left the entire first floor free as an elegant ballroom for its earlier inhabitants. The original chandeliers from pre–Civil War days remained, as did the splendid oak parquet floors. The only occasion on which I clearly recall the great hall doors being pushed back will forever be etched on my memory, for it was the day of my father's funeral.[2] He lay in state there under the life-size oil painting of my great-great-great-grandmother, Elisabeth Hammond Long.

Grandmother's family had known wealth and accomplishment, and her life seemed to reflect the corresponding falls and tragedies to which such a family is heir. She buried four of her six children: a son at age two, my father at twenty-nine, and then two of her beloved daughters in their early midlife. She had been inexplicably and tragically alone in raising them, and then she saw all six of her grandchildren half-orphaned through these early deaths. These personal losses were suffered in this house and were part of its history. Even with the almost unimaginable toll that these losses would take on a mother's heart, what I sensed as truly tragic, though, was Grandmother's unspoken *regret*, stoically borne—regret at having disobeyed her family to marry my grandfather.

Against her parents' will, she eloped with him and was disinherited for a time, according to the custom of that day. Her family's wisdom quickly proved right. Although Grandfather was from a highly respected and devout Christian family, my great-grandparents must have recognized something amiss with this particular son's character.

Grandfather was born in 1867 and christened William Thomas Mabrey. His father, Henry Yeakley Mabrey, served for many years as county judge of Wayne County, Missouri, and was also a Baptist minister. Rev. Henry Mabrey was a remarkable man whose many accomplishments included a ministry of healing of families torn apart during the Civil War, something almost impossible in his time.[3]

So my grandfather had much to live up to in his family and apparently decided not to try. He was the "black sheep" in a Christian family of achievers, and unlike his own siblings, was throughout his adult life oddly indolent and ineffective. He, like Grandmother, was college educated and for a time taught school in Missouri.

Grandmother Rose's family, though no longer people of means as before the Civil War, relented fairly soon after her elopement and endowed her with cattle, family heirlooms, and I believe some land. This proved to be a mistake, for Grandfather quickly went through the inheritance. Destitute, he moved his family to Little Rock, where his wife and children, because he did not support them, experienced the direst poverty. Grandmother never divorced him, but they separated when my father was quite young.

She made the barest of livings renting out sleeping rooms to night nurses in the antique mansion.

I saw Grandfather two or three times and shall never forget the first. I must have been seven or eight and was stunned by the news that he was coming—it was as if I were about to learn something of my own father. When he finally arrived at our door, I tried terribly hard to gain from him something of what his son had been, gazing with all my being upon this handsome old gentleman, but nothing of my father was to be found. Afterward I must have voiced my disappointment to Mother, for she tried to comfort me by telling me that my father had been disappointed and terribly hurt by him. Then she quoted from 1 Timothy 5:8, that if any provide not for his own, and especially those of his own house, he has denied the faith and is worse than an infidel. I remember being sort of frozen in sympathy and horror for this poor old man, as was Mother.

Grandmother, had she returned to Wayne County, Missouri, where the large families of the Mabreys and Fultons lived, would have been happier, it seems to me, and surely her circumstances would have been easier. But I believe that she did not move back because she felt she had, so to speak, made her own bed and would lie in it. So Grandmother Rose, courageous even as my mother had been, did not have the comfort of her siblings and their families near. She had long since conquered anything impulsive in her nature, but was fated to see it later in some of her offspring, myself included. Her one surviving son, Uncle Fulton, no doubt broke her heart when he ran away at age fifteen to fight a war on foreign soil.

Willa, the oldest of Father's sisters, was quite unlike any other member of the family. She did not marry and leave the old house but seemed almost to have been swallowed up into it. She was fascinating in her reclusiveness in that she retired to the mammoth attic and built walls around one corner of it—her own hidden little nook staked out under the high overhanging eaves. As the eldest child, the adversities of the family had fallen too strongly upon her, and this partial retirement from the world seemed to be the result.

Though she went out occasionally, or sometimes brought in a group of Sunday school children for classes, she was a semirecluse. Women like her show up almost as a type in English literature: for example, the character of Cousin Mary in Elizabeth Goudge's extraordinary novel *The Scent of Water*. In her nervous kind of way, Aunt Willa loved the children of her siblings and usually had a Christian lesson for our benefit. Not one of those do I remember, but I will never forget one thing she said to me with surprising fervor and passion. I was with her in the great old attic, awed by the huge water barrel that once provided the house's "running" water and was at the same time looking into the fierce countenance of a stuffed owl when she suddenly burst out, "Leanne, don't ever marry a German! Our blood doesn't mix!"

I was too stunned and immature to ask her what she meant by this, but did manage to find out that she did not believe that Scots-Irish (Celtic) ancestry mixed well with the Germanic. Long before I was born, she had shocked the family by leaving her husband-to-be quite literally at the altar on her wedding day, and I wondered if this poor humiliated man might not have been German.

It took me years to figure out what she was saying, and now I think I know. Though English in manner, she was in thrall to the Celtic emotions and intuitions that were unintegrated in her personality. I believe she was trying to figure out the whys and wherefores of this rift between head and heart that so afflicts moderns and separates the headier types (possibly in her mind, the German) from the more intuitive souls. This was something, of course, with which I would later be so greatly preoccupied.

Etched in my memory is another incident that has to do with the huge basement. It was securely padlocked, and we never entered it. This sparked great curiosity in me because it housed interesting, shadowy shapes and a territory waiting to be discovered. From the rear of the house, some of the basement could be barely espied through windows that had not been cleaned from the inside in almost a century. One day the time finally came when Grandmother took up large keys, opened the door, and down we went. To my astonishment, this had been the slave quarters and the original kitchen of the house, the place from which the dumbwaiters, filled with delectable plantation dishes, had at one time risen on their pulleys to the dining room.

For some reason, these quarters had been preserved exactly as they had been on the day the slaves left. There was undoubtedly confusion and hurry, for pans and huge utensils were strewn on the floor. The whole history of this house seemed yet to live in it, ours superimposed on the earlier, and I was never able to find out why the owners decreed that things should be left as they were.

Perhaps the greater mystery is why Grandmother lifted the veil that once. The basement and all it contained were never again mentioned. Why was Grandmother so reticent about such an unusual situation? Surely the early history of this house permeated it. Did she, I wonder, realize this? I think she did. My father's family did not share the North/South prejudices common to that day and region, and she likely took care not to broach the subjects that were all too liable to come up with such a discovery.

In the plethora of material I have on my father's people,[4] the thing that stands out starkly—as it did with my mother's family—down through the generations, is their Christian faith. They too were a people vitally committed to the will of God as revealed in Holy Writ. Both sides of my father's family were clergy families and descendants of pastors and vital Christian leaders. There was the same Christian orthodoxy as to be found in the history of Mother's family, but unlike her family, it did not end in the type of narrowness that tolerates isolationism. My father's family maintained an ongoing commitment to education, the liberal arts, medicine, and law and did not isolate themselves from professional vocations or from civil and social institutions. They too, however, suffered greatly in the Civil War and its aftermath and encountered vocational restrictions in the following financial depression.

In the marriage of a man and woman, two spiritual, moral, historical, and genetic histories come together, and these histories, mind-boggling to study in themselves, converge in the most phenomenal way of all in and through their offspring. The enormous task for the infant, of course, is to overcome the problems inherent in such a heritage and to take full advantage of the gifts that come with it. The more one thinks of the spiritual, intellectual, psychological, and physical implications of this in the child, the more wonderful and terrible it all seems. To know even a little of one's genealogy, say, for example, just the past two generations, not to mention the past several hundred years or so, is to be overwhelmed at the magnitude and the variance of the "strains" that have gone into one's making.

The way these differing strains were to be integrated and worked out within my teenage soul would be, as we shall see, far from ideal. I had a few large lessons to learn the hard way.

7

The Fateful Move

It will always help us if we regard this world as organized not for our comfort but for our training.

William Barclay

Shortly after I graduated from grammar school, around my twelfth birthday, we moved into a tiny apartment nestled in the home of our beloved Aunt Rhoda, the sister next to Mother in age. Aunt Ellie had quite despaired of getting her family back to Little Rock, and so our abode beside wood and creek finally had to be sold. Though it was likely Mother had little choice as to where we would move, there were a number of positive reasons for going where we did. Three of mother's sisters lived with their families within two blocks of one another, and the house was situated on the streetcar line, important for commuting to work, church, and our new schools. But perhaps the most pressing reason, and one that went unstated, was that Mother hoped to find moral support and encouragement from her sisters in regard to Grandma.

The main problem with this move, one that for me ultimately proved insurmountable, was that it limited us to extremely small living quarters. To make matters worse, there was only a strip of yard—there was no garden, not even a basement or attic to retreat to, and no forbidden great tree or creek bed where solitude could be found.

The apartment consisted of two small rooms with a bath and a side porch converted into a tiny kitchen. The one bedroom was crammed with two full-size beds, a steamer trunk for storage, a dresser, and a chest of drawers. Absolutely nothing else could be fitted into it. The treasured piano now crowded our small living room. No one had any private space. Oddly enough, this did not seem to bother my sister, but in me it not only stirred up my old reactions to being closed in—no small difficulty—but also greatly aggravated my difficulties with Grandmother.

From this point on, I seemed to have no resting place, no home. C. S. Lewis describes this condition when he writes of life at Campbell, the second boarding school he was sent to as a young boy:

> From my point of view the great drawback was that one had, so to speak, no home. Only a few very senior boys had studies. The rest of us, except when seated at table for meals or in a huge "preparation room" or evening "Prep," belonged nowhere. . . . One was always "moving on" or "hanging about"—in lavatories, in storerooms, in the great hall. It was very like living permanently in a large railway station.[1]

How Lewis would have reacted had he remained longer than one short term we will never know, but it took me three years to devise, albeit unconsciously, a way to burst out of my confinement.

I still looked forward to weekends with Mother, although with the move our Saturdays changed; now with Bible and commentaries in hand, she walked the two blocks to Aunt Maude's home to find the privacy to pray and study for her Sunday school class. Now on the weekdays I would come home from school and stand outside the house, dreading to enter. The thought of going in and facing Grandma with no place of my own was utterly depressing. To have had even a tiny portion of a room somewhat cordoned off, a desk for my books, a closet, or even a dresser that was not shared with three others would have helped in this critical period after the move. Emotionally for me it was a necessity.

My sister and I still had strict boundaries around our activities, but I found a way around them through earning money. I secured every job possible to a twelve-year-old—beginning with babysitting, which for me amounted to being paid to hang out in other people's homes, and within a year I was working several hours a week at the corner drugstore. My ingenuity in finding and learning different jobs was thought quite remarkable. No one seemed to know what lay behind this extraordinary energy.

Nor did Mother understand why, when she would give the reasonable time to come home from visits with friends, that I almost invariably went over time. She sensed I was compliant and wanted to keep the rules, so it simply didn't make sense to her, or to me, that I couldn't or wouldn't watch the time when I knew full well that my behavior would result in my being grounded—restricted to the tiny rooms. I could no longer enjoy playing my beloved piano, at least not for long. Mother apparently had no idea of the emotional trouble I was in.

Things were finally easing up for her a bit, as with the rest of the country. With the end of World War II, she was no longer working the midnight shift at an army installation and had managed to find work as a clerk in a Civil Service office. Jobs and opportunities in the South, for the first time since the Civil War, were opening up. As a consequence, my fears and concern for her were dissipating. This meant I could have "bothered" her with what was troubling me—if only I could have understood or imagined what it was. I remember desperately wishing I knew what to say to Mother when she questioned me about being late. From the time we moved, I simply yearned to be somewhere other than home—where, I didn't really know. But that is not something I ever once intimated to Mother.

Adolescence is the period when we are least capable of imagining the best way out of difficult circumstances, and this of course is the root of teenage suicide. On his own the troubled adolescent cannot envision that things will change, much less for the better. He has entered that sensate, autoerotic stage in which the "feeling being," at the mercy of rapid hormonal changes affecting the mind as well as the body, lords it over his higher and more authentic ways of knowing. In such a time, it is common for youngsters to make statements such as, "Where are you, God? I don't *feel you.*" It is a time in our lives when our parents must point to and light the way for us. They can see the light at the end of our tunnel, and blessed are we if they realize that at this time we cannot.

In this period, thoroughly uprooted from the school and home I knew, I did not successfully put down new roots. The background of our lives had shrunk to such a diminutive size and solitude was nowhere to be found. Understanding that these two conditions could play such a big part in my profound unrest was simply not available to my adolescent thought processes. The fact that these circumstances were added to the main thing missing, a father to affirm and point the way into the future for his daughter, was perhaps the proverbial straw that would break the camel's back. If we had not moved, I would still have had a rocky adolescence, but undoubtedly the uprooting and crowding had crucial ramifications for a child such as I.

It is true, of course, that if I had been a better, wiser child, I would have done several important things differently. For starters, I would have loved

Grandma better and overlooked her foibles instead of coming to see her almost as a symbol of the quiet desperation I felt on entering our home. But that was not available to my understanding either—it simply did not occur to me. What did occur and was ever present to my mind was the thought: *If I were a real Christian, I wouldn't be like this.* That was the way I interpreted the feelings plaguing me.

These feelings were simply human ones that had arisen in response to legitimate human needs. Human answers could have been found, but locked in with the difficulties I faced, I could only spiritualize them. I've come to speak of this condition as an *experience orientation.* No one before or after C. S. Lewis explains it as brilliantly as he. It is, he says, an attempt to repeat one's experience, striving to "have it over again"; then the looking inward to find nothing except "the track" that the experience left in its wake. Instead of looking up and out to God, the Christian looks inward to gauge his progress in the Christian life and misreads the empty track. In Lewis's case, these attempts were to repeat past aesthetic and poetic experiences; in mine, it was to repeat spiritual experiences in order to prove myself a Christian.

The problem of striving to *feel* God's presence and thinking that He was far from me when I did not sense Him in some way got worse as I strove to be a better Christian.[2] This introspective habit, so prominent a part of my adolescent difficulties, is fatal to learning to hear and be led of God. Such an orientation prohibits emotional maturity as well as spiritual growth.

A firm principle in acknowledging that God is always with us is that we seek God alone and never an *experience* of God. Once we learn to walk in the trust that He is indeed with us irrespective of subjective feeling or experience, we open the way for any special (usually rare and always unexpected) manifestation of the Lord's presence, one that can well set every fiber of our being atingle. But the faith lesson to be learned thoroughly is that God, the Objective Real, is the most concrete reality we can ever know; He is *really there* and is with us irrespective of our fickle moods and feelings.

The background to my experience orientation lay several years in the past. Back then I had received what would now be referred to as a baptism of the Spirit. And a most remarkable one it was. It occurred during special meetings where the preaching of the Word was greatly anointed and the Holy Spirit was powerfully drawing souls to Christ. In fact it was a time of genuine revival in that region and of uniquely powerful manifestations of the Holy Spirit in the lives of many.

One night when seekers or needy souls were invited to come down the long aisles of the church to pray at the altar, I felt a mighty compelling to go forward, even though I was already a Christian and unsure whether children were meant to go. As a child of eight or nine it took more courage and understanding than I had to step out, and only a powerful move of the Holy Spirit could have impelled me. Once started, however, I all but ran to the altar, and after kneeling in prayer, I forgot any other concern or inhibition whatsoever. Praying with all my might, I cried out for God to come. It seemed that I prayed in this fashion for a long time.

At one point I recall opening my eyes for an instant and seeing the astonished evangelist looking down on me and stretching his hand out toward me. Such a grace and power to pray was upon me, however, that I instantly forgot everything but the prayer once again. It culminated in the Holy Spirit's descent upon and into me in such a fashion that I was literally laid backward, awash as it were in Glory. It was as if the presence of God entered into me as a holy fire throughout my whole being and, filling me, ascended up through me both as a holy shout and a holy wine, bubbling up in sheerest, most incredible joy. My very fingers and toes tingled with God's cleansing, purifying fire and joy.

The weight of that hallowing presence seemed to rest on me for the longest time, and I lived in the awe and glow of it. As the sensory experience faded, however, I tried to recapture the experience. These unsuccessful attempts, along with my continued spiritualizing of my confused feelings and difficulties, led me to fear that God was no longer with me.[3]

I was well out of the teen years before I found the answer, the same that Lewis found and expresses so simply and well in a letter to a lady overawed by her sensory experiences:

Accept these sensations with thankfulness as birthday cards from God, but remember that they are only greetings, not the real gift. I mean that it is not the sensations that are the real thing. The real thing is the gift of the Holy Spirit which can't usually be—perhaps not ever—experienced as a sensation or emotion. The sensations are merely the response of your nervous system. Don't depend on them. Otherwise when they go and you are once more emotionally flat (as you certainly will be quite soon), you might think that the real thing had gone too. But it won't. It will be there when you can't feel it. May even be most operative when you can feel it least.[4]

As I continued my attempts to *feel* God, a mural-size reproduction of Holman Hunt's painting of Christ *The Light of the World* spoke to my condition. In the painting, which stood in our church, Christ holds a glowing lamp as he knocks on a door, asking admission. Briars and weeds have grown around the door, for it has not been opened in a long while. Losing myself in the painting, I would ask: *Is Christ knocking on the door of my heart?* I would respond, *Yes.* How could I open it to Him? Had I? How I wanted to! Bogged down in all the confusing feelings and subjectivity of an adolescent, I lacked the objectivity needed to affirm God's presence with me and within me, thereby coming present to my own heart and its capacity to listen to God. He had entered my heart in my initial regeneration, and, in a never-to-be-forgotten way, He had baptized me in His Spirit. Because I did not *feel* Him, however, I called to Him as if He were only and always afar off. He was there, calling me up and out of the subjective mire of my feelings, but it would be a good while before I could once again hear Him, place my hand in His, and in His strength ascend.

This confusion over "experience and its track" was the chief problem C. S. Lewis grappled with in his youth. In *Surprised by Joy*, he explains from his own life the darkened tunnel through which the teenager passes, what he refers to both as a childhood sleep and the "dark ages" in every life. For him it is that period "in which the imagination has slept and the most unideal senses and ambitions have been restlessly, even maniacally, awake."[5]

The higher meaning of the word *imagination*, as Lewis uses it, signifies the soul's capacity to intuit (receive hints or glimpses of) objective truth and reality, that which calls us up and out of introspective and egoistic subjectivity. For this faculty of the imagination to sleep, in Lewis's terminology, is to lose Joy—momentary glimpses or even impartations of glory, beauty, goodness, truth—as they dart down into our lives. These descents of the transcendent leave us in a momentary state of awe, looking up for that which lies outside the self. These intuitions are utterly *other* and impart meaning and therefore transcendent dimensions to our lives. Sensory and even false substitutes for the truly imaginative (for example, occult experience) spring up like weeds in our lives when the true imagination sleeps and Joy is but a faint memory.

Like Lewis, I was cut off from the truly imaginative in adolescence. Whereas previously he had "received" impartations primarily through nature and poetry (his early Christian belief giving to him a moral framework), my intuitive experiences were most often centered in religious faith. I did not trade good poetry for bad novels and an interest in the occult; rather I slowly replaced striving for spiritual experience with figuring out how to get out of school, where to go that was more interesting, and experimenting with cigarettes.

During this period I would have been helped had great books (great ideas whether through prose or imaginative works) been part of my new school experience, but they were not. The poetic and intellectual stimulation would have enlarged my world and worked toward banishing the intolerable ennui of that time. Above all, it would have exercised my capacity for objectivity and with it my capacity for *seeing*—all of which could have prepared me for an earlier return to God. To keep my eyes on God, the Object, and off any past sensory experiences of Him was the lesson to be learned, and until I learned it, there could be no renaissance of faith. This lesson eluded me for a number of years—years when I made the kind of mistakes we make when we cannot hear God and walk in His way.

From thinking that there must be something wrong with me as a Christian, I began to fear I was not one. The misgivings that had led to an overly conscientious and burdensome striving to be a better Christian and then into the experience orientation ended simply in feelings of failure. As adolescence wore on, I gradually ceased the striving. I never stopped praying, but these were not prayers rooted in trustful relationship to God, of peaceful assurance that I was His child. Rather I thought of myself as lost and in danger. In reality God had never left me.

Being cut off from one's soul and failing to understand it is a very modern kind of problem, one that accompanies prolonged adolescences such as we see in our narcissistic culture. Like any materialist, I was trying and expecting to apprehend all of reality with my sensory being. I was far from being a materialist, of course, but simply was a child who yet lacked the power to integrate subjective experience with objective reality and truth. My powers of abstracting, heightened and growing during this period, were turned in upon myself.[6] Slowly I was left to my own understanding and devices, not at all a safe place for us needy ones to be.

To feel estranged from God is to end in estrangement from one's own heart, one's authentic feelings, and the very faculties of one's own soul—those faculties with which we receive from God. These resources, so to speak, are all there, waiting to be blessed and affirmed into life, but we are separated from them. Estranged from our own souls, however, we begin, in Lewis's apt and colorful phrase, to "walk alongside" ourselves. We then attempt to analyze and critique the self we are in effect cut off from—an impossibility.[7] What a predicament to be in, but one common to the introspective, narcissistic period of puberty.

The above describes the inner track of adolescent life as I knew it, but of course there was an outer one as well. There the consequences of all these misperceptions began to play out. In my eagerness and impatience to live and to know, I had been drawn toward older folk and their conversations. The move out of our geographically isolated home did give opportunity for more interactions of this kind. I got to know the new neighbors, the pharmacists and their helpers at the corner drugstore, the grocer and the butcher in the local mart, the young parents for whom I babysat. But there was no "Mrs. Jones" among them—although actually it was a fatherly and authoritative "Mr. Jones" that I needed. There were no perceptive adults with the encouragement, the understanding, and the willingness to point the way for which I was so hungry. "To be seen and not heard" was, by and large, the rule for children (and that included teens) in those days.[8]

Along with being short on good, common sense, the teen has a phenomenal capacity to self-deceive that can be rooted in nothing less than our fallenness. I don't know which was stronger in me: my overly large dose of impulsiveness or my power to self-deceive. For example, with all my heart I retained a thoroughly Christian moral framework while at the same time I ceased to obey Mother in several ways. In other words, I sinned and was rebellious only in regard to certain things, and in regard to those I don't remember thinking of myself as being willful or rebellious. Any other infraction of the law, and my conscience was as keen as ever; to this day I remember with shame the time I told Mother a deliberate lie. But Mother forbade experimenting with cigarettes, and I didn't feel guilty about doing that.

As a teen, I knew well the scriptural commandments. Yet the wondrous fence of God's law was something I leapt over in several strategic places. Lack of place and boredom were the two main outer frustrations, and it was in attempting to relieve them that, as a Christian teenager, I failed to obey Mother or respect the rules of the public school system. The problem, of course, was that skipping school or finding ways to avoid going home didn't solve my problems. The frustrations remained.

Such personal difficulties would necessarily impact my experience at school. Even so, moving to the new school formed a large part of the difficulty. The change from grammar school to junior high was not simply one of being uprooted; it was one of leaving classes about real things, the solid subject matter of history, geography, poetry, literature, and so on—all interesting and challenging to me—and going to classes where methods, systems, abstractions, and the like were put forth. Had my interest been in mathematics or the natural sciences, my time at school might have gone better. But as it was, the next four years consisted mainly of boring textbooks, boring lectures, and meaningless charts on health and science. I was utterly unable to keep my attention on them.

In school we rarely touched upon the great books or ideas of the Western world; there were no challenges or programs for reading and interacting with them. In our home we had two books (besides the Bible and commentaries) that I read and reread with great interest—Charles M. Sheldon's *In His Steps* and a novel, *The Robe*, by Lloyd C. Douglas. But the classics in the Judeo-Christian and other traditions were simply missing.

World events and new theories were affecting education as well. The war with Germany and Japan had not ended before we knew there would be grave trouble with the Communist world, and Soviet Russia in particular. Our nation entered immediately into the so-called Cold War, with its scientific race for armaments and space superiority. This, along with the educational theories of John Dewey, impacted the school system, both in the subjects taught and in the teaching methods used. Science was given first place, and sociology and psychology came to the fore, crowding out other educational concerns. The social sciences, though anxious to be called scientific, were simply rationalistic. Even as a seventh grader, I rejected them for that reason.[9]

Scientism was in. Poetic insight, intuition, and the relational ways of knowing (knowledge by union, for example, child with mother or soul with God), the foundation and moral underpinning of any true science, were thought to be childish and were thus discarded. What occurred in the school system was a headlong flight from wisdom and truth and the steep downward descent into the contemporary rationalistic philosophies of positivism, empiricism, and naturalism. The split between head and heart was now in full vogue and widening. With all my being, I rejected the abstracting that ignored their union. This split is precisely what underlies the loss of reason today and explains why even "educated" Christians somewhere along the line stopped thinking.

As a student, I was at first disappointed and then increasingly bored. I met numbers and abstractions when I yearned for the windows and doors to the world that classic studies are designed to give. "The true aim of literary studies," as C. S. Lewis states, "is to lift the student out of his provincialism by making him 'the spectator,' if not of all, yet of much, 'time and existence.'"[10] Lewis expresses this yearning, it seems to me, as only those who have deeply known it can:

> The man who is contented to be only himself, and therefore less a self, is in prison. My own eyes are not enough for me, I will see through those of others. Reality, even seen through the eyes of many, is not enough. I will see what others have invented. Even the eyes of all humanity are not enough. I regret that the brutes cannot write books. . . .

> Literary experience heals the wound. . . . in reading great literature I become a thousand men and yet remain myself. Like the night sky in the Greek

65

poem, I see with a myriad eyes, but it is still I who see. Here, as in worship, in love, in moral action, and in knowing, I transcend myself; and am never more myself than when I do.[11]

One of the remarkable things about serving God is that lost opportunities, along with the deepest desires of the heart, have a way of re-presenting themselves, and that would come for me some years down the road. But healing would have to come first, and that was a ways off.

In the meantime, the inner drama, one of unrelieved frustration, was as a cloud over the canvas of my teen years, one that stubbornly shut out the sun. The effect was to darken or make of small consequence the little joys and triumphs that dotted that canvas. Looking back, I see clearly that a normal progress out of adolescence, one without undue hazard, could hardly have been possible. Given my Achilles' heel and the fact that the frustrations found no relief, the culmination could hardly have been anything other than what it was. It was the only way of escape open to my faulty adolescent imagination: that of an early, ill-fated elopement.

In my home, economic group, and culture, it was expected that girls would marry early, between the ages of eighteen and twenty-one. It was simply an unspoken given for my sister and me (she married immediately upon graduation from high school). In my adolescent emotional state, with its benighted imaginative capacity, elopement seemed the only escape.

Even though marriage represented an escape to me, I knew that the only way of transcending, of overcoming in this life, had to do with the steep ascent of obedience to divine truth, and I never ceased hoping someday to be "a real Christian" (the way I thought of it then). Therefore marriage did not appear as an alternative way to transcend, as it were, the uncreative and mundane. Heaven's call to ascend up and out of my adolescent subjectivity simply went unrecognized and unheard, and I wore the blinders that go with such a condition. From my darkened adolescent tunnel, my ears could neither receive the word Christ is always speaking nor realize that He *was* with me.

It was several months before my class was to progress out of the tenth grade when a seventeen-year-old high school dropout with a car and a job appeared within a circle of my friends. We all liked him. The fact that he had a car was astonishing in those days and gave him immediate acceptance and status with us—though we knew not to speak of him, his dropout status, or his car to our parents. Though another young man was my "special friend"—meaning we "went steady," which included walks together in the neighborhood or visits on my front porch—I was drawn to the newcomer and he to me. Fatefully the confused and very needy inner drama being waged within his teenage soul identified and intersected with the one in mine. (In the years that followed, I never learned what his inner frustrations were, for if he knew what they were, he was never able to express them.)

In the South in those days were marriage mills where justices of the peace, for the smallest pittance, seemingly thought nothing of marrying children. These mills drew like a magnet the unstable teens of our time. One fateful afternoon, rather than meeting with friends, he and I drove to the nearest marriage mill and were married. Never, perhaps, had two more naive youngsters entered into such a union. Afterward he drove me home, and I went in alone, even getting home on time. I didn't tell Mother what we had done. She did not even know him.

I waited with my awful secret, finished the tenth grade, and then the story of what we had done got out. This time my impulsiveness had gone over the top. My Achilles' heel had propelled me onto what was to be a very difficult pathway, one where remedial suffering would eventually do its perfect work and prepare me for the pathway God intends for all who fear Him, that is, all who hear and obey. It would take about ten years of trial and discipline on this hard and stony path, however, before the scales would fall from my eyes, and in faith I could step over onto the path where He, the Light of the World, led and flooded with radiance my pathway.

8

The Remedial Path

For thou hast hid thy face from us,
   and hast delivered us into the hand of our iniquities.
Yet, O LORD, thou art our Father;
   we are the clay, and thou art our potter;
   we are all the work of thy hand.

Isaiah 64:7b–8 RSV

Today the marriage of an impulsive fifteen-year-old girl and a seventeen-year-old-boy from families and backgrounds with little or nothing in common would most likely be annulled. Then the strongest efforts through counseling would be made to help the teenagers and the families understand why such a thing had happened and to give guidance for the future. But those helps were not available to Mother, and she could think of my actions only in spiritual terms. She rightly saw what I had done as foolhardy, sinful, and as a tragic mistake, not only for myself but for all those who loved me. She did not comprehend the psychological and merely human dynamics underlying the frustrations of my teen years and the resulting flight.

Therefore what was a sham, though legally recognized, marriage went uncontested. Ill-fated from the beginning, it utterly failed after the first few years. My daughter, Deborah, was born when I was seventeen, and by the time she was a year old, I was a single mother with full responsibility for her child.

"Remember not the sins of my youth nor my stupidity, but remember me in Your mercy—in Your compassion,"[1] King David prayed, and to this day I pray that verse with great fervor, thinking how my impulsive actions impacted others and especially how they set the stage for losses to be suffered by a beloved daughter. My Achilles' heel exacted a heavy toll, one that ended in Deborah's not only growing up without a father but also being torn between divorced parents and their families. Though my part has long since been forgiven and therefore, according to Scriptures, even blotted from God's memory, it is not something I forget.

Wrong as it was, the marriage was an escape valve and, as such, provided immediate rewards. From the moment I left Mother's crowded abode to join my young husband, I experienced relief from the inner and outer frustrations I described previously. The marriage immediately released me from the claustrophobic feeling of being hemmed in and of having no place. I had space and the freedom in which to maneuver, explore, and learn. Regrets about not finishing high school were nonexistent. At first I must have been more or less stunned over what I had done, for I do not remember feeling inordinate guilt over hurting Mother or my friends and extended family. That would come with intensity and an appropriate sense of shame later.

There were other "goods," major reliefs that followed immediately as well. I had suffered severe allergic reactions resulting in headaches and respiratory and abdominal upsets since about age thirteen. These started within a year after moving into our small apartment and followed the loss of the wonderful old trolley cars that had rumbled past our house close to the window where I slept. City busses with their foul-smelling, unguarded exhaust emissions replaced these.[2] How much that circumstance contributed to my teen "pathology" is hard to say, but it may have been considerable. After leaving the family apartment, these sicknesses and symptoms greatly lessened.

Another positive outcome was my family's response to this marriage. Though they had been shocked, not a single one of them gave up on me. Just the opposite. No doubt this Scots clan, with all their good common sense and practicality, knew that I now required a closer watch than they had before maintained. So I had closer relationships than ever with Mother's sisters (though the one with Aunt Rhoda could hardly have been improved upon) as well as with some of my older cousins.

My young husband was more comfortable with his own family, so very different to ours, but the openness of mine toward him paved the way for us settling in the neighborhood within a few blocks of most of them. I thus remained in close proximity to neighbors as well as to my family, and had even closer, freer relationships with many of them. They too, though I was more or less unconscious of it at the time, were very interested in me and hoped I would do well.

Though those years were filled with the toil of working against all odds to make ends meet, I have many precious memories of the times when Deb and I would interact with the family. For example, we would crowd into one of the uncles' vehicles and drive up into the Ouachitas to the mountain cabins where the extended family met. These two country places were in the vicinity of the old homestead where my grandfather's sawmill had been. There's no outing greater than meeting with one's lively Scots clan in the mountains by the "loch." As Deborah grew older, these trips would mean all the more to us.

Finally, good accrued to me from this marriage because it was imperative for me to be "stretched." From the age of twelve, I needed to be given hope for a future bright with possible achievement and then challenged and directed toward that end. The vision or the possibility of something other than early marriage was simply missing. To be kept fully extended until some degree of affirmation, maturity, and stability could be won was paramount for me, and the teen marriage I had entered into demanded this stretching. At first we were two teenagers responsible for our own living, and simply to survive was an accomplishment.

Then within several years I was a very young single parent, responsible for both the support and the rearing of my daughter. The stretching I had to do was that which either makes or breaks a person. It was not unusual, for example, to have to walk home from my day job (clerical work for a building contractor and then in a doctor's office), carrying my small daughter several miles—simply because there was no money for bus fare.

For me to have failed the difficult challenges would have been to fail my daughter, and therefore my determination would not admit to disappointment; it was absolute and ironclad. The thought of blaming God or anyone else never once occurred to me, and if it had, I would have rejected it immediately. I always knew that I alone had made the impulsive choice to marry, and that in having done so I had sown to the wind and could only expect to reap what the whirlwind wrought. In freely owning my grievous reactions to the home situation, I was, thanks be to God, never tempted to self-pity.

Though the ability to look up in faith and see God was missing, I never stopped crying out to Him. In such an eclipse, I could only think of myself as a backslider and of God as absent—a dangerous conception for a

Christian to hold. Yet in His mercy, and knowing my confusion, He heard my cries for help even then. In these years of being stretched in every conceivable way, He helped me overcome all odds.

In the years since, I have often seen this principle of stretching at work. Oswald Chambers aptly phrases it this way: "God does not give us overcoming life: He gives us life as we overcome. The strain is the strength. If there is no strain, there is no strength."[3] That is why I think of this extended "dark night of the soul" as a remedial path, one that was necessary to my soul's cure.

Along with the "goods" of the marriage, increasingly I came fully exposed to the "bads," the very real evils. They were such that finally, though I gave it every effort, the marriage could not be saved. With the added responsibility of a child, the marriage quickly reflected a weakness rapidly developing in the culture after World War II. The trend for men was to avoid the responsibilities of fatherhood and marriage. The Hemingway Man—the one who could drink the most, seduce the most women, and shoot the most wild game—was the male glamorized on the movie screen and in the novels. In the meantime, divorce rates soared and eventually even the institution of marriage was, and still is, seriously undermined.[4] Mothering and supporting a child under these grievous circumstances provided extraordinary exercises in being kept fully extended.

As most of us find on entering adulthood and the workaday world outside our sheltered childhoods, our idealism is soon pitted against the stern and painful realities of a fallen world. Our optimism may remain, but hopefully it is relieved of its dangerous naïveté, which is a feature of impulsive behavior, or at least it was in mine. It began to fall from me as I faced individual and institutional evils foreign to anything I had ever known. For example, my eyes were opened to the injustice and even coarseness and humiliation of the courts and judicial system—where one would expect help and protection. Divorce courts in those days did little to ease the plight of mothers and children.

But those injustices, grievous and stunning as they were, were easier to endure than the actions of certain individuals with whom the marriage had brought me into close contact. I saw and experienced at close range vices such as envy, hatred, disloyalty, and lying, and these were not of a juvenile sort. Only through earnestly crying out to God was I finally able to forgive.[5]

Impulsiveness, my Achilles' heel, though relieved of some of its naïveté, was still very much with me, though repressed. All of my energy and pent-up creativity went into being a mother and striving with all my might to make a living. When evening came, I only had the energy left to care for my little one and stumble into bed. But two more potentially ruinous impulsive leaps were yet to come.

After several years I made a second attempt at marriage with the father of my child, and this action went beyond impulsiveness but included that trait. The early *thoughtless* elopement with him was just that, a thing enveloped in the misty swirls of teen craziness. This second came from a hardening of the heart—one that is bound to come about when life is difficult and we are not trusting God for our basic needs, financial or otherwise. In our fallen state, we often look to that which has consistently proven unreliable and even dangerous in the past.

In the second appearance before a justice of the peace, I made a deliberate, conscious decision, taking an oath with no illusion of love or hope of permanence of the marriage; it was wrong and injurious to my soul. I was later heartily ashamed of this action, which began and ended as merely a certificate—it was never a marriage of any kind as we never lived together. The "paper" marriage was eventually dissolved, but not before I began to fear the compromises of which I was capable. I was beginning to realize that I would never be able, on my own, to steer the ship of my life according to the standards I held dear.

With this fear and realization, the first intimation of the great good to come occurred. In the downtown district close to where I worked stood a stately old Lutheran church, a cathedral of stone. One day on my noon break I felt strongly drawn to enter it, and once inside I found myself alone. Even now I can sense the awe that enveloped me as I knelt, looked up into the heights of the nave, and began taking in the great silent space.

Around the altar and scattered throughout were the time-honored Christian images and symbols of the faith. Their message, though opaque to my mind, yet spoke something rock solid into my heart. That the space was alive with meaning, holiness, and peace I understood, and I felt the miracle of taking it in. Surely the sanctuary was hallowed by the countless prayers and the worship that had ascended up to God through it, and I was the beneficiary. Something transcendent and eternally real knocked at the door of my heart and understanding that day and began to loosen the bonds of that adolescent subjectivity and experience orientation that had long substituted for the real. What is real began its long, arduous work of breaking up the old ground of misunderstandings. Through imagery and symbol, objective truth began, if ever so slowly, to penetrate my mind and awaken in me once again the intuitive capacities of my soul—what I've earlier described as the true imagination, the power to receive from God.

This transient occurrence remains firmly rooted in my memory even now in my elder years. I believe this is because it was the beginning of what would turn my life back right side up. It illustrates the inestimable value of imagery and symbol, when that which is *real* is rightly symbolized and begins to flow into us—that for which our minds may not yet be ready or even able to comprehend fully. Simply and wonderfully, as C. S. Lewis said, "God sends us words and he sends us pictures." Pictures, that is, metaphor, symbol, myth, dreams, and visions, are a vital part of the language of the heart that God uses to reveal truth to us.[6]

One of the prime illustrations from the Scriptures of God's concern that the real be rightly symbolized is how the Lord God Himself revealed to Moses the form, measurements, and all the furnishings of the tabernacle. The tabernacle and everything within it symbolized His holiness and the way He has made for man to come to Him. So did this old Lutheran cathedral that I visited. None of this, of course, did I understand at the time.

I returned to the cathedral from time to time, and sometime after this incident, began attending a Lutheran church in the suburbs with our beloved Aunt Rhoda and Uncle Gus. Then, wonder of wonders, when Deborah reached school age, the way was made for her to enroll in the grammar school that was part of this fine old downtown Lutheran church. She loved every minute of it and all her teachers. To this day, I count that as a miracle, and oddly enough, cannot remember how those six years of schooling were made possible financially.

Once Deborah was in school, things in general began looking up for us. There was even time and energy for friends, and I made some very special ones. In church those earlier spiritual stirrings continued as the rock-solid ancient liturgies, focused as they were on God alone, further weakened the walls and underpinnings of the "darkened tunnel" I had long been in. In this way, though I didn't understand it at the time, objective truth continued its stabilizing work in me, threatening as it did the misguided religious subjectivity that had so marred my early teen years. It would take more light and understanding, however, before the self-will in which I had long dwelt would be disengaged and replaced. In fact it took one more devastating mistake to vanquish my Achilles' heel finally and thoroughly and bring me to that crucial place of death to self-in-separation from God.

Until I was twenty-three or twenty-four, I didn't date at all but put all my energy into being a mother and making a living. I had lovely women friends, full of fun and the joy of life, and we did some of those normal things I had missed out on earlier. Then, as things became a little less arduous, I began to date on occasion, and suddenly there was only one man I could see. He was an exciting and extremely handsome and personable young Air Force pilot with the Strategic Air Command who had found his way into our group. We were immediately drawn together, and I was utterly caught up into the wonderfulness, even the glamour of it all. We fell in love, and all too quickly before God's holy altar and a congregation packed full of friends and family, we were married.

I won't go into all the reasons we should not have married, only the chief one. Quite simply, I was not on the path of listening obedience to God, that place where His will, not mine, could be found. Impulsive leaps are made, by definition, according to our own mind and without counsel from God or others. Impulsive leaps are *thoughtless*. "Come now, and let us reason together, saith the LORD" (Isa. 1:18 KJV), was a word I was soon to pay particular attention to and greatly benefit by.[7] Without having learned to come present to God and to hear Him, I was without the healing, wisdom, or guidance I needed to be a wise wife or mother (I vastly overcompensated my daughter, for example).

The marriage was brief chiefly because I was not the happy worldling that my husband turned out to be and not at all at ease with his more or less hedonistic universe. I had Christian moral scruples and opinions about all kinds of things that intrigued my husband, but for which he as an ethical pagan was not yet ready. In short, he had the misfortune of marrying a sorely conflicted Christian who had lost her way and was only very slowly finding it.

In later years I had the great privilege of praying with my former husband and seeing him come to Christ, a place where today he walks faithfully with the Lord. But neither his conversion nor mine happened soon enough to save the marriage.

Truly there was nothing on this earth that could have brought me to the end of myself like that failure in marriage did. That I could have impulsively and in my own selfish willfulness made another mistake in marriage, one that would adversely affect a daughter already wounded by her natural father, was unbearable. As I sorrowed, God in mercy and great tenderness began to show me myself. Eyes long blinded were opened and dazzled by the only Light that truly transforms. The hymn writer's wonderful words, "my chains fell off,"[8] are the best way to describe what happened in my conversion, for all kinds of healings began to take place

PART 2

1958–1965

His mercy has no relation to time, no limitation in time. It is not first nor last but eternal, everlasting. . . . As long as there has been love, and God is love, there has been mercy. And mercy, in the practice and in the effect, began not at the help of man when he was fallen and become miserable, but at the making of man, when man was nothing. . . .

God . . . brought light out of darkness, not out of a lesser light. He can bring your summer out of winter, though you have no spring. Though in the ways of fortune, or misunderstanding, or conscience, you have been benighted till now, wintered and frozen, cloudy and eclipsed, damp and benumbed, smothered and stupefied till now, now God comes to thee, not as in the dawning of the day, not as in the bud of the spring, but as the sun at noon, to banish all shadows; as the sheaves in harvest, to fill all penuries. All occasions invite His mercies, and all times are His seasons. . . . God goes forward in His own ways, and proceeds as He began, in mercy. . . . Whom God loves He loves to the end; and not only to their own ends, to their death, but to His end; and His end is, that He might love them still.

John Donne

Late have I loved thee, O beauty so ancient and so new;
late have I loved thee:
for behold you were within me, and I outside;
and I sought you outside and in my unloveliness fell upon those
    things,
yet had they not been in you, they would not have been at all.

You called and cried to me to break open my deafness:
and you did send forth your beams and shine upon me and chase
    away my blindness:
you breathed fragrance upon me,
and I drew in my breath and I do now pant for you:
I tasted you, and now hunger and thirst for you:
you touched me,
and I have burned for your peace.

St. Augustine

9

Home to the Father

> "I have come to give myself up," he said.
> "It is well," said Mother Kirk. "You have come a long way round
> to reach this place, whither I would have carried you in a few
> moments. But it is very well."
> "What must I do?" said John.
> "You must take off your rags," said she, . . ."and then you must
> dive into this water."
> "Alas," said he, "I have never learned to dive."
> "There is nothing to learn," she said. "The art of diving is not to
> do anything new but simply to cease doing something. You have
> only to let yourself go."
>
> C. S. Lewis, *The Pilgrim's Regress*

What an exquisite joy to come out of the memories of the long, dark tunnel
and into the extraordinary light and liberty at the end of it. Coming to the
end of the old man or self and dying to it is next to the greatest thing that
ever happened to me. The greatest, of course, was the flooding in of God's
grace in the conversion and spiritual journey that followed, a jubilant state
that left me standing—however wobbly at first—in the true self and eagerly
searching out the will of God. There is no more exciting, buoyant adventure
on earth than that of finally giving oneself up and taking off one's rags, for
that is the prelude to hearing God. It is the beginning of "understanding

what the will of the Lord is" (see Eph. 5:17 KJV) and of learning to collaborate with Him in doing it. Looking back now, it seems as if my feet sprouted wings with which to carry me over every pebble or boulder. That is because the journey, though chock-full of obstacles to overcome, was also chock-full of discovery and of becoming. It was sheer joy.

Somewhere between the ages of twenty-six and twenty-seven, I stepped off the remedial pathway—that rough and thorny road running through a long and troubled adolescence—and I stepped firmly onto the path of obedience, the one path where Christ, the Light of the World stands, patiently waiting and tenderly shining His light to welcome home all prodigals such as I. As in Holman Hunt's painting that had so captured my attention as a child, Christ's lamp was raised and fully blazoning, but this time He had no need to knock on the door of my heart. The door had swung wide open, and a heart, hungry for the grace to repent, turn from its idols (its own will and way), and obey, simply gloried as the light began to search out every confused and darkened nook and cranny. Through chastisement, God had sovereignly brought me to this place and was doing His part. Now, in company with Him, I most earnestly desired to do mine. With my entire being, I pressed into the Kingdom, holding nothing back.[1]

As St. Augustine said after his own conversion, "I entered into the depths of my soul . . . and with the eye of my soul, such as it was, I saw the Light that never changes casting its rays over the same eye of my soul, over my mind."[2] At first, as the scales were just beginning to fall from my eyes, I could not see with the eyes of faith. Even so, I turned with all my might from my own will in separation from God's, and as I did, insight came quickly: "O Lord, you were turning me around to look at myself. You were setting me before my own eyes."[3] All my past actions, fraught with impulsiveness, came into view.

Humbled to the ground and laying my heart and soul before the Lord, I knelt in deepest contrition, repenting before Him. Painfully, and with sinking heart, I recalled my fruitless striving to experience God in my early youth; this time, therefore, I sought absolutely no experience but simply resolved with all my heart to obey what I knew of God's will. I prayed, "Lord, if I never know Your presence again, if I never come to know You, if I never make heaven, yet I will serve You. I will obey You the best I can."

I could not have prayed a more life-changing prayer. That utterance, of course, was what the Lord had long been awaiting. In carrying out my resolve, I was completely delivered from the subjectivity that comes with thinking that God was with me only when I sensed Him—from an experience orientation. My eyes were now focused on God Himself and the Scriptures that reveal His will for our lives. This is the stance out of which all valid experience of God arises. Therefore, in seeking absolutely no experience, I came immediately into the only experience that matters—that of union with God, a vital personal relationship whereby God calls us friend.

What a cataclysmic thing a dying to the old self, a full conversion of the will, *is!* It is the turning of one's entire being—spirit, soul, and body—from its inward bent toward self and straight up to God, and that through listening obedience to Him. One friend of mine pictures it as a tanker sailing full throttle ahead and suddenly turning in midocean to sail in the opposite direction. That is the way it was, and the waves from the reversal were enormous. All things were made new.

The Scriptures ceased to be a "dead letter" to blinded eyes, for to obey is to begin to see with the eyes of faith. In making my will one with the Lord's and in learning to reckon myself dead to sin (the two sides of obedience), I began to hear the Lord, to know Him. From Genesis to Revelation, God spoke truth deeply into my being, and I spoke back.

I methodically searched the four Gospels for every command of Christ's and wrote them out, personalizing them by inserting my name. I then prayed over each command until I could begin to understand its import for me in the *now* of my own present time and circumstance and thus be enabled rightly to carry it out. The joy of radical obedience to the One who is the Word, the Way, the Truth, the Life was the result. Here, in recording this so many years later, it is thrilling to see that even in those earliest days the first rudiments of listening prayer were being set in. The Bible confirms this experience: "Before I was afflicted I went astray, but now I keep your word" (Ps. 119:67).

What catapulted me off the remedial path and into the full grace of obedience to God was the experience of dying absolutely to any and all attempts to find happiness on my own. The desire for happiness is inborn, given by God.[4] When lacking faith, I was separated from the obedient heart's way of seeing and hearing God, the one avenue through which happiness with its fulfillment and affirmation of identity is to be found. I strove, as all fallen creatures do, to find happiness through those things that God has created. That is precisely what God names as idolatry, and I repented of it with all my heart.

A line from George MacDonald's *The Princess and Curdie* describes what emerged when I put to death my striving for happiness on my own: "A great fire was burning, and the fire was a huge heap of roses, and yet it was fire. The smell of the roses filled the air, and the heat of the flames of them glowed. . . ."[5] Any ideas I had of finding fulfillment, of being able to pilot my ship toward any satisfying, meaningful goal, were simply forever burned away in that holy fire, banished into nothingness. What arose from the flames was the extraordinary aroma of Christ and of eternal life. Consequently, together with the pain of seeing my old self and dying to it, Achilles' heel and all, I entered into the most enormous relief and joy I've ever known.

I know why some of the saints refer to these early, formative years of our pilgrimage as "a honeymoon with God," for that is what it was for me. As St. Thomas Aquinas said: "God and Happiness are the same."

C. S. Lewis wrote, "[I]t is, I think, a gross exaggeration to picture the saving of a soul as being, normally, at all like the development from seed to flower. The very words repentance, regeneration, the New Man, suggest something very different."[6] In turning from my own strivings for happiness to face the One who had implanted those very yearnings within me, I forsook the big, singular sin, out of which all other sins (plural) come. It is the sin of separation from God for which Christ died to redeem the whole human race. Union and communion with God come with putting to death that singular sin, which Adam passed on to all, that of making ourselves as God. I had been living as though I owned myself, making my own goals and decisions, choosing my own path in life. We are commanded to die to that whole disposition in our fallen nature, and that is what the Bible terms dying to the "old man."

In turning from this state of sin, which for over a decade had held me captive on the remedial path, I most literally and wonderfully found myself immediately on the path of life, a place where "behold, all things are become new" (2 Cor. 5:17 KJV). Oswald Chambers quite firmly remarks on this state of immediacy:

> In spiritual relationship we do not grow step by step; we are either there or we are not. God does not cleanse us more and more from sin, but when we are in the light, walking in the light, we are cleansed from all sin. It is a question of obedience, and instantly the relationship is perfected. Turn away for one second out of obedience, and darkness and death are at work at once.[7]

In this conversion my creaturely identity was reclaimed; and in obeying, I became like a little child, my hand securely in Christ's, even like a beloved child (though I could scarcely believe it) who was trustfully adoring and obeying her Father. This, for a fallen and unaffirmed daughter of Eve, is miracle. It is the miracle of redemption from sin and death, a miracle pulsating with transcendent life and full of healing balm for the soul. For all who respond to heaven's call, it is, miracle of miracles, a full taking of one's place in Christ, the obedient Son of God, and an absolutely priceless participation in His righteousness.

It is often said that dying to the old carnal self involves pain, but by that it is surely meant that seeing one's old self and reaping what it sowed is where the pain lies. If, however, it is meant that there is pain in the disciplining of oneself to obey, that was not so for me. I was too amazed to be seeing, to be understanding, and grateful beyond words for deliverance from the self that suffered from its own sin and foolishness.

That was the self that could not hear the Lord say, "Come now, let us reason together" (Isa. 1:18 KJV) or "This is the way, walk in it" (Isa. 30:21), and thereby receive the wisdom and guidance to live and to know the will of God. Much of the death to the old man or self consists in dying to its deceptive, utterly blinding ignorance. Once my eyes were opened, there could scarcely have existed a more eager learner.

In this obedience, I was profoundly resting in the lordship of Christ, and soon there was a meaningful picture to go with it. I went with friends to hear a Baptist evangelist who brought the matter of "making Jesus Lord" fully alive in my imagination. After hearing him preach on Christ's lordship as it is taught in the Scriptures, I began to "practice the presence"[8] of Jesus as Lord, seeing Him on the throne of my heart. Daily I checked to make sure He was securely seated on that throne.

The very core of me was being transformed as, in this deliberate *seeing* of Christ as Lord, the thoughts and imaginations of my mind and heart were taken captive to obey Christ (2 Cor. 10:3–6). In this "putting on of Christ,"[9] for that in effect was what was occurring, I was coming to know an undivided self. The years of painful muddle and lack of single-minded devotion to Christ were over, and the "simplicity," as Oswald Chambers termed it, of life in Christ was being set in. Eventually, therefore, the times came when on occasion I felt the presence of God, sometimes strongly. But now, by a maturing and solid faith, I knew that He was always with me whether or not I sensed Him in any way.

Here were the seeds that would be so vital in the healing prayer ministry that was to come—that of the "practice of the presence of God" and "seeing with the eyes of the heart." In the words of Oswald Chambers:

> Simplicity is the secret of seeing things clearly. A saint does not think clearly for a long while, but a saint ought to see clearly without difficulty. You cannot think a spiritual muddle clear, you have to obey it clear. . . . When the natural power of vision is devoted to the Holy Spirit, it becomes the power of perceiving God's will and the whole life is kept in simplicity.[10]

Now as an adult with more understanding, I could once again respond to heaven's call. I heard and responded to God as I opened the Scriptures, as I moved throughout the day, and even on occasion as He spoke to me in the night. I received with joy His upward summons—His guidance, wisdom, insight. Response became a way of life, response to all that I was learning, response to the way things really are. By this I do not mean that I was scaling some kind of ladder in sanctity and goodness, but that I was steadfastly oriented toward God and toward the doing of His will. And it was (and still is) in the doing of the divine will that the *real me* is called forward, that I am enabled to do the works He before my birth ordained me to do! These upward summonses or mini-resurrections—the "steep ascent" in F. B. Meyer's memorable term—not only enable us to be and to do the will of God, but contain within them the happiness we yearn for, the ennobling of our beings, and personally for me, the sense of spaciousness I had long been seeking.

God's mercy and love has an incomparable wideness, one with many facets that I would be learning about over the years. One of the most basic I realized immediately is that He sets us in a broad and exceedingly spacious place (Pss. 18:19; 31:8). Here was the healing of my old sense of being bound or closed in, of not having room to maneuver, and even the healing of my Achilles' heel with its impulsive leaps. St. Gregory of Nyssa expresses it best: "For the one who runs toward the Lord, there is no lack of space. The one who ascends never stops, going from beginning to beginning, by beginnings that never cease."[11]

The Christian life is made up of new beginnings that come as we hear and respond to the call from heaven, the word that beckons us onward and upward toward God Himself, the eternal Good and goal of our faith. This growth calls for a holy heroism, one that comes with God's grace if we live in response to His beckoning. Most modern Christians turn timid at the thought of seeking "glory, honor and immortality," but heroism with its proper goal is included in the upward call, the end of which is eternal life: "To those who by persistence in doing good seek glory, honor and immortality, he will give eternal life" (Rom. 2:7 NIV).

To seek this "weight of glory" is to seek fullness of being and honor (He will make our righteousness to shine like the dawn because it is His, and we forsake our own), and peace (a quiet mind and persevering spirit come what may). Here is the beginning of emotional and spiritual healing; here is happiness and to spare; herein lies all that is promised to those who forsake self-seeking and obey the truth, no matter how difficult that may prove to be.[12]

Although all of this cataclysmic spiritual change in me was occurring in deepest solitude, it was not happening in a vacuum. The winds of the Spirit were blowing strongly across the country, leaving in their saving wake a profound renewal of faith as individuals and whole families were being touched and changed. My sister and her husband were remarkably renewed and began hosting prayer and worship groups in their home. Eventually I would join them and other weekly fellowships, but at first I knew only rather dimly of these happenings, for God had sovereignly, through chastening and the sorrow that attended it, closed me into a very great quiet with Himself. The new self that was emerging was solitary in the sense that it remained focused on the Lord, the unseen real, and was in awe, sensing its rootedness in God, and fearful lest those roots be disturbed.

Through the church's liturgy, my roots in the transcendent were steadily being strengthened. In the worship, prayer, ministry of the Word, all culminating in the Eucharistic celebration of Christ's presence with us, I was steadily receiving from the Lord that which is good, that which is beautiful and true, that which is healing and restores the soul. And, importantly, week by week and month by month I was gaining insight into the efficacy of the Sacraments. At subterranean levels of my soul, Christ was strengthening me in my own union and identification with Him as I regularly prepared for and received Him in the Communion bread and cup.

But all of this was not something to talk about with others as yet lest speaking should muddy the waters, somehow get in the way of revisiting ancient and eternal biblical truths in the light of my new understanding. But it was also difficult to find the right words. For a period of time, therefore, though joyously aware that the Good Shepherd was plucking not only me but others of his lost sheep from the steepest mountainsides and bringing us all to safety, I remained comparatively closed in with Him, listening and growing. Those months and years were a unique time in church renewal and history, one that left a vital awareness of the power of God's Spirit in the lives of countless Christians, and one perhaps only recently beginning to be adequately recognized, understood, and chronicled.

All of this and more went into forming the new inner track in me, one that illuminated all that was occurring in the outer, workaday world, which was for me, as a single mom, plenty busy.

Eventually I had to ask myself what was wrong with the faith of my childhood. Why had it failed to mature into the identification (union) with Christ in which I was now growing? In looking back I saw that this crucial element of faith had been missing from as far back as I could remember. Memories of contemplating the Holman Hunt painting that long predate adolescence reveal an emotional and feeling content to my faith that displaced trust and urged it on toward spiritual experience. Later on, and increasingly, faith was something I tried to ratchet up because a down-to-earth (incarnational) identification with Christ, which over time would have completed and matured my faith, was missing.

Why, I wondered, did the experience orientation that evolved have such a tenacious hold in my life? Why so much confusion and striving in my faith? Why did it take so long to come to myself as the prodigal returning home to the father?

At rest and at peace in Christ, I didn't agonize over these things, but as my soul was being restored, and especially as I began to pray for others in need, I was compelled to search for answers. I knew well that, as Oswald Chambers has written, "Until Jesus Christ is Lord, we all have ends of our own to serve." That was certainly true in my life. But Chambers goes on to make what for me is a provocative statement: "our faith is real, but it is not permanent yet."[13] Had real faith been there, waiting for me all along, just "not made permanent yet"? Or was it there and simply incomplete?

I had no question of what my main problem had been; it was the universal one of being fallen, in need of God's ongoing forgiveness of sin. I never doubted that, in the words of Fr. Patrick Henry Reardon: "more deeply than it is comfortable to think, we are all rebels against God,"[14] and that at bottom, in my disobedience, that is precisely what I had been. I knew I had lost my way because I had turned to my own way (Isa. 53:6). But why, especially in light of the Christian mother, the Christian training, the true Christian experience and understanding that I had never once doubted, had the faith of my childhood been so confused and striving?

Entirely missing as I asked these questions had been even the slightest glimmer of the early wounding that had intermingled with and confused genuine faith and trust. Answers to my questions came slowly and mostly as I was helping others with their barriers to faith and maturity. In helping them get in touch with their needs, I got in touch with the subterranean diseased matter in my own soul's early life.

This woundedness essentially had to do with my father's death. I know now that the experience orientation evolved with such force in my life due not solely to the craziness and narcissism of adolescence but as well to the unresolved emotional needs surrounding the loss of my father and his affirmation. Those were the deficits I was unconsciously wrestling with as a child, and my father's absence was more or less projected onto my heavenly Father. This confusion simply worsened during adolescence, a time when affirmation by the father is all the more critical. I could not, as it were, retrieve my earthly father (as my recurring dreams plainly showed), and the unrelieved emotions of grief and loss within me spread across the face of my heavenly Father. I could not see or, even after an extraordinary but passing experience of God's presence, retrieve Him either.

Mine was an instance of the Christian imagination failing, for as George MacDonald says, "human fatherhood invites the imagining of the divine Fatherhood."[15] Because of the unhealed inner trauma, I couldn't envision the Lord with me, never leaving me. I needed the healing power of God applied to the memories of loss, grief, and all the emotional misconceptions and deprivations that accompany severe infantile traumas.

Once I came to the end of my own unconscious efforts to assuage these things and made the crucial decision to die to the old sin nature and obey God, no matter what, I came to faith.[16] I might even say, my faith was completed. Healing would now commence and continue, and wonder of wonders, what I have come to call "divine objectivity" would replace the old subjectivity of experience orientation.

It is only from the standpoint of being "in Christ," with full baptismal identification with Him in His death to sin and in His rising in newness of life, that in faith we can stand on this word of St. Paul's: "For if, when we were enemies, we were reconciled to God by the death of his Son, much more, being reconciled, we shall be saved by his life" (Rom. 5:10 KJV).

In looking for faith as an adolescent, I was not depending on Christ's atonement, that which was once and for all time accomplished, as Christ voiced in His dying words: "It is finished." That was not my starting point; rather, I had started with lack of faith: "Is Christ really there if I don't sense Him?" My faith had been completely devoid of what I've come to term incarnational reality, the identification with Christ whereby we are secure in our union with Him and can affirm in faith that He not only is with us but lives in us.

God the Father, knowing my need much better than I ever would, was merciful to me. He was with me on the darkened pathway in ways I do not understand. He never stopped calling to me, and I never stopped hoping to respond aright to Him. But the soul that walked on the remedial path lacked saving faith, the kind that delivers one from the power of sin. That is why, over time, I fell away from God. Never having rightly identified with Christ, I had not matured in Him.

I am in the ministry today because of the knowledge that within many of us is not only the rebel in need of forgiveness but an abettor as well: a wounded soul that is also an obstacle to faith and in need of being led out of the prison house. Today this freeing of the captives is often referred to as a healing ministry, but even so, it should be understood as merely a vital part of the gospel ministry that has been seriously neglected, if not lost.

That basic, vital missing part is specifically the initiation into and identification with Christ that comes with a full understanding of and preparation for baptism. In the cross of Christ is forgiveness for the rebel and healing for the traumatized and wounded soul as well. I am in the ministry because of the sure knowledge that this healing comes in and with taking our place in Him, the very identification with Christ that is at the heart of baptism and of our ongoing empowerment to live out our lives in that baptismal reality.

In wise, pastoral words, George MacDonald captures the predicament of the unhealed soul when its baptism is incomplete: "We die daily. Happy those who come to life as well."[17]

And it is in rising in newness of life, the identification with Christ in His resurrection as well as in His dying, that we are named—that the Father names us even as He named our Lord in His baptism, saying, "This is my beloved Son, in whom I am well pleased" (Matt. 3:17 KJV). That is precisely what I was searching for early on, and that is where we find most all of those who come forward for healing prayer today.

I must stress the extraordinary importance of fatherhood in a life, the capacity of human fathers not only to name but to enable us to receive the heavenly Father's ultimate naming. As C. S. Lewis writes,

> . . . the most important thing that we can know about George MacDonald is that . . . [a]n almost perfect relationship with his father was the earthly root of all his wisdom. From his own father, he said, he first learned that

Fatherhood must be at the core of the universe. He was thus prepared in an unusual way to teach that religion in which the relation of Father and Son is of all relations the most central.[18]

From the loss of my father I eventually learned the same lesson. Fatherhood is smack at the core of the cosmos, and along with misplacing our understanding of baptism,[19] we impoverished moderns have largely lost this vital understanding as well.

Today much of the Christian world falls in line with secular wisdom and sees only the wounded soul, failing miserably to see the rebel and call him to repentance. Others within the church see only the rebel and fail to follow Christ in the healing and cure of souls. Dealing with all of these things has been a large part of my story.

10

The Lighted Path

"The Spirit and the Gifts Are Ours"

You make known to me the path of life;
in Your presence there is fullness of joy.

Psalm 16:11

Prayer is the atmosphere of revelation, in the strict and central sense of that word. It is the climate in which God's manifestation bursts open into inspiration. . . . Not to pray is not to discern.

P. T. Forsyth

Running through the myriad activities of earning a wage, running a home, and mothering, including preparing my daughter for confirmation, was the single golden thread of prayer. Conversation with God was constant. Nothing was commonplace anymore—not when prayed about and committed to God. And once I found my feet on the light-strewn path, others started coming for prayer. Friends became that most necessary and extraordinary gift: full-fledged prayer partners who learned to listen to God with me. In this strengthened dimension of obedience to our Lord, their lives too were turned around, completely changed and reoriented toward Him.

By this time, I had the six-volume set of Adam Clarke's commentary on the Scriptures to go along with our King James and Amplified Bibles, and my prayer partners and I didn't just study the Word, we devoured it—often on our knees. God's word to Ezekiel, commanding him to "eat this scroll, and go, speak to the house of Israel" (Ezek. 3:1) gave us no pause, for we were living it. Our prayer meetings were too exciting for words because of what we were learning and, yes, what we were becoming. From being fearful, unsure Christians, some of whom were even afraid to go to Communion, we were being turned into disciples of the King of Kings, the Lord of Lords. We knelt in my living room, praying fervently together, interceding for loved ones and others, petitioning the Lord in matters great and small, while discovering and attempting to stand on His promises. And always, always, we sang and praised and gave thanks to God.

Everything good comes of prayer. As P. T. Forsyth has said, "Prayer is not mere wishing. It is asking—with a will. Our will goes into it. It is energy. *Orare est laborare*. We turn to an active Giver; therefore we go into action."[1] It is not surprising that Pastoral Care Ministries (PCM) was born out of these early days of prayer.

Soon there was a ministry in music as well. It is remarkable how quickly the good of one's early Christian training and experience rushes to the fore once the repentant soul, Scriptures firmly in hand, turns to God in prayer. Sacred music was one of the many goods returned to me with compounded interest as I matured and was no longer stymied by a crippling rashness. It was as if the mind of Christ had been with me all along, waiting to rush forward once I came out of the fog.

The great and ancient liturgies of the church, something I did not grow up with, gift us with ways of singing our prayers together. Once I discovered them, they were instantly meaningful and alive for me. Through them the thread of prayer fairly throbbed throughout my being as together with the congregation of Grace Lutheran and our beloved leader, Pastor E. W. Callies, we sang the Kyrie, the Gloria, the Offertory, the Sanctus, the Agnus Dei, the Nunc Dimittis, and all the other great hymns and prayers.

The opportunity in every liturgy to confess and receive forgiveness of sin is an extraordinary, indeed, a necessary blessing to the soul needing healing and ongoing illumination as to its true condition—a place from which Christians never graduate in this life. "Repentance is the *arche*, the foundational principle, of the life in Christ . . . not simply the 'first' step of the Christian life."[2] This one facet alone of the liturgy began to correct anything left of a static nature in my understanding of the Christian life. There were no instant experiences leading to "Christian perfection." To die to the old self is one thing, but the ongoing need for repentance is quite another. Repentance and holiness walk hand in hand. The thing to do was to keep spreading my heart before God for His inspection, willingly see what He would show, and then repent and receive forgiveness.

In a church where the full liturgy is sung, the responsibility for the service lies heavily upon the shoulders of the organist as well as the pastor, and at that time we were blessed with the finest in both. Carolyn Westerfield Moorman, a high school classmate of mine, had a university degree in organ performance, and her playing blessed and thoroughly intrigued me. She and the choir were situated at the back of the church and thereby provided no visual distraction for the worshipers while she skillfully and unobtrusively led us in our worship. As we filed out of the church during the postlude, however, I was all eyes in watching her octave-plus reach on the ivories. *How wonderful it would be*, I thought, *to try out the keyboards, learn the pedal work, and experiment with all the mysterious stops.* But I would never have dreamt of even asking for such a privilege.

The longings of my heart just to sit at the console and experiment a bit must have ascended before the throne of God because the opportunity to do that and much more soon came about. The one who prays simply cannot be too careful of the heart's desires, for the Lord loves to honor them. The mind-boggling challenge of undertaking the actual work of organist came to me when Carolyn needed an extended time away.

The thread of prayer, vibrating throughout my acceptance of this enormous challenge, gave me the needed courage to switch from the piano to the three keyboards of the organ (counting one for feet). Somehow with a few organ lessons, I started out with the German Lutheran preludes and liturgy. In the several years I served as organist at Grace Church, all I was learning, hoping, praying, feeling, and knowing flowed out of my fingers as prayer set to music. What I lacked in expertise and training, I must have at least partially made up for in fervor and joy, for the Lord blessed me abundantly, and according to the worshipers, He blessed the church as well. Few greater spiritual blessings can be experienced in service to others than the privilege of looking straight up to God and worshiping Him while enabling the people of God to do the same.

The ancient sung prayers have never stopped being important to me. I am grieved when, as happens all too often, I find myself in a service where the unbelief and apostasy are so strong that these prayers, muttered simply as part of tradition, are no longer sung in faith as prayer to God.

Two of my most earnest, ongoing petitions during this period were for the wisdom and knowledge that come with the fear of the Lord and for the fullness of the Holy Spirit in my life. As it says in the Psalms, "The fear of the LORD is the beginning of wisdom; all those who practice it have a good understanding" (Ps. 111:10). Diligently I searched out and meditated over every Scripture that touched on wisdom and the fear of the Lord, not only because of their utmost importance in learning to walk in the Spirit, but also because I feared and detested rashness, presumption, and the lack of knowledge and wisdom in spiritual matters. Now that I was free from the confusion of the old experience orientation, I could pray with all my heart for the Holy Spirit's empowerment in my life.

It was, therefore, through praying with all my heart and will for wisdom, knowledge, and the fullness of the Spirit that I received not only ongoing healing and restoration of my soul but the *charisms*, what I've come to call the healing gifts of the Holy Spirit. (The adjective *charismatic*, used in reference to the church, refers to the presence of the Holy Spirit and His gifts, just as *evangelical* refers to the preaching of the Word, and *sacramental* to the ongoing means of grace in worship.) These charisms began gradually and unobtrusively (almost, one could say, quite "naturally") as needed to operate in my life.

In awe and expectation, my two chief prayer partners from Grace Lutheran, Lenora and Greta, joined me in searching out and praying over all that the Bible teaches on the Holy Spirit's work and His empowerment that Christ promised. Lenora was the children's choir director at church, and Greta was a valiant mother of two who was the church's secretary. Abandoned by her husband, she too struggled as the family's sole support and nurturer. We three worked together at church as well.

Lenora, a pharmacist by profession and with no children to feed, had something neither Greta nor I had—extra change to spend on books and the spare moment to ferret them out. She did me an inestimable favor by finding and bringing home to us such treasured devotional works as those by F. B. Meyer, R. A. Torrey, and others who did their theology on their knees. Both these great old evangelical saints understood the work of the Holy Spirit. Through *Meet for the Master's Use, The Secret of Guidance,* and his devotional, *Our Daily Walk,* F. B. Meyer in effect pastored me at this critical time. He moved with all his might to bring help and healing to the hungry soul, always assuring that, "Blessed are they which do hunger and thirst after righteousness: for they shall be filled" (Matt. 5:6 KJV).

With all our hearts we sought union with God, the fullness of the Spirit. R. A. Torrey's books were faithful pointers to this good and necessary end.

I remember his book *The Baptism of the Spirit* as being crucially helpful, as was Roy Hession's *Calvary Road.*

After a year or so we found and devoured as manna from God books that so wonderfully instructed and affirmed us in the direction we were going— Brother Lawrence's *The Practice of the Presence of God* and Frank C. Laubach's *Christ in Me* and *Game with Minutes.* Sometime in those early years I found the *Imitation of Christ* by Thomas à Kempis and still have this first copy, the pages worn through by constant reading.

In many ways, we in this honeymoon period were reenacting the scene in Acts where the faithful gathered, waiting on the empowerment of the Holy Spirit to do the works of the Lord. The Holy Spirit was with us, or we could not have prayed in the way that we did; yet we knew our utter and continual dependence upon the strength and presence of the Lord. In all of this we were training our spiritual ears to listen for the wisdom, understanding, and guidance that comes from God. We studied and prayed in order to do the will of God and obey.

To listen to God in prayer and throughout the Scriptures is to practice the fear of the Lord,[3] for it is to receive wisdom and knowledge from on high. It is to be led of the Lord. It is to abide in union with Him. Therefore, the golden thread of prayer is a vital part of the practice of the presence of God, and this listening opens one to receiving, besides wisdom in general, the gifts of the Holy Spirit spoken of in the Scriptures.[4]

The gifts or charisms first released in my life, not surprisingly due to these prayers, were those St. Paul refers to as the word of wisdom, the word of knowledge, and the word of discernment. These charisms differ from the way divine wisdom, knowledge, and discernment are normally received as we grow in Christ in that they suddenly and unexpectedly manifest, leaving us in wonderment and the knowledge that divine help has come from out of the blue, a vital word from outside oneself.[5] In my experience, these word-gifts from the Lord almost always occur in direct ministry to others. The three named above often cluster and operate together.

The first time I was aware of one of these is indelibly impressed on my mind, for the situation could hardly have been a more spectacularly awful one. Although at the time I wouldn't have known what to call it, I received a word of knowledge. This knowledge was desperately needed and could hardly have come to us in any other way. A man, who, together with his wife, was dear to me, had previously received a dramatic physical healing through the ministry of an evangelist who was preparing to hold meetings in the city once again. This couple had not only urged me to attend his meetings, but had pressured me to assist the evangelist as organist for his crusade. I knew from the outset that I was certainly not to do that and was left with the burdensome sense, even the Spirit's gift of discernment, that these friends were in danger of being duped by this man—which, as it turned out, they were.

My persistent sense that something was seriously amiss was not for a moment entertained by them, and they continued supporting this upcoming event with personal funds and preparation. When the time came for the meetings to begin, the huge place and all else was readied, but no evangelist arrived in town. Not a single message came from him, nor could his colleagues be contacted. In stark concern, my friends told me of all this, and as I prayed, deeply moved for them in their distress, the word of knowledge came. I spoke it out to them as naturally and quietly as if it weren't some extraordinary knowledge: "The man is drunk and will not come."

Taken aback and disbelieving, they and others involved made a full investigation. They found out that what I had said was indeed the truth. They flew out West and found the man still drunk; he had been drinking for some time.

A word of knowledge such as this comes not of our own will and striving[6] but by and in the Lord's will and timing. Such dramatic manifestations are relatively rare, but where there is unified prayer and where the gifts of the Spirit are free to operate, they happen as needed. In this case, the Lord had mercy on some young Christians who as yet had a great amount of learning and maturing to do. He was answering my prayers as well and revealing to me the work and the gifts of the Holy Spirit.

In the years since, I've seen a succession of ministers such as this poor man, souls who were sincere when they started out in ministry. But like him, in not understanding or finding help for their own serious emotional, spiritual, and intellectual deficits, they prove to be "leaky vessels," earthen jars that, unable to take the pressures of public ministry, end in a full break. Usually, like him as well, they are not properly accountable to others in the body of Christ, or, if so, those over them are for whatever reason without the power to either discipline or help them.

This particular man was focused on the power gifts: physical healing, deliverance, and miracles, and that alone would lead to an early downfall. Besides the underlying motive, such a narrow focus leads to a carnal striving to make things happen.[7] These precious and necessary charisms or *spirituals*, like all the gifts of the Spirit, manifest as God wills. To ask God to love and heal His people, using us in whatever way He deems best, is one thing. To begin to try to reproduce any one of the spiritual gifts regularly is quite another. That person will end up jaded and spent, perhaps even under serious spiritual deception, and always sinful and in need of deliverance—precisely where this man was.

I felt great pity for the broken evangelist, who lacked self-knowledge. Here was the very point where sin and the deprivations in his life came together. With a psyche too fragile to cope with the flattering public image he had acquired, much less to keep up his frantic schedule, his infantile ego needs and driving compulsions took over. The unaffirmed and unhealed, separated from or refusing the healing administrations and oversight of a mature church and leadership, often seek to find identity, vindication, and meaning in and through their roles or gifts—not in and through Christ. This plight appears over and over again in the church. A deadly activism attempts to fill in and compensate for all else that is lacking and unhealed in a life.

In these cases, one's prime focus has shifted from the Lord and His presence with us to that of finding personal power, reputation, and success through spiritual power. Spiritual lust sets in. Attempts to spectacularize the authentic gifts then begins an ongoing misuse of these gifts, a fearful and perhaps even damnable place in which to be found—witness the fate of Simon in Acts 8 and as down through church history.

Apart from the gifts of the Spirit, I cannot tell the story of PCM and the way we have seen the Lord move so graciously to heal and deliver His people. These gifts usually operate quietly and always effectively, and without them there would be no PCM history to write about.

The two petitions, one for wisdom and the other for fullness of the Spirit, are closely linked. To seek wisdom is to cherish and seek the mind and will of God in order to obey it; to seek the fullness of the Spirit is to seek union with God, the mystical marriage of man and God that empowers us in this obedience.

In respect to the mystical marriage, every verse of Isaiah 54 turned into pure spiritual gold as I took the promises in that chapter as my own. To this present day the Lord blesses those promises in a signal way to my soul—those, together with all that speak of "Christ in you, the hope of glory" (Col. 1:27). To seek this union is to find and celebrate the *sacramentum*: the incarnational mystery or spiritual marriage that only the Christian can know. The Father is in Christ, and to abide in our Redeemer is to be drawn up into the fullness of the Trinity. Union with God, the goal of all prayer, is the spiritual marriage whereby we are divinely "ingodded" and "ingifted" and enabled to do the will of God. No longer are we estranged from ultimate truth and reality.

> Fear not, for you shall not be ashamed; neither be confounded and depressed, for you shall not be put to shame. For you shall forget the shame of your youth, and you shall not (seriously) remember the reproach of your widowhood any more. For your Maker is your Husband—the Lord of hosts is His name—and the Holy One of Israel is your Redeemer; the God of the whole earth He is called.
>
> Isaiah 54:4–5 AMP

Such goods as I've written about in this chapter do not continue in a Christian's life for very long before he or she finds out what spiritual warfare is all about. We meet the Enemy of our souls head-on in spiritual battle, and that is what came up for me next.

But God turns everything to good for the faithful. Without the spiritual warfare, I would not have learned more about the incarnational reality of which I've been writing: the experience of finding for sure, and on a very personal level, that "greater is He who is in you" than Satan and all his legions who are "in the world" (1 John 4:4 NASB).

11

Learning Lessons through Spiritual Battle

In that day you will know that I am in my Father, and you in me, and I in you.

John 14:20

For to me, to live is Christ and to die is gain. . . . I no longer live, but Christ lives in me.

St. Paul, in Philippians 1:21; Galatians 2:20 NIV

The first words my mother spoke on receiving the news in 1965 that she had not long to live were those of St. Paul: "To live is Christ; to die is gain." Always on coming to those words in Scripture before, I would stop, trying to understand them better. Now I dwelt on them in earnest. Through sacramental worship and the setting in of ministry gifts, I had been growing in the understanding of the incarnational mystery (Col. 1:27)—Christ dwelling in us—but my lessons were far from over.

In describing my childhood experience of receiving the baptism of the Holy Spirit, I've already written about my first profound lesson in incarnational reality. Now Mother's citing of St. Paul's words brought this matter forcefully to the forefront of my meditations. And there would be two more major lessons in this ineffable Christian reality, lessons that forever lifted from my mind and heart the obscuring effects of several centuries of scientism that has so adversely afflicted the Western church.

As in every other crucial moment in her life, Mother's serene faith and courage came through, and she turned even her last illness into blessing for others. Therefore, though this news and the ensuing problems were difficult and grievous, they were not part of the spiritual warfare that would shortly come my way. Rather they were a watching with her as Christ's victory over sin and death was daily manifest. As it happened, the months she was given to live were, through prayer, stretched into five additional years, precious ones in which to share this life's challenges and joys with Mother.

That first major lesson in Christ's indwelling came in utter wonderment and blessedness, never to be forgotten. These next two lessons, equally profound, were learned in the stress of intense spiritual battle.

My second lesson occurred when for the first time I had a real enemy, one whose actions issued in part out of a stupefying ignorance. I had never before known how to act or stay angry, which was the gift of growing up with Mother, who had not the least discernible particle of anger in her. Disillusioned, hurt, disappointed, outraged—all these things I could be momentarily, but these states would pass quickly. However, with this dedicated enemy, I suddenly found myself beyond anger and in the grip of a temptation to hate, a temptation so overpowering that I could not throw it off.

From this person I had suffered assaults that were irrational, full of envy, malice, lying, and slander. But then one day an unthinkable final act came to light, one designed to destroy me and all I held dear. The act went right to the core of me. In pain and amazement, I knew for the first time how one person could kill another human being. I also knew that if hate came into my heart, my walk with Christ would end.

I fell to my knees and cried out to God for help. "Please do not let me hate," I cried over and over. Getting no relief, I phoned one of my prayer partners to come over and pray with me. All afternoon we cried out to God, and there were terrible moments when I wondered what I would do if God failed to help me, if I would simply have to cry out like this the rest of my life.

Then suddenly my pleading was interrupted by an amazing awareness of Christ in me. From that center where He and I were mysteriously one, I extended forgiveness to my enemy. At that same moment, I was delivered out of the grip of the worst temptation I've ever known, one designed to engender in me the terrible capacity to truly hate another human being.

That night I was awakened by a thunderous masculine voice (one I took to be God the Father's), and it boomed out the words of St. Paul: "*To me, to live is Christ.*" Never before had I understood what these words taken existentially meant, but as I sat bolt upright in bed, a large part of the meaning washed over me, never to depart. It meant letting Christ live in me, letting Him love even my worst enemies through me.

The truth of 1 Corinthians 6:19 took on vastly more dimension and meaning: "Do you not know that your body is a temple of the Holy Spirit, who is in you, whom you have received from God? You are not your own" (NIV). Christ in me was securely linking me to God the Father in all His sovereignty and to all else in highest heaven, above and beyond me. That incarnational link had been the reality through this whole terrible time.

Had I learned to acknowledge and celebrate God's immanence as well as His sovereignty, I would have prayed more effectively, and from a much quieter, less frantic place. I would have been secure in the knowledge that Christ was closer to me than any human being could ever be; He was with me in this warfare with an adversary at once illogical and yet practiced in evil scheming.

The third lesson in incarnational reality came shortly thereafter, and this time it was not a human enemy but a demonic one. The trial seemed to last forever, though actually it spanned about a nine-month period. The suffering was worth it, however, for after it was over, I knew what demonic oppression is and, even more important, what the authority of the believer is.[1]

Demonic oppression is always an attack on the mind and thought processes of either an individual or a group, but in one of its manifestations it is an all-out maneuver to take over a person's mind, and from there control the total person. Demons project lies into the mind, leveling dreadful accusations at the individual. The oppressed person seldom recognizes the source of this activity, which makes the oppression all the more confusing.

New Christians often experience this oppression in varying degrees, and it is designed to deceive them and either rob them of their new life or at least stop their progress in the Lord. Mature Christians, those who are effectively pulling down satanic strongholds and bringing in the Kingdom of God, discover the full gamut of the Evil One's stratagems. The way I use the term *oppression*, therefore, is different from being either *possessed* (that condition whereby demons inhabit and control a person from the central core of his or her spirit) or *demonized* (when demons have invaded a person's soul and body but do not yet have full control).

The demonic spirits that came against me were not within me, but their strategy was designed to lie to me and accuse me until they could press down, weaken, and then finally enter in and take over my mind.

This extreme experience of the demonic does not usually occur unless we open ourselves up in some way to it. For example, people who come to Christ out of promiscuous and perverted sexual lifestyles have opened themselves to what the Scriptures term "unclean spirits." These people may not only be oppressed, but their bodies and minds may still be inhabited by the spirits until they experience deliverance. Another example is that of missionaries living in areas where they have to come into close contact with witchcraft and other occult practices. If they fail to understand and move in the power of God, they will soon be in serious trouble. Once they have come under serious oppression, their deliverance could easily be accomplished through authoritative ministry with laying on of hands. These souls, however, are usually sent to unbelievers for medical and psychiatric treatment. Their oppression can then turn into a real depression with the possibility of even ending in demonization.

My experience was like that of the missionary. In Little Rock I had found work as a clerical assistant on a high-security psychiatric ward that served two hundred criminally insane men, most of whom had serious records, including murder and other heinous crimes. Here I came face-to-face with evil—evil as almost a palpable presence. It pervaded the minds, the language, and the rantings and ravings of those who had lost the good of reason, the good of being human. These men heard voices telling them to do vile things; their hallucinations were the stuff of outer darkness.

One who practiced voodoo would tell the psychiatrist in my hearing of his hatred for Christians. I knew that the darkness within him recognized the light of Christ with me. He would describe how he would send out demon spirits to attack Christians and would watch it happen.

I believe my oppression had something to do with that tragic lost soul. One day as I was leaving the building, I locked the last door behind me, and suddenly something with a voice seemed to be sitting on my left shoulder. It said, "Look!" and somehow pointed to my extreme left. There, as a magician might try to raise an apparition with a wand, it reared up a cross and then said, "How ridiculous!" Just three words and then an illusion of a cross. But with that awful sound and sight, I threw my hands over my ears and ran across the lovely, well-kept grounds that glistened in the sunlight. I marveled at how normal and unchanged everything around me was, while at the same time my whole world had been altered. I thought, *Oh no! Now I'm just like the rest of them. Now* I'm *seeing things; now* I'm *hearing voices.*

From that moment on, whenever I would look at a cross or crucifix, I would hear blasphemous voices and see blasphemous things—dreadful impositions of phallic images. At night when I would kneel to pray, I would be terrified by an evil presence. In fact I had to get off my knees and crawl under the bed covers to pray. It was an experience of evil that utterly horrified me and threatened to take over my mind. I knew of no one to go to for help. Today there are people who understand how simple it is to free a person from such harassment (we in our ministry alone have trained multiple thousands). Back then there were not. My pastor, an utterly faithful, loving minister of the Word and Sacraments, would never have understood what I was going through. I knew that he would rely on the current psychological Freudian "wisdom," the effects of which I lived with daily and saw helping no one.

Of course mentally and emotionally ill people who hear voices and have hallucinations need the best psychiatric care available, care that has since then greatly progressed. But I knew that my problem was neither physical, such as related to a chemical imbalance, nor emotional. It was spiritual, and though I had everything to learn in this area, I knew the only answer was the grace of God. I cried out for it day and night, like a person about to drown, with barely a grip on a lifeline.

Then, miraculously, I happened on the answer to my problem in one of F. B. Meyer's books.[2] In it Rev. Meyer tells of St. Catherine of Sienna who, surrounded by the evil and need of her day, went up into a castle turret to pray. As she began to pray, her ears were assaulted by blasphemous words, and she cried out to God, "Oh, look, Lord, I came up here to give you my day. Now look what is happening." The Lord replied, "Does this please you, Catherine?" "Oh, no Lord," she said. And the Lord answered, "It is because I indwell you that this displeases you so."

These words brought me instant understanding of my plight. I was brought right back to the fact that Another lives in me, and that He is there even when I sense His presence the least. From that day forward, I have never forgotten this truth or relegated it to the abstract. With this knowledge, I also knew that the problem was not a condition of my heart or my mind, but that it was harassment from the accuser of my soul. Reflecting on 1 John 4:4, "He who is in you is greater than he who is in the world," I knew beyond all shadow of a doubt that God in me was far greater than the oppressing demonic spirit without. So I cried out, "Take it away, Lord. Send this filthy, horrible thing away." But the Lord said, "No, *you* do it."

It was then that I learned spiritual authority. Centered in God and He in me, I took authority over the evil spirit when it manifested itself and commanded it to leave. After several months of this, I was utterly free of this harassment.

Though demonic spirits are real, there is in the spiritual realm an illusory nature to evil. Satan, the archdeceiver, was scheming to trick and bluff me, and I was terribly afraid and intimidated. Many people lose this battle and are robbed of their minds and all spiritual progress because they do not understand the spiritual realm and the full provision made for us in the Victor. But when the forces of evil come against us, they have only the power we grant them, which we do when we fail to understand "Christ in me" and the resulting authority we have to send them away.

Prayer for the lifting of demonic oppression is one of the easiest prayers to pray. In cases where demonic oppression is hooked into serious psychological woundedness, it is the latter need where more time and energy is required. We then must find those places where there are unhealed wounds and unconfessed sin that must be repented or where there is the failure to forgive others who have wounded us.

It is important to note here that I could have been instantly helped and freed had a Christian, filled with the Spirit and the knowledge of our authority, ministered to me with laying on of hands and prayer. Such a one would have immediately discerned the oppressing demon and would have simply commanded it to leave in Christ's name. But then I may not have gone on to learn my own authority in Christ and what it means to move from the center where He and I are one. For that knowledge, the longer, more painful experience was certainly worth it. Without it, I might have needed more than three major lessons in incarnational reality before finally catching on.

From these lessons, I learned in the midst of difficult circumstances as well as in the routine of the day simply to stop, place my hand on my breast, and thankfully affirm Christ's presence within. I would then look with the eyes of my heart and see His strong presence alongside me and sense His love stayed upon me. This takes merely a moment in our busy days. We affirm what the Scriptures and our experience of walking with the Lord have shown us to be true. It is the practice of the presence of Jesus. In this way I have learned to center myself in Him and abide in Him.

The affirmation and blessing that came to me and my prayer partners from Brother Lawrence and Frank C. Laubach, who took the time to write out their experience of God's immanence, is simply incalculable. This learning, of course, never stops, for we are dealing with the greatest of mysteries here, the ineffable way in which He has both drawn us up into Himself and descends into us. It is the way of His faithfulness to those whose eyes are fixed on Him—we in Him, He in us.

What I learned from these lessons, I immediately put to work in praying for others. As I look back now, I am amazed to see how quickly I began to understand the soul and the provision made for its cure. It seems that those "who are sharers in heaven's calling" (Heb. 3:1, Barclay) go rather quickly about the Father's business in the way He purposes. Healings abounded as Christians who had long been trapped in one emotional or spiritual prison house or another were set free. And for those of us who prayed for others, Christ's prayer that our "joy may be full" (John 15:11) was surely realized.[3]

Heretofore, I've used the term *call* or *calling* in its basic sense of God's initial and ongoing summons to us: "I press on toward the goal for the prize of the upward call of God in Christ Jesus" (Phil. 3:14). This is the call up and out of our fallenness and separation and into relationship with Himself. But I use these terms in a subordinate sense as well, and that is in regard to our works and service in the Kingdom. Christians speak of "being called" to a certain work or place in this life.

Though I had no idea in these early times, or for a very long time indeed, of a particular ministry vocation the Lord was leading me toward, the basic keys and ministry were even then being firmly set in. Actually, in looking back on those times now, I am amazed to see how thoroughly this is so. I think that is true for most of us, for when made reasonably whole by the Lord, we desire what is in line with our calling—that is, in line with God's sovereign purposes and the Holy Spirit's giftings in our lives. Therefore, if not misguided or barred in some way, and if moving in the power of the Holy Spirit, we go about these works rather quickly.

The thing I did know back then, however, and which immediately propelled me into ministry to others was this: I knew what the Lord had done for *me*. I knew that if He could bring me to my senses, put me on the right path, and heal me, He could and would do that for anyone. Therefore I desired with all my being to see others set free and healed.

All of Isaiah 61 gripped me but especially verses 1–4:

> The Spirit of the Lord God is upon me,
> because the Lord has anointed me
> to bring good news to the poor;
> he has sent me to bind up the brokenhearted,
> to proclaim liberty to the captives,
> and the opening of the prison to those who are bound;

to proclaim the year of the LORD's favor,
and the day of vengeance of our God;
to comfort all who mourn;
to grant to those who mourn in Zion—
to give them a beautiful headdress instead of ashes,
the oil of gladness instead of mourning,
the garment of praise instead of a faint spirit;
that they may be called oaks of righteousness,
the planting of the LORD, that he may be glorified.
They shall build up the ancient ruins;
they shall raise up the former devastations;
they shall repair the ruined cities,
the devastations of many generations.

Isaiah 61:1–4

Christ cited these verses in Luke 4:18–19 and then said, "Today this Scripture has been fulfilled in your hearing" (v. 21). He meant that it was fulfilled in Him, the Messiah. With all my being I knew that Christ had done this for me, and would do it for all who desire His purposes.

It is a great good that we do not see what all our work in the Kingdom will entail ahead of time, for courage and God's special gifts of faith come only when needed. Never then could I have imagined doing what we do today or seeing what we see the Lord do in every healing conference. What a mercy, for I might have felt some obligation to help bring that to pass, and quite gotten in the way of the Spirit's work. Never then could I have conceived the ease, joy, and naturalness with which the Holy Spirit's gifts and power operate to bring His purposes about, and the way in which even the holy angels come to help us. Nor could I have imagined the heaven-sent ways in which educational opportunities would come my way, preparing me for the ministry ahead.

We all need time in which to grow and mature at a natural pace, even as the stately trees, the plants of the field, and the animals do. I especially needed it to win through to the Christian virtue of self-acceptance. For only in daily walking with the Lord did I find release and ongoing healing from my lack of fathering and affirmation. And only in this way did I slowly leave off erroneous ideas of what it meant to be a woman called of God, freed to become all she was created to be.

Time is a sheer gift, the soil in which the soul's understanding buds and blossoms and virtues can be realized. When missing, self-acceptance does not come overnight, for it concerns deeply held attitudes about what we can and will be permitted to do. The accepting of our identity in Christ concerns opening ourselves up to thoughts and possibilities we could not before have imagined but that manifest as we walk and talk with the Lord. What a joy that part of the journey has been and still is! Blissfully unaware, then, of what the Lord had ahead, I rejoiced in ongoing discoveries and the Lord's affirmations, while learning the healing ministry by praying for one dear soul after another.

My time would now be subject to this unrecognized vocation; it was even then brought into line with His purposes for what I would later do. I started rising very early in the morning to read the Scriptures and pray, and to practice the organ and plan music for services before getting my daughter and myself off to school and work. Often I used my lunchtimes too for study and prayer. In looking back through all the years, it is wondrous and even amazing to see how the strength of the Lord, His guidance, and the power of His Spirit were always there in line with His purposes for me. Even the spiritual warfare that came increasingly as the ministry grew, God graciously turned into additional understanding when praying for the healing and deliverance of others. As I focused on and listened to Him, all simply unfolded. And where humanly speaking, there seemed no way forward, always in the right time the means appeared.

Never have I thought in terms of making a ministry happen. Indeed, we've never had advertising or institutional support behind us. Even our translators and publishers, here and overseas, have come to us. Thus today when I see folk striving to make "their" ministries happen, I tremble for them. When I see them adopting methods and plans in lieu of the Spirit, I come near to weeping. The activism, the blood, sweat, and tears, the confusion they encounter, is wearing not only on them but on those fated to watch them. For the greatest danger is that of ministering out of one's own natural gifts and power—in which case egos, swelled intellects, and all manner of pride are involved. Thank God, we do not need to run ahead of Him or lag behind either. Most truly, it is "'not by might, nor by power, but by my Spirit,' says the LORD of hosts" (Zech. 4:6). Once we get that right, then our good educations, technologies, and even common-sense methodologies fall in line, and we know that in His strength alone the real work has been done, the vocation fulfilled.

As Jesus said in Luke 17:9–10, "Does he thank the servant because he did what was commanded? So you also, when you have done all that you were commanded, say, 'We are unworthy servants; we have only done what was our duty.'"

12

Foundational Lessons

True prayer is the supreme function of the personality which is the world's supreme product. It is personality with this function that God seeks above all to rear—it is neither particular moods of its experience, nor influential relations of it with the world. The praying personality has an eternal value for God as an end in itself. This is the divine fullness of life's time and course, the one achievement that survives with more power in death than in life.

P. T. Forsyth

The three major lessons I spoke of in the last chapter drove home to my mind and heart forever the miracle of incarnational reality and paved the way for other foundational lessons to be set in during the late 1950s. In these formative years in Little Rock, when I was in my late twenties, these other lessons were key to the scope and direction of my service in the Kingdom and the ministry as it formed. Thus it is important to explore them in this chapter before we return to the story of my life.

"Personality takes true effect in God—in prayer," as P. T. Forsyth observes.[1] In this transcendent knowledge I was thoroughly rooted, even drenched through my own healing experience. A ways on down the road I would learn to speak of this truth in terms of *listening prayer,* that we become persons as we listen and respond to God. But this view of man was in sharp contrast to those I was then daily encountering in the workplace.

During these years I worked with three different psychiatrists and the plethora of mental-health specialists surrounding them. The atmosphere was one of stark, white-walled unbelief. Two of the doctors were not just unbelievers but outspoken atheists. Perhaps the fact that I was a Christian urged them to voice their convictions or lack thereof. So far as the doctors were concerned, there was no transcendent help for the suffering soul; their faith was in man's intellectual prowess and works. Their world and cosmos were reduced to what man's brain could apprehend and his unaided psyche intuit. This, of course, is why Freud himself was depressed and pessimistic about man and the world. These doctors reflected, in one way or another, the cynicism and depression of their famous teacher.

The first psychiatrist I worked with was in private practice and quite well-known. She was considered brilliant but was seriously alcoholic. The other two were with the Civil Service and attached to the high-security hospital I spoke of in the last chapter. In the Bible Belt of that era, there were many unbelievers, but somehow most of them considered themselves Christian. The Judeo-Christian worldview yet clung to them to some extent. So it was an odd set of circumstances that in that time and place, I should be closely associated with three persons, all well-meaning but Freudian in outlook and training, who were sentenced to the bleakest of jobs: facing mental and emotional illness en masse apart from the knowledge of a Savior.

In assisting the doctors, I came to discern how differently I saw and understood both the soul in need and the human person as compared with how those bereft of faith and any transcendent hope did. Thus while daily all this was before my eyes, God was beginning to set into my heart not only increasing understanding of the soul and of its cure, but of faith in His willingness to heal it.

From early on, therefore, though truly grateful for helpful medical and scientific knowledge, I've been deeply aware of the poverty of reductionistic psychology and psychiatry, and saddened beyond words to see the way that it has affected the church. Tragically the church has deserted its phenomenal power to heal, that power provided by Christ's cross and the reality of His life with and in us.

I should note that later, as the ministry developed, Christian physicians joined us, among them gifted psychiatrists and psychologists who have been willing to donate their time and expertise by coming together in the ministry of binder of wounds[2]—the healing of souls. Their cosmos has been far from small or sterile; it is stellar and absolutely limitless, filled with the knowledge of God's eternal greatness and His participation in the lives of men and angels and all His creation. Together with this transcendent understanding, they bring their invaluable medical and scientific knowledge to the work of healing prayer.

In these formative years in Little Rock, of course, I had not an inkling of the way psychoanalysis would finally fall out, and that by and large the atheistic materialism of a Freud would quickly be overshadowed by or morphed into the gnosticism of a Carl Jung and the New Age. It is difficult for even the most hardened of unbelievers to live comfortably for long on the reductionistic scientisms (materialism) of a Sigmund Freud.[3]

Today I refer to the gnosticism propagated through Carl Jung and the New Age as gnosticism from the left. Now we are seeing, insofar as gnosticism is the promulgation of man-made myths and the insinuation of false doctrine into the true, what I've come to term as gnosticism from the right. It has issued out of the imbalanced teachings and practices of self-named charismatic "prophets," whose teachings are mainly concerned with healing, fasting, spiritual warfare, and enervating end-time speculations. This movement is fast growing, even though discredited time and again. I first saw these beliefs and practices before leaving Arkansas.

At the same time I was seeing the reductionism and problems in modern psychological thought, I was learning to recognize the spurious in Christian "revelation" and teaching. I was holding on to 1 Thessalonians 5:19–22: "The Spirit do not quench; prophecies do not despise; But test all things: hold fast to what is good, keep away from every evil form."[4]

As I sought to understand the gifts of the Holy Spirit, I realized how carnal imitations and perversions, when untested and unchallenged, would threaten the church's ongoing renewal and damage the individual soul. With everything to learn in these matters, I certainly did not come to these insights overnight. We in the renewal lacked historical background and the language with which to adequately describe the power of the Spirit in its movements. And helpful and much needed books, such as *The Holy Spirit and You* by Dennis and Rita Bennett, were yet to be written. Folk in the early times of renewal were mostly experiencing the *spirituals* apart from needed understanding, guidance, and correction concerning them. Unfortunately, that is still largely the case.

As the truly grace-filled winds of the Spirit continued to blow in the early days of renewal, transforming lives and families and empowering God's faithful people for service, we were amazed to see denominational barriers between Christians begin to crumble and fall. Christians from totally different backgrounds were coming together in great joy to worship and study the Scriptures, and we learned from one another. In the presence of the Lord, love abounded and lifelong friendships were formed.

On rare occasions, however, someone would turn up with extreme teachings and false practices in regard to the Holy Spirit's giftings. These errors and excesses would almost invariably be in respect to the charisms of prophecy and physical healing or the ministry of "deliverance," and these in tandem with "end-time" pronouncements and extravagances. These folk came from backgrounds like the alcoholic evangelist (described in chapter 10) and were associated with the lesser sects among Pentecostals. The impoverishment of the intellectual, emotional, and just plain human dimensions of their beings left them prey to serious imbalances and over-spiritualization. Their deep-set sense of social inferiority left them with unmet ego needs that easily turned into a lust for the spectacular and for power. All of this fed into prideful (albeit unconscious) agendas—inordinate needs to prove themselves, to teach, and to lead others.

My experience with the alcoholic evangelist and then with a "prophetess," which I describe below, opened my eyes to these problems. From that time on, my concern over and discernment in regard to these terrible minglings of truth and falsehood have increased. I recognize the carnal operations when they either mix with the true or involve the demonic (as divination does). This recognition is merely the gift of discernment all Christians are to have and grow in. Pastors, teachers, and lay leaders must immediately exercise this discernment (as the gift of exhortation, a neglected gift that is largely unexercised today), thereby helping others to recognize, name, and dispel the false.

Insinuations of the carnal or the demonic into what parades as the true, when it goes undetected, is one of the most effective tools in the Enemy's arsenal in terms of its power to dishearten and confuse Christians and, even worse, bring them under pride and permanent deception. The most difficult thing is that these mixed words will often have an amount of truth and give some help. This was the case with the woman who thought of herself as a prophetess, and there were genuine healings (even miracles) in the ministry of the wounded alcoholic evangelist. I personally know of one miracle, medically attested, that took place in his services.

The prophetess was a classic example of the mixture of flesh and Spirit that we see in much of the "prophetic" today. She came early in my experience of a larger prayer group, claiming to have a ministry of prophecy and deliverance. All of us, full of Christian charity and eager to learn, gave her our full attention. She spoke a bit, and then in old King James prophetic phrases, straight out of the Old Testament, began loudly and sonorously, with a long and drawn out, "Yea . . . Thus saith the Lord!" to "prophesy" over the folk there. Being the writerly type, I wrote out these utterances for prayer later. She prophesied various things, words that flattered the ego and promised success—all the carnal, self-serving temptations to power and glory, such as Satan used in trying to tempt our Lord in the wilderness. Some of her proclamations were: "You are going to raise up a great church" or "You are going to speak before multitudes" or "You are going to be prosperous."

Interestingly, I was the only one of the group over whom she was unable to wax grandiose. She had nothing particularly good to say about my future, even though at the time, naive as I was and eager to learn, I was not judging her or in the least bit offended by her lack of enthusiasm about my future. I was simply thinking deeply about what she was saying over people I loved and writing it out for their discernment later. After all, a *real* word from the Lord is to be remembered and cherished, prayed over and garnered within the heart. So I thought then and so I know now.

Was she a false prophet? Her "prophecies" were certainly mixed with the carnal and mostly proved false. Some of her prognostications may well have caused well-meaning folk to seek grandiose and wrong paths for themselves. The fact is, the poor woman did not understand what the New Testament charism of prophecy is. She was, in effect, doing what seers with crystal balls do: telling fortunes. The sorrowful thing is that she was well-meaning but theologically and psychologically ignorant. She had learned her routine from others. Since then I've met those like her in whom spirits of divination are involved; I don't think that was so with her yet, but it would only be a matter of time before those deceiving spirits would flood in. Her false prognostications were a travesty on the true gift of prophecy; they were an imitation of a word that comes in the power of the Holy Spirit, one without flattery and subtlety and is so phenomenally precious and humbling when graciously sent by the Lord.

Although I never saw that busy, earnest little soul again, I learned through others to whom she ministered that her teaching and practices regarding exorcism and deliverance were spiced with the man-made myths and superstitions that arise out of ignorance. Isaiah's word is pertinent here: "My people go into exile for lack of knowledge" (Isa. 5:13). This is true in all things concerning the people of God, and especially so with falsifications and wrong motives in regard to the work and power of the Spirit.

The gifts of the Spirit, long neglected in the discipling of Christians, were now being travestied by impoverished souls who had tasted something of the goodness and power of God and were now attempting to have it over again by their own efforts. The prophetess and others like her were lone rangers; they operated without the oversight of healthy church bodies, and in effect built their own little kingdoms. I learned much from this incident as I prayed over what I had seen and heard. I came to conclusions that the ensuing years have proved to be correct.

As theologian Gordon Fee so wisely says in *God's Empowering Presence*:

> There is no Pauline evidence for the phenomenon known in contemporary circles as "personal prophecy," whereby someone prophesies over another as to the very personal matters in their lives. Where such might appear to be the case (e.g., 1 Tim. 1:18; 4:4), there is community affirmation (testing?) by way of the laying on of hands by the elders. Otherwise prophecy seems to be a strictly community affair, for the sake of the community's corporate life.[5]

In the so-called prophetess, I saw the seeds of what would later tragically blossom and be incorporated by John Wimber into the Vineyard Christian Fellowship. From there these practices moved into many other groups that he influenced as well. Pastor Wimber, activistic as most moderns are, anxious about a son, weary and in dire need of rest, had a false prophet by the name of Paul Cain thrust upon him by influential men in his inner circle. John, a dear brother and previously effective servant of the Lord, said later that his embracing of the "prophetic" movement was the worst mistake he had ever made. Some of the severest warnings I have ever given to a leader I gave to this dear man, but he was too far into the fog of deception to hear. I warned not only of the divination involved in what he was calling a prophetic gift, but of the consequences if he chose amiss. He could not receive this counsel, but instead invited me to come and join him. Seeing what has now come of that mistake is one of the great griefs I've known.

Even as I wrote the above paragraph, feeling grief anew at the necessity of writing on this difficult matter, I received an email informing me of the fall of Paul Cain. He, the star of this monstrous "prophets movement," lauded internationally up to now in these circles and still among this original group, is according to them not only alcoholic and homosexual but obstinately unrepentant. Even so, this group is claiming him as having been a great and effective prophet and healer. Those to whom he passed on his imitations and perversions of the Holy Spirit's gifts, as well as spirits of divination, have a way of continuing on unabashed, apparently learning nothing from their numerous previous scandals.

This darkness that we discerned and understood back in the fifties as a regrettable offshoot and result of "redneck religion" is now, well over half a century later, vaunting itself and gaining in strength.[6] These folk are now aggressively knocking on the doors of stalwart evangelicals—those who earlier refused any knowledge of the gifts of the Spirit—tempting them to join them with their fastings, prayers, and flamboyant teachings. The evangelicals' intense hunger for knowledge of the Spirit and renewal after a long drought leaves them vulnerable and all too often without discernment. And so in need are they now of a healing ministry to care for the myriads packing their pews caught up in sexual and other sin that they are welcoming what they used to reject.

Back then, this truly great worldwide Christian revival was short on leaders. The renewal was referred to as "charismatic," for it forcibly brought the power and gifts of the Holy Spirit before the attention of a Western church grown materialistic and heady. By and large those pastors and leaders theologically qualified to direct and give sound support instead denied the validity of this work of the Spirit. When rejected by the denominational churches, those in renewal were like sheep without a shepherd, and their lack of affirmation and teaching left them prey to unqualified leaders. Forced to operate outside the church and without solid leadership, the healing ministry has eventuated in a spiritual battle of huge proportions—one that is raging through the so-called prophets movement, through the misguided spiritual-warfare movement, and through healing movements that reflect the extravagances and imbalances of strongly egoistic and even narcissistic leadership.

One of the prominent things to be noted in these movements is how ego and showmanship play such a huge part. And modern technology has amplified this problem today. By and through these teachers, the gifts of God are spectacularized and perverted, and the ministers themselves aggrandized. They call themselves end-time prophets, apostles, and whatnot, and their teachings result in bogus "prophecies" that all too often involve the sin of divination and other aspects of the occult. The mixtures are gnosticlike in that they blend the true with the false. For example, the occult practice of divination is called prophecy and aimed at flattering the one who receives it. Benighted souls often think of themselves as encouraging others through these "prophecies," but the lives they speak into begin to be controlled by the false words in the same way people are influenced by horoscopes and the like.

These groups have long since lost the classic dimensions of the faith and replaced them with the subjective and experience-oriented myths and practices so increasingly amenable to the mind-set of our age. These teachings are heretical and dangerous in that they court the demonic by wrongly focusing on it while at the same time claiming to exorcise it. These teachers fail to realize the illusory nature of evil and that concentrating their minds and imaginations on it leads to spiritual deception and sooner or later to tragedies in their own lives.

In contrast, the true prophets are the healers, preachers, and teachers who are "binders of wounds," because they call people to genuine transformation and repentance. True prophetic words point to sin, to what is amiss in a life or in a culture; they warn of the consequences if one fails to repent (here a predictive element can come in); they reveal what one must do to clean up one's life; they console; they encourage. They do all this in conjunction with the fundamental truth that *the testimony of Jesus is the spirit of prophecy.* Their words, whether they come through preaching, teaching, or the prophetic speaking in a charismatic gift, come with the Spirit's anointing. In this context, words can come that would seem grandiose (such as Gabriel's word to Mary that she would conceive the Son of God), but they do not constellate a carnal drive to power. Indeed, they do just the opposite. They bow one in deepest humility, a humility that continues to cloak the word. These words bear the costly witness and testimony of Jesus.

In that vein, I received two true prophetic words before leaving Little Rock that had extraordinary predictive elements and that over the years have come to pass beyond anything I could have ever imagined. Neither was hyped and both could easily have been missed had I not been listening closely and been in the habit of praying over what I heard. One came through a minister who, along with his prayer group, prayed over me; the other through an aunt just as I was leaving Little Rock. I told not a single soul about these but hid them away in my heart. In fact they were so astounding and precious that I did not even confide them to my prayer journal! They were kept *that* hidden.

As both prophetic words came to pass, I marveled over them, giving thanks and remembering the dear ones who had given voice to them. These prophetic words helped me accept the large responsibilities that went with them. Both are even yet unfolding, amazing me as I'm in my seventh decade with no abatement of either word received. Like so many of the true words that come as *spirituals,* the minister himself was "unconscious" of the word; he later told me he did not recall having given it. But the Lord God sovereignly spoke through this pastor whose work was never tainted by the lust for power and has produced godly, lasting fruit down through the years. And as for my Aunt Rhoda, she denied she ever said it! After her word started coming to pass, she told me in her very practical Scots way that I was quite mistaken; she had never spoken or even dreamt such a thing. But, she—precious child of God—did! And I was the beneficiary of that word from God.

It is my experience that we are the most useful in the Kingdom when we least know it. In contrast, when it happens that we are conscious of a supernatural working of the Holy Spirit, we know of a surety that it has nothing to do with "our gifts" (or with some title we've given ourselves) but with the presence and direct word and/or action of a Holy God.

Along with the profound lessons in incarnational reality, Christ's indwelling of the believer, came a deepening awareness of another foundation stone for the believer—our ongoing need to acknowledge the "old man" within and to "reckon" ourselves dead to him. What Fr. Patrick Reardon says is true of all of us, "I am still a sinner and will be a sinner until the day I die, and the subtler impulses of my heart are quietly conspiring to conceal that truth from my mind."[7]

In the language of the King James Bible, Paul teaches us to "reckon" ourselves dead unto sin, but alive unto God (Rom. 6:11). In the South of my early years, the word still had general currency, and not just for theological purposes. I love that old term, *reckoned*. It has depth and a good, strong history. I am loath to let go of it. It was through the stern lessons of learning to *reckon* myself dead to that old self and alive to Christ that I found a new self and a hope, and watched with the Lord as He put the broken pieces of my life back together and gave to it eternal meaning. In that time and place, however, I found most Christians readier in one fashion or another to "reckon" themselves "once saved, always saved" than to reckon themselves in need of an ongoing confession of sin. The result is that they were stuck somewhere in the process of their conversions. It is as though their baptisms were never completed.

The powerful emotions that had threatened to overwhelm me in the face of my first dangerous enemy confirmed and furthered my understanding that as a Christian I needed regularly to kneel before the Lord as sinner and confess myself one, whether conscious of any willful sin or not. After all, as King David cried out: "Who can discern his lapses and errors? Clear me from hidden [and unconscious] faults. Keep back Your servant also from presumptuous sins; let them not have dominion over me!" (Ps. 19:12–13 AMP).

To go back to the early days of the conversion of my will is to recall once again my eagerness to get to church and how the liturgy of the Word and Sacraments led up to that moment when the entire congregation would

117

kneel to repent of sins, known and unknown. Turning and facing the pews, we knelt on hardwood floors as we prayed the prayers of repentance. In memory I can still hear the rustle and bustle throughout as infant and elderly alike, regardless of bulk and age, settled themselves to their knees. When finally quieted and after these prayers, the comforting moment always came when Pastor Callies, full of the love of God, would say,

> Upon your confession, I, by virtue of my office as a called and ordained servant of the Word, announce the grace of God to all of you, and in the stead and by the command of my Lord Jesus Christ I forgive you all your sins in the name of the Father and of the Son and of the Holy Spirit.

To which we would all say, as one, "Amen."

This regular practice, written into the ancient and classic liturgies of the church, began and continued a healing in me incomparable in scope. Though there was no conscious, deliberate sinning on my part, in this way I had regular access to the "sinner," the old identity that is always there but is not our prime one. As sinners saved by grace who have died to our old sin nature, we continue in that death through ongoing confession and remission of sins and weaknesses until we are completed in Glory. This is baptismal piety, largely missing from the church of today.

Apart from these ongoing acknowledgments and prayers, we lose touch with our own hearts and do not know them. Many Christians then and today attend churches with astonishingly incomplete worship liturgies. They therefore do not have regular opportunities for rightly examining their hearts, repenting, and then receiving forgiveness.[8] In fact some even teach in a way that discourages folk from this needed practice. But to rightly examine one's heart is to avoid the egoistic "disease of introspection"[9] that so many Christians suffer due to always feeling (and being) guilty and in need of forgiveness.

These scriptural lessons in Christian spirituality underlie the practice we in PCM have of training prayer counselors in the hearing of confessions and in the proclamation of forgiveness of specific sin in such a way that the confessing soul can receive it. This is the first healing session in all of our conferences, one that prepares the soul for the healings that follow. I shall never forget the first time when at least six hundred people surged forward to make confession, totally overwhelming our prayer counselors and leaving only about three hundred folk still seated. This ratio has continued, showing the astounding need for the confession of sin in the church of today. For many, including pastors and other Christian professionals as well as laity, this is the first time ever to make confession of sin to another

Christian, one ready to hear their cry and to proclaim Christ's forgiveness to them in an effective way. Major healings of the deep mind and heart—and even the body—start from this very point. The repentance of sin and the reception of forgiveness make up the first principle and basic key in the healing of persons.

In dying to the old man and rising in the new, the Christian has found himself in Christ, and thereby, as he obeys, finds that he is securely anchored in the transcendent, the Eternal, the real. I was maturing in all this as daily I reckoned myself dead to sin and alive to Christ. Though I could not then have verbalized the sacramental nature of what was going on, I was merely filling out or completing what had been lacking in my understanding of, preparation for, and experience of baptism. I was daily taking my place in Christ's death and, as it were, dying with Him to my own sin and to the sin of the world. I was taking my place in His obedience to the Father and thereby rising with Him in newness of life! This is baptismal spirituality, baptismal piety. It is the basis for all sacramental prayer, worship, and actions.

As Paul said in the letter to the Romans:

> How can we who died to sin still live in it? Do you not know that all of us who have been baptized into Christ Jesus were baptized into his death? We were buried therefore with him by baptism into death, in order that, just as Christ was raised from the dead by the glory of the Father, we too might walk in newness of life.
>
> Romans 6:2–4

Never shall I forget the first ordinance I came to when I started through the Gospels, intent on finding and obeying our Lord's every command. That is because it involved water baptism, the meaning and efficacy of which was, to say the least, opaque to my mind. Besides that, it was found in the context of our Lord's own baptism and revealed His earnest intent to obey every command of His Father! The command was not a direct one in that it was nestled away in our Lord's "autobiography," His incarnate story; yet it revealed not only something incumbent upon Him but upon all who, in His likeness and strength, desire to obey.

> Then Jesus came from Galilee to the Jordan to John, to be baptized by him. John would have prevented him, saying, "I need to be baptized by you, and do you come to me?" But Jesus answered him, "Let it be so now, for thus it is fitting for us to fulfill all righteousness." Then he consented. And when Jesus was baptized, immediately he went up from the water, and behold, the

heavens were opened to him, and he saw the Spirit of God descending like a dove, and coming to rest on him; and behold, a voice from heaven said, "This is my beloved Son, with whom I am well pleased."

Matthew 3:13–17

Here in our Lord's story, we see Him, the God-Man, immersed and rising up from the waters of earth, the opening of the heavens, and then, from the highest heavens we see the descent of the Holy Spirit, and the voice of God the Father acknowledging, affirming, and naming His only begotten Son. It was utterly cosmic and stopped me in my tracks.

In his *Confessions,* Augustine lamented the sins of his youth with all his heart and soul. In trying to figure out what had made his early years so difficult and crazy, he grieved over the fact that the waters of baptism had been withheld from him as a young lad whose heart was tender toward the Lord. He realized that if he had had a full initiation into Christ, he would not have wasted so many years of his life.

My laments and questions had been as agonizing as Augustine's, but were the opposite in that I *had* been baptized. I labored to understand why, with the godly mother and teaching I had, as well as water baptism, I could have gotten so confused and off track. To what effect had been my baptism? *Should I be rebaptized?* I wondered (a common reaction). No, I began to realize. Rather I needed to complete my baptism.

My attempts to understand this indirect command of our Lord's, His "let it be so now," brought me face-to-face with the fact that in the church I had been brought up in, rites such as baptism and the Lord's Supper were just that, simply formal rites. And they were strangely ineffectual even as memorials. The Christians there sought to keep the commands of God by once or twice a year observing these rites, but they did not think of them in terms of incarnational reality. That is, they did not view them as worship, prayer, and symbolic actions through which Christ Himself is renewed in us, and they did not thereby expect healing and blessing to follow.

The Eucharistic liturgy (an extension and reenactment of baptism, though I didn't realize that as yet) in my Lutheran church meant so much to me, and I took great care to prepare my heart for it; yet in seeing the preparations for baptism and the rite itself, I felt something surely was lacking. It wasn't that I doubted its necessity for infant and adult alike, but rather that I knew there must be so much more available to us than we were realizing or expecting. And I knew that the loss was even greater for the nonsacramental churches. As *the* initiatory rite into Christ, I saw our enactment of it as weak and anemic. I had little doubt that the outright unbelievers and pagans (like a Freud or a shaman) do a much better job of initiating their young into the darkness of their worldviews than we as Christians do into the light and life of Christ and the Judeo-Christian worldview.

This was the raw material in my mind and heart on finding my first command in the story of Christ's baptism, those extraordinary verses where we first see the full Trinity in action: the Father's voice from highest heaven, the Holy Spirit's descent upon Christ in the form of a dove, and the naming of Christ by the Father. To have been so exercised by this first command to be baptized gave me a heightened eagerness to find the rest of the commands and write them out in my journal.

I started out wanting to obey the Lord. I ended in finding that, once again, the answer is baptismal: I die with Him to my own will, and I rise with Him—in His saving obedience.

Healings of a spiritual, psychological, and emotional nature are what the Bible describes as deliverance from sin and its effects. This and everything that I have learned and experienced in the healing ministry are rooted in baptism and are found it its early liturgies. Every conversion or restoration of the life of God in a soul, every liberation from darkness and despair, every exorcism and/or deliverance, every healing of memories (forgiveness of sin), every physical or psychological healing, every holy anointing or baptism of the Spirit, every putting on of the righteousness of Christ ("the white robe" in the liturgical rite), and every sacramental action such as the use of blessed water[10] are merely a completing or fulfilling of holy baptism. All these ministrations, so desperately needed by the unhealed Christians filling our church pews, not to mention the pagans who come our way, are all provided for in baptism rightly understood, practiced, and lived out sacramentally through the Word of God and the Eucharist.

What is being described here is what I grew up hearing about in the great old sermons on holiness as "nailing the old man" to the cross (Gal. 5:24). This good image alone, however, given in a church that has lost its sacramental and much of its charismatic structure, leaves out the prime image that the cross signifies: that of a baptismal, incarnational image of being *in* Christ, participating in both his death and his rising. It includes the reality of our participation *in* Christ's obedience to the Father. These realities, absolutely unique to Christianity, are vital to keep before the mind and heart.

The term *healing ministry* would hardly be in use today if the cure of the soul had been maintained as Christ and the apostles instituted it in the church. That is why, in every Pastoral Care Ministry School we conduct, I take care to say that everything we do and teach is rightly part of baptism, a filling in of the knowledge and the practices in the rites of baptism and confirmation, and is ongoing in full worshipful Eucharists as well. The Eucharist is an extension of baptism, bringing Pascha (Easter) to us continually. As Fr. Alexander Schmemann cries out, with great grief, very few Christians even know today that our Easter Eucharistic liturgy, in its fullness, was originally the liturgy for baptism.[11]

Therefore through the liturgy at Grace Lutheran in Little Rock, the *sacramental structure* that had been so lost to me was restored while the *charisms* of the Spirit were being imparted. To lose the charismatic structure entirely is to lose that which is truly sacramental: it is to have only the form without the essence. The *evangel* (the Word) and the *Sacraments* are, apart from the Spirit, without life. These three structures were being unified and balanced within me, making this time in my life extraordinarily wonderful and blessed. To lose any one of the three is to weaken all three, even eventually to risk losing all. The evangelical, sacramental, and charismatic structures, in unity and balance, restore to the church the healing, saving gospel of Christ.

Thus I left Arkansas having learned invaluable lessons in sacramental truth and reality, and even then knew something of the magnitude of the loss of this vital understanding in the church in general, whether in denominations still maintaining a baptismal and Eucharistic liturgy or in the many Protestant churches with hardly any liturgy or none at all. I now know more of the vastness of the loss we have sustained in our understanding and practice of baptism, and therefore of that which underlies the church's loss of its own Judeo-Christian symbolic system and worldview, for baptism (in its liturgy, in its symbolism, and in its essential efficacy) encapsulates and captures it. All other sacramental actions are rooted in and stand upon this initial rite, for it celebrates and passes on to us the knowledge of incarnational reality—Christ in us and we in Him—and brings fuller understanding of the Incarnation.

Back then I also realized something of the dangers of having grown up on truly great and wonderful Wesleyan holiness sermons when they are wrenched apart from sacramental worship with its ongoing means not only of repentance but of reception of the very presence of the Lord in the Sacrament of the Eucharist (the Lord's Supper). The Wesleys possessed this understanding and an incarnational worldview; therefore their sermons, writings, and music issued out of that spirituality. For them, the three major structures of the church—the evangelical, the charismatic, and the sacramental—were yet largely intact and were integrated into their lives as one marvelous whole. Most truly, sacramental spirituality and holiness go together, and it is hazardous to our souls to separate them.

As I look back, I marvel to see how the Lord set into my mind and heart, at such a relatively young age, these foundational lessons—the true healing of the soul, the warnings against the perversion of the gifts of the Holy Spirit, and the need for a true completion of our baptism. Little did I know the adventures that lay ahead of me outside the familiar surroundings of my family and my heritage in the South.

13

The Unthinkable Looms

Time to Leave Home?

Happy are the people whose strength is in you! whose hearts are set on the pilgrims' way.

Psalm 84:4 JB

After I had found better and more secure employment and then received a modest promotion or two within the Civil Service, things were looking up for Deb and me. By 1960 we had our first car, one of a succession of old jalopies. This one, a vintage Pontiac we came affectionately to name Betsy, had been used for pulling logs up in the Ouachita mountains and had all the scars to prove it. But we got her for a little over a hundred dollars, and I don't remember such exhilaration over car ownership since. She was the most reliable old thing and seemed to run no matter what I failed to do.

After several years, however, she stiffened up to the point I could hardly turn the steering wheel. As I worried aloud over that, an uncle asked me when last the car had been oiled. Amazed, I told him that I didn't know it needed oil. He was stunned to silence. So a little greasing of Betsy's aging joints and an oil change fixed her up fine.

We had a dog the likes of which books are written about. She was a beautiful boxer we got as a tiny pup and named the Duchess of Arkansas,

Arkie for short. She understood English, showed every human emotion imaginable, and could communicate with us as well. She was wonderful out in the countryside, the best dog for taking on anything she deemed a threat, a real plus in the woods and hill country surrounding Little Rock.

Indeed, she may even have saved my life one day when I was out in the backyard hanging up clothes on the line. All of a sudden Arkie leaped on a huge snake (perhaps a mountain rattler or spreading adder), catching it behind the head just as it was striking at my ankle. Then ensued a fight that was one of the most extraordinary things I've ever seen. It seems odd now that I could note the strange grace between large snake and large dog while being so thoroughly terrified, but the picture is still in my mind. Both creatures proved to be champions, but Arkie won.

Exactly how she won I shall never know. In the midst of the battle, I ran in to phone that time's equivalent of 911, as I feared that the snake's fangs were striking Arkie in some of its thrusts. When I got back to Arkie, after frantic attempts to convince rescue workers that they must come, the snake had been thoroughly banished and Arkie simply looked satisfied. And by the time two police squads got there, Arkie was not even panting or showing any signs that she had just been in a phenomenal battle. I, however, was thoroughly traumatized and wouldn't let the police go until they checked every inch of her for fang marks, and until they scoured several acres of the surrounding wooded hillside to make sure the monstrous snake was nowhere about. Not a sign of the snake was to be found, nor a single fang mark on Arkie.

Arkie did not take to old Betsy. If forced to ride, she hung halfway out the window while gulping air. One day she took a long leap all the way out of the car and survived it, and so we simply never took such a chance again.

All this to say that the days of crowded bus rides and long walks home from work were over, and there was even the occasional pleasure of motoring outside the city as well.

The next year we found a Baldwin organ, one voiced for church, and then, wonder of wonders, saw it installed in our living room. A used car I could have imagined beforehand but never the miracle of this instrument. Now we could have musical accompaniment to our singing in our prayer group, and I could get music ready at home for Sunday services. The organ brought other blessings as well. On many occasions when my invalid neighbors across the street, a father and a son, were placed in wheelchairs on their front porch, I would open wide my front door, pull out all the organ stops, and play the great hymns for them. This eventually paved the way for a deathbed conversion of the unbelieving son, when God brought him out of a coma to receive Christ. He died the next day.

While our lives had taken a turn for the better, conditions in our country had turned quite grim. These late 1950s and early 1960s were tumultuous times and slated to get worse in terms of civil unrest and general moral decline. In Little Rock we had entered this period in a spectacularly earth-shaking way in 1957 when military troops, guns at the ready, marched into our city and up to Central High School to confront the state governor for his refusal to end segregation. Throughout the country, racial unrest continued to escalate. Once integrated, the public school systems were chaotic, and the emotional upsets for all families, black or white, mounted year by year as drugs started flooding into the high schools.

The dreadful sixties with all their riots, political divisions, and lawlessness were upon us, a time from which we have not recovered. Since World War II, the Hemingway Man had been glamorized. Women were largely portrayed as silly or sulky sex objects. By the sixties the sexual revolution was fully underway, and it resulted in the loss of moral character and in the vileness of public discourse and behavior we see flooding through the media and pop culture today.

By 1962 Deborah had graduated from her Christian grammar school, been confirmed, and was soon to enter high school. For me, life was the best yet; never before had I known such blessing, such fulfillment. Even as a high school dropout, I could now make a tolerable living— no more serious worries about where the next meal was coming from. Yet my concern for Deborah's future was urgent. As a single parent I knew I could not give her all that she needed to withstand the pressures of the public school system, chaotic as it was. I longed to further her opportunities for a thoroughly Christian high school and university training and yearned for strong godly father figures for her. Hoping to find a Christian high school, I began checking out Lutheran boarding schools, all of which seemed to be in the far North. The expenses would equal or surpass my salary, so I put this desire on hold and continued to pray about the matter.

As time went on, I prayed with all my soul about Deborah's schooling and searched out every lead. Soon all this led to what, apart from prayer and the Lord's guidance, would have been utterly unthinkable. God in his mercy opened and revealed the way and granted the impossible. He gave me a desire of my heart and in the end granted even desires buried too deep for me to know about, much less pray about. Deborah and I, who had never driven farther than thirty miles away, packed up all our belongings and drove north across three states.

By the time of this momentous decision, I had quite thoroughly taken in every scriptural reference on guidance and F. B. Meyer's commentary on it. As he says in his book *The Secret of Guidance*:

> God's impressions within and His word without are always corroborated by His providence around, and we should quietly wait until these three focus into one point. . . . The circumstances of our daily life are to us an infallible indication of God's will when they concur with the inward promptings of the Spirit and with the Word of God.[1]

My debt to F. B. Meyer is enormous. Most everything he taught I already knew in some fashion, but from Mother's womanly perspective. As a godly man, F. B. Meyer, holy and utterly orthodox like her, somehow ministered to me the things a godly father would have given. It was as though I were sitting and learning guidance and wisdom for life's journey at his knee. In him there was a holy strength and wisdom together with a masculine authority blessed by the Spirit of God. He was, in the finest Christian sense, a healer, one of the truly great old evangelicals.[2]

I now knew how to wait, how to pray, and more important, I knew that Someone else was *there* and was hearing my prayer. It was easy, then, to wait for God's answer, and as I waited and listened, the way was shown. A very ancient and grubby scribbling of Isaiah 30:21, well worn, fell out of papers saved from this period: "And thine ears shall hear a word behind thee, saying, This is the way, walk ye in it, when ye turn to the right hand, and when ye turn to the left" (KJV).

In and by God's providence, I glimpsed a help-wanted advertisement tucked into the back pages of a Christian magazine. It had been placed there by one Dr. John Blanchard, headmaster of Wheaton Academy, and he was in need of a dorm mother. The academy had been historically a part of Wheaton College and located on their grounds, but had been moved to a rural area just outside the city of Wheaton, Illinois, a western suburb of Chicago. It was a nondenominational, evangelical high school dedicated to preparing students for college and had a long history of boarding children of missionaries and of other Christian leaders serving abroad. I wrote inquiring about the school and the position, along with the possibilities of my daughter attending high school there. After several letters and a phone call, I was flown to Chicago for an interview and a weekend with the headmaster and his wife, Barbara.

It was a most memorable time with this dedicated Christian family, and a quieter one than would have been the case had the school not been closed for summer vacation. The job, however, would be quite earthshakingly different from anything I had yet attempted or ever imagined. Sixty-five girls were signed up to be in the dorm, many of whom were coming in directly from foreign countries where they had grown up as children of missionaries. An even greater number of boys were to be housed in a separate dorm, and would be looked after by Wheaton College seniors, all male and most of them athletes, many of whom were headed toward Christian ministry and missions. Deborah would live with the other students, rooming with several other girls in the dorm. My hours would be long and the duties many, but there would be some free time during school hours. There would be room, board, educational benefits, and a very small stipend but no pension.

Some of the awesomeness I was feeling over this possible transition was reflected in my prayer journal on awaking after the first night spent during that interview weekend in an otherwise empty dormitory. There is an eerie sort of stillness when a student dormitory, full of life during the school term, is bereft of its lively inhabitants. In that extraordinary quiet, a deeply sobered soul wrote: "Sat.—Aug 10, '63 Flew to Chicago— met Dr. Blanchard and family—saw the school—was told all problems involved—my heart was very heavy when I spent my first night in the hospital infirmary [dorm] . . ."

By the next day, however, my spirits must have revived a bit, for I wrote, "Aug 11th, Sunday—Wonderful day—Heard Pastor Blanchard preach at the Bible Church in Chicago. . . ."

I returned home, certain that I would be accepting the position.

Everything, like the flat plains country surrounding the little white chapel and school, reminded me of how very different life would be. No hills to look to or walk over. Rich dark soil everywhere, without the mixtures of reds and browns I'd grown up with. Lush cornfields lay everywhere around, intersected by an interesting country road, dotted with beautiful trees and farmhouses, which I looked forward to exploring.

There was, however, a tie or two with this unknown part of the Christian world that held me in good stead. I knew that F. B. Meyer and R. A. Torrey had connections with Wheaton College, and that Torrey had even visited here and prayed over its hallowed grounds with the likes of Dwight L. Moody and an early president of Wheaton College, who was also a Blanchard. *Perhaps,* I thought, *maybe, just maybe, as a Lutheran with a Wesleyan holiness background, I might fit into this part of the church.* Of course I realized that they might find me a bit strange. It was apparent that the great renewal I had experienced was not yet part of the life of this place. Even so, my ties with their eighteenth- and nineteenth-century church fathers led me to hope all would be well.

My family met me on return from Chicago with their hearts in their eyes. Would I really be leaving home and a good job—a job with a pension? To a person, they were aghast. They feared I had reverted to type and that my Achilles' heel, with its incorrigible rashness, had reappeared. (I should add that no one feared that more than I did.) But the Lord called me forth, leading me away from family, home, church, friends, prayer partners, all dearly beloved—a thing, which, apart from the Lord's leading, could not have been done. Without F. B. Meyer's help with discernment and having lived for several years listening for God's will, I would have had much more difficulty dealing with my family's understandable consternation.

This is undoubtedly where the "sanctified abandon" that Oswald Chambers speaks of comes in. Yes, without a qualm in regard to future security, I said I would be leaving because Deborah needed a good educational environment and the call "Come ye after me" was clear and strong. I knew these precious ones would understand in time but felt bad that they were so concerned.

Once they accepted my decision, however, the family pitched in and helped me pack up and move. My brother-in-law found a well-used VW Kombi (we called it a wagon or bus), sold old Betsy, and helped load up our belongings. Believe it or not, we even managed to squeeze in the church model organ—the pedal octaves are removable and can be stood upright.

By this point, our beloved Arkie had been consigned to the hills of Arkansas. We had been forced to send her away after she, overly protective of Deborah and me, bit the postman for the second time and had very nearly bitten other well-meaning strangers as well. We gave her up into the hands of an Arkansas State policeman, whom we knew and trusted to love her as we did. After a little training, she accompanied him on his trips to root out illegal stills, thoroughly intimidating the miscreants but making fast friends of law-abiding folk. I think the Lord was looking after her as well, for she was shot once, but vets removed the bullet from under her pelt with no deep injury to her.

At that time the hill folk had the habit of going into town on Saturday morning where the men would gather to smoke and hear the news of their neighbors. According to legend (for Arkie became a legendary figure), every Saturday morning she would walk the long trek into town, arrive at the meeting place before them, spend the day there, and then travel back home on her own. How she acquired the weekly time clock, no one knew! Having had a dog like her has left me knowing that no other dog will ever live up to her. Truly in every great and noble beast I meet, I see a little bit of the Duchess of Arkansas.

Finally the momentous day arrived and it was time for us to leave. Our family, friends, and neighbors gathered around the old VW bus that was packed so tight that we could not see out the rearview mirror. I had a good side-view mirror on the driver's side, but the one on Debby's side was missing. So besides being the official map reader, she had the responsibility of sticking a hand mirror out her window when needed, which of course was often.

Leaving Mom was most difficult, but by then, I think she knew there was something of the Lord in this move and she no longer voiced any dismay. Besides, my brother-in-law had built her a home next to theirs—her first home. They had the time, the means, and the full will to make sure all was well with her. Never was a mother more respected and cherished by her children, and that fully included her son-in-law.

In the midst of all our good-byes, I switched on the ignition, and with an alarming hesitation and groan of the engine, the old bus slowly moved forward. With hearts full to bursting with the love of family and the adventure ahead, Deb and I traveled over the Arkansas River, a part of the world dear to us, and onward north. We passed through some lower country and by cypress bogs with turtles sunning on whatever dry spot they could find, and on up through the hills of Arkansas and Missouri. Then we crossed the great bridge spanning the Mississippi River before entering into Illinois. The trip took three days, for we were slow moving and were unused to such a long drive. We prayed all the way that the old Kombi bus could stand the trip.

Finally, passing what seemed like endless miles of beautiful farm country, we made our way off the main highway and onto the rural road leading to the academy. As the white chapel and school came into view, we were at the end of a momentous trip, one of the great transitions of our lives. The staff of the academy were there to help us unload and were mightily amazed to find a church organ as part of the task.

14

Life at Wheaton Academy

What is true religion? It is not the religion which contains most truth in the theological sense of the word. It is not the religion most truly thought out, nor that which most closely fits with thought. It is the religion in which the soul becomes very sure of God and itself in prayer. Prayer contains the very heart and height of truth, but especially in the Christian sense of the truth—reality and action.

P. T. Forsyth

God's call is always to prayer, and responsibility for a dorm jam-packed with adolescent girls was an incentive to prayer far beyond the ordinary. It was a propelling into the biblical admonition to pray always, in the spirit and with the understanding. I look back on these challenging yet wonderful years as a time of continuous prayer, of leaning upon and into Christ as never before. Of all the memories, the most vivid are of walking the several miles up and down the beautiful rural road and praying for the school, the girls in my care, and of course the young lads whose lives intersected with theirs.

Most of these precious teenage girls were gifted and ready for more education, but some were emotionally uprooted and confused. Others seemed homesick and greatly in need of their parents, while a few others

133

were reacting to their past and were angry, rebellious, and self-destructive. These latter, who were mired in resentments against their parents, the church, and their circumstances, proved the most difficult to help. In those years I learned much about the needs of the human soul for godly affirmation and the maturation and healing that comes only through a vital relationship to Christ.

The forerunner of the PCM newsletters started from the time I arrived at the academy, for it was the only way I could correspond with all the family and friends back home. In one of the first, after getting to know the faculty and staff, I wrote the following:

> Talk about brains! It's wonderful to be around "sanctified" brains—don't know what else to call them. Master's degrees and Doctorates are the common thing around here. I have never been so conscious of my English; I eat at the same table as the Faculty. They all say I have a southern accent—they don't know it is they who have the accents!

Indeed, the two years I spent at Wheaton Academy were eye-opening in a variety of ways. They were a preparation for and introduction to the world at large and, quite literally, to the people of the world. The students given me to care and pray for included both children of missionaries and youngsters from many nations, including Africa, India, Egypt, China, Korea, Japan, Thailand, Indonesia, Philippines, Germany, France, South America, and various parts of the United States and Canada.

Two women who helped in the dorm also had international roots; one was Dutch and the other was German, and both had been taken prisoner in World War II. The Dutch lady, Mrs. Greve, was mother of several day students in the school and taught knitting, embroidery, and crafts to our girls during some of the weekends. She and her family had been living in Indonesia when the Japanese invaded and took them prisoner. They lost everything but were among the fortunate few who lived to tell of their imprisonment. It was a joy to "take tea" with her, and I remember to this day the wonderful ritual of a perfect cup of tea around her table. She brought all the best customs of her native Holland with her.

The German lady, in charge of housekeeping, was a woman who had suffered greatly. For years she endured the horrors of rape and outrage in a Russian prison camp and had given birth to a child as a result. A sudden outcry from one of our young girls, common to adolescents and not alarming to others, brought back the memories and left her open to fresh, fearful trauma all over again. I prayed with her and recall making comforting potato dishes that seemed to help her stomach.

I wish I had known then how to prepare dishes for the Asian nationals, for they could only suffer through the diet American teens relish. Three lovely Thai girls immediately come to mind, along with their difficult attempts to supplement the academy diet out of packages faithfully sent from home.

It was easy to empathize with our foreign students, for Deb and I shared a great deal of their culture shock. Southern to the core, we had to adjust to the Northern customs. For example, a few days into the term, Deborah was stunned in class when accused of "smarting off" by replying "Yes, ma'am" to her gym teacher. The young teacher, fresh out of college, was unfamiliar with Southern decorum and its way of showing respect in addressing one's elders. I too learned quickly that being "Southern friendly" earned suspicions that one is soft-headed or worse, and this was especially noticeable on the part of store clerks or those one is jammed up against on crowded commuter trains. Even more concerning, this was true of a few of my own dorm girls.

One occasion early in my tenure forcefully brought home the notion that I needed to toughen up a good bit. The school nurse, an utterly precious and petite Baptist lady, civil, polite, and lovely at table and in staff prayer meetings, ascended the stairs to the girls' dorm, took one whiff of a girl who was neglecting to take showers, and cried, loud enough for the whole dorm to hear, "Get in the shower!"

I never quite learned to handle problems in such a direct Northern fashion even though it was obviously effective, but I did learn to moderate the Southern habit of circumlocution, that wonderful way of helping misdoers save face. Here such language simply wasn't understood. All of this cultural changing and learning was as nothing, of course, in light of the large benefits coming from this part of my education.

Life in the dorm was seldom if ever placid. My two years there would fill a book in itself. To be so closely involved in so many teen lives at any time is not for the fainthearted, especially in the era of the sixties. Christian homes were not exempt from the drugs, sexual experimentation, and rebellion of the youth culture as a whole. In addition to these problems, a few students were there who, had the extent of their problems at home been known, would not have been admitted.

For example, it was during these years that I first saw the rebellion that would cause a child to turn to Satan worship. Due to this need, it was here that I first used holy water and learned the way the Holy Spirit uses blessed water ("Let this put you in mind of your baptism") and a blessed crucifix in the deliverance of souls. I could have learned these lessons earlier from Martin Luther and others, but such teaching had long been relegated to the archaic past and was not passed on as the vital help it is.[1] It was here too that I faced the difficulties of a full-blown hysteric for the first time. I would later write about such things in *The Broken Image,* as they are found in neuroses rooted in severe separation anxiety.[2]

But the more normal experiences of teen life outweighed the more difficult ones. Below I tell my prayer partners of the type of thing that parents of healthy teens face, which would not have caused nearly so much trouble for the miscreant if she were home rather than in a dorm where there are bed checks.

March 16

Week before last was a very rough week in the dormitory—we expelled two kids—so this week I have just been lazy . . . emotionally all "drug" out—but now I feel all rested again.

March 17

I got a wonderful rest just to prepare me for last night I guess! Yikes— you have no idea what it is like to search for a missing girl all by yourself at 2 a.m. thru a creaky old building til you have done it! One of my dear little ones decided she would go out and look at the stars from the football field—she opened big, old creaky doors to a spiral slide fire escape, and in the dark she couldn't see that some of our other little "Dears" had emptied their dust pans into the slide—therefore she stepped into all this loose dirt and with lots of clanging went down the fire escape at much greater speed than anticipated. I was waiting in her room (she had a big teddy bear under the covers) when she returned but had been out searching in the darkened spooky regions for her before this time—she came back up the fire escape and needless to say my presence was quite a shock to her and I'm not sure whose knees were knocking together the hardest. She is expelled for three days and I guess it will take me that long to recover—such is the life of a housemother. Never ever a dull minute. Sometimes I laugh til I cry—other times I weep til the Lord turns it into rejoicing.

This next entry illustrates the rebellious child's struggle to grow up:

One of my brightest students has been dabbling in the fields of existentialism, agnosticism, reads everything from Freud to the Scriptures, thinks she wants to become a psychiatrist. She is so thirsty for all knowledge, is full of rebellion towards fine Christian parents, unwilling to accept "childish" faith, etc.

Anyway, she had a quarrel with her boyfriend who wanted to break up their friendship. She came upstairs, took 30 aspirin tablets, and was planning on getting sick, throwing up, and really making her boyfriend sorry. She couldn't throw up the aspirin—got very frightened—came to me and told me she didn't mean to try to take her life—just wanted to make (so and so) sorry. We rushed her to the doctor and got her stomach pumped—two days later her ears were still ringing—of course she could have had a toxic reaction and died. The Lord once again was good to us here at the Academy.

This story had a good ending, as most did, for it proved a turning point in the girl's life—an answer not only to my prayers and those of my prayer partners but also those of her friends in the dorm who loved and faithfully prayed for her. The few who couldn't make it were the ones we sorrowed over.

As Deborah and I adapted to life in the North, we had another great adjustment, and this one was related to more than just cultural differences. We simply did not fit into the Lutheran church in our area. This was shocking, but leaving was made easier by knowing that we had our church back home once Christmas and summer vacations came round. Although this was a disappointment to me, it led to one of the truly great and propitious blessings in my life, one that occurred soon after we arrived and that only our Lord could have so quickly engineered. Namely, I got to know and work with the Reverend Richard Winkler for the few more years he would be in Wheaton. He was the Episcopal priest who has been referred to as the grandfather of the great renewal that had touched me so profoundly back in Little Rock and was then sweeping the old-line churches. Through Fr. Winkler I came to know of and meet many others gifted in the time-honored Anglican tradition of healing prayer, including Catherine Marshall, Agnes Sanford, and R. A. Torrey III, missionary and founder of Jesus Abbey in Korea.[3] And it was through Fr. Winkler that I joined the Episcopal church. In doing so, God gifted me with some of the most precious and gifted prayer partners one could ever hope for, faithful friends who walked with me through the tumultuous upcoming months and years. (More on Fr. Winkler in the coming chapters.)

Truly, at this time an embarrassment of riches poured over me, grace upon grace, strengthening me for ministry. Another blessing came about through one of the teen boys in the academy dorm, the son of Assemblies of God missionaries to India. He told me of his pastor, Rev. Wayne Kraiss, founder of their denominational church in Wheaton, who was in need of an organist on Sunday mornings. This worked well, as my dorm girls were in their respective churches at this time, and it did not interfere with my being a full member in my own church.

After meeting Pastor Kraiss and attending his Sunday morning service, I knew it would be a rare blessing to serve as organist there if he thought his congregation was ready for German Lutheran chorales and hymn preludes. As it happened they were and Deborah and I, with grateful hearts, attended their morning service. Together with being a fine expositor of the Word of God (I wrote home, "He's the best minister of the Word I have ever heard!"), Pastor Kraiss preached and taught under a great anointing of the Holy Spirit. That church and her people were most precious to us the several years we were there, and Pastor Kraiss proved to be the kind of pastor one never forgets, one who ministers into the lives of the neediest, the widows and orphans.[4]

The redirection in terms of church connections, coming as they did with such phenomenal benefits, was only the beginning of the blessings that came with obeying God's call, his leading of my footsteps to Wheaton. Integral to my housemothering years were these two new church situations, for they provided the backup of intercessory prayer and encouragement I needed while at the academy. They also proved to be gifts that never stopped giving, extending beyond my years there.

In addition to these blessings, I had a totally unexpected personal bonus—the introduction to the world of higher education and the joys of learning in the Christian liberal arts atmosphere of Wheaton Academy and College. As it turned out, that which I had so fervently petitioned the Lord to do for Deborah was also available to me.

The few hours of free time I had came mostly when the students were in class, and so I sat in on a literature and a history class and simply gloried in it. Dr. Blanchard, seeing my delight (and need of diversion), worked out a program whereby I could take freshman classes at the college for high school credit at the academy. By 1965 I had more than earned a high school diploma.

I first heard of C. S. Lewis in 1963, the year of his death, for folk at the academy mourned his passing. By 1965 I had read *Surprised by Joy* with eye-popping interest and had written a paper on it. It got a big, fat *A*, along with the professor's commendation: "You should write more!" Of course I didn't believe him, but as things would turn out, I was finding my niche in more ways than I could have imagined at the time.

It is hard to believe that so much blessing could rain on one with so little free time. But it did! And the Lord engineered all these things, the very times and schedules included.

As housemother I learned deep lessons about the human soul that have not been wasted; the varied experiences I had with the girls and those surrounding them are surely among the reasons the Lord directed me to the academy. For example, I have fond memories of interacting at table with several of the faculty and the Wheaton College seniors in charge of the boys' dorm. These latter were highly motivated, bright, and gifted young men, all sportsmen with much to impart both consciously and unconsciously. Though surely unaware, they provided for me quite a study of the young male and his maturation into adulthood.

As I mentioned above, it was at the academy that my search to understand separation anxiety began, a condition that can severely afflict those who have known deprivation of mother love in their first months and years of life. I wrote home that I was "seriously considering keeping notes on adopted children and writing a book on their particular problems. If I could write, I could sure sketch out a dilly. . . ."

It was in regard to an adopted girl that God so amazed me with my first great lesson in the nature of time, one that led me a great step farther toward understanding the way He so wondrously heals old traumas, those memories that can result in serious bouts of separation anxiety. I have written more fully about this lesson in time previously,[5] but it is worth summarizing the experience again as it was so seminal in my life.

During one of the summer holidays, I was deeply perplexed over a precious girl whom I had been unable to help. She would repeatedly fall into sexual sin, a thing uncommon at that time in Christian schools, and then would repent with all her heart. I knew her desire to change and as well God's freeing power of forgiveness, so I couldn't understand her inability to stand in Christ. I did not know why her pain ended in sexual compulsions that drove her to throw herself away with men time after time.

Whenever we would pray about her "falls," she would invariably begin to wail as a terrible early memory came to mind. It was of the police coming into their home and taking her drunken parents one direction and her beloved baby brothers another. She never saw them again.

While on a camping trip in Oklahoma, I had been asking the Lord why this girl, Edie, remained so troubled, why she couldn't receive from Him what she needed. The answer, though it took more time and another key lesson or two to understand, came in a most remarkable and unforget-table way. In the process of cleaning up the camp, I walked out onto a huge boulder to empty a dishpan. The chore finished, I stepped back, and when I did, I stepped back in time. In doing so I saw two Indian men and they saw me. I glimpsed the terrain as it had been hundreds of years ago. I knew instantly that it was long before the white man had come, and that these Indian men had never before seen a white person. We were mutually astonished.

All this happened and was over in an instant. Amazed, I ran back to my old camper wagon and prayed. I asked the Lord what had happened and I knew it was exactly as it seemed to be: I had looked down through time; they had looked up through time and seen me. As I prayed, the Lord assured me that He had allowed this experience and that it was in no way engineered by the powers of darkness.

The Lord was showing me that all times are one with Him, that He is eternally present to all those moments where forgiveness and healing are needed. He was showing me that the hurts that Edie had suffered as an infant were encapsulated in the root memory behind her compulsions, but that He had not abandoned her in the worst of moments. I eventually learned how to pray for healing for these traumas held in the early memories in people's lives. Inviting God into the memories, we would then ask for the power of the Holy Spirit so that they could not only extend forgive-ness to the perpetrators but receive healing into their deep wounding and incapacitating sense of rejection. After this we would pray for them to receive God's healing love, and then we would see Him minister that love into their deep hearts.

Truly God heals even the traumas we can't remember. He is present to all our times—past, present, and future. We must simply learn to collaborate with Him in prayer, as I was learning during those years.

By February of 1965, I knew that I would be transferring from the academy to the college, and plans began working out toward that end. For financial reasons, the academy was to be separated from the college and restructured along lines that would eliminate the huge deficits from run-ning a dormitory school. Dr. Blanchard would be leaving, and everything would be changing for all of us, staff and faculty alike. I tested for a job at the college, and by August 1, I was in the Dean's office, responsible for student scholarships. The job paid only a small salary, and we still had not found a place to live by the time school let out for the summer.

The stress financially was a faith-building exercise in how to depend daily upon the Lord: for a place to live, for a school for Deb, and all this in a high-cost part of the country. There was simply no affordable apartment in the area. Our resolve to stay was sorely tested, but neither Deb nor I felt it was time to head back home. My staff position at the college would make it possible for her to attend there. She had brought her grades up, had even made the honor roll, and was looking forward to her senior year in high school and then college.

At this time, in beseeching the Lord for help time and again, I received these wonderful words in prayer: "Arise and walk with Me, walk with Me in the garden, in the garden of your fears; together we shall pluck your fears." This word that came in such a stressful time is the genesis of the "garden of the heart prayer" that the Lord has used so effectively at PCMs. We seldom omit this precious, simple exercise, for it never fails to bring extraordinary healings in those who need it most. We regularly see people being delivered from life-constricting and even primal fears.

God's provision of a home came by means of two very special pastors. First, Rev. Alvin D. Schrodt, connected with the General Baptist's home for missionary children, invited Deb into his own home until we could find an apartment. Deb loved being there, helping with the smaller children, the housework, and the cooking. After two years in the dorm, she gloried in having her own private room and enjoyed being part of their family. They were wonderful to both of us.

I moved into the spare bedroom of a friend's home while continuing the search for an apartment. It was our own Pastor Kraiss who found the solution. In connection with the church and adjacent to it, he had just completed the building of a nursing home. It had a two-room apartment in its basement for housing nursing personnel that wasn't needed at that time, so he offered it to Deb and me at a price we could afford. He knew Deb wanted to be a nurse, and he gave her the opportunity to work part-time as a nurse's aide during her senior year. Here again she was thrilled with the opportunity, and the patients loved her. I donated my church model organ to the home, played it for the patients, and Deb, with a beautiful singing voice, would sing for them. Our lives were full to the brim, and there could hardly have been two more grateful souls when we finally moved in. While answering our prayers, the Lord had thrown in all kinds of extras.

My challenges did not stop, however, with my new work, and I quickly sent an SOS to the prayer partners back home:

I need special prayer in regard to my job—I have been given responsibility for all loans and scholarships to Wheaton students—I have not had training in this and the little lady who has done it for 16 years has just retired. The other staff member who knew anything about this job was transferred to California. This is an urgent prayer request—please don't forget me. There are scholarships yet to award this year—I get sick thinking about it!

Only by God's grace did I succeed and meet the deadlines, which won me great regard on the part of a number of college officials. At the time I could not know how important God's gift of favor was. These officials would later affirm me most wonderfully in a critical decision that would set the course for my entire future life and ministry. Most truly, in the words of the English poet William Cowper, "God works in mysterious ways, His wonders to perform."

15

The Birthplace of Renewal

Of all the good that came to me with the need to seek a new church in Wheaton, the greatest blessing was getting to know and work with Rev. Richard Winkler, Rector of Trinity Episcopal Church. Fr. Winkler provided for his people an ongoing place of Eucharistic worship and healing such as I have not seen equaled before or since. It grew the people of God who participated with him in prayer for healing of the sick in body, mind, or spirit, and its influence grew the church nationally and internationally.

Being so graciously accepted and received into Fr. Winkler's weekly prayer circle meant that, although I was living and working in a religious setting untouched by the charismatic renewal, I was an active participant in one of the most vital renewal groups anyone could ever hope to discover. In and through this fellowship, the Holy Spirit was free to move quietly and profoundly through God's servants to heal the sick in mind and body. For me, it was not only the opportunity of a lifetime, but a divinely appointed one for learning to move more freely in the Holy Spirit's charisms, and thereby in the discipling and the healing of persons.

This prayer group was a continuation of the book of Acts, replete with miracles, such as our small prayer group back home in Little Rock had known. In contrast to the latter, however, there was a crucially important difference that more nearly mirrored the early church's example. By that I mean it was the first time I had experienced the charisms in operation when

143

fully integrated with the liturgy of the Word and Sacraments. Liturgy, both formal and informal, provided the means whereby rare, wise, and humble clergy and elders passed on the discipline, wisdom, and knowledge of ages past in regard to the church's ministry of laying on of hands; anointings; prayer for emotional, spiritual, and physical healing; and deliverance (including full exorcism) from sin and the demonic in a life. Most in the renewal of that time had to struggle along not only without this kind of leadership and direction but with the disapproval of their respective church bodies.

People, including well-known leaders (clergy, physicians, nurses, theologians, professors and teachers, authors, and lay leaders), traveled to Trinity Episcopal Church from the ends of the earth to visit, learn, and receive prayer for restoration and freedom from whatever chains bound them. Indeed, Fr. Winkler laid hands on, anointed, and prayed for countless numbers of priests to be baptized in the Holy Spirit, and they in turn ministered to others. One of them was the Reverend Dennis Bennett who took the ministry forward in wonderful ways—but especially through his book *Nine O'Clock in the Morning* and his ministry to orthodox priests.

The fellowship and friendship with Fr. Winkler, his wife, Dorothy, and the other dear ones were simply priceless. They backed me with prayer support and counsel that was desperately needed in the work God had called me to at the academy—a work fraught with teenagers' needs and problems, some of them severe.

In our prayer circle we saw incredible emotional and physical healings.[1] But a simple point needs to be made: to see these people healed, we only needed to come into freedom in the gifts, in greater part what I write about as *listening prayer*. That was the "secret" of this powerful healing ministry. We prayed for whatever was needed, whether salvation, healing, baptism in the Spirit, or guidance.

We were always too many for whatever room was available, so chairs had to go and most stood or sat on the floor. We were discreet about our meetings so as not to provoke the hostility of those who hated healing prayer and ministry to the sick. We came together, quite simply and informally, to pray for people, many of whom had come secretly, especially church or school officials from groups who would not approve. With great joy we would sing, laugh, give testimony, and read the Scripture.

Then came the moment when what chairs we had were formed into a circle. The regulars sat down there and "agreed in prayer." We would pray right around the circle, each speaking out in a tongue, an interpretation, a prophecy, a Scripture, a song. This is just like in the Scriptures.

By the time we went around the circle, the Lord had given us the very wisdom we needed for the healing prayer to follow. We would know the theme—most wonderfully given—and receive the special faith for whatever was needed. We would then seat those who needed prayer, and after ascertaining what the need was, five or six of us would pray. Whatever gifts of the Holy Spirit were required came to the fore and operated. For instance, a demon-possessed prostitute, who was so horrifying to look at that I could barely stay in the room, was utterly transformed. It seemed that most of the gifts came into play in praying for her. The next day I literally did not recognize her—and neither did the others who prayed with us.

How this all fits in with learning to hear God is truly unique and amazing. In effect what happened in that circle was that we entered into listening prayer, and as we did, the gifts of the Spirit operated. Fr. Winkler invoked the special healing presence of the Lord, we began to pray in the Spirit, and our conscious minds were enlightened. Participating in this group brought me into a freedom in listening prayer and in the gifts of the Holy Spirit that I have since endeavored to pass on.

In our group we were blessed with our "Anna" (see Luke 2:36–38) who was always praying in the church. Her name was Helen Galloway, an elderly woman who received the baptism in the Holy Spirit when she was dying in a hospital. Her husband, a pharmacist, came to Fr. Winkler saying that his wife was dying. He told him that something else was going on with her as well, and asked Fr. Winkler to visit her. As Fr. Winkler leaned over the dying woman and heard her low speaking, he realized that she was praying in a prayer language—and that the Holy Spirit was wonderfully upon her. He prayed for her, and she was miraculously healed.

After that, nothing could stop Helen Galloway. She had more strength and energy than anyone of her age I have ever known. She went from hospital to hospital, praying for the sick. She was all things to all people in the best Pauline sense: she met evangelical Protestants, Catholics, Jews, and those without Christ right where they were, bringing in the healing Christ. She was a great power in prayer behind Fr. Winkler as well as a great discipler of those anxious to pray aright for all who need and seek God.

Fr. Winkler and Helen Galloway exercised the Spirit's charism of exhortation, and they exhorted fearlessly. If someone was out of order, or not quite on target, they were told. This is extremely important to learn; we all need it. The following is an example. When I first came into the group, I did not dare open my mouth. On the third time around when I did not participate, Helen Galloway reached over, shook my knee, and said, "Next time, you speak or you don't come back!" I was not about to be left out of that group, so the next time I prayed with all my might, and the people were blessed with the prayer the Holy Spirit gave me to pray. It was not long before I was moving freely in the gifts of the Holy Spirit as well.

On another occasion, a young Pentecostal man came in who had prayed all his life for the baptism in the Spirit but had never been able to receive. He started wailing and doing all the things he had seen people do—fleshly actions that had everything to do with emotionalism and nothing to do with receiving from God. I shall never forget Helen's matter-of-fact and objective response. She reached over, gave the young man a shake, and said quite firmly: "Stop that behavior, young man! It is not necessary!" In utter astonishment he stopped his shaking and crying. She then quietly prayed for him and he received.

The unity in this group was phenomenal. We were as diverse as a group could possibly be—different denominations and races. It was here that I learned the Jesus Prayer: "Lord Jesus Christ, Son of the living God, have mercy on me, a sinner." When at odds with someone, a rare occurrence, we were taught never to sin against that person with our tongues but rather to pray the Jesus Prayer for him or her. Then we would pray, "Lord Jesus Christ, have mercy on" that person, until he or she straightened out or until we knew what to say to help. In this way no one sinned against another, and the unity of the Holy Spirit was kept. Out of that unity flowed incredible healing power from God.

While I was in this prayer group, the Lord freed within me the precious prayer languages. Note the plural, for the Spirit's gift of speaking in unknown tongues, when freed within a person, manifests the Spirit's presence in many languages. I remember so well the first message in tongues I received, along with its interpretation: "Come, follow me, and I will make you fishers of men" (see Mark 1:17 NIV). The puzzled soul may ask, "Why receive as a charism of the Spirit a Scripture so well-known in Jesus's calling of the first disciples?" But there was no question in my mind about it, for I had long been praying fervently, "Lord, someway, somehow, love Your world through me."

This therefore was the Lord's word, affirming me as a woman obedient to His will in regard to a more specific call to service on my life. I was far from being able to comprehend then that in a few short years I would no longer have paid work, but would be in full-time ministry without a salary (much less pension!). In its full vocational sense, "Come, follow me" was a drastic call in terms of where it would lead.

I wrote home to share my experience:

> Thursday night I attended the healing services at Trinity Episcopal and stayed for the prayer meeting later. The prayer meeting was over about 1 a.m. Friday! I guess there were about 45 persons there, all of whom had been filled with the Holy Spirit—and talk about sweet communion and fellowship! There were ministers of other faiths or rather denominations there and some of the finest people I have ever met. As the Spirit moved, there were tongues and interpretations, prayers, a beautiful song in tongues with accompanying interpretation and we just quietly worshipped and praised the Lord together.
>
> Then the Episcopal priest [Fr. Winkler] asked if anyone needed prayer. His wife mentioned that I desired the gift of tongues. He laid hands on my head, asked the Lord for this gift for me, admonished me to yield my tongue and my lips to the Holy Spirit, and then effortlessly and easily came a language I have never known. This done, he laid hands on my head and prayed again that I might interpret. This I did. WOW! All this was quietly, sweetly done.
>
> I may never again interpret (I certainly hope this is not the case) but interpretation seemed to be a matter of yielding to the Spirit with English forthcoming instead of another language. Every soul there did their own interpreting—first the message in tongues and then in every case the same soul received the interpretation. Talk about intercessory prayer for the saints—we prayed for about 180 souls by name.

One of the things I didn't mention was that after I had received the first language and interpretation, Fr. Winkler prayed for me again, asking for a completely different language to come forth. He wanted to bring me into freedom in the gift. I have followed this course through the years when praying with folk, for although many have the gift, it can be bound within them. Furthermore, they often yield to it in such a way that it comes out strangely garbled. These are beautiful languages that, when yielded to properly, are to be fully enunciated.

Often when I am led to speak in tongues in public ministry, these languages are recognized and understood as known languages. To the amazed soul who hears and recognizes the language, these messages come as special and blessed signs that strengthen them in the faith.

I have many stories of these occurrences, and I remember them especially as they impact those assembled. Recently this happened in a PCM in Denmark. Besides being translated into Danish, we were translated into Dutch for attendees from the Netherlands and South Africa. In one of our healing services, my Dutch translator heard me praying in an unknown tongue but was astounded to hear me at the same time speaking in English. She shook herself, began to analyze what was happening, and the phenomenon stopped. She went right back into the prayer, and once again the phenomenon occurred. She, a Dutch woman hearing the unknown tongue, was at the same time hearing it not in her native language but in English. She then would hear me pray in English for the sick of spirit, soul, and body—the same prayer that she had just heard in tongues. This continued throughout the healing service.

Astounded, she said nothing to me about it until the same thing happened again the next day. Always she saw that the prayer in the Spirit gave me the way to pray in English. Still in awe, she told me of what had happened for the second consecutive day. Immediately I responded, "For some reason, this has come as a special sign not only to you and the Dutch team, but to the Danish speakers and to all of us here present." And that indeed was the case. I later felt led to tell the entire assembly. Immediately came some of the most remarkable instantaneous healings of severe mental illness we have ever seen.

The midweek Eucharist at Trinity Episcopal Church always provided an opportunity to receive a sacramental laying on of hands, whether for service, for healing, or for just plain strength for the battle. We who were members of the prayer circle often needed the latter. In his commentary on Psalm 4, Fr. Patrick Henry Reardon states that the "man of faith begins and ends his day on the battlefield; warfare attends him everywhere."[2]

Those who served on the prayer team were deeply aware of this warfare, as was Fr. Winkler. He was to suffer a national pillorying that was a type of crucifixion for a man such as he, one with the Spirit's charisms of love, compassion, and gentleness toward his fellow man that were far beyond the ordinary.

These virtues made Fr. Winkler known to police officials and medics involved in saving lives in our area. There was a saying about him that if he could only reach the hospital in time to see a newborn who was dying, the baby would invariably live. The infant would be healed as Fr. Winkler baptized it.

He had unwavering faith in God's desire to heal, and therefore we saw miracles almost as a matter of course. In listening to God and praying as he was led, Fr. Winkler's gifts of healing and faith for whatever was needed were truly great ones. He was of the humble, serving sort that the Roman church seeks to canonize.

Fr. Winkler's prayer group gave me the opportunity to see some of God's choicest, humblest servants in action. My astonishment knew no end when at one prayer and healing service, R. Archer Torrey III appeared as both speaker and Anglican priest. He was the grandson of Rev. R. A. Torrey, whose writings had meant so much to me and my prayer partners earlier on.

That night at the healing service, Rev. Torrey taught most wonderfully on the importance of unity in the church and in our prayer groups, and how this unity even affected the priest in his laying on of hands for healing of the sick. In great enthusiasm I wrote home about this precious unity, the sweetness of which I was already experiencing in our prayer group. I then went on to describe that remarkable evening with this dear man:

He brought out one point [about unity] that I had never heard or thought of before—that of Ananias and Sapphira when they lied to the Holy Ghost. People can lie today and hold back from God and not drop dead; the reason they dropped dead was because of the POWER of the HOLY SPIRIT in those believers at that time—there was so much power there that the Church could not become corrupt!

He was like Praying Hyde, emaciated and spent from ministering night and day in Korea, but what a witness! He and his wife are missionaries to Korea. He is an Episcopal priest and heads a seminary for Korean ministerial students, and their "Jesus Abbey" is a communal home to teach the natives to glorify God in the home; the primary purpose of this place being to show them how Christians live and treat each other.

When Pastor Winkler or Pastor Torrey anoint and lay hands on your head and pray for you, the healing power of God for body, mind, and spirit is made real—I know beyond a shadow of a doubt that I gain great strength for service through these prayer and healing services.

After the prayer service at Church, we went to a private home for our Prayer and Holy Spirit Meeting. We have to do this in secrecy now since part of the congregation cannot yet understand these things and get very upset. Very often we are admonished to love, understand, be patient and so on with those who do not yet understand. Only love can do it.

So Pastor Winkler asked me to slip out the door and take Pastor Torrey with me to the place we would all meet—was I thrilled! I told him on the way that I couldn't wait to tell certain of my friends back home who was riding around in my old Volkswagen since his Grandfather's book was so famous to us! It is a small world. He told us so much. His grandfather helped found Moody Bible Institute and Biola. Actually Dwight L. Moody called his grandfather to head up Moody Bible Institute at its founding, which he did. He later left, however, and went on to be the first dean of Biola. D. L. Moody, R. A. Torrey, Jonathan Blanchard, F. B. Meyer, C. I. Scofield, and James Gray were all associates. Out of this group of men came Moody Bible Institute, Wheaton College and Academy, Biola, and other institutions.

Pastor Torrey . . . told of how many persons were baptized in the Holy Spirit at Moody's meetings and of how Scofield and Gray—although friends and fellow workers with Torrey—disagreed with him on this. MBI's [Moody Bible Institute's] huge auditorium is named Torrey-Gray after these but Torrey pulled out and started Biola because of this difference. There was no trouble but he wanted freedom along this line. Now Biola is strong, wonderfully so, but also was eventually, like MBI, taken over by the other teaching that the Baptism of the Holy Spirit comes at conversion.

I interrupt this letter from years ago to make clear that the Holy Spirit baptism can come then if the second Sacrament of baptism is not eliminated from the conversion experience. As Alexander Schmemann writes in *Of Water and the Spirit* (chapter 3), early baptismal liturgies have two Sacraments—one involving water and the second a chrismation, a laying on of hands for the reception of the Holy Spirit.

Pastor Torrey quoted his grandfather as saying that Scofield and Gray definitely erred in their exegesis of the Greek on their doctrine and of course the same Greek is still there to study. MBI asked permission of the Torrey family to edit Torrey's books so that they could use them for textbooks. The family flatly refused as they wanted to edit out you know what. Torrey's parents were missionaries to China and they experienced the Baptism on the way there and knew whereof their father spake. Pastor Torrey said occasionally when he goes to Moody, students whisper, "Do you believe what your grandfather believed about the Baptism?" and when he says yes, they say "we do too."

I wish I could put the next paragraphs of my letter in bold and large typeface, for it concerned something very special:

It was great and very informative to hear the two priests talk over old times—they have been friends from way, way back. I found out that Pastor Winkler was the first Anglican Priest to receive the Baptism, to anyone's knowledge, in this present-day movement! Pastor Torrey was the third. Pastor Winkler told of how Torrey had been one of the most influential men in the healing and Spiritual revival movement in the Anglican Church today.

You know, I felt like I was looking at the personages mainly responsible for the Liturgical Church's revival—these two men have been greatly persecuted but because they have been faithful, Christians are being revived and empowered to live the life of Christ. I had wondered why and how R. A. Torrey's grandson had become an Anglican Priest—it is plain to me now.

Through the prayer group I had heard remarkable things about Agnes Sanford but had not read any of her work before first meeting her. Nothing I'd been told, however, quite prepared me for this truly unique servant of the Lord. Fr. Winkler asked me if I could accompany Agnes and him to a church in another city where she would be speaking. It was a large, liberal-leaning church, but a group of their pastors had prevailed on her to come. Etched in my mind is the picture of her as the three of us walked to the car. She was a small but softly rounded grandmotherly figure, utterly unpretentious, quietly walking and conversing with Fr. Winkler and me. She was not at all what I'd imagined a speaker would be who would take on such a project as this church.

Learning more of her background later, I realized something of what I had been sensing as puzzling in her demeanor: *Of course*, I thought, *how else would one raised by missionaries in China and cared for by a beloved Chinese amah be?* She had the faint air of walking in traditional Chinese dress (with obi sash) and as if at any moment she could place her hands in her sleeves and bow pleasantly.

On arrival, we climbed the steep steps up into a large cathedral-like edifice where many were already gathered. Fr. Winkler and I sat on the front row just before a long, rounded altar rail, while Agnes was escorted up to a huge chair built like one for visiting bishops. She looked ever so small, somehow unaware of the great throng gathering, not looking around but quiet and fully at peace, while I was needlessly more than a little concerned for her.

Much I don't remember about that day, but three things stand out:

First was my utter amazement at the topic she chose to start with. It was about prayer for the healing of her ailing tree! And, of course, the miracle of its "healing." *My word*, I thought, *couldn't she have started out with the healing of souls?* But of course, she knew what she was doing and she also knew something about her audience. There was great quiet as she shared her utter joy on the recovery of her tree.

Second, apparently having discerned a number of occultists there, she warned them not to come forward for laying on of hands lest they die! She went on to say, in words suitable to those hearers, that the power of the Holy Spirit to heal was infinitely greater than the occult powers they possessed, and the collision of the two would do great harm to them. She even told of a death or two resulting from such attempts—shades of Ananias and Sapphira! I believe there was not a soul in the house who didn't believe and accept her warning.

The third thing I remember so vividly was her inviting the pastors who desired laying on of hands to come forward and kneel at the altar. Twelve came forward—I remember thinking of the twelve apostles as I counted them. But these were not apostles; they were needy men. Fr. Winkler and I, being so close, heard every word of her prayers. She went right down the line, stopping to lay hands on each of them while praying. She took the time needed for each individual, and it was evident that their entire lives and special needs rose up before them. I sensed this because of the way she spoke so uniquely and differently into the life of each one and also because they each responded so deeply. Each man knelt down one person and rose quite another. It was one of the most unusual and powerful healing of souls I have ever seen.

As we left, all of this seemed to have been nothing out of the ordinary to these two servants of the Lord, but I was stunned—and God only knows how changed—by what I had heard and witnessed.

I did not see Agnes again until after my first book, *Real Presence: The Holy Spirit in the Works of C. S. Lewis*, came out in 1978. After reading it, she invited me to visit. But that story is for later.

On May 16, 1964, the *Saturday Evening Post* hit the newsstands with a story entirely unforeseen by us—one that would have enormous consequences for those of us involved in healing prayer. Introducing the author of the lead article, the *Post* wrote: "To observe the Charismatic Renewal, *New York Times* reporter McCandlish Phillips traveled 10,230 miles by car and plane through 11 eastern, Midwestern and Pacific Coast states, interviewing hundreds of ministers and attending countless prayer services."

On the front cover, these words heralded the lead article: "Mystery that baffles Protestants." The mystery was about one charism, "glossolalia" or "tongues," and it was further headlined with a Scripture from Acts of the Apostles: "And there appeared to them tongues of fire." McCandlish Phillips's article spread across six pages of this oversized magazine and reported on many renewal groups across the nation. I believe it was one of the first of its kind spotlighting the mainline churches.

One full page of the article brought us trouble; it pictured Fr. Winkler laying hands on a priest before the main altar at Trinity Episcopal Church in Wheaton. The caption underneath wrongly said, "To transmit the experience that inspires *glossolalia.*" One of the things causing our severest difficulties within the church was that this particular sacramental laying on of hands had nothing to do with glossolalia, and the priest pictured as receiving it was not part of the prayer group, nor was he sympathetic to it. But this was merely local; our difficulties didn't stop there. Vitriolic reactions came toward us from far and near.

McCandlish Phillips, in being particularly blessed by visiting our prayer Eucharist, must have taken the picture during the Sunday Eucharist itself (something not permitted during sacred liturgy). Too, he must have had no idea of the way the article would be laid out and hyped or the difficulty its publication would cause our group, one that shunned publicity and was freest in doing all to the glory of God and therefore most productive in our hiddenness.[3]

Other pictures appeared with the article, none from our group. But because of the full-page photo with its mistaken caption, Fr. Winkler, a man who had never sought the spotlight, was suddenly in it. The persecution of him and of our prayer group that resulted from the *Post* article was scarcely believable. In those days many Christians did not look kindly on these kinds of healing ministries, and some were in our own congregation. In listening to God and praying as he was led, Fr. Winkler exercised a truly great gift of healing. The worldly pride in the church was such, however, that many people despised him for doing so. It was chilling to see folk who knew of a dying baby being restored, and yet who hated the ministry and the one who prayed for the infant. These people did not attend the healing Eucharistic liturgies and prayers and formed no part of the prayer group.[4]

After the *Post* article, the vitriolic hatred hurled at us from fellow Christians, who were outside the renewal, forced us underground. We had to meet more secretively than ever, even as the early Christians did in the catacombs. Taking a cue from them, we posted the sign of the fish to places where we would be meeting with others for healing prayer.

The ones hardest hit were Fr. Winkler and our dear Helen Galloway. Fr. Winkler, not a young man, left the church in Wheaton in 1967, largely because of the division the ministry of healing caused. He and Dorothy moved to Hawaii where he pastored a small congregation on Maui. There he found recuperation, recreation, and rest from the notoriety and anger directed toward him.

A very precious man of God he was and never one to vindicate himself in the face of public disapproval. He left all that squarely up to God. However, he may have been a bit naive. I, for example, expected that fury and hatred would be directed at him due to the *Saturday Evening Post* article, but he, with such unselfish and liberal love toward others, did not. He was a just, simple (in the best sense of "ye must become as little children") man, who would never be other than the man and priest God had called him to be. He was not one to take up a cause or defend himself. Now with the Lord, he has gone to his reward, having left quite a legacy, but one that is largely hidden—just as he would have wished it.

The last visit I had with him, he was strong in body, full of joy, and determined that several of us should hike with him into and up through the famous extinct volcano, Maui's beautiful Haleakala. Fr. Winkler was a man, like most saints, who was not only close to God but also to His marvelous creation. He thrived wonderfully during his last years.

In the cycle of Psalms to be prayed, Psalm 27:4 seldom if ever fails to cause me to cry it out as petition: "One thing have I asked of the LORD, that will I seek after: that I may dwell in the house of the LORD all the days of my life, to gaze upon the beauty of the LORD and to inquire in his temple." Places hallowed by the continuous prayers of the faithful, and the regular proclamation of the Word and Sacraments, are extraordinary treasures.

As Western Christendom continues to decline, I meet people all over the world who are desperately searching for these places of deepest quiet, those permeated with the holy because hallowed by the presence of God. There, coming in out of the clamor of the modern world, we can indeed gaze upon the beauty of the Lord, and our prayers as inquiry are quickened. This I found with Fr. Winkler. There was always a quiet in the Sanctuary. One could go in at any time, kneel and feel the hallowedness of all the prayers of the people, all the sacramental blessings over the elements, the anointings for healing and deliverance from oppression and depression, the ever deepening forgiveness of sins. The simplicity and quiet were healing. No noise, no technology apart from lighting and heating, only symbols of the Holy, the sacred, of redemption and resurrection.

Back then there were at least three Episcopal churches in our area where one could enter their chapels and meditate upon the beauty of the Lord. Today there are none. There are no Eucharists in which to receive a sacramental anointing for healing. The altars are still there but now are desecrated, dedicated to among other things, the politically correct darkness of sexual perversion and permissiveness.

There are few blessings on earth to compare with fellowship in a church where its three vital Christian structures are intact, unified, and in a balance that at once preserves and reflects the gospel message and issues forth in divine wisdom. These provide the basis for all other blessings. As I've mentioned earlier, these structures are the evangelical (the Word), the sacramental (regular reception of the Eucharistic real presence), and the charismatic (empowerment of the Holy Spirit). All three are necessary to the ministry and worship of the church.

In such a fellowship, the saving, healing gospel of Christ abounds and flows forth to the world at large. Healing of spirit, soul, and body abounds as the wisdom and knowledge of God increase, and all service in the name of Jesus is done to the glory of God. One's cup can only brim over with meaning and divine grace. Such was my experience in Fr. Winkler's group.

PART 3

1965–1976

I will remember the deeds of the LORD;
    yes, I will remember your wonders of old.

I will ponder all your work,
and meditate on your mighty deeds.

Your way, O God, is holy. . . .

You are the God who works wonders;
You have made known your might among the peoples.

Psalm 77:11–14

16

Choosing a Goal

My Wheaton College years (1965–74) turned out very differently than I could have imagined. If anyone had told me that in less than a decade I would have earned a BA, two MAs, studied overseas twice, taught a Sunday school class of unbelievers in which revival broke out, and written a book on the Holy Spirit in the works of C. S. Lewis, I could not have believed them. Furthermore, I would have been utterly stymied in *trying* to accomplish it all. These things came about through listening-obedience; the deeds are the Lord's, and the way is Christ Himself.

The gracious winds of the Spirit were yet blowing strongly throughout the land, while at the same time the sixties' rebellion was wreaking its lasting havoc. For me personally, it was a season of great wooing by the Spirit of God: His "Come, follow Me, and I will make you a fisher of men" continued to sound in my ear. My journal pages record the battles, the victories, and the teachings as I followed step-by-step. His encouragement was always to practice His presence, and dotting most every page was the scriptural promise, "I am with you." It was a time of special grace, when my ears were straining to hear and obey the Lord's slightest whisper.

I dearly love all the Scriptures that speak of the way, the path on which we are to walk, and of the space or wideness under our feet. I remembered all too well the old path where space and opportunity were so limited and my feet restricted. Truth is so beautiful and without limit, and our walk is in the presence of Truth Himself. He directs, guides, teaches, reproves, and never stops speaking wisdom and knowledge into the darkened spaces of our minds and hearts. And always, even when we are the weakest, He gives strength for the journey—not only for the terrible spiritual battles but for the great victories as well. His path is a blessed one; it is fruitful and it is holy.

I'm very grateful that I had no idea of what lay ahead as I began work in the Dean of Students' office at Wheaton. Faith has to do with childlike trust in the Lord for all that is to come, which is why attempts to divine the future knock us off the path. Christ had taught me the one work God called me to, and his words in this regard topped my prayer journal to be meditated on regularly: "Jesus replied, This is the work (service) that God asks of you, that you believe in the One Whom He has sent [that you cleave to, trust, rely on, and have faith in His Messenger]" (John 6:29 AMP).

I practiced His presence in every way I knew how and delighted in trusting Him. The above verse was closely accompanied by His scriptural encouragements to persist in prayer and to listen for his voice. In this way I was prepared for the jam-packed days and years to come. Our tiny apartment was often filled with enthusiastic young voices, Deborah's friends and mine from both high school and the college. And they were all eager to walk in the Lord's ways.

It was helpful to come on staff not as a stranger but as one familiar with many facets of the college through having taken courses for my high school diploma there. I could not have had a greater cheerleader than the dean, to whom I was responsible, and we got the work of awarding scholarships and loans up and moving in record time. An important personal benefit of working there was the privilege of taking a course each semester as part of my remuneration, so I continued studying, often attending class during my lunch hour.

While on staff, my after-hours vocation of prayer with others was mushrooming, and much of this with Wheaton students. My prayer journal of 1966 records with apprehension: "Morning, noon, and night—souls are waiting to be prayed with." Having taken classes with the students, I knew the intellectual challenges they were facing and the spiritual battle being waged for their young minds. In response to these needs and the hunger apparent everywhere, I began regular prayer meetings where folk could receive prayer with laying on of hands and, in turn, learn to minister to others.

One example of the need came through a theology class I took alongside earnest and gifted young evangelical students. In it we studied the thought of Rudolph Bultmann, Karl Kundsin, and others who formulated the methods involved in historical-critical theology. These theologians removed, on the principle of not being rational, the supernatural from Scripture. As the semester proceeded, I grew increasingly alarmed as I saw some very bright students who knew and revered Holy Writ begin to waver in their faith. This was because eliminating the supernatural from the Scriptures had affinities with their own experience and training, which had been rigidly anticharismatic and given to rationalism. When these students failed to understand and accept the indispensable work and movement of the Holy Spirit in the New Testament and in the lives of the faithful (that is, the supernatural dimensions of the faith, including sacramental reality[1]), they were left vulnerable not only to liberal theology but also to the matching reductionistic ideologies that govern the social sciences.

I recall the day in class when Karl Kundsin's writings on the charisms of the Holy Spirit were discussed. I've forgotten all the details, but I know that I did not remain silent. Shock waves reverberated throughout the classroom when I stated firmly that any statements about the absence of the charisms in the history of the church were absolutely false, that, in fact, they had always operated in some lives if only ever so quietly and that, in fact, they were daily present in my own life. The students reacted to my words by being even more afraid of me than of Bultmann and Kundsin at first. Then, however, being unwilling to see Holy Writ ripped apart and hungering and thirsting for Christian reality and authenticity, they began to rethink these matters.

In consternation over their plight, I cried out to them, "If you do not begin to live and move and have your being in Christ and in the knowledge and power of the Spirit He has sent upon the church, you *will* capitulate to the scientisms (materialism and rationalism) of the day; you will be the liberals of the future." I, of course, did not fail to point out that these gifts operated in Martin Luther's life, as well as in the lives of the great old evangelicals involved in forming Wheaton College, such as Dwight L. Moody and R. A. Torrey. The prayer meetings I had started were especially crucial for these students. There we invoked and welcomed the presence of the Holy Spirit and gained supernatural help and understanding from above.

The students faced other problems that challenged their faith besides the study of Bultmann and company, which were allied to the more or less rationalistic theology that had overtaken much of the church. These other challenges had to do with the sixties rebellion.

These were difficult days on the nation's college campuses, for the students were rebelling against all things moral and time-honored. The Christian mind-set and worldview were light-years away from the nihilistic ones being broadcast daily through the media and lived out on the campuses. Though ostensibly the rebellion was a response to the Vietnam War, in effect it was a casting away of faith in a holy God and a turning to Baal and the idol gods of self and sexual permissiveness.

The insanity of these days undermined the moral and spiritual good that, though already seriously watered down, had illumined the past and made the nation stable. These times exposed the weaknesses of our national academic and political leaders, those who had not the moral or intellectual strength to stand for the time-honored truths, even for the good of reason. It was a time that also taxed even the best of Christian leaders.

After a somewhat delayed reaction on our Christian campus, the rebellion came to us as well. A few students, yielding to the spirit of the age, descended into a mocking cynicism, the demonic power of which formed a dark cloud over the campus for several years.[2] Though their main venom was aimed at those in authority, the darkness of unbelief within them targeted all who held to a transcendent and life-giving faith.

I believed then, and have generally seen it proven since, that cynics are made before a cause arises that engages their contemptuous disbelief. These students were bitter toward parents, the church, and the culture before arriving on campus.

As expressed in *Webster's Unabridged Dictionary* definition, the cynic holds a low opinion of mankind and believes that only selfishness motivates human actions. He disbelieves in or minimizes selfless acts or disinterested points of view. This definition characterized the Wheaton cynic of that time. Rationalistic and devoid of the knowledge of the unseen realities of faith, such a one was an unbeliever in the Christian sense of that word.

The word *cynic* is not in the Scriptures; there the word is *fool*. As it says in Isaiah, "The fool will no more be called noble. . . . For the fool speaks folly, and his heart is busy with iniquity, to practice ungodliness, to utter error concerning the LORD, to leave the craving of the hungry unsatisfied, and to deprive the thirsty of drink" (Isa. 32:5–6).

Nationwide, there could not have been a more frontal assault on the Judeo-Christian worldview, one that still targets the transcendent optimism and hope and lifestyle of the Christian. The Holy Spirit's renewal had prepared many for the difficult days in the sixties, but those untouched by it were extremely vulnerable. This was, therefore, a difficult time of questioning for the earnest, developing Christian who had not this maturity or experience of the Lord.

Nothing apart from God Himself could satisfy the hunger and quench the thirst of the students and adults who were searching for more of Him in their lives. They longed to be affirmed in the nobility of who they were in Christ. In this milieu, then, they turned to God in earnest. Their craving could be met only through the gracious, ennobling presence of the Holy Spirit, supernaturally linking them to transcendent goodness, hope, beauty, and love. And this is what the prayer ministry was (and is) about: restoration of the image of God within the soul of the believer. I love the way the Isaiah passage ends: "But he who is noble plans noble things, and on noble things he stands" (v. 8).

It was in this context, then, that the prayer ministry grew. Students with special problems, many of them gender related, began coming, and a quiet word got around that those with homosexual struggles could be helped. Previously these issues were simply unheard of on Wheaton's campus, and our officials could scarcely believe they existed. But this generation of young people had been born into a secular culture that had affected the church, where divorce had become prevalent, fathers were absent, and mothers were taught to choose careers over breastfeeding and nurturing.

This prayer ministry did not continue, however, without spiritual battle, and the first one was fierce indeed. I suddenly became fearful that, in laying on of hands and prayer with others, I had fallen into pride. My own heart seemed continually and obsessively to be accusing me: *Who are you to reach forth your hands and pray for others?* And especially, *Who do you think you are, a woman, praying for others—even for men—and laying on hands for healing?* I did not quickly discern Satan in his role as the "accuser of the brethren," for this battle came with demonic force.

In the midst of it, I prayed continually without relief and studied all the scriptural references on humility as over and against pride—but to no avail. Finally, I ended up in bed, quite ill and weeping before the Lord with the thought that I must cease to minister to the students. The study of the Scriptures had not helped because the accusations were not coming from my own conscience. Lying in bed, feeling as defeated as I ever have before or since, I cried out to God to give me His definition of humility. He did, and I leaped up from bed, grabbing a pen:

My humility is God in you the hope of glory . . . there is no other glory but Me . . . to glory in anything else is vanity . . . dwell on My Presence within you . . . therein is power and humility to spare . . . I will heal you [that is, deliver you from the Accuser] as you come to Me, practicing My Presence and rejoicing in Me.

What a definition! Not one that would make much sense to many today, but it was the answer I understood instantly, for it was *incarnational,* the dwelling of God in his people. And it was the very reality that I was busy passing on to others, in both teaching and in prayer with laying on of hands, that was under attack. I was instantly set free by this word, as Satan, the archaccuser of God's people, was put to flight. I knew that Christian humility is the dying to self so that Christ might live mightily through his people (see Gal. 2:20). The church tends to fall away from this message, the very one I had been asking God to restore.

What would have happened if I hadn't learned to *listen* to God? All who truly learn to listen know how careful we must be and how we must test what we hear. The great saints in history are those who know best that what we hear is liable to error, and it needs to be spread out before the Lord and tested. Like Mary, we learn to hide these words away in our hearts when need be.

How many valid ministries are stopped just as they begin, perhaps through just such a battle? Apart from being able to receive that word from the Lord, I could have quit, for the teaching prevalent then, as it has been off and on, was against women freely collaborating with the Holy Spirit. I had already learned major lessons in regard to demonic oppression, but throughout life, the Enemy finds ways of embattling us. Nothing apart from the discernment that comes with a word from the Lord spares us and the ministry. Then the Word Himself sets us free and heals us of the wounds sustained in the battle.

As it says in Hebrews, discernment, constantly exercised, is one of "the basic principles of the oracles of God," and our powers of discernment must be "trained by constant practice to distinguish good from evil" (Heb. 5:12, 14).

Following the resolution of the spiritual battle, though now fully free to teach and pray with others, I remained pensive before the Lord, deeply thoughtful as to where He was leading me and in need of His affirmation as prayer with others increased. In response, he gave me several words over the next months that brought understanding. A prophetic word to be journaled and prayed over was: "I have chosen you for a peculiar work [purpose], one that will drain you of all unnecessary tasks." This word helped me accept the fact that what I was doing most often would not fit into the official ministries of the modern church. It has proven all too true, not only for then but throughout the years.

That message came at the end of words of affirmation and instruction, oft repeated in one form or another since: "Trust in Me and do good— continue to break the chains that bind the wicked, the oppressed, and the downhearted. I will give you strength as you look unto Me. Know that I am with you." Such words I received with all of my heart. But I knew weariness, and that brought yet another unusual word, one I would have to come into line with: "Do not be overcome by weariness but overcome weariness by good works."

Another word was a puzzler, one that I didn't understand for a while. I was to *choose* and set a goal with the Lord. With Deborah now in her senior year of high school, my set goal was that of getting her through college, still a considerable way off. So this I continued to place before the Lord. Also a verse by Alexander Pope had been so impressed on my spirit that I placed it in my journal so as to pray over it almost daily:

> A little learning is a dangerous thing;
> Drink deep, or taste not the Pierian spring:
> There shallow drafts intoxicate the brain,
> And drinking largely sobers us again.[3]

I knew I too was to study, and that I would never be satisfied with "shallow drafts." But I was already drinking at the Pierian spring through taking courses, so I didn't set a goal past that. But this word of setting a goal was the last gentle nudge. It would come again soon, and not so gently.

As 1966 wound to a close, Mother, though ill, had a great desire to be with Deborah and me at Christmas and to see the area where we had settled. She flew up, and those days were precious. Throughout my youth, Christmases were magical (in the sense of being awe-inspiring) because Mother ensured they were. I remember the yearly climb up the steep steps of the State Capitol in Little Rock to the crèche scene, holding tight to Mother's hand. This trek was at night, under the stars, where we would arrive at the panoramic scene amid other awed pilgrims. The greatest and most beautiful hymns of Christmas would be pealing through the air as musicians played their instruments with gusto.

Now in the Chicago area, Mother had it in mind that we three should go see the Christmas scenes and decorations for which Marshall Fields was justly famous. But the problem was that the trip and walk of even a block or so in the icy Chicago winds would be far too much for Mother. Yet she was determined to try it.

Somehow, we managed to get her there and into the store, and besides enjoying the Christmas scenes, we reveled in a festive meal in one of the store's restaurants. But as we feared she would, she paid a terrible price in terms of physical pain. In writing this just now, I weep to think of her love for us in determining to visit and her courage in doing so. Mother died a little over four months later.

In early March, just over two months after Mother's visit, the Lord dealt with me yet again about choosing a goal. I received a word of knowledge—even as I was playing the organ for the Sunday church service—to the effect that the goal I had set with him long ago had been met.

This was no small nudge from the Lord. I am not a crier, but the impetus from the Spirit was such that I began weeping so profusely that I could hardly see the music. For three days I wept before the Lord as He said, "Choose." I implored Him to choose for me, and He said, "No, you choose and I will bring it to pass." No one forgets a nudge from the Lord so strong as that one, but that doesn't necessarily mean we understand the command. I remember asking, "What does such a word mean, Lord; I have to get Debbie through college." My imagination simply didn't extend past the four long years ahead.

Even so, in obedience I finally wrote out before the Lord that together with my desire for learning, "I want to see Your world and Your people before it is too late." This time *learning* meant choosing an education and gaining a liberal arts degree, something that had seemed so impossible to attain for myself. Before, I had thought in terms of the sheer love of learning, of finding more truth and ministering it to others. Now I knew that the Lord was preparing me for even more. I was to see His world and His people, but I was also to take the message of healing prayer forward. How this could come about was safely up to the Lord. It was in His hands; I had chosen.

These petitions, literally wrung out of me over a three-day period, were not brought up easily. Clearly the Lord was forcing up the deepest desires of my heart. His patient dealing with me over setting a goal ended in a major healing, one necessary to the maturing of the work required of me: that of bringing up repressed desires. It was here he taught me how to deal with them, whether in myself or in helping others. Today we teach and minister this in our PCMs; it has long been one of our important healing exercises. For if we pray, listening to the Lord and seeking to obey Him, he deals strongly with repressed desires, for He expects us to ask largely of Him.

On the heels of these three unusual days of prayer, tears turned to elation when Deborah received her acceptance letter to Wheaton College, where she would begin in the fall. We went into joyous celebration mode, and Deb fairly glowed with happiness over her friendships and accomplishments in her senior year.

Then a short two months later, in the midst of the time crunch that comes with the awarding of scholarships and loans for the upcoming academic year, Mother died on May 5, 1967. Deb and I flew home to Little Rock.

Though I didn't know how it would be possible, I played the organ for her funeral. Deborah too received the same divine strength, and sang one of the arias from Mendelssohn's *Elijah*: "O Rest in the Lord." How could we do it? We simply had to honor her in this way, and feared that a stranger would drone out the hymns—all those that Mother loved so well and sang with such joy. God rewarded me richly, for at the end, during the "Halleluiah Chorus," the Holy Spirit fell on me and a palpable joy came that lasted for more than a year! I couldn't grieve as one normally does. I could only rejoice that Mother, with the Lord, no longer suffered and knew the healing of a lifetime of hardship.

The funeral was a huge one, with a crowded funeral home and miles of cars lined up for the procession. Along with the extended family and friends were the many souls she had taught in her Sunday school classes throughout the years. All the folk who attended were in awe over the blessing of the Lord on that occasion—something Mother had always said should be part of a Christian funeral.

On our return to Wheaton, I faced the immense challenge of catching up at work. After this was accomplished, and after such a year, I must have needed an enormous boost, for the Lord moved mightily to give me a very great gift indeed. In late July and early August, I flew to Europe.

Only four months after the desire to see the Lord's world and his people was forced up and out of my soul and placed before the Lord as a goal, I was on my way to Europe through a remarkable provision. And the incredible introduction to Europe and its people—through its greatest museums and opera houses—went hand in hand with education: I earned twelve credits in Art and Music Literature by going on the college's Fine Arts Tour.

This was an intensive study course, and I could hardly overstate the impact it had on me. Principally, beginning with three days in the Louvre in Paris and then on through Switzerland, Italy, Austria, and Germany, the history of the Western world, especially as it concerned Christianity, was flung wide open to me through great art. It was a phenomenal time of learning and sheer joy.

The paper I wrote for the course, titled, ambitiously, "The Arts of France: A View towards Understanding the Religious Influences That Formed and Influenced the Arts of France," gives ample evidence of the explosion of thought it wrought in me. My Professor, Dr. Cronk, then head of the Music Department at Wheaton, wrote on my term paper that I "really undertook too much; you covered *too large* a territory. However, you did it well and *interestingly* . . . we learned interesting things from this." And he gave this overly enthusiastic, aging freshman twelve credit hours, all A's—no small encouragement.

On return, I wrote the prayer partners back home quite a tome as well, beginning with:

> I frankly haven't fully assessed this trip and all it means to me—am still a bit dazed over it all. I know this was in God's plan for me because I had definitely not even thought of going. Eight days before departure I was in the middle of early Saturday morning devotions when I was thunderstruck with the idea to go. I don't yet know how arrangements were made at that late date—reservations all through Europe—not to mention shots, passport, packing, and etc. But the Lord impressed me to go and so I did. There were so many things against me going—work, finances, leaving Deb, and so on, that the impression to go had to be very urgent to get me moving. After praying all Saturday and Sunday about it, I put all my efforts into getting ready.
>
> On this trip I was made to see again so clearly that there is nothing that this world has to offer—riches, travel, learning, great art, great music, the power of kings, nations, or popes, that has meaning or that can satisfy outside of Christ. The privilege of travel once more affirmed this truth to me.

The P.S. to this very long letter was in response to seeing the dark history of "Christian" kings and popes as portrayed, so powerfully, through the great art of the West:

> It seems to me, so clearly now, that the world has not so much rejected Christ as they have rejected that which poses for Christ and Christianity—I can see why Voltaire evolved and thrived—why Communism tries to free men from "dead" religion—some of it not only dead—it is death itself. If and when we Christians ever confront the World with our Christ Who is Truth

Itself—the world will change—it is dying for this truth, this confrontation. Christianity has not failed but Christians sure have—we have almost let the world be overcome with that which passes for or calls itself Christianity.

Deborah attended Wheaton one semester, loved it, and yet instead of finishing school, she decided to drop out and marry. My counsel, along with that of the dean and the young man's parents, was to wait and finish school. Deborah had considered Stephen a best friend since her junior year at the academy, and he, now a college junior, was determined that they should marry early in the new year and go to England. Deborah agreed with him.

Though I knew that my daughter now had a solid Christian foundation, I was still floored and at a loss in the face of this development. Years before I had begun to pray and work toward the seemingly impossible goal of a good education for her, and my being on staff at the academy and then the college had made it possible. The goal had propelled me to leave my home in the South, my dearly loved friends, and church home and journey across the country to a new home in the North. It had been quite a pilgrimage, and apart from that goal and the precious and extraordinary leading of the Lord, I would never have summoned the courage to do it. Like the proverbial rug, the long-term goal had slipped out from under me; it had vanished just when we were in sight of it.

My prayer journal at that time reveals an irrational confusion: "I realize I no longer have a reason for being at Wheaton. I must wait before the Lord for where to go and what I should do." Later, as I earnestly prayed for guidance, the Lord got through to me anew that a formal education *for me* was where He was leading. After I had worked for so long toward that end for a beloved daughter, however, now it all seemed that no matter what I did, it was only for myself. What a strangely irrational feeling for a Christian who endeavors to do all to the glory of God. But I record it here because I know that many mothers are tossed into just such a muddle when their nestlings fly away.

This must be the empty-nest syndrome, and in my third year on staff at the college, I had it in full. One of the deans I worked with, who had a doctorate in psychology, sought to help me by recommending that I give thought to remarriage! That counsel, long since forgotten, I found in my prayer journal, and it makes me realize how evident my trauma must have been to all those around me.

The odd thing about my surprise over Deb's leaving school to marry and my being so at sea afterward is that the Lord had so faithfully and fully prepared me by having me set yet another goal. His dealings with me in the months leading up to it were those of a merciful and all-seeing God.

Deb's marriage to Stephen, a young man who grew up on the Ecuadorian mission field, took place on February 2, 1968, in a beautiful church wedding, jam-packed with fellow students, friends, and family up from Little Rock. Their decision to marry rather than finish school was so they could sail for England and enter a ministry there.

After the wedding and reception, the wedding party and my family went to the nursing home (where we still lived in the small apartment), and the ambulatory patients were gathered to wish Deb and Steve good-bye. I shall never forget their joy in seeing the bride and groom in full wedding attire. Deb sang for them once again as I accompanied her on the organ. By this point, I was resigned to their determination to marry and could enter into their joy with all my heart.

The upshot of all this? I became a full-time student.

17

The Joy of Academe

All men by nature desire to know.

Aristotle, *Metaphysics*

Man's ultimate happiness consists in contemplation.

St. Thomas Aquinas, *Summa Against the Pagans*

Though I had been slow to understand the extent of my next goal, I began to pursue it quickly once Deborah married Stephen and moved to England. On March 5, 1968, I was admitted to Wheaton's Liberal Arts College as a full-time student, and on the very next day I moved from my apartment in the nursing home into a bedroom just off campus.

Always mindful of my old Achilles' heel, impulsiveness, I had first carefully counted the cost in prayer before the Lord, according to His words in Luke 14:28: "For which of you, intending to build a tower, sitteth not down first, and counteth the cost, whether he have sufficient to finish it?" (KJV). I placed all my fears before the Lord—those things or hardships that could keep me from finishing the tower—and after praying I was at peace about the road ahead.

This cost counting was important because the new goal required a special leap of faith: to become a full-time student I would have to resign my job in student personnel. I received a state scholarship that helped greatly

171

toward tuition, and all kinds of encouragement from the deans and other college officials, but how I managed the tuition, fees, books, and living costs I cannot now remember. This is why I cited Psalm 77:11–14 at the beginning of part 3, for it is the flagship Scripture for the whole of my story, not only my time at Wheaton: "I will remember the deeds of the Lord." Indeed, they were His deeds, and perhaps that is why I can't now recall how it all came about.

I do know that the greatest financial help, even beyond the state scholarship, came through an alumna of Wheaton College who had graduated in 1907. She was Stella Woolfenden Alexander, then in her nineties and long widowed. I moved into one of her upstairs bedrooms at a cost of five dollars per week, with an additional ten dollars per month for kitchen privileges, almost a giveaway even in those times. My tiny room looked over the roofs of several houses and out onto the bell tower of Edman Chapel. It was sheer joy to gaze out that window, whether praying, reading, or studying, and to hear the bells as they chimed great hymn tunes on the hour.

Those who have studied early American literature will understand my observation that Mrs. Alexander was like ten of the sternest Puritans one would ever meet, all rolled into one. She had a backbone of steel and a faith to match, and she could easily intimidate even the hardiest of souls. During World War I, besides raising their three sons, she took her husband's place as head of the entire Chicago school system and continued in that capacity after he returned maimed from the war. In addition, she taught at College Church in Wheaton for over half a century and daily interceded for an astonishing number of missionaries, some several hundred. I came to admire her tremendously.

She was not easy to get to know, but we became much better acquainted after an extraordinary incident in her home. In working with youth I was getting somewhat inured to these unforeseen encounters, but for her it was certainly a first. Without knocking, a young man burst through her front door, rushed straight up the stairs to where he heard I was, and threw himself headlong into my room. Knowing the young man and of his Christian background, I realized that to do such a thing meant he was in serious trouble. As it turned out, he was on an exceedingly bad drug trip. That day, on a dare, he took his first dose of drugs, and it had resulted in psychic and demonic activity of the most frightening kind.

As I called on the presence of the Lord, my eyes were opened and I saw the horrible dark spirit that was oppressing him, the same that he was seeing, and commanded it to leave. I then anointed him and prayed for the healing of his mind. He came into normalcy, repented with all his heart, and left in great quiet. It was an experience that changed his life for the better.

As he was leaving, Mrs. Alexander was waiting at the foot of the stairs to escort him out. She then turned to me in the sternest manner possible and stated with considerable authority, "Mrs. Payne, we do not allow gentlemen in our rooms!" I wasted no time in replying, "Mrs. Alexander, I couldn't help it. He was on a bad drug trip and literally threw himself headlong into my room and onto my floor!" I then told her of his deliverance and healing.

It was wonderful how she—aged, set in her ways, and so formidable—put aside her ironclad rule and thanked God for what had happened. From that time on, she was interested in my prayer ministry with troubled youth. Indeed, she actually counseled and encouraged a few of the women. More importantly, she interceded for all those she knew about, adding them and me to her extensive prayer list.

This woman of God is the only person I've met who seemed to hail from a totally different age than the modern one—she could have easily fit into the pre–Revolutionary War period. But I'm most grateful she lived in my time, for knowing her was like an introduction to the earliest Wheatonites. I could more fully understand how they sent out such vast numbers of missionaries and why the school gained its fine reputation.

Though close intimacy in friendship was not in her character, Mrs. Alexander became a staunch friend to me in ways that particularly counted. For example, when one of her longtime church associates offered a harsh statement of me as a "charismatic"—a dreadful word back then—she gravely reprimanded the person by saying, loudly enough for me to hear, "I shall go to my grave a different person because Mrs. Payne lived here!" The "different person" she spoke of could only have come about because she witnessed the work of the Holy Spirit in the healing ministry that, along with me, entered her life. I can only give thanks to God that she took me into her home and then, full of godly courage and disdainful of criticism, kept me in it.

She was a precious saint, one whom, as she grew even older and deafer, I would hear interceding through the night hours. This was the dread time of Martin Luther King's assassination and the great civil unrest that followed. Though I did not know the specific burden of her intercessions, I had the strongest intuition and need to pray for the sufferings in the dark of night, especially on behalf of the helpless children in Chicago's inner city. I added my prayer to hers.

The leisure to learn in a liberal arts college—one imbued with a liberal spirit in the classical Christian sense of breadth of mind and heart, of magnanimity and humility, of fair-mindedness and absence of bigotry—is an enormous privilege never to be taken for granted. My experience at Wheaton College was an exquisite gift for which I, to the best of my ability, took fullest advantage.

In such a freeing atmosphere, I learned to stand and defend what I believed to be true. I knew that great truth—no matter what the field—culminates in great theology, and I judged every class and book according to that measure.[1] And I knew that great theology, like Holy Writ, was filled with openness to mystery and to the supernatural even in the very present moment. But I was not seeing this clearly delineated in the mainline evangelical theological texts we were studying at the time—nor in the philosophy texts. There the abstract substituted for the transcendent.

I was passionately concerned about how the loss of the transcendent impacted Christian formation, spirituality, and discipleship and knew that what lay behind it was the appalling lack of understanding and experience of the work of the Holy Spirit in the modern Western church. I tried to understand the resistance to experiencing and learning to collaborate with the Lord in such a way that sick and lost souls could find healing.

There were great old evangelicals on campus, such as Chaplain Evan Welsh, who could have easily stood beside the evangelicals of the past like R. A. Torrey, who depended on the work and presence of the Holy Spirit. But I wasn't seeing the dependence on the Spirit duplicated in the evangelical youth following them. Yet the young people were yearning to know how to do just this.

I was concerned for the students because I knew how boring and misleading abstract theology and philosophy could be when it is not rooted in the ever present reality and mystery of God in and with us. With all my being I knew that true knowledge and wisdom come from God as an intuition of the unseen Real, that it comes with seeing with the eyes of the heart and hearing with spiritual ears attuned to honor and obey the God Who is with us. This wisdom doesn't come easily in a fast-paced and materialistic culture, but only through patient listening through the Scriptures and waiting upon God. In short, it doesn't come so much with study, though that is necessary, but with prayer, with meditation, with the practice of the presence, with learning to collaborate with Him in the doing of His will.[2]

My challenge, in a heady and abstract age, was to find the words to rightly express such things. Early on, one kindly prof, after struggling with one of my papers, told me solemnly that I was a mystic. But I knew

I was a very ordinary, down-to-earth Christian. I continued my search for better ways to express what the Bible so plainly reveals as to what is not only possible but expected of us. Needless to say, I had tussles with one or two professors that did not turn out so smoothly.

In the wonderful leisure to search and to learn, I was soon to find and study one of the greatest gifts to our lost and darkened modern centuries: the works of C. S. Lewis, one who knew what the great Christian philosophers knew and who wrote in terms that many modern Christians could begin to receive. To have the opportunity to study the entire corpus of his work, published and unpublished, was a gift straight from God, and nowhere else on the planet could I have done just that than at Wheaton, thanks to a truly extraordinary Wheaton English professor. But that story must wait for the next chapter.

In 1968, my first year of full-time studies at Wheaton, I immersed myself not only in theology but in the history of the Western world. Impressed by the teaching and work of Dr. Robert E. Cooley, who headed up Wheaton's archaeology program, I then ventured into biblical archaeology, courses that included fieldwork—such as digging on ancient Indian sites in Illinois. Dr. Cooley soon went on to teach elsewhere,[3] but not before imbuing me with the thought that just maybe I could survive (not flunk out of!) the scientific fieldwork of Wheaton's upcoming dig in Israel, a part of the graduate school's Institute of Biblical History of both the Old and the New Testament worlds, with campuses in Jerusalem and on Tel Tekoa.[4]

This culminated in one of the most extraordinary summers of study I could have imagined. This was not only because of the timing and the exceedingly dangerous political climate following the Israeli Six-Day War, but because of one of our leaders, the Old Testament graduate school professor, Dr. J. Barton Payne. He was a brilliant man but seemingly without fear and definitely without the usual cautions. Before the trip Dr. Cooley alerted us: "Dr. Payne won't leave a foot of Palestine uncovered." That was exciting to contemplate, but the import didn't fully register until I was there. So determined was Dr. Payne that we would miss none of the biblical sites that we even climbed through barbed wire fences to off-limits places where gunshots took lives daily, and, led by Israeli soldiers, formed one of the first non-Muslim expeditions into the Sinai desert in many years.

Before going to Israel we traveled to Greece, Lebanon, Egypt, and Cyprus, visiting archaeological and biblical sites in those countries. To see Athens and Corinth while keeping St. Paul's journeys and ministry in mind was a moving introduction to our summer studies. It was peaceful, even serene at points, and as such was not a harbinger of what was to come.

In Egypt, on more than one occasion, we could have easily come to serious grief. We were there during the reign of Gamal Abdel Nasser, the second president of Egypt. The situation in the country was perilous as Nasser had introduced a police state and emotions were running high following their devastating loss of life in the Six-Day War with Israel. On our arrival, therefore, as a group of North Americans who desired to visit the famous Museum of Egyptian Antiquities, we were not welcome. In fact we were refused entrance and were stunned to have the huge doors slammed in our faces.

It is hazy in my mind just how a Canadian archaeologist and I got separated from the rest of the group. The two of us were spotted immediately by a great throng of beggars who came running down toward us, shouting, "Baksheesh! Baksheesh!" (their term for money or alms)—an amazing and piteous scene. The archaeologist threw me into a tiny, rusty old car for safety and climbed in behind me, and instantly the beggars surrounded the car, knocking on the windows. With the huge numbers surging up to us, the beggars were in danger of being crushed. So terribly needy were they that I gathered up the few coins I had in my purse and started to roll down the window. The archaeologist, however, shouted, "No! Stop that! Throw coins out and they will tear us apart—and one another, trying to get them!" Finally the police, slowly and grudgingly, came to our rescue and broke up the mob.

Even with such a welcome to Cairo, none of the plans for our time in Egypt were omitted, and off we went—all my "housemotherly" instincts (especially for the young women students) now elevated to the max. After an eerie night in a hotel in Cairo, we rode camels out to the Pyramids, and concern over my camel driver (who was unduly focused on me) left me with little energy to fear my ill-tempered beast who liked to run. Sharing something of this experience with the folks back home, I wrote:

> Cairo is really something. First of all—if you want to get back alive, you don't utter a peep. The situation is extremely tense and Americans are not welcomed. Nasser's picture is everywhere and you could get clapped up by the police if you even uttered the word "Israel." Several times I wondered if we would get out of Cairo and back to Lebanon.

In contrast to Egypt, Lebanon was a lushly green land, serene in its Mediterranean beauty. Our tours of the archaeological sites went unhindered. From there we flew to Cyprus where our study and work experiences,

My mother, Forrest Irene Williamson, on the occasion of her high school graduation.

father, Robert Hugh Mabrey

mother, the toddler sitting on the American , with four of her siblings: Rhoda, Clara, ode, and Grace.

My father (the infant) with three of his siblings: brother Fulton and sisters Hazel and Willa (younger sister, Mary, yet to be born).

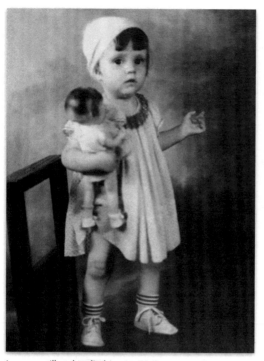

Leanne, still at the climbing stage.

My paternal grandmother, Rose Fulton Mabrey, beside the old manse.

If not climbing, always pointing up and out. If one arm doesn't do, two will.

...y childhood in Little Rock—three generations of feminine souls ...der one roof.

...y maternal grandmother, Mary Williamson.

My mother, cousin Loriece, and Aunt Rhoda on the back row; Nancy and I on either side of Grandma Williamson on the front row.

My mother, Forrest Mabrey.

My sister, Nancy Jane, and I (I am on the left).

Maternal clan gathering, featuring my cousin Lloyd's new bicycle, with Lamar Porter Field in the background. I am on the far right, a fourth- or fifth-grader; Mother is taking the picture.

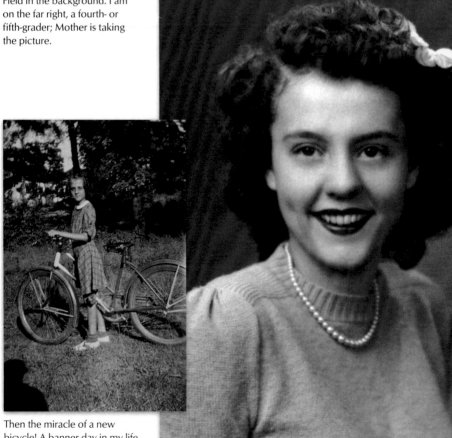

Then the miracle of a new bicycle! A banner day in my life.

At age 15, a few weeks before the elopement.

My daughter, Deborah, at seventeen months and then as she is growing up.

A photograph of me in 1956 or 1957, the years just before stepping onto the shining path.

Now securely on the Lord's path where great good, like the privilege
of worship and making joyful music, is restored.

Debbie, in the center, with our friend Gayle Sampson
and I on either side. This photograph was taken after
Debbie's graduation from Wheaton Academy, before
she entered Wheaton College.

Deborah's confirmation. Now prayers
for a Christian high school and college
for Debbie are speeded up.

ith my grandchildren,
a, aged 6, and Joseph,
3 months.

Joseph, Sara, and Joy, on
the occasion of Sara's
wedding.

Joseph and Sara
at the June 1994
PCM in Wheaton.

Working at C. S. Lewis's desk in the early Lewis collection. The many files housed his letters, which I was indexing.

Dr. Kilby and his parakeet Peter.

Beloved Professor Clyde Kilby, who founded the Lewis-Inkling (later the Wade) collection. This fine portrait by Deborah Melvin Beisner, which hangs in my library, is bequeathed to the college after my death.

With Dr. Kilby and his wife Martha, upon my graduation from Wheaton College in 1971.

In 1986, after completing ministry schools in Northern Ireland and London, I traveled down to Malvern for a visit with George Sayer and his wife, Margaret. George had invited me down for a walking trip through the Malvern Hills, a walk that he and C. S. Lewis had often taken. It was on first arriving there that I learned of Dr Kilby's death, at age 84. It was more than comforting to be with George Sayer, a devout man who well knew the greatness of Dr. Kilby's mind and heart. We celebrated his life and accomplishments as we walked through those marvelous hills and visited such places as Kilns, Lewis's home in Oxford, where we are pictured below.

In Belfast, Ireland, with Rev. Cecil Kerr, after speaking at Queens University. His ministry of healing the rifts between Protestants and Catholics in Northern Ireland is so wonderfully ordained of God and has borne extraordinary and lasting fruit.

In 1975 or '76, Debbie Melvin (Beisner), fresh out of college, invited me to sit for her first life-size portrait (a learning experiment), after which she painted the splendid portrait of Dr. Clyde Kilby. This one of me was not completed until 1982, her marriage and children having intervened. It too is slated to be part of the Leanne Payne Papers collection at Wheaton College.

Ministering with Fr. Winkler in Hawaii
in the summer of 1972.

With Agnes Sanford at the Three Rivers School
of Pastoral Care in 1979.

The prayer ministers in Hawaii receiving
laying on of hands by Fr. Winkler.

With Agnes at her home in California.

is a typical picture of the U.S. PCM team from the 1980s. After a PCM, tired, but filled with the joy of
ord. Bottom, left to right: Patsy Casey, Lucy Smith, Jean Holt, Barbara Pain (a guest). Middle: Connie
ner, Lynne Berendsen, Leanne, Larry and Claudia Evans. Top: Clay McLean, Bob Boerner, Ted Smith,
o Bergner, John Fawcett, Gerry Soviar.

e 1990 California PCM, with Desert Stream.

Ivy Upton, my friend extraordinaire.

Ita Fischer, Signa Bodishbaugh, and Sile Ni Chionna at a European PCM in 1996.

The 1993 PCM in Allerheiligen, Germany, at the International Headquarters of the International Catholic Programme of Evangelisation (ICPE). From left to right, back row: Henry Cappello, Dr. Daniel Trobisch, Leanne, Ariane de Chambrier, Esther Fong, Mario Bergner, Connie Boerner, Dr. Jonathan Limpert. Front: Stefan Attard, Patsy Casey, Anna and Mario Cappello, Christiane Mack.

Oxford PCM, 2001. Ministry team
and musicians heading toward
Magdalen College and the Cherwell
River after the conference.

With Ted and Lucy Smith
in Edinburgh, Scotland,
sightseeing before a
conference in Perth.

K., U.S., and Dutch team members departing after the Belgium PCM in 2003. From left to
nt: Patsy Casey, Valerie McIntyre, Carla Waterman, Ron and Lin Button, Rev. Conlee Bodish-
ugh, Jean Holt, Jetteke Noordzij, Mark Pertuit, Signa Bodishbaugh, Gwen and Sandy Purdie,
v. Norman Arnold.

Gathering of some of my cherished prayer partners on the occasion of my seventieth birthday. From left to right, Lucy Smith, me, Carla Waterman, Valerie McIntyre, Patsy Casey, and Connie Boerner. Wheaton, June 2002.

Christa Bernitz and me in December 2007, just as I finished the first draft of this autobiography, at age seventy-five. Christa founded and brought incredibly gifted leaders into the burgeoning German PCM ministry.

With Rev. Conlee and Signa Bodishbaugh, Wheaton PCM, 1999.

though good, were marred by the ongoing bouts of civil war that wracked that island, splitting it into Greek and Turkish sectors. From Nicosia we flew to Israel and our main campuses for the summer, one in Jerusalem and our prime archaeological site on Tel Tekoa.

Living and studying those first weeks at the Mandelbaum Gate, an entrance to the old walled city in Jerusalem, provided a wide introduction to the many facets of Arabic and Israeli culture, both old and new. Quickly we came to know the old city within the walls with its Palestinian population; facing outward from the wall, we could see the entrance to the Orthodox Jewish section. Besides being warned of treading on hidden mines (present in our own backyard, a bombed-out area), we were told about dangers to avoid once the Jewish Sabbath began. As I wrote home: "At sundown police guard the road entrances so that no car passes through. You would be stoned if you drove through!" Studiously avoiding the pitfalls, I quickly learned my way around Jerusalem and loved to go to certain sites unaccompanied so as to meditate alone on all I was seeing.

In a letter home during this time period, I told about one of the hair-raising experiences that were becoming almost commonplace:

> Yesterday we were at Qumran[5] and Jericho on the Dead Sea. Approximately three miles from there is the Jordan River where there are daily skirmishes between the Israelis and the Arabs [El Fatah]. This site on the Jordan is thought to be the place where Jesus was baptized. Now, the government has the road blocked and guarded by Israeli soldiers so that no civilians can go down. We went! Dr. Payne got special permission for us from the Governor and in his words, "Off we go!" We went likety-split barreling down that road, ran down to the Jordan, quickly waded or dipped our fingers in, praised the Lord, and ran like everything out of there.

That very weekend we learned that twelve people were killed on that day, within a few miles of where we had been on the Jordan River.

On July 13 it was time to climb up to Masada. Knowing its phenomenal history, we were all looking forward to this climb, but we hadn't planned on doing it in 120-degree desert heat at high noon. The Arabs could only shake their heads at us Americans and look for shade. This day, however, had only just begun to present its hazards. When we started back to Jerusalem, the Israeli military stopped us and took away our Arab bus driver.

Hurrying then to meet the curfew, we didn't get very far before the bus broke down.

> You will never believe what all happened to us yesterday. We were at Masada on the Dead Sea and our bus broke down. This area is heavily patrolled and there is an absolute curfew after dark. So, here we were, in an Arab bus after curfew. The guys put it back together with *baling wire* and off we went [going barely ten miles an hour]. The Judean hills and sky are beautiful at night—of course no lights anywhere except an occasional Bedouin lamp. Well, all of a sudden we were drenched in spotlights and surrounded by soldiers and guns. Wow! After checking our passports and everything carefully, we were allowed to proceed.

But the worst was yet to come. After some time, creeping along ever so slowly and fearing the bus would give out altogether, we were inching up an incline. I still remember how surreally the moon lit up the hill, revealing Israeli tanks circling us, deftly closing in, with great guns aimed right at us. At a dead halt, we watched as they slowly tightened the circle around us, their guns aimed at each of the bus's windows.

> Israeli eyes were staring in every window of the bus, and vehicles surrounded us. I was electrified. [A gun was shoved right in my window!] I thought sure we were going to be put into a Palestinian *hoosegow*.
>
> After much English-Arab-Israeli speaking [mostly Dr. Payne with the military], we were "escorted" by these armored vehicles, and their spotlights were searching for "Fatahs" on both sides. I tell you it was an eerie sight. Then gunshots rang out and everybody [on the bus] ducked. . . . then I heard two thumps [gunshots] hit the top of the bus. . . .
>
> As it turned out, the Israelis had two boys—frightened half out of their wits—screaming, "We are Americans!" They were from the Bronx—hitchhiking to Eilat and had somehow or other gotten to this territory and were stranded. The Israelis put them on our bus and they had to backtrack all the way to Jerusalem with us. This one guy was saying, "They almost shot us!" It all struck me as funny at that point—Americans can sure get in a lot of trouble over here. I'll tell you, the Lord is really looking after us.

For us in the archaeology program, all was leading up to our move to Tel Tekoa, once home of the Old Testament prophet Amos, but now a huge mound under which seven civilizations were buried. Our object was to uncover and find out as much as we could about those civilizations. The Tel now provided a seasonal home to Bedouins and their camels. Wheaton

College had a ten-year lease on the Tel, and the archaeologists were antici-pating years of exciting digging and great research in the Jerusalem library facilities[6] into this historic biblical site.

We moved on July 14, and in my journal that night I described our exodus from Jerusalem:

> As we came through the shepherds' fields in Bethlehem, we sang Christmas carols: "While Shepherds Watch Their Flocks by Night," and "Oh Little Town of Bethlehem," etc. It didn't matter (much) that a desert sun was streaming down instead of stars or snow. . . . In that heat, I felt chill bumps as we sang . . .
>
> We then came to the Mound of Tekoa. Ascending the mound, we saw the huge amount of stone from a crumbled civilization. This city had had monu-mental structures [the last city on this site was destroyed in A.D. 1138]. . . . The walls, barely perceivable to the uninitiated, of a Byzantine Church, are part of the rubble. What looks like a stone baptistery is standing and the only visible object in good condition.
>
> The view to the east is of the Judean mountains, the Dead Sea sparkling as far as one can see to the North and to the South, with the higher moun-tains of Moab behind. Due North is Bethlehem plainly visible situated on two hills or mountains and further to the northeast one can see the towers of the Russian Church and Lutheran Hospital atop the Mount of Olives. Frank Mt and the top of it is plainly visible.

Our experiences here could fill a book. While on the Tel, we came into contact with the Ta'amari[7] sheik and five of his sons, who were nearly always with him. He had several wives and a number of children we did not see. I was much taken aback when he mistook me for a second wife of Dr. Payne! Very soon we were involved in controversy between two tribes, one being the Ta'amari, who inhabited the Tel, and the other being the Sa'ir, who claimed to be part owners. They were demanding payment, and Dr. Heicksen, our archaeology professor, was soon drawn into court and entangled in Bedouin Arab legal matters—no small problem. But work went on, and I was amazed at the giftedness of our professionals in the archaeological field. Soon the apse of the church was uncovered and the walls of what was almost certainly a Byzantine church were appearing.

By July 24 I wrote home:

> Things are hectic atop Tekoa and right now we are learning more about the present people than the archaeology of pre-history. In the last letter I told you of the problems with the men of Ta'amari and Sa'ir, the two Bedouin Arab clans that we are mainly dealing with. Things have gotten to such a

pitch that our work is stopped until we get military protection. Early this morning we went out to the dig with about thirty of our Ta'amaris. . . . The men of Sa'ir came to Field I and ran off our Ta'amaris, threatening to stone and shoot them if they continue to work for us. These Arabs are marvels at stone throwing—they *never* miss and have lots of force behind the missile. After that they went to the tomb area and told the workers there that if they didn't come out of the tomb that they would roll stones over the mouth and bury them alive. Needless to say, all came out in a hurry including the archaeologists. Later today over fifty of the men of Sa'ir came out, pulled up our grid lines and stakes and threw stone boulders down into one of our excavations. This is of course a dangerous situation and Abu Khalil, our Inspector who is always with us (works for Israeli Dept. of Antiquities) says this is the worst situation he has ever encountered in his 33 years of archaeology. We may have to leave. . . .

Hoping for Israeli protection, we were much surprised when Moshe Dayan, the famous Israeli general with his trademark eye patch, and his soldiers showed up on the Tel. For reasons we could only speculate on, he failed to intervene, and we were forced to move from Tel Tekoa back to the Mandelbaum Gate.

That we could not complete our weeks of fieldwork on Tekoa was a disappointment, a very keen one for our archaeologists and the more scientifically minded among us. For me, however, the people themselves together with their culture and their land turned out to be the compelling interest. I realized how the Lord was answering, in such a phenomenal way, my heart's desire to see His world and His people before it was too late. There had been so many lands, so many peoples, and in such a short time since the Lord had dealt with me so strongly in regard to pressing up and out my heart's desires. God's grace abounding toward me was more wonderful than I had words for, and there was much more yet ahead—even on this trip!

When signing up for Wheaton's summer studies in Israel, we had not the least hint that our field trips would include one to the Sinai, much less all the way to Sharm esh-Sheikh on the Red Sea, the end of the Peninsula. Under the political circumstances long before and then following the Six-Day War, there had been no possibility of going. I can only guess that Dr. Payne, his extraordinary ingenuity never flagging, conceived and engineered this trip at the first possible moment such a request could be made of the Israeli government. Somehow we got not only their permission but help in going.

Our main goal was to follow (as much as possible) the route of the Exodus, and to end up at Mt. Sinai and St. Catherine's Monastery. Besides two Israeli buses, we had a special military vehicle for the interior, a bus that could traverse the great rolling sands of the wilderness. With us were three Israeli soldiers, as armed escorts and guides, besides our two bus drivers and mechanics who I believe were also part of the military.[8] War-hardened and used to this desert and primitive conditions, they at once inspired my confidence. We were only the second expedition allowed to go, the first being the military.

Leaving Jerusalem, we descended from the mountains to Ashdod and Askelon, land of the Philistines, then on to the Gaza Strip where the Egyptian-Israeli war began. Soon, at El Arish, we made our first foray into the interior. Writing home later:

> My, what a desert—but the thing I will never forget is the remains of the six-day war . . . I could never have imagined the sights I saw there . . . hundreds of miles of burned out tanks, trucks, Egyptian barracks, personal things like helmets, shoes, etc. . . . . Trenches dug, they were fully prepared to take Israel—10,000 young Egyptian men died on the Sinai desert! What a horrible thing war is. The Egyptians . . . were "fully prepared" with Russian tanks and etc. to make good their boast to push Israel into the sea.

> We took Hagar's route into the Sinai—were forced to backtrack due to sands over the road—we couldn't get off the road—mines everywhere—I saw huge shells lying everywhere that had never gone off. Awestricken or numbed by the sadness of it all, I picked up an Egyptian shoe. . . .

> Proceeding on down from the Suez Canal and into the Gulf of Suez, we came to Abu Rudeis and camped there, about where the Israelites camped when they came out of Egypt. The next morning we started on the adventure of my lifetime! We left the coast and (in a special vehicle built for roadless desert travel) went into the wilderness where Moses fled, where Jethro his father-in-law lived, where he later brought the Israelites into the wilderness and to Mt. Sinai. I remember so clearly bucking up and down over endless sand dunes, all of us trying to hang on to our seats as we sped toward our goal. Several times I wondered if we would die out there—it didn't seem possible to get where we were going, no water, no shade—nothing but desert mountains on either side of the plain of Fienan which we were on and wonder of wonders—a time or two we saw a camel train with riders and their provisions and we'd wave back and forth.

After a ride that left me sore just from trying to hang on to the bus seat, we reached Mount Sinai and the ancient Monastery of St. Catherine's. The Lord led the children of Israel into a wilderness I don't think I could have imagined apart from traveling through it. I can see why they were tempted to murmur! The monastery, a great fortress, nestles in at the foot of Mt. Sinai, and what an awesome sight it was to approach!

Since 1968, when we were there, a road has been built on which pilgrims can travel to Mt. Sinai. I'm sure this has wrought changes. My impression then was that it was a place transfixed in time, being so very isolated. I felt to the depths of me the strangeness and wonder of it all.[9]

The library was closely guarded, and for good reason. It was here that the famous Sinaiticus and Vaticanus codices of Scripture were discovered by the German nobleman and scholar, Count Tischendorf, perhaps the greatest find in all antiquity and one that put the first translation of the New Testament books fewer than three hundred years from their genesis. These are the entire New Testament. This library, therefore, was a focal point for all of us. Few of us could have read the ancient texts, however, and so we were not overly disappointed that we weren't allowed to browse in that extraordinary part of the monastery. It also is a place of priceless icons and artifacts. The privilege of staying within it was quite an awesome gift from God.

Within the fortress is a small cemetery with a tiny chapel and ossuary. Never before had I been into an ossuary, or even known of one. In our tour through the fortress, and with no idea of what we were walking into, we were suddenly presented with all the bones of the monks who had lived there throughout the centuries. I must have been in conversation with one of our armed, war-hardened military escorts, for one of my most vivid memories of the place was his reaction to what was before our eyes. With a strange groan, he sagged against me before quickly recovering. All the hundreds of skulls were neatly stacked in one section, all the long-bones in another, all the short in another, and so on, and in the center was, as if seated in a prominent place, the skeleton of a sixth-century monk, in full black vestments and with a prominent cross. Due to the lack of burial space, the monks are buried and then exhumed; their bones are then placed in the ossuary (or charnel house, as it is sometimes called).

There was nothing Dr. Payne and the theology profs were looking forward to more than *the climb*. We arose at three in the morning to climb Mt. Sinai, and I recall Dr. Payne's excitement over the prospect and his energetic—even formidable—leadership. We were rationed out Israeli army crackers and cheese, our fortifier for the grueling trek. Climbing Mt. Sinai in the moonlight, and watching the sun slowly rise is no small experience, especially when we came to the really rugged parts of the ascent. It takes two hours of hard work to get to the top, and I didn't make it all the way. Indeed, I thought of Moses, and wondered how he made it. Experiencing all this was truly an inspiring experience, and surely, all the more so for the great Old Testament scholars amongst us.

One of my most cherished memories of this trip came with a stop on yet another oasis, as we started back toward the coast. They were so rare, and when one appeared on the horizon, our anticipation of stopping was unbelievable. As I wrote home, "Here people live—just as they lived hundreds and even thousands of years ago—beautiful people they are . . . tiny little girls under their little long robes—brown eyes looking out with faces half-veiled; proud, sturdy young boys, standing next to their fathers, looking ever so ready to take charge."

At this oasis we were received with great hospitality even though the group seemed never to have seen Westerners before—nor a camera either. One of our expedition thrilled them by taking Polaroid pictures and then handing these over to them as gifts. They had never before seen a picture of themselves—a happening that must have seemed supernatural. Here I especially remember one tiny little girl, her adorable little sun-browned hand holding a veil half across her face, looking with sheer wonder up into mine. What a treasure to bring home a memory like that—seeing God's world and the beautiful people, made in His image, full of wonder and life and the extraordinary ingenuity it must require to survive in the Sinai wilderness.

It is deeply moving to think about how thoroughly God brought to pass what I had chosen as He directed me. Truly, I learned to be properly mindful and prepared for the consequences of answered prayer. It is awesome even in retrospect to think back on all the peoples of the world I was privileged to meet and the remote places we visited where Westerners had not been for many generations.

But the new people and places didn't end there, even on this trip. After winding up our time in Israel, we flew to Rome to see special archaeological sites, and then I left the group and flew to England for more than a week. I was ecstatic to be reunited with my children, Deborah and Stephen, who were now well acclimated to their new country and skilled in finding the right trains to the places we longed to see.

When the repressed desire to see God's world and His people first surfaced, there was no place of greater interest to me than England—her religious history, cathedrals, museums, and great writers. I could scarcely wait to get to Westminster Abbey, not only because it was drenched in history and full of the tombs of the greats, but because I was intent on finding the Stone of Scone under the ancient throne chair of English kings and queens.

As a child, I often asked Mother to tell me the entrancing legend of the stone, one said to have been Jacob's pillow on the night of his vision of angels ascending up and down a ladder from the earth to the heavenlies (see Gen. 28:10–22). With my urging, she would tell of the conflict between the English and the Scots over the keeping of the stone. Thinking of Mother's stories, I was overjoyed to find the relic in the Abbey, tucked under the ancient Coronation Chair. But just as I was delighting in the stone, another visitor came up next to me and began insisting that it was not really Jacob's pillow, but merely a stone dug up out of the Scottish hills. I much preferred the great old story and left this Englishman quite unthanked for his offering.[10]

My love of English literature and history left me without a need for a tour guide, and together with my children, we visited London and her most memorable spots. We had an incredible day in the British Museum, seeing the phenomenal archaeological artifacts. While there I also discovered the German swastika on an ancient artifact, revealed to be the symbol of Baal. That was a valuable bit of knowledge I carefully filed away.

Then I rejoined my group in Paris and flew home from there.

After so much travel, it was wonderful to settle back down in Wheaton. I studied without letup through 1969, even though in March I had an enormous distraction, the intense joy over and yearning to see my first grandchild, Sara Marie, born in the south of England.

In 1970, being a declared English major, I met for the first time Dr. Clyde Samuel Kilby, one who would impact my life far beyond anything I could ever have imagined. In the spring I took his poetry class and then in the fall his class in modern myth, this latter a gift that has never stopped giving. In it the dreadful rationalism of the day had no part. In it I found an academic niche, for in C. S. Lewis especially, I came home to literary and philosophical brilliance that gave me the language I was seeking with which to speak to modern Christians of the supernatural, the transcendent.

But before telling of my work with Dr. Kilby, I must not leave out the way travel kept coming into my story, for that would become the pattern of my life from henceforth. In the summer of 1970, between the two courses with Dr. Kilby, I flew to England to meet my little granddaughter Sara, whom I already knew by heart from her pictures and her mother's letters, and to be with Deborah for the birth of our second little girl, Joy Anita, who arrived in July. My cup of joy indeed ran over, and that joy ended up naming our new little one.

Before going back to England on this trip, I knew in prayer that I was to do graduate work and thus wondered, since my family was in the U.K., if the Lord would lead me to do it there. Therefore I planned to scout out universities in England, Scotland, and Ireland. By now, I knew that God would make the way when His will was in it.

On this trip, I traveled on an exceedingly cheap student charter flight and stayed in youth hostels. I was to be five weeks with the children, arriving shortly before the birth; afterward, I planned to travel up through Oxford and into Shakespeare country and then on up and through Scotland, visiting universities on the way.

After my delightful time with the children, and an unforgettable introduction to Oxford University, I reached London and stayed overnight at a youth hostel close to St. Paul's Cathedral. I wanted to look more closely at Holman Hunt's painting of Christ, the Light of the World who knocks at the door of our hearts—the representation of which had so impressed me as a child. The painting spoke hugely to me once again, in great blessing. And on the day I visited, Anglican bishops gathered at the cathedral from all over the world. I climbed up into a balcony just as they were processing into the building in their colorful regalia, and I was thrilled as the organ and choir gloriously gave voice as we celebrated the liturgy.

I mention this because it added to my joy—my heart was so full of thanksgiving anyway, having enjoyed my first grandchild and attended the birth of my second. Also, besides the meaningful travel up from the south of England, the Lord was blessing my time with students in the hostels. All of this, I think, prepared the way for another extraordinary experience in regard to time. It occurred less than a week later as I crossed the Scottish Highlands.

I took the Flying Scotsman, the train from London to Edinburgh, basking in the glow of all these things. After several momentous days visiting that wonderful city, I took a bus across the Highlands en route to the Isle of Skye and the Hebrides with the intention of visiting the Isle of Iona with all its rich Christian history. I was still much in prayer with great thanksgiving, meditating on Holman's painting and the meaningful interactions with other students along the way, when suddenly the scenery changed. We entered mountains that were solid purple with heather, and the smell of the peat fires wafted into the air. In an utterly profound experience of somehow *knowing* this place, of somehow having come home, I could not keep the tears from flowing and flowing. It was as if my roots went down to the center of the earth there. This surfacing of an ancestral memory, along with the incident while camping in Oklahoma during the academy period (see the story about Edie in chapter 14), prepared me to understand and move in the healing of memories, which was yet to come.[11]

On my return home, I looked into my genealogy and found that indeed, the great majority of my ancestors are Highland Scots. And furthermore, according to my Aunt Grace (the amateur but gifted DAR genealogist), I am descended from the last tutelary chieftain of the McFarlane clan, who migrated to the United States early on.

Besides staying in youth hostels and cheap bed-and-breakfasts, I even hitchhiked along with other students. I would never have done this apart from the leading of the Lord, and here again, He sent me with most remarkable results not only in terms of witness but in what He was teaching me.

The flight home in the student-chartered airplane stands out in my memory all these years later. I rejoined the same group of students, who now looked considerably more bedraggled and in need of home, showers, and a few good meals. They were tired and grumpy, and some were loud and rowdy. While the summer had so increased my joy, it didn't seem to have done the same for them.

As we neared the States, I became burdened. I strongly felt that something was wrong and I wanted to get off that airplane. It made an unscheduled landing in Boston, and I asked to get off, even knowing I would not be able to get my luggage. But they would not allow it. Then as we sat on the tarmac at the Boston airport, the Lord sent a sign that he often sends at times of concern such as this—an incredible, double rainbow. Never have I seen one so brilliant. Even so, my concern increased as we neared New York, where we were scheduled to deplane, and I cried out to God. Finally, we landed safely, and my relief was immediate.

I later heard that the plane was to fly to Washington, D.C., where it would pick up more students, but that it crashed, killing all the crew. This was tragic, but at least no students were on board. Somehow I believe the Lord held that plane together through the power of prayer. I have never before or since (even when flying on rickety craft in the Mediterranean) had such a sense about an airplane.

On returning to Wheaton, I entered the modern myth class with Dr. Kilby, and, wonder of wonders, he selected me to be his assistant, not only in modern myth, his class on the Oxford Inklings, but also for the now-famous literary collection he founded in 1965. This collection gathered the works of C. S. Lewis and his friends, the Inklings. My job would include the enviable opportunity of reading the voluminous numbers of Lewis's unpublished letters and cataloging them for researchers to use. No adventure on earth could compare to the mind adventure I then undertook into the works and world of C. S. Lewis. Academically speaking, I had come home to joy.

I had found scholarship that not only always points to the holy and the transcendent, but that adequately exposes the reductionisms coming through secular, materialistic anthropologies, sociologies, and psychologies (Freudian), and that raised great protections against the new gnosticisms (Jungian and feminist). Here was the language that honored the Real and the reality and the truth that streams from it.

The experience of seeing God's world and His peoples, the very desire I had put before the Lord, prepared and affirmed me for the world of C. S. Lewis in ways I can't define. In granting my desires of both education and travel, God the Father had further affirmed me, not only as His child but in His call on my life and the message He had given me, even the scholarship and ministry that I was already engaged in.

The remarkable answers to prayer, together with the day-by-day means of support, prepared me for even greater leaps of faith that he would require of me in the near future.

18

Modern Myth with Professor Kilby

A perfect good, as well as a perfect anything-else, is mythlike. The call of conscience toward perfect goodness is a mythic call lying beyond the best possible set of rules and regulations. Systematic philosophy and systematic theology are no more than statemental pointers, dry bran, beside the reality toward which they point.

Clyde Kilby

Rooms large enough to hold all the students wanting to crowd into Dr. Kilby's senior seminar on modern myth were simply not to be found. Literature majors had first priority, but history, science, premed, and all the fine arts majors wanted in as well. He took the largest space available and in sorrow had to turn students away once the limit was reached. The class outgrew all the classrooms and so had to meet in a larger space. With the large numbers crowding into his classes, Dr. Kilby needed help. As his assistant, I sat up front and to the side perched on a high stool so as to see all the students and learn their names.

The class reading assignments, besides Mercia Eliade's *Cosmos and History,* a comprehensive account of myth, began with C. S. Lewis's space trilogy (*Out of the Silent Planet, Perelandra,* and *That Hideous Strength*), *The Abolition of Man,* and *Till We Have Faces,* and went on to J. R. R. Tolkien's trilogy, The Lord of the Rings (*The Fellowship of the Ring, The Two Towers,*

The Return of the King), and from *The Tolkien Reader* his "On Fairy-Stories" and "Leaf by Niggle." We then proceeded to Charles Williams's *Descent into Hell* and George MacDonald's *The Princess and Curdie* and *Lilith*.[1]

One can hardly imagine a classroom where students were more avid readers—or listeners and note takers—than in this one. Dr. Kilby's lectures were full of his love and knowledge of the mythopoeic, and he knew and had corresponded with Lewis and Tolkien and had an extraordinary ongoing correspondence with and visits from other Inklings such as George Sayer, Owen Barfield, and close friends and family members of deceased Inklings. His lectures were full and overflowing with much that had not as yet seen the light of print.

With Dr. Kilby in charge, the class itself was a mythical experience. Here, the Christian supranatural, full of mystery, nobility, magnanimity, and truth, burst forth through great story, great symbol, great myth. I was in my glory. If anything could cure a soul of its introspective ways, point it to the objective real outside itself, and liberate it from abstracting away the unseen ultimates (in all that *is*—man, Scriptures, and creation), this was the class for it.

Myth, as great story, is concerned with *being*; it is about meaning. It speaks deeply to man's condition, and through modern mythmakers such as C. S. Lewis, J. R. R. Tolkien, and George MacDonald, myth speaks to modern man's desperate condition and plight. What Dr. Kilby wrote in his personal notes on myth is an example of how he spoke in class:

> The easiest and perhaps the best way to suggest man's present dreadful loneliness and fragmentation is to say he has been demythologized, that is, that he has lost essential meaning. Myth is concerned with essential meaning, and this meaning is no longer his possession. He has learned—or so he feels—to live by bread alone and he is finding the bread pretty indigestible.

Another characteristic of myth is timelessness; it is, in the words of Mercia Eliade, "a revolt against concrete, historical time" and a "nostalgia for a periodical return to the mythical time of the beginning of things, to the 'Great Time.'"[2] The students, reveling in meaning and entering into the timelessness in these Christian authors, began to experience the transcendent. Especially from Lewis and Tolkien, they received back the symbolic knowledge of Jehovah as the God of Hosts: space itself regained its meaning with its heavens full of angelic beings and the "assembly of the holy ones" (see Ps. 89:5–8). The students' minds, now resymbolized according to a Judeo-Christian view of reality, were able to intuit the eternal, with all its imagery and glory.

Being a fine evangelical Presbyterian, Dr. Kilby, sensing at the final session of class the extraordinary reviving of souls amongst these keen and precious students, asked me most solemnly if we should have an altar call. Knowing all that God had done by way of healing, I cried out immediately, "Oh, no, Dr. Kilby, we should have a dance!" Restrictive notions about dance prevailed at that time, but our students had entered the Great Dance of the Cosmos, that which C. S. Lewis captures in his space trilogy, by name and in paeans of praise in *Perelandra*.

To say that my debt to Dr. Kilby is very great indeed is to understate the case. The privilege of knowing, studying under, and working with this great man was a blessing, the enormity of which is difficult to put into words. And who can adequately laud the gifts he came bearing? I am convinced that apart from Dr. Kilby's vision and labors, the Christian world would know very little about C. S. Lewis today. We certainly would be devoid of much of what Lewis wrote. In these our times, it is hard for me to imagine how deep would be the hole in the fabric of Christian learning and discipleship without the man so aptly referred to by Chad Walsh as the "Apostle to the Skeptics."[3]

The astonishing thing was the down-to-earth, Hobbit-like fashion in which Dr. Kilby, although clearly erudite and scholarly, went about working all this academic magic. Besides that, he had distinctly elfin traits. Because he was so exceptional in the ordinary things of life (a kind of genius here), he ended up, almost as a matter of course, doing very great things indeed. As his student assistant in both his modern myth class (1971) and in the collection of Lewis's works and the works of the Inklings (1971–76), and then later as a friend, I had occasion to see all this up close over a number of years. I watched him as he combed the world from east to west and from pole to pole for Lewis and Inkling letters and then went about preserving and making them available to everyone else. Time and again, with seeming effortlessness, he would get an idea in the middle of conversation, turn in his chair, pluck up his tiny, ancient manual typewriter, plop it in his lap, and in seconds complete word-perfect letters of inquiry to academics (such as a Tolkien or a Barfield) and folk the world over. I never once saw him hurried, and there was a simplicity and glee in the doing of the impossible task of gleaning the world for Lewis and Inkling lore and literature.

Dr. Kilby wrote in his book *The Christian World of C. S. Lewis* that he found in Lewis "a mind sharp as a scalpel and as intent as a surgeon upon the separation of the diseased from the healthy." Further, his "impression was of a man who had won, inside and deep, a battle against pose, evasion, expedience, and the ever-so-little lie and who wished with all his heart to honor truth in every idea passing through his mind."[4] Most assuredly, what Dr. Kilby said and thought of Lewis was also uniquely true of himself.

With all his heart, Dr. Kilby loved truth and the reality it is about. He had a lifelong vendetta against the modern's propensity toward separating the two: that fateful way of reducing reality (including meaning itself) to mere statements of fact about it. He came against this blindness in all of his courses as his bright students, heavy into analysis and sorely introspective, dropped their blinders, looked up, and began to see. They were infected by what he called "our present one-dimensioned age." They had come to value and develop the mind's power to abstract and analyze while at the same time ignoring and even denying its imaginative (that is, its intuitive) ways of knowing—those with which we apprehend the Unseen Real.

Dr. Kilby, together with Lewis and other great Christian mythmakers, *knew that imagination, understood in its highest sense as the mind's power to intuit the real, is key in all of this.*[5] Lewis calls the imagination "the organ of meaning," and it is not to be separated from reason, "the natural organ of truth," without losing the good of both. They knew the Lord requires the whole of us.

Just as we do not reduce trees to their number of feet in board lumber and therefore think we know what a tree is, so we are not to reduce the great realities of our faith to dry statements of fact about it and think that we know God. Dr. Kilby was never preachy nor did he even specifically teach about these things. He didn't have to. He was an evangelist simply by pointing his arm alongside Lewis's (MacDonald's, Tolkien's, or others') to the mystery. The students in his classes could at last look up and see.

Presbyterian saint that he was, he was as near as anyone to being a St. Francis when it came to his relationship to nature. After modern myth class I had the enviable privilege of accompanying Dr. Kilby back to his and Martha's rooms across from the campus. There I would help grade papers and plan out upcoming classes on Lewis, Tolkien, Williams, and MacDonald. But first I had to run the gauntlet of Peter the parakeet. Dr. Kilby, who came from Mississippi, was the quintessential Southern gentleman and would invariably open the door and usher me through first. That meant, however, that I would get a face full of furious feathers. No canine ever greeted its master with more avid expectation than this winged creature who would fly freely in the Kilbys' apartment. The feathers were furious because Peter was jealous of Dr. Kilby's attention, plainly revealed by flying at and almost through me to get to him.

And it didn't end there. As we settled down to work, Peter would dive-bomb me in an unfriendly fashion, nip angrily at the students' papers, and then fly back and nuzzle Dr. Kilby's ears. When that didn't get his master's attention, the bird would walk atop his head, take hold of a strand of hair, and hang upside down while attempting to poke his beak in Dr. Kilby's mouth. Dr. Kilby would keep on talking, paying no attention except to me and our papers. At this point I always feared lest the bird miscalculate and lose his head. When this maneuver didn't stop Dr. Kilby, Peter would fly to his ear and pluck at the hair in that tender spot. This finally won him Dr. Kilby's full attention.

Somewhere in the midst of this, his remarkable wife, Martha, herself a saint and solidly one with her husband in his endeavors, would make one of her rounds. With napkin in hand, she would wipe off our shoulders or wherever else Peter misbehaved. And this is partially how we operated and prepared for modern myth, one of the most popular and influential courses ever given at Wheaton College. Of course Dr. Kilby thought nothing of this unusual way of doing things and never once indicated that such a situation was out of the ordinary. But it was! It was downright mythic.

He loved the *is-ness* of that bird, its very essence, and that bird existed to enter into his presence. Peter was fully affirmed in his "birdness" as a real thing, resplendent with meaning, and in Dr. Kilby's love and recognition, Peter the parakeet seemed to gain human characteristics. Of course Dr. Kilby's appreciation of God's creation extended beyond his home and even up to the cosmos itself. In a series of statements he passed out to his students, he wrote such things as the following:

> At least once each day I shall look steadily up at the sky and remember that I, a consciousness with a conscience, am on a planet traveling in space with everlastingly mysterious things above and about me.
>
> I shall open my eyes and ears. Once every day I shall simply stare at a tree, a flower, a cloud, or a person. I shall not then be concerned at all to ask *what* they are but simply be glad *that* they are. I shall joyfully allow them the mystery of what Lewis calls their "divine, magical, terrifying and ecstatic" existence.

He celebrated the *is-ness* of creatures and creation until he died at age eighty-four. On one occasion he greeted me with the exciting news that two squirrels in his yard had just turned backward somersaults, "Just for sheer joy, Leanne! Just for sheer joy!" Martha chimed in, "That's right, I saw them do it." The spring day was splendid, but note that such antics occurred in Dr. Kilby's presence. Though the squirrels were no doubt full of the joy of life for a number of reasons, a large one was because he was standing there, delighting in their existence. Even the descendants of these squirrels seemed different, more approachable, for decades after.

Lest I leave an imbalanced picture of Dr. Kilby, I should underline that he was a unique evangelical saint, for he celebrated not only the existence of all that God created but supremely God Himself. He was a man who talked to God. The academics, authors, and others with whom he corresponded would have been surprised to know of his prayers for them. This, of course, was true of his students and colleagues as well.

Among the rare opportunities Dr. Kilby made possible for me was that of a semester's tutorial work on Charles Williams. I was only the second student to be allowed to do this, and Dr. Kilby must have had great difficulty in putting this through, for he thought I'd be the last. He was willing to arrange it due to my deep concern with theological problems in Williams's writings. One was the doctrine of the "reconciliation of opposites," amounting finally to a marriage of good and evil, the very thing that C. S. Lewis so brilliantly and rightly divorces. While Lewis stands for orthodoxy in regard to the mystery of evil, Williams attempts to reconcile all opposites, including and especially those of good and evil. His was a poetic attempt to find "the unity of all things," but his efforts were wrongheaded and even gnostic.[6]

The other theological problem was Williams's doctrine of "substitution," a mistaken notion of what it means to love others and to "carry the cross." This misconception is dangerous to anyone and especially to Christians in the healing prayer ministry.[7] This latter problem showed up when several of our idealistic and loving students, influenced by Williams's novels and concerned about a friend's need, started to practice substitution. That is, they asked to take into themselves the darkness (physical, spiritual, or emotional) that someone close to them suffered, and thereby carry it for them. They quickly got into trouble, however, and would come to me for prayer.

Mothers and nuns seem the most prone to do this sort of thing, but in healing prayer with others, we find it across the board. Unbelievable problems can come about because demonic forces take advantage of it. Good doctrine is vital; the dangers in heresies take terrible, even fatal, tolls.

I should note that as part of PCM's healing workshops, we try always to include the teaching on and renunciation of these substitutions. It is amazing the miracles that we witness, even on occasion instantaneous healings of terminal illness. Substitutions are attempts to do in our own bodies and minds what our Divine Substitute, Christ, has already done.

Dr. Kilby made possible all manner of opportunities for me. Excerpts from a letter I wrote to Aunt Rhoda and Uncle Gus (April 5, 1971) refer to them:

> I had a wonderful experience Friday night. Dr. Kilby and I drove up to Trinity Seminary where he and Dr. John Warwick Montgomery (the theologian who debated with Bishop Pike and Altizer over NBC)[8] were giving the oral examinations of two students for their Master's degree. One concerned Charles Williams, the author that I am researching, and the other was a thesis on a theory of aesthetics—the problem in literature that is most frustrating to me at the moment. They had two hours each in which to defend their thesis and they had to have encyclopedic knowledge of the same. Wow! It was really something. Of course, I know that I have that to look forward to—nice thought! There were several questions that I could've answered that stymied them and encouraged me—but there were several that they answered which I couldn't have.

Looking back, I'm more amazed than ever at how Dr. Kilby invested in me—a senior undergraduate who was an older student and by then a grandmother of two. Apart from him, I would never have had such a unique opportunity to study C. S. Lewis and all his friends.

By the summer of 1971, graduation was just a few weeks ahead and I was much in prayer over "What next, Lord." By then I knew I was to continue in my study and felt it should be master's work in both English literature and in theology. I had been offered a full scholarship to Wheaton's graduate school, and the dean, Dr. Will Norton, had arranged that I could take a theological degree, directing my work toward the special Lewis collection. This amazing offer came after I had asked the Lord why, with everything right there at Wheaton, did I have to go to some other graduate school in order to bring literature and theology together in a study of C. S. Lewis? So it seemed logical to do that master's first.

So with such a boon as this, the decision about what to do next seemed obvious. But the Lord led very strongly in prayer that I was to do master's work in English first. How could such be managed? And how could I leave

Dr. Kilby, the work in the library and in the collection, the scholarship and work in the grad school, Mrs. Alexander and friends, and go to another college? I was now beseeching the Lord most earnestly to show me where to go and how to manage it financially.

Though I continued to pray, no understanding could I receive except that I was to go away for a while and then return. Even after an absolutely glorious graduation day on June 14, 1971 (I processed with the group although my graduation date was after the summer's completion of my tutorial thesis), even then I did not yet know where I was to be later in the fall.

Then, after the tutorial and all my academic work were completed, in my tiny little room in Mrs. Alexander's house and while kneeling in prayer, the Lord sent a very special Messenger indeed.

My eyes were suddenly opened to see a huge angel (much taller than the home I was in). My awe to be in the presence of this unfallen being was such that I could not look all the way up to his face. I also felt a distinct physical change in the power of my eyes to focus—to *see*—for he was robed in a white that was whiter than white. It was as though my eyes had the power to zoom in and see a very small portion of a huge wing, one with an indescribable texture and beauty.

I should note that the appearance of the angel is not necessarily the way angels really look. Rather it is the way that the Lord enables us to see them: in this case, a way fully symbolic of the holiness, the purity, the heavenly beauty that normally we would be unable to picture. I come close to tears just in recalling the beauty.

I realized immediately afterward that the angel had brought me the knowledge of where I was to go, and even whom to contact, though he had not spoken to me. (I'm not sure I could have borne that and lived.) After the visitation, I simply had the answer; the knowledge was there in my mind, and I knew he had brought it.

During this visitation and for a brief period afterward, as I continued in prayer and worship, I sang in the most incredible tongue, one that seemed to chime (bell-like) and resonate with the very sounds of Heaven, one that I somehow knew was an angelic language. It was as though the angel had imparted his song to me. There simply are no languages like it on earth.

My awe at the degree of his presence and the superimposed spiritual plane (not level as we know level) was such that it remained for weeks and seemed even to spill over on to the exceedingly few others (only the closest prayer partners and Dr. Kilby) with whom I shared the experience. It took weeks to get over this physically, but the hand of the Lord and a great and most precious quiet was on me. Gradually the deep inner assurance and quiet gave way to sheer joy.

God guides us so dramatically only when necessary. We are not to seek an angelic visitation; we seek only God and His will. Because I was required to make such a leap of faith, I could probably have received the message in no other way.[9] The message: I was to apply to the University of Arkansas graduate school, and I was to go to the Episcopal priest-chaplain to find a place to live without cost. I applied late but was accepted.

Of course I couldn't go without telling Dr. Kilby why I would be leaving Wheaton College and the work in the special collection, not to mention the generous graduate school offer. Thus I had to tell him about the way I received the guidance from the Lord, something I wanted to do anyway but over which I had some fear and trepidation. That was not because I feared that he wouldn't, after looking at me long and hard through his properly skeptical Presbyterian eyes, believe what had happened in the end. I knew he would, for he understood the intuitive ways of knowing that are important to God's people. But even so I knew that an experience like this is simply not to be shared, except as the Lord leads. It is too sacred and meaningful, and indiscriminate sharing can bring one into spiritual battle. I also had a sense of lingering awe and the gifts of silence and serenity that went with the experience.

Anyway, as I attempted to unfold what had happened, the awe fell freshly on me again. I'll never forget coming to the matter of the song. In joy I cried out to Dr. Kilby that I had sung in an angelic language, that the angel seemed to have passed on to me his song. It was only then that I was conscious of a fair amount of Reformed skepticism in the air. So I branched off into C. S. Lewis and J. R. R. Tolkien's stories and their Christian myths that have such an uncanny way of portraying these experiences, all of which he dearly loved. Tolkien, writing of the Elves and the glorious singing in the elfin languages, comes as near to capturing the experience of that singing as can be done through story. I said, "Surely, Dr. Kilby, something like this must have happened to Tolkien for him to have written in such a way!" Dr. Kilby, who knew him personally and had even worked with him in regard to trying to put the *Silmarillian* together, said rather emphatically, no, he didn't think so. He had the highest regard for Tolkien's poetic intuitive capacities but apparently balked at this.

But if Dr. Kilby failed to accept any part of this angelic visitation, he didn't show it. He too was convinced I was to go to Arkansas—and later, after all that happened there, any lingering doubts he might have had were fully and forever vanquished.

And so in late August, my car packed with all my belongings and with hardly any money, I left Mrs. Alexander and my dear little room that held so many memories and headed out toward the hills of Missouri and Arkansas and a very different environment indeed. Once into north Arkansas, I ran into unbelievable traffic. All the chicken farmers from Arkansas, Missouri, Oklahoma, and Texas were crowding into that beautiful part of the country for a special meeting. It seemed they could have filled a city. It was good to be back in the mountains of Arkansas, heading into Fayetteville and Razorback country.

19

Revival!

Having no place to stay—and every motel room in northwest Arkansas occupied by a chicken farmer—I made my way directly to the Episcopal chaplain. I simply went in, introduced myself, and told him I needed a place to live that would not cost money. Apparently I didn't come across as completely crazy, although legends about this meeting sprang up later. He was stumped, but as I continued to quiz him, he suddenly recalled that several weeks previously an older woman had visited his office with a request. He saw her as a colorful character, one well-known in those parts. She was a leader in the Christian Science movement in North Arkansas. A fairly recent widow, she was offering a room free of charge in exchange for help in the household. As he told me about it, he looked very doubtful that I would find it suitable. But I cried out, "That's it!" and went to see her. I moved in immediately.

Mrs. Ruth Gilbert loved beauty and goodness. She excelled in craftwork, creating her own patterns and styles and then marketing them expertly. She fashioned flowers from silk, and presented me with a unique corsage and matching red rosebuds for my hair. Through the years I seldom had occasion to wear the corsage, but in order to show my appreciation for her artwork, I wore the rosebuds occasionally. I mention this because these feminine touches—along with the long skirts I favored—inadvertently helped to create something of a mystique surrounding me that I would have gladly avoided had I foreseen it. But even that later worked to the glory of God.

Mrs. Gilbert and I were a million miles apart in theology and practice, but I knew right away that none of that would get in the way of our arrangement. Furthermore, we had one strong common desire—to see people healed. She couldn't hear enough about the healing ministry as I had known and lived it. It was, without doubt, the Lord's will for me to be there, and it ended up being a very great blessing for both of us. I had a lovely room and the easiest duties—I think she mainly needed someone congenial living in her home—a spacious, quiet, and peaceful haven, one that I would sorely need in the days ahead.

Earlier I wrote of the culture shock Deb and I experienced when moving from the South to the North. That was nothing compared to what I experienced in moving from a fine Christian liberal arts college to a secular university still in the throes of the sixties that had largely imbibed the "Berkeley language" of profanity. I think all my professors were unbelievers in the sense that they had lost the Judeo-Christian worldview, though several attended the Episcopal church where I went.

Within a week I grew intensely concerned for the naive Christian students who clearly lacked the language and ability to refute the materialistic and even atheistic onslaught. I don't recall being worried about some students, such as a doctoral candidate who sat next to me in class and had no shame about writing pornography to pay his way through school. He had chosen hell and darkness, but the naive ones—those who did not deliberately rebel against God—were the ones for whom my concern knew no end.

My first response was to cry out to God, asking Him why on earth He had sent me there. Never before or since have I so repeatedly and earnestly asked Him a question. I was alternately on my knees and then pacing through Ruth Gilbert's spacious, beautiful home when she was away, crying out loudly and telling the Lord I couldn't bear it. This went on for a week or two.

My second response was anger. Never before had I been angrier at lying rebellion and darkness and the awful state it leads a nation into: one of the loss of reason, and with it the moral and spiritual good. My realization of what a wretched anthropology secularism leads to—the loss of the holy and a view of man that ends in his destruction—utterly weighed me down. And then the anger came, an anger for which I never had to ask forgiveness. It drove me very quickly to the rector of the Episcopal church where I was attending.

Meeting with him in his office, I asked him if he had any idea of the responsibility he bore for the university students who sat under his ministry one mere hour each week on Sunday. Having a very large idea of it myself, I told him in no uncertain terms what they were receiving in class—some from several of the professors who attended his church. I named one woman in particular whom I saw tripping down to receive Communion each Sunday, yet whose profanity often echoed through the school hallways.

The rector, orthodox in his priesthood and preaching, leaned far back in his chair and heaved a long and audible sigh. He then told me of the adult Sunday class that was made up of about a hundred skeptics with at least two outright atheists. He stated, very simply and tersely, that he could do nothing with them.

We sat in silence until I spoke out, "Why don't you teach them the works of C. S. Lewis? He is, after all, the apostle to the skeptics of our age."

The Rector countered, "Why don't *you* do it?"

The upshot was that he sent me in to teach the Sunday school class that several of my teachers attended, along with at least one who would later help decide whether or not I graduated with a degree. Though I trembled at the thought of teaching such a class, it was not for fear of the loss of a master's degree. I phoned and told Dr. Kilby what I was about to do, and in considerable amazement and concern, he began to pray for me (as did all my prayer partners).

Never before or since have I taught a class that surpassed this one for sheer bone-rattling excitement. The spiritual and intellectual debate was extraordinary. As the worldviews clashed, it was clear that none can ever equal or stand up against the Judeo-Christian's—which, of course, C. S. Lewis, in impeccable prose, symbol, and story, shows fully.

I could not go in and teach the Word of God because they had rejected the Scriptures. (Of course, most were rejecting what they had never really known.) I therefore went in armed with C. S. Lewis's space trilogy that ends with *That Hideous Strength*. These books show how in a brave, new world, created by a scientific mind-set that rejects transcendent good and moral values, man is corrupted and totally dehumanized. After the trilogy I taught Lewis's immensely important book, *The Abolition of Man*, which through prose explores the issues of *That Hideous Strength*. Speaking to the unbelievers, I told them: "This is exactly where you are spiritually and intellectually and in your worldview." The class was utterly electric with the presence of the Holy Spirit, which I never failed to invoke on beginning.

At this point, early in my second semester in February of 1972, a few began to hear the truth and requested that I meet with them separately. Conlee and Signa Bodishbaugh[1] were members of this class and opened their home for these meetings, during which the Holy Spirit fell in a most extraordinary way, ushering in revival. I could then—outside the regular Sunday class—teach the Scriptures and disciple these precious folk with abandon. This group grew and soon began to meet in the church. The presence of the Lord was such that some people walking outside the church, knowing nothing of what was going on within, were drawn in as by a magnet. They, too, became part of the revival.

Momentous and holy happenings usually have their share of amusing circumstances, and this was no exception. Our Sunday school class continued on with all of the folk still attending, even though the members who had been "born from above" seemed to have turned alarmingly fanatical to those who maintained their unbelief. Therefore, though puzzled that the group remained intact, I continued teaching the works of C. S. Lewis to great effect. Only later did I learn why the group stayed together. The rector was a bachelor whom they all loved, and they had heard rumors that there was finally a woman in his life. They thought I was that woman! So here I stood with long flowing dresses and Mrs. Gilbert's red rosebuds in my hair, while they waited to see what would become of their rector.

The things that happened during this year were so numerous and remarkable that I'll never adequately describe even the high points here, but suffice it to say that how I ever earned my degree in the midst of it all was only one of the Lord's miracles. Indeed, one of the strange coincidences that worked to my good was that I was unable to take a master's degree in English as planned but had to get all my English courses through an education degree in the Teaching of English. Therefore, the master's I was taking, even though it made available the same English literature courses, had less stringent requirements, and I did not have to write a comprehensive thesis. In that year and the next, no master's or doctoral degrees were open to students in the United States in either English or history for the reason that too many were being graduated in those fields. It was wrongheaded, but it took some pressure off me.

Therefore I was taking three graduate courses in English literature plus the other required education courses. The amount of reading for one literature course alone can be staggering, and shortly before the renewal broke out, I wrote home the following:

Dearest Aunt Rhoda and Uncle Gus,

How is everything? All is well with me for the moment but it is probably the last time I'll be able to say that for another semester. I've just been assigned 37 novels—and this doesn't count outside reading and research and papers—for only 3 of my classes. The semester is 16 weeks long—please pray that I can read fast and retain my sanity. I'm plowing through one book that is 785 pages long—and it is horrible. Despair dripping out of every page.

I *must* retain time for the Sunday School Class. And I *must* work [earn money]. I wish I could take tension and pressure better. . . . Have gotten a good number of hours in working for which I'm grateful.

It was into this scene that the revival broke out, and immediately I was teaching two groups and was busier than I've ever been in my life. I was discipling those in renewal both in the Scriptures and in the gifts of the Holy Spirit, which were in operation and set in from the very beginning. These precious converts were seeking the Lord with all their might, and I taught them what I would later present in schools of pastoral care.

We saw healing after healing—even miracles. There was the extraordinary deliverance of a parishioner whose neediness had long been apparent. Most of those being discipled participated in this ministry to her. She was a woman of means who in her youth was reputed to have been a beauty. Her home was filled with expensive Hindu idols that she had gathered up from temples in the East. She was fully delivered after I told her she must destroy (not sell or give away) her idols, which she finally managed to do after an intense battle. Her ability to think, to come up and out of an utterly paralyzing darkness, was completely restored, and she became a wise and valued member of the prayer group. Her true giftedness came out as well, and she was once again a beautiful woman as well as successful in her career.

Now, rectors don't often see these kinds of conversions played out in their churches, but this dear pastor did. And he hung in there with us through it all. In God's mercy, he soon had a great ally, for a bishop well-known in the Episcopal world suddenly appeared in our midst.

The Right Reverend William C. Frey, liberal in his education and outlook, together with his wife, four sons, and daughter, had barely escaped with their lives from a South American country. He had taken a courageous stand against that nation's top leaders, speaking out against the assassinations of those who opposed them. He and his family arrived in our midst badly battered, in great need of prayer, with little more than the clothes on their backs. They came right into our prayer group and received healing and laying on of hands for the release of the Spirit in their lives.

This bishop then began to lead renewal, not only in that church but later on in the church at large, becoming the bishop of Colorado before being named president of the conservative Trinity Episcopal School for Ministry in Pennsylvania. Next to the descent of the Holy Spirit on the group of believers, nothing could have been more electrifying for that church body as a whole. Bishop Frey, of course, gave full legitimacy to the prayer group and spread his protection over it.

Later I wrote to Fr. Winkler, when I was sending out an SOS for his help:

> Our Church is shaken to the roots—drastically changed. There aren't enough hours in the day or days in the week to minister to all who are coming. Bishop Frey is ministering in the power of the Holy Spirit on Campus and in the Church, and our meetings are so beautiful and fantastic—it's hard to believe. Dozens more are ready to receive the laying on of hands. Some are being filled as they worship and one as she went to receive communion. I have never seen a renewal of a whole church before—and this is so beautiful. They are stunned and praising God—and are now busy ministering to others. The parish members are beginning to minister on campus—other church members are joining us in the prayer groups. Churches in other cities are wanting us to come help them get started.

Soon there were glorious Eucharists during the week with Bishop Frey officiating and all of us sitting on the floor. Everywhere renewal occurred in those days, it was like this—never enough room for folk to be seated in chairs. Students from the university were now joining us. I shall never forget the singing at those meetings. While in the presence of the Lord, the Holy Spirit gave us the gift of singing antiphonally in tongues, something too beautiful for words. The classical musicians in our midst were stunned, for the perfection and originality of it and the depth of worship in it are simply indescribable. This is surely how the early antiphonal chants came to be—they were given by the Spirit for the blessing of God's people and for the enabling of their worship.

I recall a young student from India, learned in various of their languages, who interpreted the words at one point. She understood and translated them as one would interpret a message in tongues. Nothing could have banished the doubts of this young convert as did this sign from the Lord—given surely for all of us but especially for her. Bishop Frey was almost dancing for sheer joy, and on my reporting these things to Dr. Kilby, he too was spellbound with amazement and thanksgiving out of what comes from teaching C. S. Lewis to a class of unbelievers. It has been my unfailing experience that when one teaches his work in the same faith he knew, the eternal truths of our forgotten past are restored and great rejoicing and healing result.

The Word of God, along with the full Judeo-Christian symbolic system, was restored to these dear ones in our prayer groups. Their minds were informed and their imaginations baptized in the holy, the transcendent, the good, and the true.

So without an income, how did I make it financially? Folk began to ask me to speak, and gifts started coming my way. I was slated to visit and speak on Oahu and Maui along with Fr. Winkler, for example, and a Wheaton professor donated the roundtrip ticket to Hawaii. These gifts just never stopped coming, but only as needed. One of the many delightful provisions was that several people, including my sister, gave me dresses. And Signa Bodishbaugh made several beautiful ones for me as well.

In beginning to minister in other churches in Fayetteville and Little Rock, I first ran into the problems of suicidal depression brought about by extreme teachings on the submission of women. One evening a woman came up to the altar for prayer and told me that she planned to kill herself if she did not get help that night. She was badly battered and abused by her husband, but the pastor in her church (not the one where I was ministering) said that even so she must submit to her husband. When the ongoing situation didn't change, *she* was blamed because the prescription hadn't worked. She received the counseling and prayer she needed, but I was fated to meet many more like her. This brought forth a number of lectures that I ended up giving even in other countries. Many church leaders here and abroad were influenced and swayed by some powerfully misguided teachings coming out in that day.

Many incidents arose out of people's need for prayer. One situation drew on my understanding of the problems experienced by the Wheaton students who were influenced by the doctrine of substitution as found in the works of Charles Williams. In the South in those days, many of the churches had long altar rails where people could come up, kneel, and receive prayer. On one occasion, a young woman had long awaited her turn, and when I finally got to her, some of the folk still there were ignoring what was going on at the altar. In other words, they were not praying, a dangerous thing when serious prayer for healing is being made. This young woman had suffered severe pains in her midsection and had seen many physicians but received no help. I anointed her, laid hands on her, and she was released from the severe pain.[2] Immediately, however, a woman who had been talking with her friends screamed out with pain. A demon lodged in the body (not in the spirit) of the first woman had left her and entered the other woman. Of course we then prayed for the other woman and saw her released. But first we brought visiting to a halt and asked everyone to pray.

I should add that among Christians, most often needs for physical, emotional, and even serious psychological difficulties and illnesses are not connected with the presence of the demonic—that for which deliverance is required. But on occasion they are, and this incident shows graphically how, in substitution, one becomes open not only to emotionally and psychologically induced illnesses but to demonically induced ones as well.

Fainting at the sight of "the fields white to harvest" (see John 4:35 KJV) and earnestly wanting to respond to the calls for help, my mind turned to the diaconate. I have always had a great need and desire for the support of the organized church, and my first effort to bring the ministry that God charged me with under the hierarchy of the church occurred at this time.

To me the diaconate seemed the only way it could work. Even back in Wheaton, overwhelmed with the burgeoning prayer ministry and the sense of aloneness once Fr. Winkler and the prayer group were gone, I had thought of becoming a deaconess, for it seemed that is what I had been, unofficially and in effect, for a long time. That the church was the place for the ministry (in effect, one of healing and evangelism) goes without saying. Now in Arkansas, I thought long and hard, and in late April of 1972 submitted a plan to the Bishop of Arkansas. The excerpts reveal not only my thoughts about the way forward but my deep concerns for renewal itself:

Dear Bishop Kellar:

I have so much to say I hardly know where to start: But I will begin by saying that we are certainly looking forward to your visit to Fayetteville next weekend and to the service of Confirmation. Also, I hope that there will be time in your busy schedule for exploring with me the possibilities of my being ordained as deaconess.

I am now nearing the end of an MA program at the University of Arkansas. I came here determining to do little else but study so that I could quickly "clear out" and return to Wheaton or some other Christian school and teach the works of C. S. Lewis, Charles Williams, and J. R. R. Tolkien.

As matters have fallen out, however, my study here has been a mere adjunct to the work that God has dropped into my hands to do: Everywhere I turn on campus, in the church, in prayer groups in the state, I come face to face with hungry and questioning people and my studies in literature paled into insignificance when compared to the spiritual needs of those God sent me to. During my preparation for college teaching, both at Wheaton College and here, the thought of becoming a deaconess has recurred to me. Each time I have thought the notion a strange one and have asked that the Lord direct my career plans.

Since coming to Arkansas, groups of people who have received the Baptism of the Holy Spirit have been asking me to come and teach them. In doing so I have found Episcopalians who . . . have been saddened that their wonderful new faith and zeal was not being integrated into their own churches. Sometimes I realized that the training they were getting was not at all what it should be. I feel that our church and way of worship is ideal for establishing the balance that the Christian who is new in the Gifts of the Spirit needs. Also, I have realized that often these estranged ones were not altogether happy in the groups that they had come to be in—groups that . . . leave out our sacramental truths. More and more the Lord seems to be leading me towards reaching out to these persons and teaching them.

Instead of accepting a teaching position in a college next fall, I feel a desire towards doing the work of a Deaconess, towards teaching in the church, towards ministering to Episcopalians who are receiving the Gifts, towards setting up prayer and healing groups, towards being a "liaison" (hopefully of love and understanding) between these groups and our church where necessary—all of this seems to be the end toward which the Lord is leading me. . . .

If I should be ordained Deaconess, this would assure the others who have received the Gifts of the Holy Spirit that they are indeed accepted by the church. As deaconess I would be better situated to be a liaison between a priest and any group that might be in the midst of misunderstanding one another. Due to many factors, these newly Baptized in the Spirit believers can come into misunderstandings. The church, depending upon many local circumstances, either rejects or accepts them in differing degrees. However, rather than a passive acceptance or rejection, these precious ones need positive leadership more than they ever did in their lives if they are to become balanced groups and remain free from false teachers. . . .

The Church has need, I believe, for an ordained—an authorized person

1. to work with the people who have received the Gifts
2. to teach them
3. to channel in the right, orthodox literature
4. to help the priest of the parish to understand the problems or the needs of these persons and their wonderful potential in the church

5. to arrange or recommend visits or missions by some of our clerical leaders in the charismatic ministry.

... It is a most exciting day to be a Christian and to experience the great renewing of the Body of Christ; I surely want to be in the center of God's will and do His work in His way. I know, Bishop Kellar, that you are God's anointed servant and that whatever you decide in this matter will be right. I will praise the Lord either way that you decide knowing that that is my answer from God.

From this plan, it is easy to see that the enormous needs there in Arkansas were deflecting me from my original sense that I was to return to Wheaton. But besides the fact that "the need is not the call," I was to learn time and again that the denominational church was by and large without the mechanisms or the knowledge needed to come in and make a difference in this largely lay-led revival. The tragedy of that pains me to this day. But the Lord, and Bishop Kellar who was very gracious toward me as he pondered all this, knew that the organized church did not have the structures or the will in place to accept this plan.

Structures in lieu of the experience and knowledge of the work of the Holy Spirit reigned then and yet do now. I know that structures are important but have never thought first in terms of them. Rather I think in terms of invoking the Holy Spirit and the enabling that comes in the proclamation of *truth*. It is unthinkable to me to consider that for lack of a structure—one that assures the freedom of the Spirit within it—the church by and large foregoes the ancient rites of healing and of the ministry of the Holy Spirit.

My particular plan didn't work, not only because under these circumstances there was no place for a diaconate in the church, but also because God had other plans for me. I was not hearing His still, small voice telling me to keep to my original plan, and so even before hearing from Bishop Kellar that a diaconate was not then to be, the Lord spoke powerfully to me through a phenomenal dream.

After I took my finals in Fayetteville, the dream came when I was on an eventful two-and-a-half-week trip to Wheaton in June. I made this trip to meet numerous ministry appointments and to get the last of my belongings (two spare tires and a set of dishes) from Mrs. Alexander's basement, with the plan to return to the ministry in Fayetteville. But on this last night of the trip, the dream came in vivid Technicolor, stopping me dead in my tracks.

Extraordinary by any kind of measure, the dream (or vision) I awakened with was powerful. The archetypal imagery in it was far beyond anything I could have imagined. It was mythic and at the same time heavenly; it was plainly from the Lord, and I needed to know what it meant. The phenomenal scene was chiefly of a large and majestic Bird in flaming reds, unlike any earthly bird, and it was rising up out of a muddy mire. Surrounding its feathers were plumes that were as living flames, and the mire could not adhere to the Bird, but flowed down from it. Under the flames were revealed the glistening plush red feathers that were not of this earth—they reminded me in texture of the angel's wing in the visitation. The Bird, when fully risen, stood glisteningly clean.

I looked away to the left and then, turning slowly back again, I saw the Bird bound and fettered, yet determined to fly up and over a fence. This fence and the terrain were as we would see them, meadowy and earthy. In trying to fly, the Bird's feathers were dropping out as they rubbed against the cruel fetters. It finally got up and into the air but could not gain the needed height to surmount the fence, so I ran to try to help it fly up and over the fence. And that was the end of the dream.

This dream that awakened me shook me to my foundations and stayed with me. As in the angelic visitation, the message was simply there: I was to return to Wheaton as originally planned, and the new word was that I was to write. The full meaning of the vision, however, I was yet to understand.

Two days later, back in Fayetteville, I realized even more fully that the vision had to do with the Holy Spirit and the way the resurrected Christ's gift of the Spirit was bound within the hearts and minds of most Christians in the Western church of today. In rising from the mire, the heavenly Bird was very like the Phoenix rising from the ashes, an ancient archetypal image adopted early on by the church as a symbol of Christ's resurrection. The flaming reds surrounding it were fires of the Holy Spirit cleansing away the mire that in turn revealed the heavenly reds of the feathers of the divine Bird.

A mere four days after I recorded the dream in my prayer journal, I had enjoyed two glorious prayer meetings with the renewal group. By then I knew that I was to write about how, in the church and its peoples, the Holy Spirit (the beautiful, magnificent, huge, red Bird) was bound—mired down in the reductionistic theologies and so-called social sciences and rationalisms of the day—and must be freed. Christians were, in effect, fenced in by the rationalistic naturalism and the unbelief that comes with it. The Holy Spirit, though bound by our unbelief and loss of understanding of His work, was attempting to fly, as it were, through the church.

The Lord continued to give me understanding of the dream, but that was the gist of it. I see and understand even more now, more than three decades later, as in retrospect I write about it.[3]

How is it possible, I often wonder, that so much can happen in an academic year? At the end of my time in Fayetteville, I flew to Hawaii for the incredible reunion and ministry on Maui with Fr. Winkler. Before going, my dear friends in Fayetteville, including the Bodishbaughs, sent me off in style. They presented me with a lovely seed-pearl purse that contained the gift of a financial collection they had taken up. Then in Hawaii I was laden down with leis after being met at the airport by Fr. Winkler and so many of the Wheaton prayer group members who were now at home and ministering on Maui. Together with combing the island, whale watching, and swimming, I once again had the priceless privilege of prayer with these dear ones whose fellowship had meant so much to me.

After speaking in Sunday services on Maui and on Oahu, I returned Stateside, directly to Wheaton College and the life of a student once again. I enrolled in the master's program and once again assisted my beloved friend, Dr. Clyde Kilby, in the Lewis and Inkling literary collection. In addition, for the next three years, on a fellowship provided by the English Department, I taught freshman writing at West Suburban Hospital to Wheaton's nursing students who trained there.

It seemed an eon had passed since first leaving Wheaton College, but now I nestled back in as if I'd never been gone! Time as *chronos* is oddly confused and strangely unmeasurable when *kairos* is so very prominent—those points when God moves so powerfully to redeem and restore his people.

After the year in Fayetteville, I received far more invitations to speak and teach than I could have accepted, though I yearned over most all of them. My desire to be with God's people and proclaim His truth and the reality of His presence far exceeded my physical strength to go. But the writing, though the hardest work in the world, once in print, has the power to work while I sleep.

It's interesting that, once I arrived back in Wheaton, the Lord continued to send dreams about what I was to write. It was an assignment that would stretch me to the limit and compel me to confront a writer's block, the roots of which went back to wounds from my early years.

20

"In the Night
My Heart Instructs Me"

Is any pleasure on earth as great as a circle of Christian friends by a fire?

C. S. Lewis

In the fall of 1972, back at Wheaton, the times were rich and rewarding, full of researching, locating, and reading everything that C. S. Lewis had written—published or unpublished—and full of friends with whom to be in communion and great dialogue. Of these, thanks be to God, there was no dearth. This is what made leaving Wheaton College always so difficult: the intellectual stimulation of Christian minds and hearts—those resident on campus or visiting from the world over. I treasured the special occasions and conversations with scholars, ministers, and artists, some of whom became cherished friends.

Visitors from abroad seldom failed to visit the Lewis and Inkling collection[1] where I was busily indexing Lewis's unpublished letters, of which there must have been thousands. These visitors included one or two of the Inklings themselves, as well as those who knew and were close friends of Lewis, J. R. R. Tolkien, Charles Williams, Owen Barfield, and Dorothy Sayers. My job was most enviable. And Lewis's extraordinary capacity and talent for friendship seems wonderfully to have survived him. As we study his works we come to know him not only as a friend but as one of our greatest allies in the battle for truth; we then go on to make friends with others who have experienced the same.

Later, at the end of August 1974, Lewis's desk and wardrobe arrived for the collection, the latter now immortalized in the Narnia books and the filming of *The Lion, the Witch, and the Wardrobe.* We had only one fair-sized room at the time, so placing these items of furniture presented a problem. We solved it by making use of them! In a journal entry I noted: "The CSL Wardrobe and Desk arrived. I felt weepy as I placed my things in it." Amazing as it seems now, in the small space, I worked at his desk for more than two years.

Since those days, as on occasion I need to search through the expansive research and notes I made on Lewis, I almost invariably end up teary-eyed—most unusual for me. In awe, I weep over the magnitude and clarity of such a mind and heart and imagination and his magnanimity and humility. My response is not alone, and this surely is what makes the Lewis collection such a phenomenal place, one where friends and often seekers after God are brought together by Lewis.

On returning to Wheaton, I needed friends who could hear me out as I processed all that had happened in the revival of the past year. A goodly number of prayer partners were very helpful in this. Also it was a very great blessing that I could speak freely of the work of the Holy Spirit in the renewal with Dr. Kilby, Dr. Will Norton, dean of the graduate school, and our revered Chaplain Evan Welsh, who was then semiretired.

My chief concerns were for restoration into the church of the healing prayer ministry and for the formidable barrier to that happening: modernity in its forms of naturalism, materialism, and rationalism. The healing ministry, with its prime emphasis on repentance (thereby naming and confronting sin), together with its sacramental laying on of hands and prayer for restoration of man's spirit, soul, and body, is at the very heart of the gospel—of baptism, discipling, and evangelism. I could see that Western man's attempt to replace the work of the Spirit with that of his own studies, education, and capabilities blinds the church and hinders any healing ministry.

Soon after I arrived back in Wheaton, I received from the Lord the first of a series of dreams that had to do with this twofold, overriding concern. The dream, which was more than a dream in that it was an impartation, showed me beyond all shadow of a doubt what I was to do—that is, what I was to write.

In this dream, I was merely a spectator in a hospital delivery room when a nurse handed me a baby boy. He was a beautiful, vitally healthy baby, an exceedingly precious gift that surely couldn't be mine to keep. This extraordinary baby looked up at me with clear, great, sparkling depths to his eyes, and he smiled. From that moment, I was, in C. S. Lewis's words, "pregnant with book." The baby was wholly gift, coming to me from without.

The academic work for the master's degree was foundational to the book in the dream, which would focus on Lewis, and was almost entirely a pleasure, for it brought together my keenest theological and literary interests. In March of 1973 I completed a theological paper, "The Sacraments and Their Relationship to the Holy Spirit: An Exploration," followed up in May by one entitled "Incarnational Reality: A Study of the Holy Spirit in Man."[2] Dr. Robert Webber, the theology professor for whom I had written these papers, then asked me to write a book with a title such as "Sacramental Reality: The Spirit and the Eucharist," a suggestion that left me greatly encouraged but also quite dazed and unbelieving. Being "full of book" already and concerned that his suggestion was beyond me (which it was), I racked my mind for others who might write this book or the others he suggested. But his enthusiastic encouragement, together with that of the dean, Dr. Norton, affirmed and cheered me on.

Once birthed, the extraordinary baby boy given to me in the dream was named *Real Presence: The Holy Spirit in the Works of C. S. Lewis*.[3] After all, who knew and wrote better about my deep concerns than Lewis, and he from the standpoint of academician extraordinaire: historian, philosopher, and "mere" Christian? My book would be, I hoped, a bridge to help evangelicals regain incarnational (including sacramental) reality, the understanding of the real and immanent presence of God with us, and therefore a renewal of the knowledge and experience of the healing work of the Holy Spirit. It's interesting that *Real Presence* also became a bridge for Catholics to better understand evangelical strengths.

The delivery of this book did not come about without the strongest of birth pangs, which anyone who has ever suffered writer's block will know all about. To be "pregnant" and unable to give birth is a wholly terrible condition.[4]

What seminal years the four back at Wheaton turned out to be (from the fall of 1972 to the summer of 1976)! During them, while collaborating with the Lord, I was able to resolve the block and complete the book on incarnational reality in the works of Lewis—this great apostle to the agnostics of our day as well as to the inadvertently skeptical Christians, caught up as we all are to some extent in the naturalism of our age.

Besides the master's work and that in the Lewis collection, I taught freshman writing to Wheaton's nursing students at West Suburban Hospital in Oak Brook, Illinois. It was a large class, and what students they were! I dearly loved them. My one regret is that I had to keep them to Wheaton College's Bachelor of Arts standards in writing. In my opinion these young women were being called on to do the impossible, for their nursing studies included working on the hospital floors, often at night. I assigned several of C. S. Lewis's novels, on which they successfully wrote their papers. I heartily wished I could give all of them *A*'s.

Apparently I was not cut out for professorial work, that is, to teach literature as planned earlier. I had no trouble stimulating people to dig deep into the great minds and hearts—past and present—and to think and write on these things. But not to assess work and award grades, or even to follow the rules in the ways one is supposed to teach, especially in writing.

Indeed, once Dr. Kilby shook his head and said to me, "Leanne, it's no use; you are a preacher and not a teacher." He said this in response to the long lines that would sometimes form after my classes as the students waited for prayer. How could it be helped, especially when using the works of Lewis, for truly, as George Sayer says, he "combines a novelist's insight into motives with a profound religious understanding of our human nature."[5] There's nothing like a full Christian anthropology and psychology to constellate insights both into our need for healing and wholeness and our intense desire for it.

In those days I was wearing the long skirts and dresses made for me by Signa Bodishbaugh, and I didn't realize what an impression they made until one day I showed up for class in a just-below-the-knee dress. The students' shocked disapproval was astonishing. With one voice, they lamented that I should do such a thing!

I learned so much in the three years of teaching freshman writing, and not the least was that Dr. Kilby was likely right, as he nearly always was, about my being more of a preacher than a teacher. And though I was slow in catching on, this was the last job when I would earn money other than that which came through ministry. The pattern of my life was to be one of utter financial dependence on the Lord, such as I had already experienced in the gaining of my education.

Once again, miraculously it seemed, the Lord provided a place for me to live free of charge. Otherwise, my part-time teaching job would not have covered expenses. In January 1973 I moved into the home of a young mother with two little girls. Deserted by her husband and fearful to live alone, she needed another adult in the home. Her plight was particularly hard in that she had grown up under Communist rule and was a stranger to our country. She was a beautiful young woman, the equivalent of a Miss America as she had won the national beauty title in her country. It was precious, sitting at table with her and her little girls and sharing Christ with them.

Here again, I have many memories of experiencing God's grace in this home. I remember much prayer in the night seasons, incredible dreams and guidance from the Lord, prayer with and loving those little girls, and of having Dr. Kilby over to meet the family. He was thrilled over this young mother's entrance into the Christian faith and was eager to hear her story firsthand.

Living in this way, in people's spare bedrooms, was made all the easier as I now had an office for all my books, teaching work, and research. In connection with the teaching of writing, the college assigned me a tiny third-floor office in the Music Conservatory. Besides work and study, much healing prayer and counseling went on in it. There I could look directly out onto the face of Edman Chapel and, once again, as from Mrs. Alexander's house, see the Bell Tower as I meditated.

On one occasion when I was praying at my desk, looking up and out of the huge window, the Lord dealt with me uniquely. This came just as the last of winter's gray and cold gave way to the warmth and glory of spring's first appearing, and it lasted over the period of Holy Week. Most preciously, the Lord instructed me to get a ring with a crucifix and wear it on my left hand—as a sign of being married to Him and to His will alone. I did this immediately, and I have worn such a ring ever since. This was more of a turning point than I realized at the time, for I believe I received a very special gift with it, one that would banish any thoughts, should they have ever come my way, of remarriage.

During the summer of 1973, I attended my first School of Pastoral Care, founded by Agnes Sanford. She was retired by this time, and folk who had worked with her in the past were leading it. For me, it was a time ordained of God. I received a healing of memories in which I experienced the power and ease with which God can place his finger on a core memory, no matter where in the infant soul it might be.

The group that gathered consisted of ministers, nuns, monks, deacons, teachers, and various professionals in the medical, health, and educational fields, all of whom, like me, were involved in prayer for healing of the sick. The leadership team was made up of Barbara Schlemon, who had been active in Fr. Winkler's prayer group and was by then a leader in Catholic renewal; the Reverend Herb Nabb, pastor of a Congregational church and a very effective, humble, and devout man; and the Reverend Herman Riffle, a Baptist pastor who ministered with his wife, Lillie, and who was greatly gifted in the understanding of dreams.

Toward the end of the week, Barbara prayed a healing of memories prayer over the group, and she formed it chronologically, beginning in the present and going back down through the years toward birth and conception. I was greatly blessed by the prayer, but had previously confessed every known sin in every period of my life and had received not only forgiveness but the healing of every known hurt and even disappointment. Absolutely nothing came up until Barbara got down to between age three and eighteen months. Then up popped the clearest voice imaginable from my deep heart that literally resounded throughout my being: "Forgive your father for dying!"

How strange, I thought, *to forgive one's father for dying.* But I did it just the same: "I forgive you, Daddy, for dying, for leaving me." The clarion quality of that command is something I've never forgotten, much less doubted or denied.

On the following day, Barbara's teaching related to the fact that children take the loss of parents, however it comes about, as a personal rejection—the very thing God had so clearly shown me in placing His finger on this traumatic time in my life.[6]

This healing of memories and the knowledge that came with it shot fathoms deep into my being, touching down into that underground river in my soul of grief and loss, of which I wrote earlier. I would need this knowledge to overcome the painful block to completing the book on C. S. Lewis. I had not had a writer's block when I wrote thesis papers or tutorials, but it is one thing to write about something that one is vitally interested in and quite another to write it for publication, which tapped into my old unconscious fears.

From the time of this healing of memories, the Lord began to send the most remarkable dreams, dreams that brought up from my unconscious what I needed to deal with in resolving the writer's block, even before I was fully forced to acknowledge its existence. In these dreams I clearly saw the traumatic effects both of my father's death and my difficulties with Grandma.

I had never had one single ill feeling toward my father. That, however, is not the point. He certainly had not sinned against me in his death, but I had experienced his death as a sense of personal rejection, and in releasing him fully in the presence of the Lord, I was released from inner stumbling blocks, such as fears of exposure, and all that I had experienced in both his death and in the way our little family was thrown out into a world hard put to receive us. Those fears were a vital facet of my writer's block, together with fears of rejection.

During the four years back at Wheaton, I recorded in my journal more significant dreams than I've received in the entire rest of my life. All of them helped in overcoming the early repressed grief and fear of loss, and in doing so, released creativity, thus clearing the way to respond to the Lord's call in the quickly expanding ministry. Herman and Lillie Riffle's friendship and expertise in dreams was an invaluable help and a very great gift.

My understanding of the dreams increased as I wrote them out and continued to lay them before the Lord in listening prayer. Busy as I was, it would have been easy to neglect this, but then much of the understanding would have slipped back down into the unconscious recesses of my soul and I would have missed the ongoing healing and understanding. As I continued to listen to the Lord, I saw that the feelings and fear left by the loss of my father and the difficulties with my grandmother had been unconscious or unacknowledged barriers to moving forward with the work the Lord had so clearly assigned to me. Now they would no longer hold me back.

Also the healing of memories brought in its wake, immediately and remarkably, a special anointing together with the insight and understanding of how to pray ever more freely for the healing of men—and to write, in later years, *The Broken Image* and *The Crisis in Masculinity*. In this way I was freed, as a woman, to pray for and with men and to understand gender inferiority (whether in man or woman) and the imbalance of the masculine and feminine within the soul. This knowledge also paved the way for the insight into how to pray for souls who fail to come to a secure sense of being in the early months of life.

All who have been blessed in prayer for healing of memories owe a great debt indeed to Agnes Sanford, who pioneered this way of prayer, one that brings emotional and spiritual healing to the deepest levels of the soul.[7] Such is the result of the forgiveness of sin, either our forgiving another or receiving forgiveness for ourselves.

After attending this school, I was invited to teach in future schools. Only a few months later, I was a leader in one and in several per year for the next decade, both here and abroad. These were remarkable times of experience and learning.

I hadn't been back to Wheaton long before I inadvertently caused a bit of a stir. Several faculty members in my prayer group belonged to a small church that was without a pastor. They wanted to hear the material I was teaching, both in Fayetteville and now in Schools of Pastoral Care, and they prevailed on me to fill in until they could locate a new pastor. This was not something I felt good about doing, principally because of the time involved, but these prayer partners were persuasive, and I still had a few more lessons to learn in regard to withstanding such. I ended up conducting their Sunday services. It looked very much as if I was pastoring a church, a no-no for women in this part of the evangelical world, and it took a while for a few folk to get over their grievances that I would do such a thing.

I kept hoping to be released, but a new pastor failed to show up. And of course things other than the Sunday service came up needing attention. As it turned out, something very dark was going on, and the longtime members told me of their sense of something demonic in nature. They felt that it, though unknown, was what had so disheartened and discouraged the former pastor.

As we prayed and asked for discernment, the Lord moved strongly, and the awful matter came to light. A man in the congregation had been sexually abusing a severely retarded child in the congregation, an unthinkable crime for the folk there to face. In working with the leaders of the church to resolve this terrible thing, my work there was finished and I was released. Once in a while the Lord seems to require things of us we had rather not do, or at least, He comes to our aid when we find ourselves doing them.

At the end of 1974 I completed the master's program at Wheaton and soberly reflected on it in my prayer journal on December 6:

> It is 7–8 yrs from March 5, 1967, when the Lord impressed me to seek a goal and He would bring it to pass. The goal was education. Today ends with the completion of the 2nd Master's degree—A BA and 2 MA's in 7-1/2 years.
>
> Just as He brought to pass the goals I set with Him earlier, now He has brought to pass this goal. He is faithful. I do not know if this is the end of formal education. Also, have had several moments when I felt I might be out East in School. My Master's orals ended with Dr. Norton strongly recommending that I go on for Ph.D. research degree at Oxford. Several profs have indicated they took more or less for granted that I would go on.
>
> Father, what goal would You have me now set with You? Send me, Father, to do Your bidding. Send Your Holy Angel with a live coal from off the altar that is in Your very Presence, and *cleanse* me. May all excess baggage fall off; prepare me to collaborate with Thy Holy Spirit. Show me any other preparations necessary. Praise and Honor and Glory be unto Thee now and forever more. Hallelujah. Amen.

After graduation, I remained another year and a half at the college to write, teach, and work in the Lewis collection. It took sixteen more months to complete *Real Presence,* while working through the writer's block and dealing with more significant dreams than one would expect to have in a lifetime. In fact the prophetic nature of one of the dreams revealed two more books being formed in me just as I was completing the book on Lewis.[8]

I dreamt of a large baby buggy. I looked in and saw what looked to be a grown baby at one end. But down at the other end I saw tiny, tiny twins. They were dark—like young embryos—and were in little squares that appeared rather like manuscripts. On awaking, I instantly knew that I was "pregnant" with two more books, though I had no sure idea what they would be about. My awe and consternation were considerable, for I knew that once engendered, the birth of these twins must come to be.

Two terse, solemn lines mark the date in my prayer journal when *Real Presence* was completed: "March 27, 1976 Came to the end of the book on Lewis. There is much polishing yet to do on the last chapter but—this is it. Hallelujah."

The celebrating would have to wait for its publication, for I now keenly felt my responsibility to see the newborn in print.

A few days later, another terse line appears in my journal:

March 31 Dream: an exceptional young baby boy, a perfect little boy aged two, lost.

I had sent the larger part of the manuscript to a publisher who was most enthusiastic about it, but this dream warned me to send my "lost baby" elsewhere. And it proved correct. Truly, in answer to fervent prayer and when necessary, the Lord instructs us, even in the night and in our sleep, often using the symbolic language of the heart. As it says in the Psalms, "I bless the Lord who gives me counsel; in the night also my heart instructs me" (16:7).

These years at Wheaton were filled to the brim with opportunities and blessings, and I would leave with a heart chock-full of thanksgiving to God, yet greatly sobered in knowing how very much I would miss Dr. and Mrs. Kilby, the C. S. Lewis and Inkling collection he founded, and my many friends and prayer partners.

I would leave with yet another block to surmount, one that had been with me now for a number of years. It consisted of the deeply held need and belief that I should work directly under the hierarchy of the church.

My desire to work under godly, divinely appointed masculine authority stemmed from the fact that the church has always taught that regardless of the gifts and calling God has bestowed on someone, these should be exercised under the oversight of proper spiritual authority. But I kept running into a brick wall. The burgeoning ministry God had visited upon me could find no resting place in the church. It would take two long years of financial hardship and exhaustion before I was forced to face and accept this dilemma.

PART 4

1976–

Delight yourself in the LORD, and he will give you the desires of your heart.

Psalm 37:4, NIV

. . . truly, I say to you, if you have faith like a grain of mustard seed, you will say to this mountain, "Move from here to there," and it will move, and nothing will be impossible for you.

Christ our Lord, Matthew 17:20

> Dying you destroyed our death,
> Rising you restored our life.
> Lord Jesus, come in glory.
>
> Lord, by your cross and resurrection
> You have set us free.
> You are the Savior of the world.

The Eucharistic liturgy

21

The Search for Home

As each has received a gift, use it to serve one another, as good stewards of God's varied grace.

1 Peter 4:10

The next several years were showered with God's blessing, his varied grace streaming down upon this ministry of healing prayer. Sparkling with all the rainbow colors of the Shekinah glory, this grace was sufficient for the inevitable spiritual battles as well as the tough and exciting lessons that accompany ongoing renewal and revival. But my unresolved block—my desire for the ministry to be under the hierarchy of the church—proved to be a barrier to health and well-being. With no salary, I could not afford a home, and therefore I lacked the solitude and quiet I needed for rest as well as for writing the books that were clamoring to come out. Never robust physically, I grew increasingly exhausted.

This block, of course, had nothing to do with past trauma. Rather it had to do with my need to face the tenor of the times and where they were heading, a direction that would continue to militate against the venerated healing rites and prayer practices common to the church throughout the centuries. Generally speaking, the church, whether Protestant, Anglican, or Catholic, was eschewing the knowledge of the healing gifts of the Spirit. Instead, it was satisfied with its psychological, sociological, and counseling programs that were replacing all that involves the transcendent, the supernatural power of God. The exception would be in institutional churches where priests and pastors such as Fr. Richard Winkler were in charge, but we've seen already the battle he faced, which ultimately forced him to leave his church.

Therefore I left Wheaton College in July 1976 looking for home, which I believed would be where both the ministry and I could be an integral part of the institutional church. The irony in leaving Wheaton was that I was at home there, and in going on missions from that base, I was doing precisely what I had been called to do. But with blinders on and hoping to find a suitable diaconate open to my work, or even to found one, I left.

I moved to Episcopal lodgings in the West, hoping eventually to find there the spiritual covering I longed for. In exchange for room and board (but no salary), along with others in the community, I became deeply involved in the ministry of the diocese. I told my friends and family of my new surroundings in an early newsletter, written in late January 1977:

> I'm writing from my tiny office in my home that I share with (at the moment) sixteen others. From my window the snowcapped Rockies smile at me, beckoning me to "come up higher." Colorado is breathtaking in the winter. A sad commentary on the times, however, is the fact that here in Denver we often see this grandeur through a blanket of smog. Drive a few miles outside the city proper, though, and one transcends it. Today—no smog. And the sun is beaming on us.

When I wrote this newsletter, I had been living in this community for just six months. But my feelings of exhaustion kept increasing, and the lack of solitude was sapping my strength. This is apparent in my handwritten postscript to Aunt Rhoda and Uncle Gus:

> It has been terribly hectic since coming back here [following a visit to Little Rock]. Sometimes I wish I could come home and hide from all I'm being called to. Or maybe a cabin up in the mountains here—hide away with pens, paper, and books. Ah, I'm dreaming sure enough now . . .

In Colorado I continued with what I had been doing in Wheaton: living by faith and in other good folks' homes. Within a year of leaving Wheaton, I was crisscrossing our great North American continent, from the northernmost reaches of British Columbia (even up into Alaska) to the southern tip of Florida, and from Quebec and the far northeastern reaches of Canada to the southwest coast of California—with lots of points in between. In 1977 alone, besides four full Schools of Pastoral Care (those that Agnes

Sanford founded), I was involved in at least ten more conferences and made appearances on radio and television. I was getting letters literally from all over the globe—my mailbag alone required secretarial help. And so in the midst of the blessings of the ministry, I became increasingly weary.

Meanwhile I hung on to the hope that I could eventually earn a living within the established church, one with a godly, scripturally authoritative hierarchy. This striving remained as a block until early 1978, even though, here again, the Lord was warning me about this goal through dreams. The blind spot connected to my strongly held conviction, however, prevented me from understanding the dreams. To look back now and read my notes is to marvel that I could ever have missed the meaning.

The growing ministry—though unincorporated and unfunded—brought in priests, pastors, physicians, and others in the healing professions and ministries, as well as gifted lay leaders to minister alongside me. They were all men and women of prayer who knew that God desired to bring wholeness to His people through prayer for their deepest spiritual, mental, and emotional needs. The ministry simply was blessed beyond all knowing as we were able to move freely and fully in sacramental worship and the healing ministry with the laying on of hands, and with the charisms of the Holy Spirit quietly and profoundly in operation.

Most of this, however, took place outside the institutional churches, whether in the individual missions and schools that I conducted or when working with others in the Schools of Pastoral Care. The spiritual formation and transformation of lives coming out of these truly remarkable healings characterized every conference, and where there was adequate leadership, resulted in ongoing renewal that people took back to their churches.

In late April of 1977, I was at the zenith of my need to find a home for solitude and rest. I was also deeply disturbed over the introduction of Jungian psychology into the Schools of Pastoral Care. These neognostic influences were being introduced mainly by Morton Kelsey, one of the teachers in SPC (I write more fully of this disturbing phenomenon in the next chapter). Against all common sense and still having some hard lessons to learn, I had been persuaded to work with Morton in an "Advanced School" the next month. In the angst of all this, I was off to Chattanooga to teach in a school alongside Dr. Howard Rhys, a revered professor of theology at Sewanee Episcopal Seminary; Harry Goldsmith, the wounded soldier for whom Agnes Sanford prayed in her book, *Oh Watchman;*[1] and Edith Drury, Agnes's assistant, who lived with her in California.

Once the Chattanooga conference ended, Edith and Peggy Rhys (Dr. Howard's lovely wife) proved intent on helping solve my problems, and I certainly needed all the help and prayer they could offer. As part of this, Edith invited me to her summer home on Cranberry Island, off the coast of Bar Harbor, Maine, for a full month of rest and reflection. Peggy and I prayed about this gracious invitation, and we decided I should make every effort to go in July.

In between our prayer times in Chattanooga, Edith regaled us with stories of Agnes. Wonderfully interesting to me was the description of how Agnes went about her writing. When she was about to write a novel, she and Edith would first act out the characters. This skit-playing continued as the writing progressed. When Agnes was actually writing, however, Edith was not permitted to say a word. Silence reigned in the house. This routine worked very well for both of them.

Besides the skits for her novels, the two enjoyed acting out spontaneous ones just for the fun of it, ones that featured such characters as "Dr. Sigmund Jungstinker, psychiatrist," and "Wheeler," an imaginary whale who sleeps under Edith's bed, replete with descriptions of what it is like to step out of bed onto wet flukes in the morning.

Edith also cited the limerick Agnes loved to give the folks preparing to leave one of her schools. She knew the tendency of some after the conference would be to strive to stay on a mountaintop high when their next step must be to descend, full of God's grace, into the valleys of life, there to work out their healings and transformations. Therefore she counseled the participants to go home, get their hands in the good earth and plant, build, and clean. In short, do all the earthy human things while integrating what the Lord had done in the school. This, of course, was one of the great secrets of Agnes's own spiritual strength and balance. The limerick brings squarely home the extremely odd and unfortunate falls folk take who fail to learn this incarnational lesson:

> There once was a monk of Siberia
> whose existence grew drearier and drearier
> 'Til he burst from his cell
> with a ter-ri-ble yell
> And eloped with the Mother Superior.

So in the summer I was off to Cranberry Island, Maine, with a stopover to celebrate the Fourth of July holiday with friends in Washington, D.C., never dreaming of all they had in mind for us to do. After visiting the Smithsonian and revisiting many of the famous monuments on such a meaningful weekend, I was amazed to spend the evening of the Fourth at the White House as a guest (among many others) of the newly elected President, Jimmy Carter, and his wife, Rosalynn. They were hosting the press corps, of which one of my friends was a member, and to be there on such an occasion was momentous indeed. Writing home to Aunt Rhoda and Uncle Gus, I described meeting and shaking hands with the President and his wife, meeting their little daughter, Amy, and being shown her tree house, and my awe at the privilege of watching the festivities and fireworks from such a historic spot.

> There were others from the press and staff and their families and we put our blankets down on the beautiful lawn and watched the festivities. We looked down in a direct line to the Jefferson Memorial and outside—between the White House lawn and the Memorial—were 210,000 people watching!

That day, so full of meaning, and at the height of the world press's enchantment with our new President, was a magnificent yet sobering and eye-opening experience. It was sobering because I sensed an enchantment—even a lust—for worldly power on the part of the press and the politicos, together with a lack of comprehension and acknowledgment that if we failed to attribute our democracy to God, it would fail. At the same time, I realized the demonic temptations hovering over all this (as in Eph. 6:12). I could only reflect on how weak our democracy is apart from our Judeo-Christian roots and a vital church at prayer, and wondered how long we would retain our freedoms.

The Fourth was surely special, but the day before was even more memorable to me. My friends had arranged for us to meet with a clergy acquaintance of theirs, Fr. Henry Atkins, with whom they thought I would resonate. He conducted Eucharists at the now fully constructed Washington National Cathedral, and our visit was arranged for after the Communion service. I remember as wholly special the time with him and the extraordinary tour he gave us of that beautiful place, for he was a humble servant of God in whose presence we were blessed by the holy and the good. When I unburdened my heart in regard to the spread of Jungian spirituality, not only did he understand, but he was the first (and for the longest time the only) one whom I knew to be aware of the problem.

But there was more to come. I believe it was during this tour of the cathedral that I met Henri Nouwen for the first time, together with the writer Elizabeth O'Connor[2] and the Archbishop of Brazil, Helder Camara. I was most impressed with all of them. Fr. Nouwen, one of the most well-known spiritual writers of our time, invited me to get in touch with him at Yale, and though I don't remember all the details, our chance meeting and visit no doubt had much to do with my later appointment as a research fellow at Yale.

Though I had known nothing of Archbishop Camara, I sensed a greatness of the love and presence of God in him.[3] He was so immediately a brother in the Lord with us, and love seemed to pour through him. Years later, I learned that he had received world renown but also constant death threats for his work of defending the poor and championing human rights in Brazil. The day was altogether a sheer gift, right from the heart of God.

My heart was full to the brim as, on July 5, I flew from DC to Bar Harbor, Maine, where Edith was waiting for me. After cramming my luggage into her little yellow Fiat, we were off to catch the boat over to the island. On board the wind whipped up such a gale that we couldn't put in at the usual place and had to move into a more protected harbor. It was an altogether exhilarating introduction to Edith's sun-drenched, ocean-washed island, only about three miles long and not more than a mile wide. Here the sea utterly dominated, and the people, only about 145 souls in all, gleaned their living from it. Along with the island air, I breathed in the wonderful sights of the fishermen's sturdily built houses, their fishing boats from huge to small trawlers everywhere about, and all their paraphernalia—the most conspicuous being lobster traps.

Edith's home, the oldest on the island, had been built by a sea captain to withstand any Atlantic wind. Inside it showed some resemblances to a ship's cabin. Wild berries grew in profusion in the yard, and an artesian well offered the most delicious water imaginable, a thing of great value on such a small island.

I had not known Edith personally except for the time spent together at the SPC a few months before, but this unique home, full of her family history, was in itself quite an introduction. Just inside the door hung a picture of a young woman standing arm in arm with Eleanor Roosevelt. That was Edith's mother, Cornelia Wolcott, daughter of Roger Wolcott, who had been governor of Massachusetts from 1897 to 1899. Her father, the Reverend Dr. Samuel Drury, though he had been a missionary in the Philippines, was best-known as headmaster of the famous St. Paul's Boys School in Concord, New Hampshire.

Edith's regard for her father, like her regard for Agnes, was boundless. After his death she had dismantled his office on the mainland and reconstructed it on the island. Situated a ways off from the house, it served as her personal prayer and retreat place. Edith had, before coming to Agnes's assistance, worked as a missionary up and down the coast of Maine on her boat, the *Sunbeam*.

Edith's property extended over a great part of the island, with acres and acres of shoreline that spanned almost the width of the island in several places, giving her great privacy. She had built two little studies on the property in addition to the reconstruction of her father's office—one in the woods at the back of the house and one down on the beach. They all had fireplaces, and two of them had beds, writing tables, books, and, as I wrote home to Aunt Rhoda, "all sorts of great things." I had one study all to myself and could go there to pray, read, and write. This was the one she built for Agnes for privacy to write and study when she was there.

But for prayer and reading, I liked my second-floor bedroom in the old house best where, again writing to Aunt Rhoda:

The air is so fresh and so pungent that I just sit in my little window and gulp it in when I'm not out in it! Biologists have a field day when they get here—the heath has incredible varieties [of plants] as do the thick forests. The fragrance of the balsam pines and other trees and the wild flowers that grow profusely at this season is overwhelmingly wonderful to one just out of the big cities. There are deer and mink here and beautiful birds. The white-throated sparrow is so beautiful! There are huge sea gulls of course—always wheeling about, and there are funny black birds that I thought at first were small, black ducks.

Here Edith was in her element. Together we explored the island, which she knew like the back of her hand, and took exhilarating forays out to Preble Cove and other spots for picnics, where we pulled up traps full of lobsters, took quick dips in a very cold ocean, and, most fun of all, dug up buckets full of clams. I learned all about the digging up, cleaning, and cooking of clams! The last part was the most difficult—boiling the little creatures. The wild cranberries that give the island its name were not in season then, but we picked and ate wild blueberries and raspberries to our heart's content.

All of this—feasting on the island's abundance, the forays and great exercise (besides hiking, I would ride Edith's bike into the little village and there meet some of the island folk), together with the great privacy for prayer and meditation, good conversation at specific intervals, and reading great books (many long out of print)—is surely an example of the way God graciously orchestrates time and circumstance to one's need.

This was the setting He gave me in which to begin working through my block to accepting the fact that the ministry would have to operate apart from the established church.

My stay on Cranberry stands out mainly as a time of asking questions of God. None of them were new, but having reached the breaking point physically and knowing things would have to change, I asked with a fervor and urgency as never before. I had to go through all the soul searching that ensues for a woman like me to live out her calling apart from finding proper church authority and support. With no duties or interruptions to seeking Him, I was able to get all my concerns before the Lord and listen for His word. As I read them now, I realize anew the blessing of the words He sent in answer and the accuracy with which they came to pass.

"Where, Lord, is home? Will I ever have a house of my own? Is that a soulish desire? Lord, be in my desiring. Do I need an independent income? Is it even possible physically to continue on as I have been? From whence, and *how* could a salary come?" These questions and prayers are lifted right out of my prayer journals from Maine. "Lord, at age 45, I have three degrees and feel proficient in nothing. I feel at home nowhere and have no idea where home might be." I queried Him as to whether I should pursue a doctorate and teach, as the dean of my graduate school had strongly recommended. Also I asked whether I should consider applying for scholarships here in the Northeast, having some premonitions that I would be in school here.

Knowing, of course, that my true home was in God, I renewed my trust that He would work these things out. In response he gave me Isaiah 43:19–20:

> Here and now I will do a new thing. . . . Can you not perceive it? I will make a way even through the wilderness and paths in the barren desert . . . I will provide water in the wilderness and rivers in the barren desert.

I should reiterate that I had not lost trust in God, nor had I made an idol of the church. Yet I knew that the church and proper authority ought to be there. That I kept knocking against the fact that I couldn't find real spiritual authority no doubt helped fuel the inspiration later to write *Crisis in Masculinity*, for it is the true masculine that is lost when churchmen capitulate to the spirit of the age, and, like politicians looking for votes, fail to stand for truth.

My thought was: *I am brought low that I might once again trust only in the Father* (not in the hierarchy of the church). "Jesus," I prayed, "I would see none but Thee: build a booth to no other. Other booths are being built, O Lord. Booths to Jung, to Buddha, to Krishna, etc. The fact that Christians build booths for Jung has upset me, Father, caused me to reexamine everything so as not to be 'narrow,' unloving, etc. Thank You, Lord, for bringing me back to this one essential: utter, childlike dependence upon You and my oneness with You through Jesus."

This brought me to the place of trying to figure out my particular gifts or ministry. I complained to the Lord, laying before him the fact that I was not the "usual lit teacher, not a teacher or writer, not a preacher or pastor, though I do all those things." I cried out:

> What is my name? My new name, Father? My name surely contains the work I'm to do [that is, what *is* my gifting, my calling?]. Who am I, Lord, in Your Kingdom [what kind of ministry is this You have visited upon me?]? It is full-time work, and yet I have no salary coming in that could allow rest and time for writing. What am I not seeing? Understanding? Thanks for Your wonderful promises.

If the ministry of healing prayer could not be part of the diaconate in the church, then my fears of becoming a so-called Christian personality came strongly to the fore. So I laid before the Lord what seemed to be the two parts of me: the one being the "charismatic" speaker (certainly I depended upon the Lord's healing gifts), the other being the contemplative, the student, the thinker. "Lord, I leave all this with You," I prayed. "Fill my hands with the work You have for me."

These were just some of the ways I was praying. Then, after much reflection, I would tell Edith the difficulties I was having with living out a full-time calling with no salary and therefore no place to call home.

"Junior is putting up one heck of a row," she commented, borrowing Agnes's language and term for the unconscious mind. Edith went on to say that Agnes had discovered painfully in her own ministry the real necessity to earn money for material gain, not only to support herself but for psychological reasons. To give out so much with little or no return, she had said, simply doesn't work.

One option before me was to follow my professors' advice and earn a doctorate and teach great literature. I knew that, by God's grace and a good scholarship, I could do that. But as Dr. Kilby had said, "Leanne, you are a preacher and not a teacher." I would be living out my call and vocation in the classroom, critiquing everything from the standpoint of the transcendent and the true, which causes all literature to leap alive. But, of course, not all in a university setting would appreciate it if revival were to break out in the literature classes.

My calling, I reasoned, was as one sent out. That is what God sovereignly did with me: He sent me out, blessing whatever He sent me to do far beyond any natural capabilities of my own. People like me do not seek ordination and neither do they minister extensively within the home church, but mostly are called out on missions. And as a woman, I never once initiated a conference but went only at others' invitations to come and with the Lord's confirmation. And, as St. Paul spoke of himself in his letter to Titus, I knew with all my heart that, though my servanthood could not compare to his, it was "for the sake of the faith of God's elect and their knowledge of the truth, which accords with godliness" (1:1).

In addition, while at Cranberry I faced the fact that my ministry had a very strong prophetic element, in that God had "made my forehead very hard" (see Ezek. 3:9) against sin, heresy, and the like. I also knew that, as part of the Lord's gifting, I saw the heretical coming down the road long before others did and sounded the warnings. With all my heart I hated the shallowness and faddism that many seemed to see as harmless. I saw the unholy mixtures in it and knew where they were leading. I knew their dangers and took strong stands against these things that many seemed content to ignore, and therefore I appeared extreme. Did others simply not see the problem? As I brought all these things before God, I was recognizing how "extreme" the *true* prophetic appears to moderns and, in fact, actually is: as extreme as salvation and reality itself, as the holy in an unholy, fallen world.

In this way, and in meditating on the gifts of the Holy Spirit as they operated variously and in differing lives, I struggled to understand, as a woman, my calling and the way God's grace, uniquely and according to His will, flowed through me.

I left Cranberry Island grateful for Edith's gracious hospitality that had enabled me to lay my concerns out before the Lord while resting and being renewed. I hadn't fully come to the end of my block that had so long held me back from the incorporation of this ministry, but all this struggle had further loosened it. My time on Cranberry would prove a crucial foundation to my decisions in the months ahead.

The Lord has a wonderful way of redeeming our mistakes, even turning them into miracles—all part of what the apostle Peter refers to as God's varied grace (1 Peter 4:10). My block, the failure to see and rightly assess the whole picture and adjust accordingly, did not slow down the ministry; perhaps it even speeded up the pace. As Herman Riffle was fond of reminding folk, if we cannot hear that still, quiet voice of God, He will send us a dream. If we can't hear that, we will learn on a bed of suffering. My suffering left me desperate for place, for solitude, for home, and for the means to obey the Lord through writing the books that He was birthing in me. It was, however, a suffering that, in being redeemed, left me with the outright gift of a beautiful home, extraordinary prayer and ministry partners, and expert help in founding a parachurch ministry—all riches that I would not have known had I attempted to start an organization on my own.

The block was removed only after I faced the realities of why the healing prayer ministry could not—apart from holy, scripturally well-balanced, authoritative, and courageous priests and pastors, such as Fr. Winkler—fit into the institutional church. In the Episcopal church there was no longer a diaconate for women with ministries such as mine; there was only the priesthood or the pastorate to pursue, neither of which I would ever have considered.

Even priests such as Fr. Winkler, were they to be found, were having great difficulty going forward due to problems at higher levels of the institutional church. I was searching for godly authority, which is what hierarchy is supposed to provide, and, like Fr. Winkler, could not find it. Increasingly, faulty seminary training together with political correctness had robbed even the better clergy and bishops from the ability to rightly name sin, confront it, hear confessions, and minister into the lives of penitents—the basis of all healing prayer rites and that which brings into our midst the power of God to heal.

I was only able to face these facts as I confronted the shocking realization that, for the first time in my adult ministry life, I could not hear the Lord or receive guidance or assistance from Him on a critical and growing difficulty in my life: that of a debilitating exhaustion and need for solitude to write the books. This understanding came at the end of my last attempt to bring the ministry under the institutional church. I could hear Him loud and clear on other matters but not on this one. Crying out to God, I determined to find a teaching job (in order to have a private apartment) until I could hear the Lord aright in this matter.

My deafness on this matter had been such that in late January 1978 I literally had to pack up my car and leave the place where I was staying without knowing where I was going. With everything I owned in my ancient car, I drove across country and began to experience once again, step-by-step, the leading of the Lord as to where to go. It was an incredible experience.

It was as though my feet had long been ensnared in a net and I was not free to fly—to soar—until I acknowledged the block for what it was and willed with all my might to come free of it. In my heart and mind, I saw a little brown bird, wild and untamed, its throat pulsating and throbbing with song, but its tiny claws ensnared in a net and its song restricted—an apt picture of what attempting to fit the ministry into the institutional church would do. This image was from a dream that even after several years I had not forgotten, and now I knew what it meant.

I ended up spending the first two weeks with family and friends in Little Rock where we prayed and listened together for the Lord's direction. And then, at yet another invitation and strong urging of close friends in Milwaukee, I drove my packed car up there after considerable hesitation—not knowing what would come of it and needing a salary to pay for a place to live. Once again I would be staying (who knows how long) in someone else's home, traveling from there to the many upcoming conferences and missions, and in a city even farther to the north than Wheaton.

Before going to Milwaukee, and perhaps one of the factors in my going that far north, I had a dream so vivid it was akin to a vision. In it I saw a very large boat on a great body of frozen water, and it was cutting large swaths of the ice away, cleanly and evenly, to make a channel for other ships to get through. The words in the dream were audible and as clear as crystal, with the message: "When I found this region, I would find my pen." That is, I would be able to write the books. What a strange dream to have, for never had I witnessed such an ice-cutting scene. I was not sure if this was from the Lord or from my need to get the books written, several of them now within me and in my imagination getting hopelessly tangled up together. At this point I knew it would be a job just to get them separated.

So having accepted the invitation of gracious hospitality from my dear friends, I was now in Whitefish Bay, a northern suburb of Milwaukee. A member of the church we attended lived close by in a beautiful home on Lake Drive, fronting Lake Michigan. This home had what amounted to a tiny, unfinished attic apartment, and the friends offered it to me free of charge for as long as I had need of it. It had two windows only, but one was magical. It looked out over Lake Michigan, and so I placed a large, fine round table under it for all my writing materials. I shall never forget the day, seated there with pen in hand, that I watched winter roll in over the lake toward Whitefish Bay with winds that began to freeze the waters offshore. I don't believe that since that year there has been another winter so cold as to ice over the bay. Looking from the lake to my pen, I remembered the dream of the ice-cutter in vivid detail, realizing now that it had indeed played a part in my coming this far north, and that it had indeed been sent from the Lord.

In Milwaukee, I knew finally that I had made my last attempt to be under the covering of the institutional church; my block was therefore completely removed and things began to move fast. My prayer partners and I could hardly get our petitions out to the Lord before He answered them. That I was not to find a teaching job was soon clear to me. By this time, my manuscript on C. S. Lewis had been accepted by a good publisher, so that was an additional spur toward getting the other books written, an exciting prospect.

It was in Milwaukee, then, that the Lord began opening doors, one after another and almost faster than I could walk through them—each door in succession bringing in more of the vital help needed to sustain life and ministry. Greatest of all, He gifted me with the most precious prayer partners, truly extraordinary ones, fully and deeply converted and with one desire: to fulfill the Lord's will for their lives. They soon saw that my health was giving way, and they formed, as it were, a golden prayer shield around me and this ministry, and soon they began to play vital roles within it.

22

Beauty and Truth in the Midst
of Spiritual Battle

One word of truth outweighs the world.

Alexander Solzhenitsyn

During those momentous years after leaving Wheaton in 1976, I experienced spiritual battle on a number of fronts. At the same time, I felt nurtured, strengthened, and even at times drenched in God's beauty and truth. These drenchings came first of all through the ministry itself, through its schools and missions and the precious souls who were drawn to attend from the four corners of the earth.

Together with seeing the beauty of the Lord as He touched and transformed lives so profoundly, I was awed and blessed beyond words by His beautiful world. In traveling afar and experiencing more and more of God's creation, much of it in pristine territory in British Columbia and the far Northwest, beauty and truth came together for me as never before.

Once I gained a home in the little attic aerie, writing and praying at the magical window overlooking Lake Michigan, this sense of God's creation pointing to the transcendent and the true was almost divinely heightened. The solitude I now enjoyed, together with the beauty flooding through my window, was priceless. In a winter newsletter I wrote:

Greetings from the land of snow and ice. I expect to look through my mullioned window any day now and see a polar bear floating on one of the icebergs in Lake Michigan. The North Pole could hardly have more to offer such a creature. At times the skies and lake blend together in varying shades of icy blue, while the quiet deep white snow lies all about—then it is that the whole scene takes on the aspect and feel of "faerie." And God is in it all. "He gives to the earth snow like a blanket of wool," and the psalmist admonishes the snow, along with water, ice, winds, and all of nature to praise the Lord! I praise the Lord for the gift of life, and the gift of this place—a warm, quiet place in which to write and from which to go on missions.

That window had a magical tree as well. In the spring of that same year I wrote in a newsletter:

Spring is greening and blossoming here in Whitefish Bay. Just outside my window a Mountain Ash is leafed out and pregnant with thousands of little green buds that will soon flame forth in red berries. From then on to late fall, I'll see the blues of Lake Michigan and the sky through the graceful branches, green leaves, and red-red berries of that incredible tree.

After learning that this ash is the Rowan tree often spoken of in ancient tales and myths, I looked for information on it and found that

others besides myself have found it a spellbinder. . . . That beauty points to the supernatural is surely verified in the history of this tree. The Europeans, under the spell of its beauty, began to think *it* had supernatural qualities, and the tradition sprang up to the effect that it had healing qualities and could even exorcise witches! Therefore it is sometimes called witchwood. Such is the effect of beauty on us poor mortals whose vision of truth is more often than not wanting in theological detail. And what wonderful tales we weave in lieu of it!

Dostoyevsky once said, "Beauty will save the world," and Alexander Solzhenitsyn, just coming out from under Communist rule, commented on that enigmatic statement in his 1970 Nobel lecture:

Perhaps then the old trinity of Truth, Goodness, and Beauty is not simply the dressed up, worn-out formula we thought it in our presumptuous, materialistic youth? If the crowns of these three trees meet, as scholars have asserted, and if the too obvious, too straight sprouts of Truth and Goodness have been knocked down, cut off, not let grow, perhaps the whimsical, unpredictable, unexpected branches of Beauty will work their way through, rise up to that very place, and thus complete the work of all three?

At that window, sustained by the Lord and His beauty and truth, I wrote *The Broken Image*, reluctantly setting aside work on *The Healing Presence*. That was because of the overwhelming need for accurate information on the healing of homosexuality. I kept waiting for Christian psychologists and psychiatrists to write *the* book that would set all these matters straight, but nothing appeared. Finally, after several years I was more or less forced to do it myself, having received direction from the Lord.

The guidance I was listening for came with a dream. In it, I was traveling on a bus with many people, including Mother, a beloved prayer partner, and most unaccountably, my new infant, a tiny little reddish-haired baby girl who was quite homely. I carried her to our seat at the very back of the bus, tying her safely in her carryall chair. Amazingly, however, she sat up straight as can be and began to speak to all on the bus—to each and every one individually in a most insightful way. Mother and I and all on the bus marveled at her. At first so unattractive, she was now speaking to the hearts of everyone.

I awakened knowing that the homely little baby girl was the book I had to write on the healing of homosexuality. I could no longer wait for someone else to write it. I had several other dreams in relation to the book; one even came the month I started to write. It came with a huge warning that the book itself could be lost and showed how that could happen. "He who has ears, let him hear," our God is always admonishing us (Matt. 13:9 NIV), and thanks be to God for the differing ways in which He speaks to us.[1]

So once again I was "pregnant" with yet another book, and this time I knew only too well how homely the subject of healing homosexuality would be to many within the churches. At that time it was not because folk had been brainwashed into saying that sexual perversions are normal and moral, but that Christians by and large couldn't believe that within their own churches and pastorates such problems existed. Had they conducted healing services that included hearing confessions of sin, they would have known the extent of the problem and that it was growing alarmingly. But they had not, so even Christian leaders were often loath to hear of the subject (and were even irritated by it), much less that I should be urging them to learn how to pray for those suffering with such problems.

And thus I wrote *The Broken Image*. The spiritual battle that came with this writing was well-nigh overpowering, one I had to fight every time I sat down to write. "Who are you to write the book?" the Enemy would chide, echoing my own thoughts, and I could only daily pray through it. To state the obvious, there was tremendous and vividly apparent opposition from the Evil One, because I was breaking new ground while speaking the ancient truths about gender and homosexuality.

Though few could see it, the sodomization of American culture was then underway, a movement increasingly politically organized and savvy. Its leaders moved strongly against therapy and help for those desperate for the healing of sexual neuroses and the deliverance from sheer lust. Their attack was not only on those who sought forgiveness and healing but on the family and on gender itself. Indeed, every attempt was made to silence ministers or therapists who knew there was help for these needy folk. In contrast, I saw regularly in the ministry that there is, in Christ, abundant healing for those unaffirmed in their gender identities and that, furthermore, there is healing of infantile memories of severe trauma, those resulting in the symbolic confusion and diseased fantasy lives found not only in homosexuality but in other reactions to woundings in the past. At that point people were coming from all over the world for help with these problems, and I had to give my utmost energy in training others to pray for them.

A most fortuitous thing occurred a year before I gained the solitude of the attic aerie and the chance to write *The Broken Image*. A young woman who worked with Youth With A Mission returned to the United States from England, carrying with her a very large tome. Titled *Clinical Theology: A Theological and Psychiatric Basis to Clinical Pastoral Care*, it was 1,282 pages long and was written by Dr. Frank Lake, a Christian missionary to India who, on returning from the field, became a psychiatrist. He was well-known in England but not in the United States. How this young woman came into possession of such an expensive book, I do not now recall, but she gave it to me as if she were carrying out an assignment.

These sovereign acts of God never cease to amaze me. This was pure gift, from this youth and from the heart of God. I quickly read every page of it and was thoroughly affirmed in all I believed and had learned through the healing ministry. Not only that, through it I was given the language I needed with which to speak of the terrible failure to come to a sense of well-being, or even more critically, of being itself, in those first months of life. Out of that failure the severest emotional and psychological illnesses emerge. No one, it seems to me, writes better than Dr. Lake on the separation anxiety these sufferers know, and the reaction patterns to it—the homosexual, as well as the schizoid, hysterical, dissociative, and paranoid.

Later I corresponded with Dr. Lake and we were planning to meet soon on his next trip to the United States, for he was anxious to know more about the way of prayer for these healings. Sadly, however, his death intervened. We had much in common, both attempting to speak that "one word of truth that outweighs the world" to a culture rapidly turning from God and preferring its man-centered and permissive (even gnostic) psychologies. Later, in 1981 at Yale Divinity School, I heard the great evangelical world leader, Donald Coggan, the Archbishop of Canterbury, then retired, praise Dr. Lake as a great man and influence for good in England.

The spiritual warfare over writing *The Broken Image* was fierce, but the most deeply wounding battle came through two very close family members. Over a number of years they had become increasingly possessed of an irrational and even virulent opposition not only to the ministry but to me personally. This conflict came to a grievous head in these years as they separated completely from me. Though it had started earlier, this battle, utterly shocking and unexpected, was first publicly evident in response to the ministry and resulting revival in Fayetteville. In other words, open warfare came when this ministry of healing prayer with its emphasis on forgiving others and receiving forgiveness for ourselves became more widely received.

I write of this in *Restoring the Christian Soul*. There, under the rubric of "When the Enemy Is the Beloved Enemy," I write of forgiving and learning how best to pray for these dear ones.[2]

These first two spiritual battles were fought more or less in the privacy of my own heart and mind. Not so the next one. It involved vital ministries and many new Christians in renewal as well as the church's overall ministry in helping folk not only name sin aright but confess and repent of it. This battle forced me to study, name, and confront Jungian neognosticism as it flooded into the church's pastoral, counseling, and healing prayer ministries.

Early on, the Lord assigned me a heartbreaking front-row seat from which to watch these neognostic inroads into the faith. To see these for the occult religion that they are, was to receive the mandate to confront, speak out, and write about it. Every way I knew how, I tried to warn the church and all who value objective reality and truth.

Gnosticism is and has always been the deadliest enemy of Christian orthodoxy, and this influx, coming when the church was largely separated from its own infinitely superior psychology and understanding of Christian formation, was not being recognized, discerned, or counteracted. The so-called Age of Enlightenment and decades of materialistic incursions had already taken a huge toll on the great psychological teachings of the church, together with the necessity of a heroic, radical conversion and communion with the Holy Trinity—the only kind of conversion the early church knew anything about. It was almost impossible, therefore, to find great courses on Christian formation, those that fully and unabashedly taught these things together with what it meant to seek and be empowered by the Spirit to do the works of Christ. In evangelical schools the virtues and vices were never mentioned, much less taught, and even Catholic schools were losing sight of Aquinas's brilliant teachings on these matters. With these losses, Christians were starved for knowledge of the soul and of the transcendent power of God.

I was told time and time again by Christian scholars on both sides of the Atlantic, orthodox and liberal alike, that gnosticism ended in the first two or three hundred years after Christ's death. I would then present them with the work of Jung or one of his current promoters, and they would say, "No, that is not gnosticism." But I knew it was and battled it with every resource I could muster.

Gnosticism's beguiling effect is always to loosen, if ever so subtly at first, the Christian's moral and spiritual framework. It does this largely through resymbolizing words and other symbols, changing their meaning. For example, sin gains new names, perhaps "respectable" psychological ones, and thereby gains acceptance in a life. In this way gnostic systems reconcile good and evil, and the obscene insinuates itself into lives. The sense and knowledge of the Holy One is lost, together with the good, the true, and the beautiful.

A very small amount of gnostic leaven goes a long way. To allow the least bit in is fatal for true and lasting renewal in the individual or group that fails to discern and renounce it. That is because those who employ a gnostic reading and use of the symbols and images of the heart—whether appearing in dreams or those arising from an unhealed soul or the unconscious—turn it into a source of mixed and even outright false revelation. They soon neglect objective, divine revelation in favor of one's own heart becoming the sole revelator. Simply, man would be God. This is the subjective stuff of the New Age, the old but ever-present paganism ready to rise up and conquer when the church fails to name and confront heretical elements. The church's love and power to heal and disciple thereby becomes neither hot nor cold through compromise with the spirit of the age.

I was seeing Jungian neognosticism rush in as a mixture of the true and the false, the good and the bad, for that is its nature as a syncretistic, parasitic religion that can thrive only as it attaches itself to the real and the true Judeo-Christian faith. For example, one of its chief promoters, Morton Kelsey, had many true things to say of this era, such as:

> Our "Christian" religious practice has been largely cerebral for so long that we have built up a sizeable tradition which scorns and rejects the body. We have almost lost any understanding of the relation of the body to the religious encounter.[3]

Such statements as these were followed up, however, with teachings on symbol and imagery, myth and story, man's imaginative faculty, the body and the unconscious, which, while speaking to people right where their hunger was (and is), fell far short of Christian orthodoxy.

As clearly as I could in response, I set orthodox spirituality and psychology over and against this current gnosticism. I had long since written of incarnational truth and reality as the *real* (no greater connection to the body than this) and of story, symbol, the true imagination, and the healing of memories and one's unconscious. Having to deal with this onslaught of gnosticism, however, no doubt sharpened these teachings as I set them over and against the neognosticism of Jung and his followers.

In teaching on our infinitely glorious Christian reality and the symbolic system that attends it, I began to realize how most Christians had compromised or even lost their own symbolic system and their understanding of the imagination. In fact many feared rather than treasured the enormous gift of an imaginative faculty. In response, I formed lectures on symbol and imagery and on the true imagination, and I conducted healing sessions whereby needy, empty souls, plagued by diseased imagery and fantasy lives, could be delivered and begin to regain the most glorious imagery and symbol known to man, that of the Judeo-Christian faith. Such is a dire need of the church today.[4]

Christians cannot live as simply hyperactive, heady rationalists. To eschew the gifts and power of God and the true and great mysteries of the Christian faith with its profound psychology and understanding of man is to be given over, sooner or later, to the occult and capitulate to the "supernatural" and "mystical" within it and thus to fall heir to idolatrous symbolic systems that are conduits of false revelation.

No one was more skilled in introducing Jungian psychology into the church than Morton Kelsey. He was an Episcopal clergyman and, by the time I met him, professor emeritus of the department of graduate studies in education at the University of Notre Dame. He had studied psychology at Claremont College, California, and then under Carl Jung at the Jung Institute in Switzerland. Morton was a priest in Agnes Sanford's parish and, before she retired, had become a lecturer in her schools. After her retirement, he came to the fore and conducted what were called Advanced Schools.

Though a practicing priest, he was an enthusiastic disciple of Jung. In the schools, his lectures, like his books, bore the stamp of the Jungian analyst, synthesist, and promoter. Such a combination always undermines Holy Writ and is thereby in opposition to a Judeo-Christian worldview and symbolic system. It leaves no room for a truly scriptural and orthodox Christian theology, spirituality, and psychology.

As a leader in the Schools of Pastoral Care, I began to read and then scan his works. I saw first of all the way in which he was reconciling good and evil, sometimes subtly, sometimes not. I became increasingly concerned about his influence not only on the schools but on the church and his many readers. This forced me to delve more deeply into Jung himself. By October of 1975, after finishing Jung's autobiographical work, *Memories, Dreams, Visions*, my concern knew no end. I saw clearly that this gnosticism ends in what I've come to term Baal worship, *phallicism*, and the worship of one's own genitalia, and I knew with sickened heart that sexual perversions and falls would be the outcome. This proved to be the case—far beyond even what I had feared or could have imagined.

As I mentioned in the last chapter, in May 1977 I was teamed up with Morton Kelsey in one of the Advanced Schools. It was of course a foolish mistake to have attempted this. To say that there was an evident dissonance in our lectures and interaction is an understatement, and it took months for me to come to terms with my chagrin in ever thinking such a thing could be managed. It was more than slightly catastrophic, and to this day I can only hope that God covered it and that some, in spite of the apparent friction, got help.

Actually, I do recall meeting with folk individually and beautiful things happening. One priest, in a later news report to fellow clerics on the SPC, told them, with tongue in cheek: "If ever you want to find healing, just meet Leanne Payne on a stairwell and ask for prayer!" I remember that stairwell as a rather perilous place to get lost in prayer for healing, and though I have no idea what it was we prayed about, it must have been highly successful. So the Lord did work His will, but certainly not in the way I had experienced in every other school.

At this Advanced School, I could not be in the same room with Morton without strongly discerning the demonic that was empowering the Jungian archetypes and psychology. These dark powers were effectively at work in Morton's eclecticism: his "Jungian Christian" psychology that was a subtle, clever, and enticing synthesis of good with evil, of dark with what is all light, of the gnostic and occult with what is all truth.

In the weeks and months after this school, I experienced excessive spiritual warfare. I believe that all effective ministries experience severe testings such as this—times when our very calling and the unique ways in which God would use us—are hit hard and called into question. The Enemy was accusing me of "narrowness," of "failures to love," of "causing conflict and division," and these accusations only magnified the other concerns and questions I had in regard to living out my calling—all the accusations that afflict our souls when we take important stands for vital truth. This stress is doubled and trebled when brothers and sisters fail to understand, and even more so when they join in the accusations. At this time of testing I found great comfort in the Scripture's portrayal of Christ being led by the Spirit into the wilderness, there to be tested and there victoriously to overcome the tempter.[5]

As the intense warfare continued unabated, I met with a Christian pastor for help. As soon as we had gone to prayer, his eyes were opened and he saw the demons who were empowering the Jungian archetypes and synthesis surrounding and coming against me. In the power of Christ's name, he commanded them to leave. He then prayed most earnestly and powerfully that the Lord would hide me—spirit, soul, and body—from these malign forces.

As I followed up that prayer with the ongoing thanksgiving and knowledge that the Lord was indeed hiding me, this intense oppression lifted. This prayer, asking God to hide me—spirit, soul, and body—from evil forces, is one that I've often prayed since, when in intense spiritual battle, and I find that our Lord loves to answer it. In battles such as this, I need to emphasize that we must first discern the spirits and what is going on before we can effectively pray such prayers. And when we are in the heat of battle, we often need others to pray for us in this way.

Thomas à Kempis's influence in my life had long since instilled in me prayers for hiddenness, for besides the need to be alert to any tendency to seek the limelight or the recognition of man, I felt strongly that such spiritual direction particularly pertains to the welfare of the true feminine in every woman who is called to public ministry. Now I saw more clearly the necessity of these prayers for hiddenness concerning demonic forces in spiritual battle as well.

In retrospect I can see why the mistake of attempting to work with Morton Kelsey was a necessary one for me to make. Suffering[6] through it and its aftermath actually empowered me to face the inevitable criticism and lack of understanding as I continued to say, "Jungianism *is* gnosticism," a thing no one seemed to understand or agree with at that time.

To this day, I see Morton as the Pied Piper, whistling a tune that led many students and leaders right over a cliff. He especially drew in unaffirmed men: priests, pastors, and psychologists, as well as those in the religious professions, such as nuns. Where Morton, acting and speaking as priest, needed to teach them how to die to the old man, thereby bringing them into full conversion and a growing intimacy with God, he taught them rather to look to their own hearts and dreams and to interpret the imagery there in such a way as reconciles good and evil. He was leading them away from where true renewal would bring them.

Morton's influence spread quickly as he trained countless Christian psychologists, pastors, and counselors. These leaders then went back to their home churches as so-called experts, counseling and teaching in the renewal prayer groups. Before long, the largest audience for Jungianism was among Christians, both Catholic and Protestant.[7] Christian Retreat Houses here and in the United Kingdom were more or less taken over with Jungian retreats, conference speakers, books, and magazine articles. Christian publishers began to list books under the heading "Jungian spirituality." Catholic, Episcopal, and Methodist seminaries, among others, were soon seriously compromised by these teachings.

The rationalist theologies, having lost the *real* and transcendent, could not stand against the gnosticism. Even after Jung's psychology was discredited, his gnostic heresies lived on as, for example, feminist and homosexual "theologies" and ideologies. The spirit of the age took its all-too-tragic toll.

I warned of Jung and his reconciliation of good and evil in my first book, and in all the later books.[8] For he is the "John the Baptist" of the New Age movement; through his psychology he managed to make the occult seem scientific and respectable, even to many Christians.

After my experience with Morton Kelsey in the Advanced School, not only did I fully recognize the danger to the schools but also I saw that its present administrators were not confronting this danger. With Agnes no longer in charge, there was no adequate "watchman on the wall" (as in Isaiah 62:6: "On your walls, O Jerusalem, I have set watchmen; all the day and all the night they shall never be silent"). Due to Agnes's age and knowing that she had long since let go the reins of the ministry, I hesitated to turn to her in this matter, but when I did, I was richly rewarded. She had read and written a blurb for *Real Presence* while it was yet in manuscript form and was thereby aware of and agreed with my assessment of the Jungian problem. She invited me to her home in California, but even before I managed to make the visit, I knew she felt that there was little then that she could do about the problem with the schools (more about this remarkable visit in the next chapter).

As a laywoman, I never expected to stand atop the walls or at the gates when heresies loomed large and attempted to enter, but that surely is the lot of any orthodox person in the healing, counseling, and pastoral care ministries these past decades. Together with Agnes's prayers and the help of Edith Drury, we did manage to make some badly needed administrative changes. But what was taught depended on the leadership of any given school. I was sad about this, because Agnes had founded the schools as a counter to the liberalism and unbelief in Episcopal seminaries.

I did many more missions of my own apart from the schools and gradually I no longer worked with them at all. Other reliable, orthodox leaders dropped out in the same way. And as my own ministry began to form, the Lord sent precious leaders of like mind to work with me.

To have to speak of the nature of gnosticism—whether coming through a Carl Jung, an Elaine Pagels, or a Dan Brown, author of *The DaVinci Code*—is to be horrified afresh at its parasitic nature, the fact that it can only prosper on the soil of host religions. It has absolutely nothing to give but, in the end, Baal and Ashtoreth worship (sexual orgy and utter ruin)— and in the final end, the Goddess Religion only.

The battle against it, as the early Christians knew, is ugly in the extreme. In these years, I was for the first time praying for priests and nuns who were falling into sexual sin. With nuns, this had been virtually unknown before. It was heartbreaking. A hardened feminism—the Goddess Religion—flourished and grew into what we have now.

In all the ugliness of the battles, God's beauty and truth more than sustains those with eyes to see and ears to hear. The presence of the Lord to glorify and point always to his beauty, goodness, and truth, primarily through his Word and his creation, together with his power to save and heal the sick of spirit, soul, and body, is strength and beauty enough to awe one right to the ground. The great Advent hymn, "On Jordan's banks

grains. These were in reserve—to be planted later. The seed in the basket was even then being sown.

This dream has often recurred in different forms, though always as a word from the Lord and always with an abundance of the seeds I am to sow. Sometimes the seeds in the basket that I hold before me have become loaves of bread, all differing, and I have the knowledge that the Holy Spirit will help me serve the loaf of which each individual is in need. All these seeds pertain to the eternal *evangel:* "Christ has died, Christ is risen, Christ will come again." Thereby, Christ has made a way for us to the Father and to our eternal becoming in Him.

Often when I'm sent out on a mission, or "pregnant" with yet another book, I see those golden seeds again, held high above my head and supernaturally adhering together in this huge golden disk. I cry out, "Come, Holy Spirit, come," knowing that only if He does, will the seeds be planted in the hearts of those who hear or read; only then will the seeds live and multiply, sprouting up unto eternal life for all who receive. I remain amazed at the blessing and ongoing effects of this important dream-word God sent so deeply into my spirit.

Even as the dream came, I was eagerly anticipating a visit in March with Agnes Sanford in her Monrovia, California, home and preparing for extensive ministry at a huge evangelistic center within fairly easy driving distance of her home. The ministry center, Melodyland, was located next to Disneyland and was a place where literally thousands of needy folk were streaming in from the California counterculture. Many of those coming to Christ were in very great need of deliverance and healing from the effects of drug and alcohol addiction, perverted sexual lifestyles, and all manner of darkness. Besides conducting five meetings for the larger groups, I would be making six radio programs and training the many ministers and laypeople to pray for the masses who were coming to Christ.

This ministry hotline was taking in ten thousand calls a month, and that same number of folk gathered every Sunday to hear Rev. Ralph Wilkerson preach the gospel. At that time, Drs. J. Rodman Williams and John Warwick Montgomery, theologians and academicians I deeply appreciated, were conducting a school of theology there, and to my surprise, I was being considered for the faculty. Working with such great hearts and minds would have been quite a draw had I not finally found a home in Milwaukee. Also my schedule was already jam-packed with what I was called to do.

So the vision of what was in my heart to accomplish and the more-than-ample, glorious seeds the Lord would be sowing were given as always in God's wonderful timing. This was a visionary encouragement for now and for all time, however, and as I was coming back again in a few months to

Melodyland to give more training, I was freed to broadcast these seeds with great abandon, knowing I'd be back to tend them.

Perhaps I would never have received the vision of the golden, living seeds apart from a prayer I had many years been praying. It was one that I was half afraid to pray. I feared the audacity of such a prayer, even that I might be praying amiss. Once I stepped onto God's path for my life, I took great warning from Christ's parable of the sower and the seed:

> A sower went out to sow. And as he sowed, some seeds fell along the path, and the birds came and devoured them. Other seeds fell on rocky ground, where they did not have much soil, and immediately they sprang up, since they had no depth of soil, but when the sun rose they were scorched. And since they had no root, they withered away. Other seeds fell among thorns, and the thorns grew up and choked them. Other seeds fell on good soil and produced grain, some a hundredfold, some sixty, some thirty. He who has ears, let him hear.
>
> Matthew 13:3–9

Praying for the soil of my heart and the seed that God was sowing there, I meditated on every phrase of this parable, praying that no seed would fall on anything but good soil in my heart. I gave great attention to the soil, asking God to till, soften, and enrich it—whatever He needed in order to prepare it for the seed being sown in it. But there was one problem. I could never pray for the seed the Lord sowed in my heart to produce only a hundredfold. That's where I feared I was being presumptuous—or worse. I would pray for a hundred times one hundredfold, even a thousand times one thousandfold.

I realize now that the Lord could answer that prayer only by making me a writer or a public speaker, one who would broadcast the everlasting evangel as carefully as possible—that is, to sow all these seeds to sprout in the hearts of others. What else explains such a dream-vision, coming as an answer to prayer, or the multiplication of the loaves and the ongoing effects of it?

It simply explains the ministry itself, and the way it has so quietly yet quickly spread around the world. It explains the thousands of letters we've received over the years from people who write to tell us what happened to their lives after attending a Pastoral Care Ministry School.

I no longer feel half-wrong to pray my prayer for a thousand times one thousandfold. In fact I must pray it all the more! The Lord answers prayer when we have ears to hear what He is saying, and He seems to favor not the presumptuous prayers, but the impossible ones.

Perhaps someday, even in our backslidden West, we will once again know baptisms and daily Eucharists where there is always prayer for healing; a church where once again, in great awe and holiness, prayers of faith are released for the healing of the sick who fill our pews, so that in every divine liturgy, the spirits, souls, and bodies of men and women will be touched by the power of the Holy Spirit. Thus it was in the early church; thus it has been in every Pastoral Care Ministry School!

It was a couple of weeks after the momentous dream that I participated in the ministry at Melodyland in California. In the sowing of seeds there, I grew increasingly exhausted. When my last time to speak came, my weariness was such that I could not concentrate, prepare a coherent lecture, or plan a healing service. I could only practice the presence of Jesus and call on the name of the Lord. As I got up to speak, I deliberately reached out my hand and took His as we walked up to the podium. No sooner had I situated myself at the microphone than people all over that great auditorium began to weep. Later people rushed up to me saying, "Do you know that the whole time you were speaking Christ was standing next to you?"[1] Truly the Lord was planting his seeds.

After the conference I needed to make my way up to Agnes Sanford's house in the mountains. In my fatigue I accepted, with great relief, a ride by one of the unofficial prayer "ministers." Instead of taking me to Agnes's house, however, she took me to her own large place in the mountains that was very secluded. Utterly amazed, I found I was not free to leave! Soon I realized as well that she had a group under her control there in her isolated domicile and that they were all living in some kind of false prophetic myth that she imposed on them. I wondered then if her offer of a ride was a means by which she hoped to locate Agnes, a plan I had foiled when I told her en route that she would only be taking me to a location close to Agnes's home. Soon I discerned that this woman was intensely envious of me and wanted to "swallow up" both Agnes and me. This I write about as the "cannibal compulsion" in *The Broken Image*.[2]

The next day I managed to get to a telephone and send out an SOS to a young minister friend at Melodyland. He knew these mountains and came immediately. I stepped out a first-floor window, suitcase and all, and got into his car. Off we went to Agnes's. This incident seems more like fiction than reality! I had forgotten all about it, but it came back clearly when recently I read Jan Karon's book *In This Mountain*, where the character Edith Mallory locks up Fr. Tim in a similar situation.

Earlier I wrote of first meeting Agnes when in 1964 Fr. Winkler and I accompanied her on a day mission. I stated that nothing I had previously been told about her prepared me for this wonderfully unique servant of the Lord. She was simply not the *usual*. The following is a good reintroduction to Agnes before I tell of my second memorable time with her. A young seminarian, whose rector was part of the incident, first told me this story.

Agnes went into the church where she was to speak, accompanied by the priest sponsoring her mission. He genuflected before the Reserve Sacrament over which the candle was brightly flickering. Agnes, however, sailed right past without even a nod of the head. Astonished, he asked her why she did not genuflect. She said, "He is not there." Just that—and no further comment. In a few moments one of the curates walked up to this rector who was somewhat confounded and said, "Please forgive me for forgetting to put out the candle after removing the Host," and he proceeded to extinguish the candle. Utterly dumbfounded, the priest turned to Agnes and asked, "How did you know?" She replied, "Oh, I always see a white Light when He is there."

To know Agnes, if only briefly, was to know the authenticity of the story, for Agnes knew the presence of the Lord. With as thorough a knowledge of the Scriptures as one could have (she had memorized more of it than anyone I've ever known), she knew and lived in the blessing of the *Word made flesh* and in the many ways in which He is present to us. Some Christians, long separated from a sacramental and incarnational understanding, dip into Agnes's books and before reading enough to realize how orthodox she is, grow afraid of her.

One of my friends, a well-known Christian author, grew up in the same town where Agnes lived before she moved to California. His family was staunchly fundamentalist, as were most of the town's Protestant Christians at that time, and could easily have been suspicious of her. Yet in knowing her personally, they all knew she was a woman of God. Also they were aware that she was as unprepossessing, unpretentious, and unself-conscious a soul as one could ever meet, and a playful one at that.

Since Agnes had selected her home in California because it was situated on the San Andreas Fault, it took a certain amount of courage to visit her.

As she writes, this fault "is a rift in the earth running north and south along much of the West Coast, and subject to disastrous earthquakes."[3] She moved from her New England home to this one to better pray for this great rift "that it might accomplish its work of relieving the tension in the earth's crust quietly, with sufficient small tremors, but without destructive earthquakes." My imagination could ordinarily work overtime in visiting such a site, but I don't recall any undue concern as my driver pulled up the last incline to her home. Perhaps the shock of being trapped in the mountain complex put the matter of the fault into perspective.

I remember well arriving at her door and seeing her, then some fourteen years after our memorable day together with Fr. Winkler. Still childlike[4] at eighty years of age, she leaped up and down as I came in, looked straight into my eyes while taking both my hands and cried, "We are kindred spirits!" I was absolutely thrilled to see her, yet so keen and so young, and delighted in such a welcome and greeting. As I wrote in a newsletter back home,

> Her wisdom is a steady and brilliant current of light—I could have listened to her from now on and been learning. But, her faith is still the most phenomenal thing about her.

Her faith, when released for the healing of man or of nature (whether it be a sick child, an ailing tree, or the very rock structure struggling to right itself within the bowels of the earth), was extraordinary to behold. She came as near to having "faith like a grain of mustard seed" as anyone I've ever met, and I believe that this special charism of faith fueled and informed her truly unique and remarkable relationship to nature.

Agnes believed that "we have a duty to the earth on which we live" and that "the Lord of this great field, the earth, has ordered us to take care of it for Him until He returns."[5] She believed that we are commanded in the Scriptures to pray not only for the healing of mankind, but also for the healing of the earth itself. Many Christians believe that, but few seem to have the understanding of how to pray effectively for the earth. She spent her last years teaching others how to do so.

To describe her relationship to earth, air, sea, water, and all that moves in it is to describe a very down-to-earth human being who was also a bona fide Christian mystic. Her respect amounted to awe not just for plant and animal life, but even for God's inanimate creation, and this was balanced by a scientific curiosity to know all about them. She studied God's creation, the vast cosmos as well as the earth, to find out how better to pray for it. Then she experimented in prayer to find the most effective ways to pray.

Her life and ministry was that of teaching others the how-tos of releasing the "prayer of faith." In doing this, her special charism of love, laced with down-to-earth common sense, made her remarkable charisms of faith and healing all the more effective.

At one point in my visit, she held up a seashell that she had discovered years before. Looking at its design, she exclaimed, "Can you believe that written into [what was] this little creature was the 'mind' to create such a design!" She was marveling over the genetic makeup that could bring forth such beauty, and she often looked at that shell in awe. Her odd way of expressing herself left some folk perplexed, ready to think her a pantheist. But she only spoke of the shell like this because she adored and communed with God as supreme and sovereign Creator. Knowing God as she found Him in history (in the Scriptures) enabled her to know Him as Creator. She was in Aquinas's class, not as a philosopher, but in regard to knowing, loving, and properly revering all that our God has created and its power to speak to us.

I can only describe her relationship to nature as that of a poet-saint; I don't know how else to think of it. She was in a respectful, prayerful, and even loving relationship with the very rock structure under our feet and knew that there is indeed "a great connection between the earth and the people who live upon it."[6] The Scriptures, such as Jeremiah 12:10–11, abundantly back her up on this.

While I stayed at her home, a forest fire far below our higher-altitude perch was quickly gaining ground and surrounding us. We had been so engrossed in conversation, prayer, and so on that I had not known of it until I looked out and saw planes below us dropping flame repellant. Agnes was as serene as could be, but I said, "Agnes, dear, I am not where you are on all this, and we are surrounded by fire, and I'm not all that comfortable." I don't recall what her words were but they amounted to the expression, "Oh, not to worry."

She and I simply looked out toward the Pacific, which wasn't too far away, while she prayed to God and then spoke to the ocean and to the unseen clouds, bidding them come and send their waters our way. And, friends, the rain came! Before this incident we were in the midst of a time of prayer that was most significant in both of our lives. We weren't finished yet, and the forest fire made hardly a ripple in it.

Soon we were arm in arm, walking together out in her backyard and preparing to pray some more when suddenly I remembered she had written of a rattlesnake that lived there: one she would speak lovingly to, and it would obey by respecting her boundaries. Once again, I voiced my concerns: "Agnes, I am definitely not where you are in regard to your snake." That a rattlesnake might need to be spoken to was more alarming even than the forest fire, but she immediately put me completely at ease. "Not to worry. . . ." And then she started sharing her need to hear from God on a certain matter, and I simply forgot all about the snake! We never saw or heard it.

As it turned out, the prayer we had in the backyard was deeply significant, and now that Agnes is with the Lord and seeing His greater glory, perhaps it is all right to speak of it, though briefly. She said to me: "The Lord has told me His first call to take me home would be at age eighty-two, and then, as I was walking in the garden, I'm sure it was the Lord, He said, 'I will extend the years to eighty-eight.' I said, 'Oh, no, Lord' (because I don't want to be a burden or to outlive my usefulness), 'how about eighty-four?'"

I knew full well the importance of this conversation and of any reply I might make. Knowing her need to hear from God on this matter and then to choose, I replied, "I'm not hearing the Lord say anything, but I feel that if He said eighty-eight, you should not ask for eighty-four." Of course I wanted to keep her as long as possible.

She then said that going "home" is something she looks forward to, that it will be her next great adventure. She reiterated that she never, ever wanted to be a burden or unable to do anything. She assured me that she would indeed like to stay to age eighty-eight if she could be useful. I believed that she could—that the Lord would give her this and use her for His glory, and said so. Indeed, she had shown me her paintings, very good ones, that now after eye surgery she enjoyed doing.

Then she had to come forward with the difficulty, which was very hard for her to express: "Edith won't let me do anything. I am caged up like a bird. I don't want to live if I can't do anything."

I had already known of some of this and had grieved over the many who desired to see her, folk like Dr. Frank Lake, for example, who were not permitted to come and visit. She may not have known he had tried to meet with her, and she would so have loved to see and pray with him and many others. How I was one of the comparatively few Edith allowed in amazes me yet. I knew only too well that Edith, now not just her secretary-assistant but caretaker, overprotected her at this point.

This, then, was the major problem. I could now pray and receive the mind of the Lord on her choice. Having done so, I responded, "I believe, Agnes, that you should choose the age eighty-four you are opting for, because there *is* something important for you to do past age eighty-two and before the Lord takes you."

And indeed, there was. I don't know what all of it was, but certainly one task had to do with a badly needed change in the leadership of her Schools of Pastoral Care.

Though Agnes had issued a standing invitation to visit her home whenever I could, I did not see her again until November of 1979 when she utterly surprised me and everyone else by coming to the Three Rivers, California, School of Pastoral Care. I was deeply moved to have this opportunity to work with her in the schools she had founded. Edith did not bring her, but another couple who knew her well did. She wanted to hear me lecture and sat with me as others taught. We had the most special time of fellowship throughout the week. To be with her was always to be nourished in the truth, clarity, and humility that so characterized her. Her witty and sparkling rejoinders in question-and-answer sessions wonderfully belied her years, as do photos taken at that time.

We had been in touch before this SPC, as Agnes had been able to read and reread *Real Presence.* I was deeply humbled when she wrote to me regarding it:

> It is a *wonderful* book! It makes the supernatural divinely natural and brings out meaning behind meaning and clear light out of shadows! And as soon as I get this long-delayed letter off I'm going to re-read it again, very slowly, a section every day until all of it sinks into my mind. Thank you for writing it! You have opened doors to the REALITY behind reality: to the Light that shineth through the dimness of our minds.

To write of these years is to marvel at them, for I do not know how so much of great moment could be packed into them. I mustered strength to go from meeting to meeting in one part of the world and then straight from there to multiple meetings elsewhere on the globe, all the while teaching and praying with people night and day. There was great blessing in working with others who were doing the same. From places where the main ministry would be to folk coming out of the countercultural lifestyles of the day, I went directly to universities or academic settings, or to where on occasion people with distinctive primitive faces from the polar regions were brought in by priests and missionaries. Of course, the Spirit was wooing them as well. In times of great outpourings of the Holy Spirit, doors like these are to be walked through when they are wide open.

In truth I can say that there was nothing of activism in all this. The cries, "Come and help us; come and help us," were being voiced from every quarter, for the harvest was ripe for the picking. And sadly, the gatherers were so few. I had been forgiven much and had learned what so many others were thirsting to know. With all my might, the power of God helping me and the gifts of God in full operation, I shared it.

Always I taught the very same things—the eternal *evangel*—all those teachings that are in the books, beginning with the presence and power of God with and within us, and the practice of that holy, healing presence. Simply to read of these swiftly moving times in my prayer journals is to be exhausted all over again and at a loss to understand how so much could have been packed into these years or to adequately describe the miracle of seeing such a multiplication of the differing loaves.[7] Always, in dream after dream, I saw the same golden seed falling into good ground.

Even so, when I did have time at home in the little attic aerie, I was getting the writing done. As I mentioned in the last chapter, once there, I started in earnest to write *The Healing Presence* as the next book after *Real Presence*, but twice I was forced to set it aside and free it from two other books that were by then hopelessly tangled up with it, and all three struggling to be birthed as one. No small problem, and it left me crying out to God for guidance.

He answered my cries in many ways—through my meditation in the Scriptures, through His words, and through the dreams He sent. For example, pasted on my computer just now is a ragged, extremely worn piece of paper with Isaiah 30:21 (KJV) scribbled on it. The black ink has long since faded to an ugly red. It is now well over a half-century old, and I had it before me back then: "And thine ears shall hear a word behind thee, saying, This is the way, walk ye in it, when ye turn to the right hand, and when ye turn to the left."

As I wrote these books, the dreams would continue to come as the "babies" grew, and the Lord would bring before me as a waking vision or dream the golden grains in the huge sheaf being sown. More on these babies and dreams in the next chapter.

As I wrote *The Broken Image*, I was full of amazed thanksgiving for the reception and critiques *Real Presence* was receiving, and as the years wore on, these blessings increased as I received word from pastors, scholars, and friends. I was being showered with other blessings too. Besides the priceless gift of the little aerie and the solitude it afforded, I was given a brand-new car. Giving thanks in my prayer journal, I wrote that only once that year had I gotten down to my last few dollars!

I had kept close ties with Wheaton College friends and had known such fruitful and precious times with Dr. Kilby, with Agnes, with dear friends and prayer partners in Little Rock, Fayetteville, and now, in Milwaukee. Actually, by now I had friends and prayer partners all over the world. Whose heart wouldn't be full? My body was exhausted but my heart was full to overflowing by the time 1979 came to a close.

Then the joy of all these years was capped off at Christmastime by a Christmas Eve concert, "The Joy of Bach," a program I saw and heard in Milwaukee. As I listened, my spirit rose heavenward. I felt that Bach composed and played in the power of the Holy Spirit, that he was a man whose jubilation flowed up to the throne of God. I think it was with this program that I first learned that he began every piece of music he composed by penciling in the initials *J.J.* (Latin, standing for his prayer, "Jesus, help me") at the top and *S.D.G. (Soli Deo Gloria)* at the bottom, meaning "to the glory of God alone."

The year 1980 took up where 1979 ended in terms of the fast pace and momentous times, beginning with the great honor of speaking to the student body of Wheaton College in Edman Chapel. I spoke on "The Loneliness of Man," and to my immense surprise that address was one of two voted as "Chapel of the Year." I had hit on a subject students were silently struggling with. Never did I dream then that in a few years the ministry I was in would be incorporated as Pastoral Care Ministry Schools and would be held regularly in that great auditorium-chapel.

Interest in *The Broken Image* was growing. I was receiving mail from people all over the world, including many Episcopal bishops, who wanted copies as soon as possible. In the midst of the missions and all the correspondence, and thinking how restful and helpful a seminary graduate school library would be, I applied for and within two weeks received a letter with the news of my appointment as a research fellow from none other than Henri Nouwen. I was amazed that I would be spending 1981 at Yale Divinity School. I wrote in a newsletter to friends in August:

This was an unforeseen *gift* straight from the Heart of the Father, and I'm still in a state of joyful trauma over it. Fr. Henri Nouwen and Dr. Paul Holmer are on that faculty, and they are two I am particularly looking forward to working with.

After this, there was quite a battle in terms of the SPCs, one I had to take a significant stand in, and Agnes (though not present in Massachusetts where it took place) stood firmly with me in it—one of the reasons she was not to choose to go home to glory at age eighty-two. I went directly from that exceedingly stressful battle, one that changed the leadership of the schools, for a long weekend at Yale Divinity School. A graduate of that institution, Rev. Paul Malicote, drove me there and gave me a wonderful introduction to the place.

After showing me about campus and then leaving me off at my accommodation, I was fully on my own in exploring New Haven and praying about the fallout of the stressful time I had just been through. We had won the battle so far, but I was burdened over what the final end of the schools would be. I could only pray that all would go well. So, on Sunday of that weekend with this still very much on my mind, I made my way to Trinity-on-the-Green and stayed for two services. I needed all the healing I could get, and nothing better for that than two Eucharists.

There I met a lovely lady, a Ph.D. in Russian literature, and she told me that Henri Nouwen would be saying Mass at 9 p.m. for students and that he would then discuss the Scriptures. She even offered to pick me up and take me there. So I had three Communions in one day—I think the only time this has ever happened—and I needed every one of them. And what a wonderful introduction it was to the way Henri brought the Word and Sacraments to Yale students.

From the weekend at Yale, I went directly to ministry in Minnesota. This was again a year jam-packed with schools and missions around the United States and Canada, up the West coast as far as Alaska.

I had a third visit with Agnes in California in November, and as always with her, it was a deeply meaningful time. In regard to the upcoming publication of *The Broken Image,* the book on the healing of homosexuality, she prayed a marvelous prayer of protection around me, an invisible shield of light that nothing evil could penetrate. Our conversations and prayer times revealed her to be as keen and insightful as ever and always with a wonderful sense of humor. She knew of my exhaustion and spoke of times of great weariness when God especially visited her with comfort and assurance.

She wanted to show me some of her treasures in her study, one that fully let the outdoors in. No sooner had we gotten there than "James," a California blue jay or mountain bird, flew into his birdbath just outside the patio doors. He was beautiful—smaller and different from any blue jay I'd ever seen. Agnes told me that he would come whenever he heard her. In her childlike way, she exclaimed several times, "He *knows* the time of day!" She was amazed that he knew her habitual times of descending into the study, either for prayer and meditation or for writing. James would light in her hand and feed from it.

She had pots and pots of orchids that weren't blossoming yet and was most impatient for them to bloom. Again like a little child, she couldn't wait.

Then she showed me her treasures; this time, *all* her seashells. "Imagine," she said, "they have the intelligence within them to do this . . . a little wormlike creature." She had one unusual and heavy brown thing—not a stone. She thought it was probably a meteor, as the Mexican man who gave it to her said it fell from the sky. I had brought her Robert Siegel's novel *Alpha Centauri,* and of course, she knew the star. Like a child, she leaped toward the book, and I knew she would enjoy it.

I'm simply amazed at the goodness of God, that He should allow me two friends with such incredible relationships to nature as Agnes Sanford and Professor Clyde Kilby. Both loved God first of all, and thereby, in special ways and with such giftedness, all that He created. That God should place my path across or alongside both of theirs for a season is greater blessing than I can measure.

Agnes died in her home on February 21, 1982. She was eighty-four years old. As courageous as ever, on that very day she was scheduled to go with friends on a glider expedition. But when they phoned before picking her up, she simply told them that she was going on another gliding trip. And as Howard Rhys wrote, "She went in joy, free from pain." Death held no terrors for her. As she had said to me when we walked and prayed in her garden, it was an adventure she looked forward to. Hers was a heroic life of prayer and of teaching others to pray.

No, Agnes was not the usual.

Internationally known as a spiritual leader, Agnes Sanford was recognized as such in a major piece in *Newsweek* magazine where she was honored as one of the six people who shaped religious thought in the twentieth century. In 1978 she was presented with an honorary Doctor of Divinity degree by the University of the South, Sewanee, Tennessee. For those who have not read her books, a good place to start is her autobiography, *Sealed Orders.* Those concerned with her theology will enjoy *Behold Your God,* her most theological work.

That year, 1980, ended with a most precious and important time of prayer with Dr. Kilby and with many others at Wheaton. I was also making preparations for going to Yale.

24

The Year at Yale

On January 5, 1981, I drove away from Milwaukee bound for New Haven, Connecticut, and a year at Yale. Friends had helped me pack all the necessary paraphernalia, including what seemed like tons of books and papers, all that I needed to continue writing *The Healing Presence* while searching through the Yale libraries. With the temperature at thirty-five below and with no more room in the car, a heroic friend put a carrier atop the car. So it was in the deep of a Lake Michigan winter that I drove from Milwaukee to the East Coast. I arrived at Yale Divinity School (YDS) late on January 6, unpacked until midnight, and awakened to a deep Connecticut snow.

The first week of classes afforded the keenest of introductions to the vast world of Dr. Paul Holmer's learning. I hung on every word as he taught on Kierkegaard,[1] Wittgenstein,[2] and others, all interspersed with great quotations from C. S. Lewis. What a privilege the time with him turned out to be! I also greatly enjoyed Henri Nouwen's classes, but chiefly gloried in his Eucharists and regular expositions of the Scriptures. The best of Henri's insights came out in these meditations, and they were not lost on the students. Interestingly, the Yale Divinity School students had the privilege of sitting in with the faculty in the interviewing of new faculty prospects. After their classes with Henri and quiet meditations on the Scriptures, they were known to ask of the prospective teachers, "Do you read Scripture *spiritually*?" A way of separating the sheep from the goats that can hardly be improved upon.

In early February, Donald Coggan, former Archbishop of Canterbury, arrived, and he together with Henri Nouwen gave what surely was one of the great convocations of all time at YDS. Many of the alumni had gathered for this, and I knew some among them. They were almost incredulous at the Yale of then compared with the one they had known earlier. Apparently, too much psychology and sociology had replaced the spiritual formation that Henri had now reintroduced, and they could see the difference. Henri was awarded an honorary doctorate by the Berkeley Divinity School, and its dean, Charles H. Clark, paid a high and honest tribute to him and his accomplishments.

In a magazine article written in 1980, Henri had said that it is "possible to experience the relationship between pastor and counselee as a way of entering together into the loving silence of God and waiting there for the healing Word."[3] And it was this statement that had prompted me to contact him earlier. This, of course, is what I had discovered in the healing ministry and what I was writing about as "listening prayer" and as a vital part of "practicing the presence." I told him that I would like to research the great pastoral ministers of past and present for an understanding of their theology of the Holy Spirit and of how that theology was worked out practically in their counseling and prayer ministries.

Within two weeks of browsing in the libraries, however, I realized that very little was to be found other than what I had previously seen. Henri had scouted out the library and realized the same. I wasn't overly surprised; this confirmed what I already sensed: outside the great old liturgies of the past and the scholarly pastoral leaders and historians who tell how these liturgies were lived out in the early church, little was available. See, for example, *Liturgy and Worship: A Companion to the Prayer Books of the Anglican Communion* in regard to liturgies of healing, especially "Visitation of the Sick: Unction, Imposition of Hands, and Exorcism" by Charles Harris.

To this day, I have found no better source on these matters. The loss of great liturgy—the living out of ongoing worship, prayer, and the fullness of the gathered church's life—runs parallel to the loss of the church's healing ministry and the dread loss of the Sacraments. As Dom Gregory Dix writes, "It is a demonstrable historical fact" that losses in the fullness of liturgy run parallel with great social changes in the piety and faith of Christians.[4]

Alexander Schmemann's books, such as *Of Water and the Spirit* and *The Eucharist,* reveal the enormity of our losses in understanding.

I remember the first history of the early church I read, T. G. Jalland's *The Origin and Evolution of the Christian Church.* It blessed me with an understanding of what it meant to the early Christians who risked their lives to come together as the church and there corporately and individually take their place "in the Cup"; that is, in Christ's dying and in his rising. It gave me an in-depth knowledge of what it means to be the church and to abide in Christ, which is largely lost to the understanding and practice of most Christians today.

But as matters were falling out, I had little time or leisure for being disappointed in one less project. Besides keenly enjoying the classes and the chapels, I was busy writing *The Healing Presence* and still attempting to overcome fatigue. I was seeing that Henri, too, was often overcome with weariness, and my thought was that it simply goes with the territory of pastoral care.

But a completely unforeseen thing happened once classes commenced. By the second week, I was praying with students who were greatly in need. Then the next week we had our first retreat with Henri, a deeply meaningful time, and I saw how widespread was the students' spiritual hunger. Many as yet had little foundation in the Scriptures or in prayer. It was as if they had come to seminary to find Christ and themselves. Several of the students came to me, asking if I would teach a group, and I did so in the context of prayer meetings. In my prayer journal, I noted that "it is perfectly amazing to see their reactions to the Holy Spirit's presence as we talk and pray." These were joyous and most fruitful times.

William Beasley, a Wheaton College graduate, was a second-year divinity student and was aware of my prayer ministry. He came for prayer and began bringing his friends with him. (Later William, as an Episcopal priest, was not only my pastor but one of the PCM team leaders for a number of years.) In his undergraduate days, his major was acting, and we had mutual friends, Christian actors and artists, who were now part of the New York Arts group.[5] Several of them came over to New Haven for fellowship and prayers, sometimes bringing a needy fellow artist. Some of the most remarkable healings and turnarounds one would ever want to see occurred during this year at Yale.

So, while still searching for great works on healing prayer, I was even busier in the ministry itself. I had come for a restful, quiet time in a library setting, but that was not to be. Of course not! I would not have had it any other way. How could I see such spiritual need as exists in the modern university, and perhaps most especially in the modern seminary, and desire to turn my head?

At this time, the galleys of *The Broken Image* were finally ready and it would soon be in print. *Real Presence* was now being sold in the YDS bookstore, and I wondered about the reception of this new book on the healing of homosexuality and sexual neuroses. By now Henri was a bit wary of me, a non–Roman Catholic woman of the sort he hadn't known before with a ministry that drew the emotionally broken for healing prayer. His uneasiness evaporated, however, after he asked to read the galleys of *The Broken Image*. We had great discussions after that. The following is lifted from my prayer journal:

> For an hour Henri talked about the book and asked me questions. He thinks it is a "pioneering work" and said, "I know of no other book that brings together the psychological and the spiritual in healing the way this does. . . . At first, I reacted against it—faith healing is outside my experience. Then, I thought, No, this is what I have believed and it is made practical. I like the theology in it. You don't *overlook the story*. Story is important to you. Sin is there, but there is *story* behind it."

Henri was deeply interested in my experience with demonic oppression, as described in the book, and he questioned me closely about it. We also discussed Francis McNutt's book, *Healing,* which he had liked tremendously. However, he was distressed over McNutt's recent loss of credibility in the Roman church, a distress I keenly shared, fearing its negative impact not only on Francis and the Roman church but its effects on the new, vitally fruitful openness between Protestants and Catholics.[6]

Henri said to me, "When I started [*The Broken Image*], I didn't believe how interesting it would be. Now, I can't wait to read the rest." He thought I was a little hard on psychologists, however, saying, "You are a little stronger in places."

This year afforded many occasions for trips to New York City. During several, I attended or spoke at the New York Arts group and had a couple of memorable visits with an author friend in Manhattan. Wonderfully encouraging were forays up to St. Paul's Episcopal Church in Darien, Connecticut, where Terry Fullam led a great congregation in renewal.[7] There were always YDS students wanting to drive up with me. There I first met and came to appreciate the associate pastor, Martyn Minns, for many years rector of Truro Church in Fairfax, Virginia.

Being within driving distance also made possible a trip to Gordon College and Gordon-Conwell Theological Seminary in South Hamilton, Massachusetts, where I touched base once again with friends and faculty from Wheaton College days, including the highly regarded professors Dr. J. Gordon Fee and Dr. Robert E. Cooley. This alleviated my homesickness for the Midwest and Wheaton. Especially memorable was my visit to the home of Dr. Thomas Howard and his wife, Lovelace. Tom, an author and professor of English literature, was a former student and close friend of Dr. Clyde Kilby's, so the conversation was keen and endearing indeed.

I had tried to keep the first semester free of longer-distance travel and had for the year planned only three long weekend conferences for the fall, taking as little time as possible from Yale and the writing of *The Healing Presence*. On March 1, however, I got an urgent message from Ivy Upton, a "loyal yokefellow" and "true companion" (Phil. 4:3), in British Columbia. She said that I needed to come and meet with her, Bishop Hambidge, and others during spring break.

Ivy's call came in a sequence of events that stretched back a number of years. Whenever and wherever I ministered in Canada, she would leave her professional duties, attend the meetings, and give all manner of extraordinary assistance. She was a very successful businesswoman, completely free of anything smacking of political correctness. Nowhere did this show up more than in her Christian witness to Jesus and His desire to heal and set free from sin. She was, in fact, loud in her praises of such a Savior, and this characterized all her life, including her business deals, which were manifold. With most folk, this lack of reserve would have hindered financial success, but not so with her. She was a most unique child of God. She simply loved Him with all of her heart and soul, and this was at all times visible and audible.

She had quite a testimony. With God's help alone, she had survived severe childhood abuse, poverty, and what was expected to be a terminal illness early on. She had experienced what can only be described as a miraculous physical healing in addition to the healing of her soul. Therefore, full of thanksgiving, she desired with all of her being to see suffering people receive the same healing and salvation that the Lord had so freely visited upon her.

I shall never forget the first time I met her. It was at the end of one of my conferences, and in need of rest, I had immediately taken refuge in the rector's private study. Sinking down into a great old leather clergy chair and relaxing fully, I distinctly remember drinking in the soft, warm sunlight streaming in through a lovely, old stained-glass window when Ivy came rushing in. She more or less flung herself to the floor in thanksgiving to God and embraced my legs and knees in a great bear hug—like an enthusiastic child kneeling at a mother's knee. Her excitement over all that she had seen the Lord do in this conference was such that she didn't have even her usual smidgen of reserve. I sensed her deep love for God and for His people and felt the full force of it coming down upon me. This love never wavered through the years, and she ended up showing it toward me in ways that likely saved my life. She continued to attend our conferences after that. Her love for this ministry, and appreciation for the understanding and training she received through it, simply knew no bounds.

A year or two before I had moved to Milwaukee, she saw that I was wearing out physically and would soon be unable to go on. It was then, when I was again on a mission to British Columbia, that she asked to take me out for a drive. We went to one of the most beautiful spots I have ever seen, before or since. It had an expansive view of the ocean and the most lush green grass sloping all the way down to the sea. The beauty of the mountains of Vancouver, snowcapped and towering above, left me gasping in awe. And in one of the more amazing moments of my life, Ivy said to me, "Leanne, I will build you a home on this property if you will move to Vancouver." Stunned, I looked at her hardly believing she could mean such a thing. She did. She said, "No strings attached; it will be given to you."

Here I was, so hungry for solitude and a home, never expecting to actually own one. But I had to say to her, "Dear one, the Lord is not leading me to live in British Columbia." After a moment or so, though disappointed, she responded, "Then, wherever the Lord settles you, I will buy you a home." Here again, my imagination failed. Who could think of accepting such a gift? Not knowing her quite so well back in those days, I feared that surely strings would somehow be attached.

Then a few years later, after I moved to Whitefish Bay, the Anglican bishop in Vancouver, Bishop Hambidge, asked me to come to his office when I was on one of my missions there. Mystified, I went, and to my utter astonishment he looked at me directly and said, "Leanne, Ivy's offer of a home wherever you decide to settle is from the Lord. You must take it."

His word went straight to my heart; I received it and thereafter accepted Ivy's gracious offer. Due, however, to the scheduled travel and ministry, I had not been able to follow through on finding a place. Then the wait was extended while I was at Yale. The home was what Ivy's urgent call to me in March 1981 was about. The monies for it had been put in trust for me, and I had only to locate and buy the house. The year before, the gift of a new Chevy Citation; this year, a home! To say that I was on overload is to put it mildly, for my poor brain and heart were fairly bursting with thankfulness, amazement, and thoughts of what to do next.

Flying to British Columbia, I met with Ivy, Bishop Hambidge, and the lawyers to sign all the papers. Then on the way back to Yale, I had to make an unscheduled layover in Chicago for a conference with my publisher, and after that a quick trip up to Wisconsin in regard to the legal matters going on in Canada. This made me a day or two late getting back to Yale. Henri Nouwen, even with so many responsibilities, was concerned that I had not returned on schedule and phoned me to see if I was all right. This was the kind of caring person he was to his many friends and students.

Precisely at this point, in the midst of matters related to bringing out *The Broken Image*, when the miracle of a gift of a new home had me completely overwhelmed, and amidst of all that was going on at Yale, God sent a dream. I was again "with book"—yet another one, and it demanded to be written before *The Healing Presence*. At this point I was almost desperate to get *The Healing Presence* up and out of my heart, for that gestation was very long, but I knew from the dream that I would be laying it aside once again. Although I didn't realize it at the time, the book-to-be, *Crisis in Masculinity,* would free me to complete *The Healing Presence* as it should be written. Otherwise an editor would have had to free it from the content that is in *Crisis in Masculinity*.

This "little one" had warned me earlier that she was on the way. Several months before, in her introductory dream, I saw a tiny baby who was precocious and able to climb up into windows many stories high. In the dream, as I was trying to rescue and protect the baby, I saw that there were actually two babies (the two embryos I had seen in an earlier dream). I climbed out of the window onto a sort of balcony to rescue them. They were so tiny they could slip right through the grillwork. The last scene was when I had rescued the two babies and brought them in to safety, but they were quite a handful by then, almost eight or nine months old. In my prayer journal, I scribbled out the dream I did not yet understand, then wrote: "Creative projects must be rescued. They could fall overboard before they grow out of infancy."

Still having no idea of what the new creative project would be about, the baby appeared in a dream five months later, in late July, and as the twin of the baby speaking to everyone on the bus (who turned out to be *The Broken Image*), she too had red hair. In the dream, and from my prayer journal:

I had a baby; she was so tiny, felt like a feather as I held her. I was very concerned to keep her safe and warm and swaddled in infants' clothing but she was so small and I didn't have the infant clothing I needed. From a small baby, she became a tiny little bird in my hand and as I was trying to fit on warm clothing she would escape from my hand. I was so afraid someone would step on her; once, when she flipped out of my hand, I fell over from a sitting position trying to get her and was so afraid I would crush her or that someone would run over her before I could see her.

It took a while to understand this dream, for indeed, as the dreams showed in various ways, the baby was an escape artist! Fearing it was something I was neglecting in my writing of *The Healing Presence*, I cried out to the Lord for what it could mean and sensed Him saying:

Little One, do not fret over the "baby" dream. I am the Midwife Who brings forth the healthy infant. I am the Father and the Mother, the Source of all inspiration. I bless this book within you, and I bring it forth in joy. Go now with mirth and thankfulness to the work of your day.

Then, two days after that dream, a comforting dream came. The baby, once again, was the tiny bird but it was in a net, and both the bird and the net were safe in my hand. Then I knew what it was, a book on gender inferiority, a subject very much on my mind, together with the identity crises and even life-threatening depressions that can be the lot of the seriously unaffirmed man or woman.

Gender (masculine and feminine) is an awesome reality, having transcendent roots. I knew that I, as a woman, participated in a special way in a feminine reality rooted in God Himself. In the healing ministry, I saw daily how even the least bit of repression of what I had come to call "the true feminine" or "the true masculine" affected lives. Indeed, we are to glory in gender identity, for there is glory in it.

Both gender and language are primordial, and the way gender affected language was mysterious to me; not something I could even begin to fathom. I asked questions of a post-doctoral student whose field was linguistics: "Don't you think language is terribly mysterious?" With great feeling he answered, "Oh, yes!" I knew, of course, that C. S. Lewis was onto all this, and only wished he had written more specifically on the transcendent nature of gender.[8]

I ended up asking Dr. Paul Holmer what writers other than Lewis had shown this understanding that gender is rooted in the transcendent. His simple answer was, "Man doesn't invent language; language, as Wittgenstein says, pictures the world. It is a picture of the world." That was all the answer I needed. By inference, of course, so is masculine and feminine. Language is symbol. And symbol is picture! Words, when unhampered by such things as political correctness, picture the real, whether on this plane or that of the transcendent. No wonder God sends dreams as answers to prayer—messages to be understood intuitively and symbolically as well as rationally. No wonder the world is in a mess when a culture produces men and women with repressed gender disorders; no wonder the church is in such a plight when she loses her Judeo-Christian symbolic system.

The final dream of a baby came two months later. In it, I had a baby girl. She was tiny, not longer than a pair of gloves but much larger than the tiny birdlike and flighty infant in the last dream. She smiled at me the most precious smile. She had blue, blue eyes that looked straight up into mine and, like her twin *The Broken Image*, light red hair.

After having been home in Wisconsin, and then back there during summer break from classes, I witnessed the truly magnificent maturing of my prayer partners in terms not only of intercessory prayer but in their ministry of healing prayer with others. In giving thanks with my entire being for what I was seeing, the Lord spoke to me very strongly, granting guidance for the future: I was to incorporate the ministry, and its name was to be Pastoral Care Ministries. This was to be done in Milwaukee, there with this team of wholly committed prayer ministers. And though my precious prayer partners did not dream of such then, they were to be a vital part of the team that goes out to minister wherever the Lord might send us. After such guidance and understanding from the Lord, I committed all to Jesus, ending with Augustine's prayer: "Command what Thou wilt; will what Thou commandest." And with all my being, I meant it.

This had been quite a year, one that included three full missions, the last of which was a trip to Vancouver, Washington. There I joined Rev. William L. Vaswig in the ministry of The Life Institute, a U.S.–based organization in Issaquah, Washington, one that he founded and directed. Having read and appreciated his book,[9] and knowing him as a Lutheran pastor and friend of Agnes Sanford, I had the year before fitted this into the Yale year. It was while on my way there, however, that I realized my exhaustion was at a dangerous point. I returned to Yale and finished up the last couple of weeks of this memorable year, after which my new friends helped pack my car for the trip back to Whitefish Bay.

There, a joyous homecoming awaited me, and somehow I knew that from here on, I would take very few invitations other than those which would be sponsored by the organization these dear ones stood ready to help me put together. Back home in Whitefish Bay just before Christmas of that year, a friend and realtor helped me find just the lovely home the Lord had in store for me, and on the last day of 1981, my friends and prayer partners gathered together and moved me in.

So, after more than three years in my attic nook, I owned my first home in Whitefish Bay, completely debt free, replete with offices, where the work of the ministry could be done. Mr. L. B. (Ted) Smith, an extraordinary Christian man, with a battery of his lawyers, helped me incorporate this ministry. He also sat on its board and drew in others who gave expert secretarial and bookkeeping help. This is how God moved, once my blinders were removed, and at what a pace! Ever after, though faithfully attending the local church, I trusted Him alone as my covering. As a friend of mine, quoting the faithful African bishops now overseeing many Episcopalians who have had to leave their churches: "Extraordinary times require extraordinary means."

Here I am tempted to say, "The rest is history!" But there is more to tell about the Milwaukee team, those incredible souls who then traveled the globe with me, bringing their richness of fellowship and giftedness with them.

25

Interlude—Henri Nouwen

It might seem odd that a famous priest and author could seek a place where he would feel accepted. However, Henri Nouwen was dogged by an undercurrent of emotional uncertainty that none of his real achievements could completely relieve or erase. Henri Nouwen searched openly for something that perhaps many long for secretly—friendship and real intimacy with other people and with God.

Michael O'Laughlin,
God's Beloved: A Spiritual Biography of Henri Nouwen

I would not have written this section on Henri had not the first biography published after his death in 1996 labeled him gay. From the beginning, even in the preface of *Wounded Prophet,* Michael Ford posits Henri's identity as that of a gay man, saying that in his research several people had informed him of this.[1] Also, early in the book, the author implies that Henri's physical gestures when speaking publicly convey a narcissistic drawing of attention to himself.[2] I've never heard anyone else speak of Henri's physical movements in public speaking in that way. Knowing Henri's special giftedness in verbal communication, I felt that this author must have known him only superficially, or even worse, had an agenda in writing about him. Either way, he misread Henri's spiritual and psychological identity. Those reading Ford's book who did not know Henri personally can only lose heart and confidence in the holiness and moral integrity of a priest whose writings have spoken so deeply to them.

The term *gay* refers to a male homosexual and implies homosexual acting out. For me, it is disturbing in the extreme to see the term applied to Henri, for he did not act out. He was a wounded man who in spite of early, unhealed trauma in the areas of personal identity (those leading to severe and recurring bouts of depression) even so remained wholeheartedly centered in Christ, thereby turning his wounds into healing power for others. His own books are his spiritual biography, writings that openly show the spiritual journey he took into assurance of God's love and abundant acceptance of him.

In part, Henri's inner turmoil resided in the very thing I was to write about next as a "crisis in masculinity," the plight of the man painfully unaffirmed in his gender identity and therefore in himself as a person, one unable to achieve the crucial developmental step of self-acceptance. Often, as in Henri's case, this leaves a man "bent" toward other men in an attempt to gain the masculine love and affirmation he so craved and failed to receive earlier. The most readily visible cause in Henri's case would quickly be seen by counselors in his lifelong attempt to find intimacy and gain affirmation from a father he greatly admired and respected but whom he perceived as cold and distant. Failing in this, he strove to find these identity-saving affirmations through his spiritual fathers and male friends.

Unfortunately, in our current Western culture, one rife with politically correct speech and the resulting loss of freedom to speak the truth plainly, the adult male's need for masculine love and acceptance is now automatically viewed as something to be eroticized and labeled gay. In fact men like Henri are now legion in a culture where fathers are often absent or are themselves wounded and unaffirmed; they are now encouraged to act out— that is, to become gay. There is even a political campaign in our schools to deliberately eroticize this condition in prepubescent boys who, in the grip of inferiority complexes of one kind or another, yet await the adolescent developmental step enabled by the father's affirmation. In this step a young man separates his identity from that of his mother and moves forward as a man, affirmed in his masculine identity, and in his very being.

An important point to make here is that this "bentness" in Henri toward seeking intimacy with men was not eroticized. Though he craved a proper intimacy with the men in his circles, he actively resisted any eroticism. The young men I knew in my prayer group were thick as thieves with him, some over a period of many years, and none sensed sexual lust in their close relationships and daily contact with this good man. It just wasn't there! His tactile needs no doubt were great; I've seen this before, as I've ministered to young men suffering as Henri did, who grew up in homes with fathers who never once touched them. I know this sounds impossible, but it happens.

Anyone having read Henri's *The Return of the Prodigal Son* and of the way he was affected by Rembrandt's famous painting of this scene from Christ's parable (Luke 15:11–32) will surely remember how struck he was by the father's hands resting on the son. Henri literally sat for days in front of Rembrandt's larger-than-life painting of the same, drinking in the meaning of the Father's touch and love. Those days in The Hermitage, St. Petersburg's famous art museum, were utterly life-changing for Henri. Men with such needs hunger for the touch of a loving, intimate father; their bodies long for a warm, loving, tight hug. The blessing that flows through an affirming father's hands carries with it the affirmation of the masculine within the son, the feminine within the daughter, naming them in their identities as a man, as a woman. By this they are enabled to come into the great virtue of self-acceptance.

But Henri's psychological need went beyond even the failure to be affirmed in the masculine and as a person. What made Henri's inner pain so excruciating and his depressions so dangerous was very early trauma whereby he failed to come to a secure sense of being, making him subject to severe separation anxiety. Such trauma, unhealed, would have disabled him from receiving gender affirmation and full self-acceptance later on, even from the warmest of fathers.

In early October 1981 I saw that Henri was sliding into depression, as I noted in my prayer journal, "in a desperate battle for his mind." I phoned my prayer partners in Milwaukee. They would hold my concerns as under the office of the confessional—they would never under any circumstances divulge them—and they went immediately into prayer and fasting for Henri. They urged me to move to help him, but I knew that in his present state of intense fear, he would be unable to accept help through me (had a Roman priest been with me, that would have made the difference). So we continued to pray. Eight days later, William Beasley and another seminarian in my prayer group, Michael McCarthy, sent for me to come quickly. Henri, in a dreadful place of fear and agony, was collapsed on the floor, and the two were holding him tight and praying.

Though I was never in a counseling relationship with Henri, I instantly knew what was going on, for I had seen this need for healing many times. It is one thing to be cut off from one's gender identity, and it is quite another to fail to come to a secure sense of well-being, or at worst, a sense of being itself.

In an effort to cry out about what is happening to them, these sufferers will often describe a split in their inner being, an open abyss, the edge of which they are desperately attempting to hold to, even as if they are just hanging on by their fingernails. To slide into the abyss is to fall into an infinite nothingness. Henri was experiencing the terror of nonbeing, the dreadful sense that he was falling into it. Anyone who prays for such a one will instinctively hold the person tight, as if to stop that slide into the abyss.

No one sees this sort of suffering and intense fear for the first time without being greatly shaken. The Christian will then have an incredible gratefulness to God for the gift of eternal being in Christ, who created all things, and for the opportunity to grow into the fullness of being that He intends for us. To love God and to love truth is never to stop growing in this fullness of being, something we never completely attain on earth, but which is eternally ours in Christ.

Once brought up out of the critical place and his intense fear, Henri, so very grateful for our prayers, grabbed and continued to kiss Michael and William's hands, a movement so full of thanksgiving that it still brings me to tears to think of it. He thanked me over and over, unable to touch or take my hand, but he surely read my understanding. I had expected this, knowing that he was at some level schizoid in relation to women.

We were totally depleted afterward, having seen the enormity of Henri's fear and need. There was much yet to be done, for Henri did not allow us, once he was up and out of the abyss, to go on to pray for a healing of memories, a bringing of Christ's healing into the prebirth, infantile, and childhood memories underlying this failure to come to an adequate sense of being. But the emergency was over for the moment, and we could only hope that he would soon allow the full healing to come. He did not, however, and soon the term was over and we were parted. I grieved over this, knowing that though he was safe for the moment, the root memories were yet uncovered, unhealed. In retrospect, I think he simply did not realize the effectiveness of such prayer.

The next day, I wrote in my journal: "Henri looks like a new person. He is now strengthened to go on. . . ." Henri's joy and thankfulness were precious to see, and that day he *could* grasp my hand, a breakthrough for him. In the afternoon, William Beasley came for prayer, still worn out and in a dread awe of what he had seen. "I've never gone that far into darkness with anyone," he said. "I had to stop (praying for Henri) and just pray for you," meaning me, for I was leading the prayer.

Failure to come to a secure sense of being in those first months and years of life results in the severest forms of separation anxiety and is related to the mother figure. How, I wondered, with such a warm, loving mother as Henri's, had this happened? I also puzzled over his irrational fear of God. He loved and obeyed God, but at that time he was yet afraid to draw too close. Henri's emotional view of God and the way God perceived him were simply off. Intellectually, and in his theology and ministry, this view did not show up. It was deep set, however, in his emotional need. I've seen this in some old European strains of Catholicism, which would cause some people to substitute Mary, the mother of Christ, for Christ Himself.

When I first saw Henri's fear of God, sometime before the incident described above, I had engaged him theologically on the matter, trying to see where this fear came from. I failed in that but did realize that he practiced a form of substitution; at some rational level he felt that in his suffering he was participating in the sufferings of Christ. We argued a bit about that in regard to himself. Any Christian who takes up the cross and follows Christ will suffer, and I believe as firmly as anyone ever did that we participate in Christ's sufferings in doing so, but I knew this was a psychological wounding we were dealing with. Henri needed to look to God and to the finest physicians to find healing and release from it.

After leaving Yale, with the ministry taking all of my energy, I did not keep up with Henri's writing and only during work on this book did I read his *In Memoriam,* in which he describes his mother's death and her abject terror of dying. This was the first inkling I had into perhaps understanding Henri's irrational and unhealthy fear of God. To have such an extreme fear of death as his mother had is to fear God in the wrong way. I think Henri took these fears into himself even before he was born, and certainly early on, with his mother's milk. Later on too she, a deeply devout and regular communicant, confided this fear to him when he was as yet a young lad. Had my devout mother shared something in confidence like that with me as a child, and had she never gotten over the fear, it would certainly have negatively impacted me. His mother would have had this fear during her pregnancy[3] and especially at his birth, and as loving as she was, this could have been one of the early traumas contributing to his separation anxiety.

277

I'm writing these things out of my experience in seeing these maladies, now over many decades, in the context of healing prayer. Separation anxiety leads to the most critical of emotional illnesses, those that prohibit coming to a secure sense of being. As mentioned earlier, Dr. Frank Lake writes of the five reaction patterns that can come about when one has failed to come to a secure sense of being early in life or failed to come to a sense of being at all: schizoid, hysterical, dissociative, homosexual, paranoid. These are merely defenses against the pain of the condition.

William and Michael continued to pray for and with Henri, and I don't believe he had another such depression until he ran into the deeply entrenched unbelief at Harvard Divinity School.

Henri Nouwen was a man of God, a great man possessed of a certain kind of genius. He was one who suffered greatly. Yet in choosing Christ and the way of life and holiness, he had a special charism of love. He who so irrationally feared that others could not love him was dearly loved by almost all who ever knew him—and they were in the thousands, for he was as outgoing, extroverted a person as one is ever likely to meet. His generosity and giving to others in need were simply epic in terms of their expansiveness; he was heroic in his never-flagging capacity to love God and others while yet craving the capacity to feel and receive love and affirmation himself. All this giving came not out of hoping to receive in return, but out of his choosing to obey and abide in Christ. Therein lies his difficult-to-describe genius as well.

To see all this played out over his lifetime, and the way it increased as he—albeit out of a restless, searching, crippled sense of being—slowly found many of the answers he was searching for, and an ever greater capacity to love and serve others, is wonderful to behold. Truly God can and will, when we allow it, turn even our gravest woundings into the power to *be* and speak his light and sheer multicolored grace into the lives of others.

In this way, and in contrast to a traumatized sense of being, Henri possessed a strong true self, one wherein there was no "crisis in masculinity" but the capacity not only to resist temptations peculiar to his needs but to strongly stand up for Christ and His truths bequeathed to the church. I am grateful to call him friend, one of many who do. To have known him personally, even if briefly, is to bless his memory.

26

Joy in the Midst of Incorporation

Pass through, pass through the gates! Prepare the way for the people. Build up, build up the highway! Remove the stones. Raise a banner for the nations. . . . See, your Savior comes!

Isaiah 62:10–11 NIV

Joyously in my new home on New Year's Day, 1982, I headed the year's journaling with the above quotation from Isaiah. The Christmas celebrations with the dear ones in the prayer group had been precious indeed, meetings filled with praise, thanksgiving, and *Jubilati Deo*, the joy of the Lord's presence with us. I realized that we (not just I!) were "passing through the gates," and that although these special servants of the Lord as yet had no idea of it, they themselves would be helping raise that "banner for the nations."

Members of the group, Lynn and Paul Berendsen, had sent their three strapping teenage sons to help me move, and they had made short shrift of hauling all my books and paraphernalia out of the attic aerie and into the beautiful new home. My dear friend and prayer partner from Wheaton days, Gayle Sampson, soon arrived bringing her bedroom furniture as a gift, and she stayed to deal with all the cleaning, organizing, and arranging. By January 2 Ted Smith had sent a huge old desk and chair that he was no longer using, and my office was up and running. By January 7 Trish

Ross, another friend with experience in interior design and great taste in furnishings, had helped me select the furniture needed for the rest of the house.[1]

Friends and prayer partners throughout the United States and Canada and other parts of the world rejoiced together with those of us in Whitefish Bay, Wisconsin. We knew and basked in the joy of the Lord and in all He was leading us to do.

Now that *The Broken Image* on the healing of homosexuality was out, letters poured in, some from places and even islands I had never even heard of before. Clearly the need for deliverance from sexual fantasies, neuroses, and acting-out was global, as was the need for healing prayer for spiritual and emotional problems in general. My phone had long been ringing with calls from Christian leaders all over the world, with one request, "Come and help us!" For a long time the requests had been more than I could handle. Now they were impossible. Very soon Lynn Berendsen was helping me not only with all the mail but with the office work. We have never advertised this ministry; it grew in answering one letter and one phone call at a time.

Within the first week of moving in, my growing fatigue culminated in severe tendonitis. It had begun two or three months before and was grievously aggravated by the travels and all the moving. Suddenly I had limited use of both arms and could lift them only waist high. Later I learned that two vertebrae in my back had more or less collapsed, and my weariness was diagnosed as allergic fatigue syndrome.[2] Ivy Upton, in her ongoing push to see me resting, had provided the home and office space where others could come in and help, and I doubt if Pastoral Care Ministries could have evolved as a corporation apart from her prayers and her extraordinary gift.

None of my physical problems, however, had the power to dampen my joy. It was as though I had gotten into the new home at just the right time, and though my health was more tenuous than ever, I knew just what to do: enter into the quiet and peace that Christ gives. This I did, praying:

> Father, Thou has given to me all that is needed. Add now Thy love, peace, quiet, word of wisdom, word of knowledge: the sureness, deftness of movement needed in prayer, study, work. Thanks be to Thee, God of my fathers.

Throughout the years in ministry, my strength and trust has been in God alone.[3] I would turn half a century old in 1982, and with no health insurance or savings for retirement. And yet here I was getting ready to incorporate the ministry! So I prayed:

> Lord, I ask for glowing good health even unto old, old age, and for sufficient funds to maintain the home You have given me. Lord, give to me the spirit of Joan of Arc, of Judith. Women capable of leading armies—Your army— against darkness and evil. Injustice. Lord, that I might take the offensive. Make strong my right arm, O Lord, to hold the sword of Your Spirit. Heal my left, Lord, that I might be fully shielded from the evil one.

I knew that somehow I must, through incorporating and the benefits that would come of that, train Christian leaders, clergy and lay alike, in healing prayer, both in the States and abroad. What was the ministry that was to be incorporated? It was *exactly* what I was already doing, mostly giving five-day schools—retreats where pastors, doctors, lay leaders, and all in the medical professions, together with those seeking healing, could come. Incorporation would provide the necessary legal and financial benefits, such as health insurance and an income for retirement.

Now that I had hit a new low physically and was forced to reach out for more help, I was astonished to see how ready those around me were to give it—far beyond what I could have asked or imagined. These were extraordinarily capable people, folk wholly given over to God and eager to serve. Only the Lord could have orchestrated such a time and group of Christians.

It seems nothing short of miraculous to me that one among them was L. B. (Ted) Smith, a man eminently qualified to know what a pastoral care board should be and do. I could hardly believe that he would be willing not only to be on the board but to take charge of all the legal aspects through his own lawyers. Ted, with a huge heart for helping individuals as well as whole institutions, was the president of A. O. Smith Corporation and sat as director on such boards as John Deere, Goodyear, Continental Can Corporation, First Wisconsin National Bank, and Smith Investment Company. And he was going to be secretary-treasurer of the PCM board! I was humbled clear to the ground with thankfulness to God for causing me to cross paths with Lucy and Ted Smith and to have a man so noted for high ethical and moral principles not only to help me put PCM together but then to direct the board in the right way. He continued in this capacity for a good many years.

It is said that every great man has a great woman behind him, and that is certainly true of Ted. Lucy, as she progressed in prayer, became a veritable powerhouse of faith and action. Countless are the souls and lives Lucy has touched, and having her as a prayer partner down through all these years has been one of the great strengths behind the work of PCM.

As if that weren't blessing enough, the Lord called Dr. Bernie Klamecki to serve with Ted and me on the board. This good man, ever so dear and full of good humor and fun, was like Ted, a wearer of many hats. He was a busy medical doctor, the father of a large family, and a leader tirelessly active in the renewal then sweeping through the Catholic church. What a friend he has been through the years, one of those who prays for me and the work of PCM daily.

How in the world did I fall in with such folk so soon after moving to Whitefish Bay? And I've only begun to name them. God alone could have engineered it.

I first met Ted and Lucy Smith, then members of the Lutheran church, when they attended classes I was teaching at Christ Episcopal Church, where I was a communicant. Lucy's immediate reaction to the teachings was a definite "Eureka, I've found it!" As she told me later: "God moved very fast to bring us together. I had this drive, that the Lord gave me obviously, to get to know Him. You opened up a new doorway for me to cross over. My life was changed as I came to know Jesus in a personal way. What a supreme gift I was given."

She had found the Truth, Christ Himself, and the teachings on His presence and power in our midst that she had so hungered for; and with my friends and me, she found the prayer group she was searching for as well.[4]

It wasn't long after meeting the Smiths that I met the others, all of whom were attending and growing in their personal relationships with Christ through a prayer group at St. James, at that time a center of Catholic renewal in Mequon, Wisconsin, a short drive north from Whitefish Bay. It was there that I met Patsy Casey for the first time, and she immediately introduced me to her family and to Connie Bense (later Boerner),[5] the Berendsens, and the Klameckis. What a find!

Patsy, full of fervor and longing to know more of the Scriptures and the Spirit's gifts in ministry to others, was already showing her main gift: that of evangelist. (In the years to come, we were always losing her, which was no small problem when traveling abroad, only to find her doing one-on-one evangelism with some avid listener in a crowd or on a plane or train.) Quickly she talked me into giving a full conference at the Sisters of Notre Dame, a massive and lovely convent located at that time just north of us on Lake Michigan.[6] With that "school" we were off and running. In it Patsy together with Connie and others provided the music, and what worshipful music it was.

Connie turned out to be our budding songwriter, one who worshiped and adored God with all her might, even as Patsy did. Once they began accompanying me on the missions, Connie became our precious song leader.

Soon Lucy, Connie, and Patsy were climbing the stairs up to the little aerie (these relationships formed before I moved into my new house), and our times together, filled with teaching and ministry, bound us into an inner core of prayer partners far beyond the ordinary, one that united us so quickly as a PCM team later. From the beginning they, like Ivy Upton, realized the extent of my physical needs as well as the calling on my life, and they gathered around me as incredible intercessors and "holders up" of my arms in ministry. I could not have been more blessed of the Lord than in this team that was so quickly, and in my eyes miraculously, drawn together.

I could write a book just on these incredible women and their walk and labor in the Lord. What one of us alone could never be and do in prayer, through the years the four of us were and did. That is what true Christian community looks like and does. In all the many, many PCM schools given over the years, the four of us have been united in prayer, interceding and receiving God's Word and guidance for them.

Recently, Lucy, Connie, Patsy, and I met for prayer to discuss the beginnings, and I asked them why they thought the team could have formed so quickly. Without taking even a second to think, Connie replied: "The one thing about Pastoral Care Ministries that is so profoundly different is that, as you practice the presence of the Lord, nothing is manipulated, nothing is controlled, nothing is sensationalized, nothing is worked by the hands of man. In respect and reverence for God and who He is in the fullness of His glory, you back off and let Him move. Leanne, that is what you exemplified. That is what we saw and hungered for.

"This ministry is so refreshing. People come to hear you, and all of a sudden they're tasting Jesus Christ, the living God. What they find is not because of anything you do, because you minister out of your weakness; there God's strength is made perfect. So that's what we experience at every PCM. The Lord is faithful to lead, faithful to show up, faithful to do, and we are all in awe. We celebrate our littleness, like children; we celebrate the wonder of who He is, and it is that simple. That's what God calls us to: He says, 'Enjoy Me, love Me, adore Me.'"[7]

Connie and Patsy were onto the truth of P. T. Forsyth's profound statement: "If God's will is to be done on earth as it is in heaven, prayer begins with adoration."[8] They had long been "pray-ers": as Catholics they had knelt regularly before the Reserved Sacrament, the sacramental presence of Christ, and there would worship and adore Him; therefore, they instantly discerned the Lord's presence—whether coming through the Sacraments, the teachings, or the gifts. Lucy, authentic through and through and now walking in the presence, had the same quickened discernment.

Through the songs she wrote, Connie taught countless other musicians besides those in PCM to follow her lead in adoring and enjoying God, even as they led His people in worship to do the same.[9] All of this, together with my teaching, gave back to many the true feminine, the saying with Mary, "Be it unto me according to thy word" (Luke 1:38 KJV).

By February, besides enlisting Lynn Berendsen (who had by then become part of the prayer group of women) as secretary, Ted had recruited her husband, Paul, as the official bookkeeper for PCM, a work he did professionally for the University of Milwaukee. I was awed by all this treasury of help and hardly knew how to take best advantage of it. Therefore Ted drew up an organizational plan for me to follow. As recorded in my prayer journal, it

1. requires an answering service on my telephone so that the a.m. will be entirely quiet and clear for prayer and writing,
2. a secretary who will pick up my mail and be here at 1 p.m., go through the calls & the correspondence with me, and leave at 4 p.m.,
3. 4 p.m.—recreation. Exercise, good reading.

After reading the plan the first time, I cried out in joy, especially in regard to number three about recreation, "Lord, I lift this up to you." It seemed too good to be true. I did my best to hold to this extraordinary reordering of my life.

In response to all this incorporating business, I had a dream, humorous in retrospect. It featured an author and friend of mine. She was as I had seen her last: weary, aging, rather awkward in movement, not always steady on her feet. But she was going to have a baby! I was astonished: "But M—— can't have a baby! She's too old." But she did. It was a large, wise baby, a unique baby. Just like M——, a writer, speaker, and observer of creation, especially mankind. The baby had a somewhat square face with a wide forehead and widely spaced blue eyes. It had a white gown on (I wasn't sure if it was a boy or a girl), exactly as babies were dressed in days of old.

Suddenly recalling the dream in full later on in the day, I knew what it meant. I thought, symbolized by M——, I'm giving birth to a corporation! Square-faced indeed. I'm too old and too weary, but a wise, healthy, large baby will be born!

In the midst of all this, starting in March were prior commitments I had made—full schools and other speaking engagements. The members of the prayer group could not be included on any of them. I had kept the slate clean for the schools to come after incorporation, and so it would be 1983 before the first school could take place that would include the members of the prayer group as prayer counselors.

With my mornings free and the luxury of knowing that someone would be in to handle the phone calls, I made good progress on *Crisis in Masculinity*. The writing was a marvelous time of thinking through the concepts of masculine and feminine. Surely that is one of the most satisfying and richly rewarding studies a person with a full Judeo-Christian worldview can make. It ends up involving the Holy Trinity Himself. As C. S. Lewis rightly maintains, God is so masculine that we are all feminine in relation to Him. God is the source of the true feminine; indeed, the source of all that is real and true, period. Masculine and feminine are rooted in the transcendent.

Soon I would be conducting a school in a large Episcopal church in Dallas, Texas, where Fr. Ted Nelson, a wonderful leader in the renewal, was rector. I was much taken aback when he informed me that Derek Prince would be with us through the week. Those acquainted with that good man knew he had taken strong positions on women in the ministry. And he would be sitting through my conference! So along with alarm bells, all my consideration of gender suddenly took on added force and meaning.

To my utter amazement and everlasting thanksgiving, I ended up friends with Derek—he with respect for me, and I for him—no small feat. It turns out that he, an Oxford graduate, knew C. S. Lewis personally, and we had great things to talk about. In the years to come, I taught classes in Youth With A Mission's Pacific and Asia Christian University in Hawaii, often at the same time as Derek. Even though he kept his wife under the kind of "submission" he favored, I came to appreciate this man as a faithful, knowledgeable, and even humble servant of the Lord (albeit extreme and therefore in error in some of his teachings on the submission of woman).

My year of jubilee was coming up in June, and Leviticus 25:10–11 with its "Consecrate the fiftieth year" and the "fiftieth year shall be a jubilee for you" (NIV) took on enormous significance for me personally. I gloried in it, sensing that the Lord had much that was special not only for now but in the years to come. In great physical need, I even so received this promise from the Lord:

> You will indeed plant the golden grains you saw in the rounded sheaf— perfect, whole, glowing with golden light and life grains. You will "broadcast" them; others will reap the harvest. I make of you a sharpened instrument.
>
> Based on Isaiah 41:15; 45:2–3

On June 8 Ted, Bernie, and I signed the Articles of Incorporation. Mike Casey was the notary, and all the prayer partners were in attendance. We had a tremendous time of prayer, much of it for Henri Nouwen from whom I had received several notes indicating depression. His good friend Michael McCarthy phoned me, and we prayed together for Henri. If only he had allowed the prayer I had offered. . . . That was always our sadness, that he had to go through so much more agony before getting the help he needed.

On June 26, 1982, I turned fifty years old. Without the least exaggeration I can say that this is the one birthday that I celebrated for an entire year. It truly was not only consecrated but a yearlong jubilee.

I was scheduled in early July to give a full school in an Exodus International conference at Trinity Western College in Vancouver, B.C., and so Ivy Upton insisted I come early in order to celebrate my birthday on the *Prince George*, a British Columbia/Alaskan cruise ship. This was a birthday gift from Ivy and her husband, George. On June 26, therefore, we three boarded the *Prince George* and sailed into the splendor of the Canadian coastline and waters of Alaska, beauty enough to break one's heart.

However, not even with days of rest in the exquisite sunshine on the ship's deck did my fatigue let up, and I was concerned for the upcoming conference. Always, in the midst of a conference, it is as though a supernatural strength comes to me, an anointing that simply is set upon my head and flows down. Surely, this is His zeal, His holy power enabling me to minister His love into the lives of the needy and the lost. I prayed, "Why, Lord, this extreme weakness?" There was no specific answer, simply these words spoken to my heart: "Your love for truth is known and blessed of God. This will continue to be so. Honor truth in every thought and word, every image of your mind, heart, tongue." This I have ever endeavored to do.

The Exodus conference was my first with this evangelical group, and I was greatly looking forward to it. The leaders had come out of the homosexual lifestyle and were dedicated to passing on the gospel and the help they had received to others involved in homosexual activity.

To say that the conference was unusually blessed is an understatement, and without the least hyperbole, I attest that incredible fruit has come of it throughout the years. There I first met all the key leaders of Exodus International, many of whom still guide and carry on the ministry. None who were there will ever forget that conference. To this day, I remember faces stunned with wonder, souls who had come desperate for deliverance from sexual addictions. They were experiencing the power of the Lord to forgive, to heal, and to cause His Word and their faith to leap alive. I was seeing ennoblement, or at least the promise of it, in the light on their faces, that which comes with life in Him.

Truly, everything Patsy, Lucy, Connie, and I had foreseen in prayer for this conference was accomplished. Ivy also assisted at the conference, and we were overwhelmed by the need of so many. However, Ivy's strength held out far into the night as she was enabled to pray with those anxious for one-on-one help. All of this she did besides handling all the books and tapes in conferences, a ministry she continued in Canada up until her death.

On my return home, something happened that made me realize my days of having a listed phone number and address were behind me. A prison inmate on the West Coast managed to get out and come straight to my door. Then other such incidents occurred, including one particularly frightening airline flight when a mentally deranged stalker figured out what flight I would be on. He boarded the airplane and found my assigned seat, and then towered over me while waving a worn copy of *The Broken Image* (underlined throughout in red) while uprooting the lady sitting next to me on the aisle (against her and the flight attendant's objections). Unfortunately we were already in flight, and the situation could not be properly dealt with. Talking loudly and full of grandiose ravings about how impressed the president (and other dignitaries in Washington) would be if he were healed, he thoroughly traumatized all the people within hearing distance. He did not omit the fact (later verified) that he was being tailed by government agents. The story is too long to tell in full, but once we were off the plane, I, together with Tommy Tyson, the well-known evangelist who awaited me, had very good and effective prayer with him! And I hope this dear man is even now somewhere in a good church and ongoing treatment if necessary, and progressing in wholeness.

In addition to this more dramatic instance, many within the church, both Protestant and Catholic, who were suffering with sexual neuroses of one kind or another, would travel from the far ends of the earth for help. Once some came from Europe to Whitefish Bay, with no prior communication whatsoever. They were simply searching for help, and such need for prayer was heartbreaking. I would soon be setting up training schools in Europe and the UK, and help would be made more broadly available—more quickly than I could have imagined. But first I had to survive, so I no longer allowed my home phone number and address to slip out. This has not been easy, and goes against my inbred Southern hospitality. But if my home was to be a place of rest, this barrier had to be raised. The restriction lent all the more joy to the planned visits that came my way.

On July 18 Fr. John Sheets, SJ, came from Creighton University (in Omaha, Nebraska) not only to visit but to talk to me about being on their summer graduate school faculty. There I would be teaching an intensive course on Christian formation and spirituality, an unusual opportunity and honor since I was not Roman Catholic. He had read and loved *Real Presence* and afterward wrote an excellent and deeply perceptive foreword for it. The book was being used in several courses at Creighton.

During the visit he asked forthrightly, as if he'd been sent to ask this very question: "Leanne, what are you writing now?" I told him I was working on *Crisis in Masculinity* and was deep into a study before the Lord of what gender is, what the true masculine and true feminine are. I knew I had some beautiful and true answers, answers that proved themselves daily in the healing ministry but were far removed from the understanding of moderns, even in the church. All of this we talked about, and I shared with him how very alone I felt in addressing this topic. He then gave me a very large gift indeed, the knowledge that Karl Stern, a German psychiatrist who had survived the Holocaust and converted to the Christian faith, had written a book on gender, *The Flight from Woman*.[10] The book was out of print, but I soon managed to get a copy. I found that I had more or less taken up where this truly great man had left off. What a soul mate Karl Stern was. The deep aloneness I had felt was lifted from me.[11]

I had been teaching on the loss of the symbolic mind and the more intuitive ways of knowing, of the loss of the intuitive feminine mind and its seemingly readier capacity to worship, saying with Mary, "Be it unto me according to thy will" (Luke 1:38 KJV). I dealt with what it meant to run from that mind-set, even to despise it. In his book Stern sketched the history of this flight from the true feminine as it can be read through literature and philosophy, along with its terrible effects on men. The rationalism and harried activism of the day, so grievous in its impact on the church, results from valuing the more masculine, analytical, rational mind, while devaluating and even denying the more feminine, intuitive, symbolic, feeling mind. I had been trying to show how the loss of the intuitive capacity that is within us all to see, worship, adore, and respond to God had now resulted in the critical loss of the invaluable true masculine—indeed, in the loss of reason itself. I dedicated *Crisis in Masculinity* to Karl Stern with high hopes that it would bring about a reprinting of his book, and apparently it did, for the book was subsequently republished and has been in print ever since![12]

After praying about teaching at Creighton, I knew that it was made to order for me. I would teach a full, extended PCM school while there, using the works of C. S. Lewis, especially his novels. They provided a way of giving back the full Judeo-Christian symbolic system, so necessary to understanding and retrieving what has been lost in understanding mystery, gender, and all the transcendent, unseen real.

I had so much to give thanks for, I thought my heart would break. Another friend, a German professor from Wheaton College, Carol Kraft, had just come up and spent hours doing to my yard what Gayle Sampson had done to my house. Carol mowed, trimmed, and planned what flowers should go where. She was the friend who a year before had given me a new car. From time to time, though she had no knowledge of it, her gifts to this ministry had come when I was down to the last dime. Times would soon be easier financially, though I could hardly imagine it then.

In July we announced the successful birthing of Pastoral Care Ministries, Inc., and asked for prayer as we made decisions on how, where, and when the schools were to be held. Due to the need for medical care, I had to take a sabbatical of several months from travel, but I ended the year by speaking at the fourth annual festival of the New York Arts group. From there I went to St. Paul's in Darien, Connecticut, a wonderful end to a great year in the ministry.

At the conclusion of my ministry at St. Paul's, I was given the gift of a very beautiful "Risen Savior" crucifix, one designed and crafted by a member of their congregation. I've worn it ever since, never exchanging it for another. God has uniquely used that blessed work of art down through the years and in every country where we've ministered, sometimes in unusual ways. Rather often strangers ask if I'm a nun, to which I have learned to say, "No, but I'm very like one." On several occasions, when waiting to board a plane and especially on days when the weather is stormy, people noting the cross come over to me and say, "We are not afraid to get on the airplane if you are going!"

On a Caribbean island, as I checked in to a hotel, the woman in charge mistook the crucifix for the likeness of some angelic being. She reached over and grasped it, then immediately released it, crying out, "Oh, it's got your energy!" She was obviously an occultist who thought at first the likeness was not of Christ crucified and risen, but of an angel of the psychic sort she hankered after. The "energy" that so repelled her, of course, was that of which the crucifix signifies, surrounding me and the blessed object. Now, almost three decades after receiving this gift, I can say it is a very rare week when some stranger has not commented on the cross I wear. A likeness of it has become our Pastoral Care Ministries logo.

From this point the ministry fanned out quickly into what it is today—with ministry teams in continental Europe and the United Kingdom as well as in North America. Through the many years of teaching a school every winter in YWAM's university, the ministry spread out through my Asian and South African students to Southeast Asia and Africa, and through the students from the Pacific countries and islands to Australia, New Zealand, and all points in between. From the extraordinarily efficient teams and translators in Germany, France, Switzerland, Holland, and the Scandinavian countries, it continues to spread to the nations once under Soviet rule. The books, long available in the European languages, are now appearing in the languages of former Soviet bloc countries. So many of their peoples are desperate for the healing power of God in their souls, their families, and their nations.

Isaiah's word, once again, heads up not only the year but the commission under which this ministry has labored to fulfill: "Pass through, pass through the gates! Prepare the way for the people. Build up, build up the highway! Remove the stones. Raise a banner for the nations. . . . See, your Savior comes!"

27

"For Such a Time as This"

Be exalted, O Lord, in your strength!
we will sing and praise your power.

Psalm 21:13

Almighty God, who inspired your servant Luke the physician to set forth in the Gospel the love and healing power of your Son: Graciously continue in your Church this love and power to heal, to the praise and glory of your Name; through Jesus Christ our Lord, who lives and reigns with you, in the unity of the Holy Spirit, one God, now and for ever. Amen.

Book of Common Prayer

In a visit to my home some years ago, a Christian biographer who was well acquainted with the work of PCM said to me quite forcefully: "You *must* write your story, for if you don't, someone else will, and they will not get it right. And when you do, you must write of what it has meant to be a *woman* in this ministry, and the special difficulties you have known because of it."

I was already aware of the need to write of this ministry, daunting though the prospect was, and not only to keep the record straight (for others were already writing and speaking about it) but once again—this time from the standpoint of my own story—to put before men and women alike the church's need to recover its thoroughly Judeo-Christian healing prayer ministry; its cure of souls.

Apart from rediscovering this biographer's strong advice to write of what it has meant to be a woman in this ministry, I would not have written this chapter. I think that is because my story has already shown it, and I have absolutely no complaints about being a woman in ministry to wounded souls, only thanksgiving and amazement over the great privilege and freedom to be fully stretched and challenged by it. In addition, I glory in who God made me to be, a woman, and need to state up front that there is not an ounce of feminism or political correctness in me.

I also need to stress how highly I value the place of man in authority and leadership; I see and grieve over our decadent culture's ongoing inability to strengthen and affirm young men in who they are created to be. There are great and noble men in my life, some of whom are active in this ministry, those wonderfully affirmed in their masculine giftings. They saw my search and knew my need for their great strengths and wisdom. There is no greater need today than for knowledgeable and noble men in authority everywhere, capable of courageously speaking the truth both in the church and in the public square. Indeed, my special difficulty has been the scarcity of men who know and rightly exercise their God-given authority in the church.

Space does not allow me to address all of the "special difficulties" I have experienced in this long line of ministry, now nearing half a century, but only the one at the top of the list—the matter of broken relationships caused by *psychological transferences*. Before writing about this phenomenon, and specifically women's heightened risk of it, I need to speak briefly of feminine gender.[1]

Woman symbolizes all that is responsive in the universe. In terms of her creation and her capacity to be the mother of life, she symbolizes all that acknowledges itself to be creaturely. In terms of loving God, she symbolizes all that is surrendered and obedient. Fr. Patrick Reardon says of Mary:

> The Church is, moreover, a house of contemplation, and perhaps we may call this the Church's preeminently Marian aspect. This does not mean that other Christians are deprived of the gift of divine contemplation, of course. It simply indicates that Mary of Nazareth became so full of God's eternal Word that He assumed flesh in her body. Her "yes" provided God's path into human existence. Consequently, when we think of the Church in terms of contemplation, we think of that Lady who "kept all these things in her heart" (Luke 2:51).[2]

Mary, with her eyes and ears open to God's will and unswervingly obedient, is the supreme symbol of the true feminine. The contemplative dimension, whether in man or woman, is vital to the ministry of healing prayer and to all of Christian life. We listen and obey, and in adoring subjection to the Ultimate Masculine, we say, "Be it unto me according to Thy will."

As always, Jesus, in prayer and submission to the Father, shows us the pathway of the holy, of wholeness and the healing of relationships. He, the Christ, is the vision of what is to be seen in every great and whole man's life, in which case that man will be in touch with the true feminine, the contemplative; he will, like Christ, reflect that wholeness in relationship to woman.

In her gender identity, the bending of the knee in worship seems to come more easily to woman. We know that her special giftings are in relating to others, and that, generally speaking, she has a heightened intuitive awareness of their needs.

To be contemplative (that is, prayerful and thoughtful) before the Lord causes these intuitive giftings of relating to others to increase, and the Lord greatly uses this receptivity in prayer for the healing of souls. This is great blessing. But there is bane within it as well, for it is in woman's special capacity for gracious and loving response to others that she is brought to the point of her most grievous sufferings: that of broken relationships.[3]

At times throughout history the Lord calls women to the fore, as can be seen in Holy Writ. Surely, as in Queen Esther's case, it is because these callings into a more public ministry involve their feminine gender giftings. I believe it was "for such a time as this"[4]—when the Western world was in full flight from the more feminine, intuitive, symbolic, feeling mind—that I was urged forward, all the while attempting to foist the ministry off onto capable men. These men were called to the ministry of healing as well, but their vocations differed from what the Lord was requiring of me.

Generally speaking, a woman, when happy to be herself and not overly influenced by today's feminism and political correctness, does not seek a cutting-edge public ministry. Rather, her gender drive with its strong desires lead her to seek a loving husband, children, and a home. Until fairly recent times, especially as a Christian, she valued the comparative "hiddenness" and needful protection that goes with such desires, knowing home and hearth to be her special sphere of greatest joy, influence, and effectiveness. This view of woman may seem to contradict all we see and

293

hear around us today, but in gender healings we see these deeply rooted yearnings unearthed.

This sense of the true feminine was never absent in me. But the Lord, in calling me to the fore, visited this public ministry upon me, and it came by obeying Him one step at a time. I've stated all of this to say that the most troublesome or grievous difficulties I've known, then, as a woman in the public eye, have come in response to being *myself*—a woman—and as best I could, bringing forth the true feminine in an age of activism and the denial of woman's special giftings.

As I wrote in the last chapter, Karl Stern's book *The Flight from Woman* sketches the history of the Western culture's retreat from the feminine and the resulting activism with its terrible effects on men. Trained to value only the more masculine, analytical, rational, scientific mind, men have more or less been forced into a full flight from the more feminine, intuitive, symbolic, feeling mind, both within themselves and within woman.

This flight, resulting in the loss of the intuitive capacity to see and respond to God as we should (paraphrasing C. S. Lewis once again: God is so masculine that we are all feminine in relation to Him), has resulted in the critical loss of the true masculine as well—indeed, in the loss of reason itself. Perhaps my mission has been to proclaim as loudly as I can that to lose the good of one mind is eventually to lose the good of the other. The masculine and the feminine combine to give us the good of reason, and to lose the feminine is to lose finally the capacity to *know* meaning at all. Women, emulating men in their ambitions and activism, are now all too often seriously cut off from their own gender identities. The overwhelming need for spiritual and psychological healing we now see in our culture—for both men and women—is related to this flight.

No man or woman effectively ministers in healing prayer apart from being in touch with the true feminine. Such a vocation from the Lord requires a contemplative relating to God and to others that is foreign today. There will be no restoration of the church's invaluable healing ministry until both men and women repent of their rationalistic activism that eschews the work of the Spirit and has lost its focus and concentration on God.

One of the things people note about the ministry of PCM (often with shocked surprise) is that the feminine isn't masked; it isn't made over in the image or imitation of men who minister out of their masculine identity with its proper giftings (much less out of an egoistic "power image" of males or females ministering out of the false masculine[5]). Women, whole in Christ and living out from who they were meant to be, are uniquely used to minister into the times that are now upon us.[6] That is because they model and minister the power *to be*—that capacity to live fully in the present moment, recognizing the transcendent, the "gift of eternity"[7] in it—that which confronts and confounds the dread rationalism and activism of our time. And when they do, men and women alike find healing, the power *to be*, and with the true masculine, the power *to do*, to act courageously on behalf of the good, the true, the beautiful, and the just. They also have the spiritual and psychological strength needed in the face of all difficulties to give thanks and to be joyful in the Lord. In the power that the Lord gives, they can initiate change and impact the surrounding culture positively— that supreme gift of the true masculine.

To illustrate the wonderful polarity and complementarity of masculine and feminine working together in healing prayer, I share an excerpt from a physician's letter. He wrote the letter as he was flying home from his second PCM:

> . . . Then came Thursday night. . . . When you began the prayer for healing of memories, I was sitting in the front row. And what a gift it was to be so close. As you invoked His Presence with us, I was conscious of an enormous power flowing over us; then, an ever greater awareness—look at the energy Leanne is using to stay perfectly focused on His will each second! People began to cry, to laugh, to crumble in pain relived and relieved. The Spirit worked as a surgical laser beam: intensity of such an *incredible* magnitude focused with a precision that melts cell by cell, memory by memory in brain and soul. The masculine creative flowing, invading, consuming—all through your praying, while balanced—and this was just indescribable for me—with your joyous laughter and encouragement of a nurturing mother.
>
> The experience of watching the Divine Masculine invade and cleanse us while the Divine Feminine sang us a lullaby just flooded over me. It was like being immersed in a tidal wave of something yet as gentle as the warmth of morning's sun. And then, "This is My heart, this is My balance, this is My tender power." Tender power—imagine!! Followed by an assurance that my healing, slow and marked by stumbling as it often seems, is being brought into fullness in the fastest way that TENDER power can bring—more speed would destroy. . . .
>
> The entire picture—your personal love gift given in obedience enabling this spectacular wave of Masculine surgery in balance with Feminine nurture, all overlaid by such tenderness—is without doubt the most powerful revelation of God I've ever seen.

He ended with this P.S. "Plane seats just don't absorb tears too well! I learned one more thing: awe places us in a receptive posture, entirely appropriate to men!"

As I said at the beginning of this chapter, chief of the special difficulties I have experienced over the years is the matter of broken relationships caused by psychological transferences. According to the *Baker Encyclopedia of Psychology*, the term "means literally to convey information or content from one person, place, or situation to another. . . . The usual pattern is for a person in the present to be experienced as though he or she were a person in the past."[8]

Priests, pastors, and lay leaders who shine as loving father figures know this phenomenon as well, and suffer through some of these worst transferences—those capable of splitting churches when not successfully resolved. If these good men are to survive the wear and tear of the healing ministry and their very giftedness in symbolizing the fatherly true masculine, they have to understand what they are dealing with and build in certain protections. For women who minister successfully in church and community situations, this protection is nearly always difficult to find. The key need is to understand the phenomenon and educate church leaders about it *before* transferences occur.[9]

As a "mother figure" who ministers into infantile woundings, I carry what we on the PCM team call a "high transference liability." I'm off the chart with it, a thing that psychiatrists and psychologists seek to draw forth, but only with the professional boundaries that protect them. (To resolve the transference completely, that protection is needed.)

Dr. Gino Vaccaro, a psychologist who for many years has been a friend extraordinaire of this ministry and is now active on the team, explains the phenomenon clearly:

> Transference is a term first coined by Sigmund Freud to describe a process by which an individual distorts a present relationship because of unresolved issues from earlier relationships. Within the context of a professional therapeutic relationship, such as psychotherapy, transference can be used to help the individual become aware of, identify, and process these unresolved issues in a safe and structured environment. The therapist and the client in a healthy therapeutic relationship have significant boundaries, including limited contact, which help to contain the client's transference to the professional relationship. The therapist has virtually no contact with the client outside the therapeutic session.
>
> Outside the safety of a highly structured therapeutic environment, transference can wreak havoc in both the client's life and upon the object of this transference. Transference often involves deeply disturbed erotic and hostile feelings toward its object. Competent therapists are trained in understanding and helping their clients make sense of these emotions and associated behaviors. Outside of therapy, however, the unsuspecting recipient of such

a transference is often unaware of what is happening and is unprepared to deal with the powerful emotions and potentially destructive behaviors that occur. While some degree of transference may seem benign, the fact that it is not based upon reality but upon unresolved early relationship issues means that it often proves to be problematic.

Transference, when properly treated in a safe, professional therapeutic relationship, can help clients identify unresolved early traumas, neglect, abuse, and loss. Then they can begin to actually name sins that may have been committed against them, confess their own sinful response to these sins, and begin the process of accepting themselves as God made them.[10]

Psychological transferences are a special hazard to all ministers but especially to those of us who minister the love and healing of God into the lives of the deeply broken, those who failed as an infant to come to a secure sense of being in their mother's love.

Dr. Frank Lake, in his extensive work, saw that the infant comes "to life as a person in the light of the mother's countenance." That "conversely, to be identified, not with a loving being, but with a mother whose painful absence shattered all confidence, was to be identified with nonbeing."[11] The most critical emotional illnesses are related to this loss, one that can be described as a failure to achieve this most basic of developmental steps. They are exactly as Dr. Frank Lake names them (as I've listed before): schizoid, hysterical, dissociative, homosexual, and paranoid. These reaction patterns are, as he states, defenses against the pain and fear of nonbeing.

In ministering into early infantile woundings, we continually see the truth of this. These dear ones, who are always dealing with intense separation anxiety, show up in great numbers in our healing conferences. Thus our "Sense of Being" prayer is one of the most basic and important ones in the cure of souls.[12] Truly God alone can speak *being* into a soul that failed to come to an adequate sense of being.

I've become the object of a transference in five especially difficult instances. These did not occur in conference settings, but where there was prayer ministry with those who had close access to me. Each was suffering an extraordinarily deep infantile wounding and repressed but intense, even murderous, rage toward his or her mother. When this finally abreacted (surfaced), I, not the mother, became the target of the rage. Related to these transferences has been some of the most excruciating spiritual warfare we on the team have known. A transference threatens the unity of the body of Christ when the opportunity to resolve it is not given—that is, where there is no acknowledgment of what is really going on and no repentance, only hatred, spite, and slander.

On comparatively rare occasions, to experience a transference that isn't resolved in further healing, though heartbreaking and full of havoc, is a small price to pay for the literally thousands we see healed. These are the neediest ones who fill our conferences. It is an ominous sign of our times that for the past decade, fully two-thirds of those who come to PCMs will have come specifically to receive a sense of being. Many are only too aware of their identification with and fear of nonbeing. Thus to see this healing that only the Lord can bring about is joy enough to cover any price we pay. As Dr. Frank Lake writes, "We must not despise the inescapable human spiritual fact of 'transference.' It arises wherever human need meets human kindliness."[13]

For men and women alike, a vital Christian ministry is from day one impossible to do. God alone accomplishes it as we collaborate with Him. Our work is to believe in Christ (see John 6:28–29). We, as it were, do all we know to do, stand back, and watch Him work. And with each task that God assigns us, as we listen and obey with all our might (that is, as we collaborate with Him), it is even as Hudson Taylor, the evangelical missionary of the China Inland Mission, described years ago:

> First it is impossible,
> Then it is difficult,
> Then it is done![14]

This saying is written in huge print and attached to the wall before me even as I write. In twelve words Hudson Taylor points to that which makes the Christian calling so incredibly exciting. We are wholly dependent upon His empowering presence with us, and only if it's humanly impossible are we called—given a vocation—to do it.

Too, for men and women alike, as Oswald Chambers points out: "Our Lord calls to no special work: He calls to Himself. 'Pray ye the Lord of the harvest', and He will engineer circumstances and thrust you out.... Prayer does not fit us for the greater works; prayer is the greater work."[15] This I believe to be true. Once we respond, listening to Him with all our might, the Lord uses us in the unique ways for which He created, fashioned, and fitted us for service—whether as a man or as a woman.

28

Jubilation!

If God's will is to be done on earth as it is in heaven, prayer begins with adoration.

P. T. Forsyth

Te Deum Laudamus

You are God; we praise you;
You are the Lord; we acclaim you;
You are the eternal Father:
All creation worships you.
To you all angels, all the powers of heaven,
Cherubim and Seraphim, sing in endless praise;

> Holy, holy, holy Lord, God of power and might,
> heaven and earth are full of your glory.

The glorious company of apostles praise you.
The noble fellowship of prophets praise you.
The white-robed army of martyrs praise you.
Throughout the world the holy Church acclaims you;

> Father, of majesty unbounded,
> your true and only Son, worthy of all worship,
> and the Holy Spirit, advocate and guide.

You Christ, are the king of glory,
the eternal Son of the Father.
When you became man to set us free
you did not shun the Virgin's womb.
You overcame the sting of death
And opened the kingdom of heaven to all believers.
You are seated at God's right hand in glory.
We believe that you will come and be our judge.

Come then, Lord, and help your people,
bought with the price of your own blood,
and bring us with your saints
to glory everlasting.

Praise the Lord, all the earth; serve the Lord with gladness; enter into His presence with jubilation, for the Lord Himself is God.

Psalm 100; Vulgate 99

Oh sing to the LORD a new song; sing to the LORD, all the earth!

Psalm 96:1

I close this memoir in my home in Wheaton, Illinois, where the work of PCM has flourished since 1989. It has been no small thing for me to look back over a long life and relive it, seeing more clearly than ever the panoramic, overarching faithfulness of a loving, merciful God.

From day one of the ministry we have rejoiced in great victories while experiencing the inevitable spiritual warfare that attends them. I have known spiritual battle before every conference and during the writing of every book, article, and newsletter. Truly, as Fr. Patrick Reardon comments when speaking of Psalm 5:7: "When the Christian rises, it is always on the battlefield."[1] Always, always, however, *jubilation*—the new song of praise, thanksgiving, and adoration that God gives to the faithful—has soon followed, or perhaps comes even in the very midst of the battle.

After a large PCM conference in 2003, the state of weariness I was in, complicated by the aging process, seemed to be as a cloud over my head, utterly closing in on me. Would I live long enough to finish even the work on my desk? How would I ever find the breathing space needed to sort out all the papers that are yet to be turned over to Wheaton College at my death?[2] Or destroy all the letters containing "confessional" material but also, alas, wonderful testimonies of healing? At times like these, I always cry out to the Lord for a new song, and if ever there was the need to do so, it was then. I was too exhausted to squeak, even to sing aloud a beloved hymn.[3] With all the voice I had left, I cried out to God for a new song and the strength to sing it; in other words, for the power to *jubilate*: to proclaim and praise Him loudly.

> Hark! the loud celestial hymn,
> Angel choirs above are raising:
> Cherubim and Seraphim,
> In unceasing chorus praising,
> Fill the heavens with sweet accord,
> Holy! holy! holy Lord![4]

Lines from Michelangelo's prayer voice in poetic form what I was crying out to God:

> The fetters of my tongue do Thou unbind,
> That I may have the power to sing of thee,
> And sound thy praises everlastingly.[5]

What I needed was a full rest, and so this prayer, the answer delayed, was yet with me as I boarded a plane bound for Scotland and a quiet convalescence with dear friends and fellow team members, Sandy and Gwen Purdie. Their home was situated in the Scottish Borders, the rolling highlands where neighbors are few and far between but four-legged creatures dot every hill and mountain for miles on end. I stayed there for a month, just breathing in the pure air and the goodness of blessed company and all the creatures of earth and sky.

During the second week, my friends having journeyed to the nearest city for supplies, I walked up into the higher hills, praying with the unique sense of solitariness that can only come in such panoramic views and surroundings as the Scottish shepherds know. It was there, with no other souls about, that the new song came, together with the full strength to sing it. Soon it echoed throughout the hills, and I seemed to have the volume of an opera diva—something certainly not with me in the natural—as I walked along, singing my praises and thanksgivings in the Spirit and with the understanding (1 Cor. 14:15).

So lost was I in looking up to the heavens and the wonder of it all that I didn't see the large herd of cattle until I was almost upon them. Perhaps this was also because the entire herd, as an entity, were standing stock-still, not a single one grazing but all looking straight up at me, sheer *awe* upon their bovine faces. Reverent as any congregation, they stood there motion-less as I continued to sing, coming to a halt in front of the low *stanedyke* (stone fence) that was between us.

This jubilation went on for a long time. Finally, still singing but lowering the volume, I turned to go, and to my dismay the whole herd, as one, fol-lowed me. I'm sure my new song changed into pleas for help, for I had no knowledge till afterward that cows don't jump. After all, in the old nursery tale "the cow jumped over the moon." I became terrified lest several hundred cows jump the low *stanedyke* once we came to the end of their pasture, one that bordered on Gwen and Sandy's garden. It is simply no small thing for a city girl to have *one* cow follow her, much less a huge herd of them. What if they followed me into the Purdies' yard? And house? To my intense relief, however, they dutifully stopped where their pasture met our garden fence and watched, awe still on their faces, as I walked into the Purdies' garden.

The story doesn't end there, for the cows did not forget. The next morn-ing, and every morning thereafter, they came to visit. As they stood look-ing over the garden fence, I sang to them. Talk about a new song and the congregation to sing it to! After I left, the Purdies had to take up where I left off. In the words of the famous hymn:

> All thy works [all creation!], O Lord, shall bless thee;
> Thee shall all thy saints adore:
> King supreme shall they confess thee,
> And proclaim thy sovereign power.[6]

Jubilation is the term Christians cherished up through the seventeenth century for the song (not restricted to intelligible words) that God not only gives the faithful but receives back, extraordinarily blessed by the Spirit, as prayer. To jubilate is to sing in the Spirit and with the understanding, with a supernatural gift of music received while singing our praises, or sometimes chanting simply, such as repeating the holy name of Jesus.

St. Augustine, St. Bernard of Clairvaux, St. John Chrysostom, St. Je-rome, Pope St. Gregory the Great, St. Thomas Aquinas, St. Bonaventure, St. Francis of Assisi, Jan Ruysbroek, John of the Cross, and Teresa of Avila: these form merely a short list of those who not only wrote about jubilation but experienced it in their lives, both privately and publicly. The list also includes most of the leading theologians, philosophers, devotional writers, and Christian mystics down through the history of the church, until the misnamed Age of Reason took its toll on belief in anything other than the material world.[7]

As we jubilate, the animals respond and all the good earth is blessed by it. The ancients in Christendom knew this, and sang to the oxen pulling their plows and as they sowed the precious seed in the furrows. There are wonderful glimpses of this in medieval writers, and in more modern-day novelists, such as Elizabeth Goudge, who note their unique songs.

Only a few days ago, while meditating on how to write of jubilation as it occurs in our PCM schools, I walked down through a prairie marsh close to where I live, a wonderful haven for migrating birds. And the following happening inspired me to tell the story of the Scottish cows.

This time it was a young deer I came upon. The animal was large and I only knew it for a yearling by its stripe. Deer always bolt the moment they scent, hear, or spot a person. In my quietness, however, the deer was not warned of my passing, and so I simply stood and gazed at it, so stunningly beautiful in that early morning light, the sun just up. Quietly, I began jubilating, praising God for such a creature. Just like those wonderful cows—how I love them now, having such a relationship with a certain herd of bovines—it looked up from its grazing and stood stock-still, simply gazing at me and listening. Believe me, if one has never had this experience, he or she has no idea of the almost human regalness an animal can possess—its face and eyes were simply aglow with a knowing or recognition that one does not ordinarily see, except in a cherished, highly intelligent pet.

Again, as with the cows, I continued singing, and the yearling would have stayed on for the day! When I moved on, still it did not bolt but only its head moved as it turned and watched as long as I was in sight. It's amazing, the reaction of all creation to God's presence in song, in prayer, in however the Spirit shines through human souls, those given dominion over God's creation. Perhaps the beasts too receive healing, maybe even a glimpse of what it will mean when the lion lies down with the lamb and all are safe from fear and alarm (see Rom. 8:18–25).

I mention healing here, for as it has been noted down through the centuries, Christian healing and jubilation go together. As the new song came forth in Scotland, I received physical strength and healing as well as great encouragement to continue on (even at my age!) in ministry. Jubilation often follows experiences of the mass healings[8] we see in this ministry. Since there are never attempts to make the new song happen, it comes always as a blessed and utterly unique surprise, bringing always more healing in its wings. I have learned to call all the *spirituals* "the healing gifts" of the Spirit, for all come forward so beautifully in times of jubilation and interact in the healing of souls and bodies.

I am greatly indebted to Eddie Ensley and his research on the writings of the church fathers and saints as he documented this vital history of the church. The following quotations from Ensley's book define this new song in the Spirit:

> Almost all the major Fathers speak about jubilation. . . . St. Augustine of Hippo, whose thought was the major influence on Western thought for nearly a thousand years after his death, mentions jubilation a number of times. . . . He says: "What is jubilation? Joy that cannot be expressed in words; yet the voice expresses what is conceived within and cannot be explained verbally; this is jubilation."[9]
>
> [For Cassiodorus (490–583)] jubilation was an overwhelming joy. He says: "The jubilation is called an exultation of the heart, which, because it is such an infinite joy, cannot be explained in words." Again, "Jubilation is said to be an excessive joy, but not the sort that can be explained in words."[10]
>
> Though it is unfortunate that theologians have not studied this aspect of patristic devotion, we are lucky to have the work of a number of medieval music historians on jubilation. These music historians have studied it intensely in their study of the roots of Western music. One of the best definitions of musical jubilation was given by music historian Albert Seay. For him it was "an overpowering expression of the ecstasy of the spirit, a joy that could not be restricted to words. . . . *It occupied a peculiar place in the liturgy, for it carried implications of catharsis, a cleansing of the soul.*"[11]

When jubilation such as this occurs in our healing conferences, the classical musicians who attend and hear it for the first time are astonished at the musical perfection and intricacies of what they've just heard. They marvel that it has issued out of a worshiping, spontaneous choir of hundreds of people, most of whom have never endured a choir practice. One musician, Robert Faub, described this experience from the 2005 Wheaton conference both expressively and analytically:

> Musical lines spinning together, like tendrils, spiraling.
> First two, then several, then many—
> > Voices raised in a pentatonic masterpiece,
> > like the sound of David's harp, only multiplied, amplified,
> > Deified.
> Conducted by the unseen Real, both Composer and Maestro.
> Creator allowing creature to collaborate in a new creation. . . .
>
> We sing a new song, with spirits rising, building,
>
> Reaching a gentle peak, volume and activity arching towards their
> > height, suspended.

304

A sweet refrain, sustained, floating.
Slowly ebbing now, flowing down the other side
    of a tonal rainbow;
Now lighter, ever softer.
Song of the past, song of the future.
Timeless—always was; always Is.
(Just a glimpse.)
Sounds trail off,
Leaving only a trace of the eternal.
But, oh! What a trace!
Christ Incarnate.
Spirit of Life.
Eternal Father.
Just a breath.
Song of the Spirit.

What happened in that moment was true worship. As the body of Christ, we worshiped the Lamb in Spirit and Truth, responding to Christ in us, unhindered by the trappings of "doing church" and freed by healings in the deepest parts of our souls. It was as if we had joined in the ongoing song of the saints, worshiping at the throne of grace, just for a moment glimpsing their heavenly worship.

The melodic material was mainly the pentatonic scale, a set of pitches that flows naturally from the people of all cultures and forms the basis of most of the world's folk music. This scale (which can be played by using just the black keys on a piano) arises from the common spoken patterns of language and is used for thousands of familiar tunes, including songs like "Amazing Grace" and "Old Man River" and the vast majority of African-American spirituals. . . . Interestingly, it is believed that David's harp was tuned to a pentatonic scale. . . .

Ultimately, words are inadequate in expressing things of the Spirit. . . . In the moment of that song, there was no analyzing; there was only the experience, the "being" of those few minutes, resting in what one can only see in retrospect as the mighty presence of God. There was peace and unity and a sense of rightness: "This is what I was created to be, and what I was created to do. I have longed for this my whole life, without even knowing it." Where words fail, the inexpressible and the unknowable was expressed through a song—a beautiful, spontaneous song.

When the Holy Spirit gives us such a song, I've seen people overwhelmed and crying out to those around them, "What was that?" Their amazement is all the greater according to how well they know the early chants and roots of Western worship music and liturgies. The beauty of it, the thankfulness, the worshipful adoration, the praise that comes of it (sometimes

305

antiphonal), simply cannot occur apart from miracle—from the Holy Spirit.

Though it seems there are no historical citings of it, I mightily wonder if J. S. Bach jubilated—such a depth of joy and worship comes through his genius and his music. There is everything about its uniqueness that makes me think it could only erupt from the labor of one who daily jubilates. Surely too Martin Luther jubilated, for he was one who prayed so effectually over the sick and understood the Spirit's charisms. As he says in his great hymn:

> The Spirit and the gifts are ours
> Through Him who with us sideth. . . .
> God's truth abideth still,
> His Kingdom is forever.[12]

The privilege of receiving glimpses of the heavenly Kingdom, if only dimly and in moments all too brief, come to us as we live in communion with the Holy One.[13] In our experience, these holy happenings occur most especially as God's holy people[14] gather in His name to worship and adore Him as the King of Kings and Lord of Lords, and, as in every PCM, we invite into our midst those who are searching for Christ or who need spiritual and psychological healing. These glimpses from time to time include seeing angelic beings, hearing angelic choirs and song, or even catching sight of loved ones who have long been with the Lord. These may be preceded by a supernatural quiet, one that comes as a holy awe over the people, after or during which the new song of joy may be softly expressed. And again, the church up to the seventeenth century experienced these things and our fathers in the faith wrote of them; they wrote also of the renewed or utterly changed hearts and healings that come with the joy, with the new song.

Now why am I telling of these things at this juncture? It is certainly not to put forward any particular gift of the Holy Spirit (again, *all* of them operate together), or, God forbid, to tempt anyone into an experience orientation. Rather it is because of our intense need, as moderns, to learn again how to worship. Nothing of lasting moment occurs apart from our being a praying people, a people who continually invoke the presence of the Holy. There is no jubilation apart from the Holy One. In the words of Fr. Alexander Schmemann,

> "Holy" is the real name of God, of the God "not of scholars and philosophers," but of the living God of faith. The knowledge about God results

in definitions and distinctions. The knowledge of God leads to this one, incomprehensible, yet obvious and inescapable word: holy. And in this word we express both that God is the Absolutely Other, the One about whom we know nothing, and that He is the end of all our hunger, all our desires, the inaccessible One who mobilizes our wills, the mysterious treasure that attracts us, and there is really nothing to know but Him. "Holy" is the word, the song, the "reaction" of the Church as it enters into heaven, as it stands before the heavenly glory of God.[15]

The more we know of the Holy One, and the longer we have walked in His presence, the more we realize how inadequate our adoration and worship of Him are. We know that we can only persevere and look forward to that time when we stand "before the heavenly glory of God," when our earthly limitations and imperfections are lifted from us. Then, with all the saints and angels, we will be freed to worship Him as we can only yearn to do now. In the meantime, however, the Holy Spirit most wonderfully assists and empowers us, and there are times even now in worship when we are given a minute foretaste or foreseeing or "forehearing" of what will be when we enter into glory.

All of this is far too vast and high and deep—far too great—for me to try to touch on, but I can't seem to close this book without speaking to the matter of our worship, both as individual Christians and as living stones in the body of Christ, the church. Modern Christians have lost, along with the memory of profound worship, the underpinnings, the very how-tos, of entering into it. We are bereft, for worship of the Holy One is all important in the healing of persons, communities, and nations.

For us as individuals, one of the greatest means to worship is practicing the presence of the Holy One. As the body of Christ meeting together, the corporate practice of the presence begins with the invocation of the Holy Spirit, for in this way Jesus is seen "huge" in our midst and the Father is glorified. We begin every PCM school with the powerful invocation, "Come, Holy Spirit, come," and then the priest or pastor carries in the cross in procession, whereby Christ crucified is lifted high. By then the people are fully prepared to continue with lectures and exercises on the practice of the presence of God with us and within us. We teach the "within us" part as incarnational reality. Thus we lay the foundations for the entire school.

These lessons and healing prayers alone, when received and put into practice, utterly change lives. As none can practice God's holy presence with unrepented sin at the top of their consciences or with long-standing inabilities to receive forgiveness, we invite people to come forward for confession of sins. And our prayer ministers receive them as they surge forward. Then the healings, even the new births replete with deliverances, break forth, and it is only the first day!

These lectures are preceded by the greatest classical worship hymns we can find, those that aid us not only in focusing on the Lord but in dying to the old man and its overweening modern obsession with the self.

But even before the school starts, we prepare to receive attendees "in the presence." No matter whether we are meeting in a church, university, seminary, or auditorium, our priests, pastors, and prayer ministers go throughout the space, cleansing it with holy water[16] and hallowing it, praying yet again for all who will attend. At times our prayer ministers are led to pray even over every seat in the house, blessing and praying for the cleansing healings the ones who will sit there need.

Because of our prayerful focus on bringing all into the holy and into true communion with God, people are taken aback by the presence of God, even on arrival. One well-known evangelical leader, harried about many things and attempting to arrive at a PCM on time, wrote to us:

> I found the church at last, ran into the building and opened the door of the sanctuary. In all my fluster and rush I couldn't have imagined what awaited me on the other side of that door. I walked in and felt . . . nearly bowled over by the peace and the presence of the Lord. I couldn't get over the contrast! On one side of the door I was flustered and exhausted by the cares of the world. On the other side of the door my anxieties vanished because I had walked into the Presence of the Holy! It was unforgettable.

A psychologist who has founded a number of clinics where Christian psychologists and therapists work comes regularly to PCMs, and he sends both his colleagues and clients to the schools. Some of his clients, being very needy, have been so hit by the sense of the holy even as they are in the registration lines that they have fled! They are unable or unready as yet to go into the sanctuary. Nothing blesses me more than reports like these—not that some have had to flee, but that they now know there is the Holy One. He *is*. And later, when the pain gets even worse, they will know to whom to turn.

I have been asked by church leaders why it is that we see healings, especially those involving sexual compulsions and perversions, and they do not. I believe we see such a super-abundance of healing in our PCM schools, not only because of our openness to the power of the Spirit in our midst, but because we are not satisfied with the level of worship or the incompleteness of liturgy that marks almost all Bible-believing, orthodox churches today, whether formal or informal.

Healing occurs in PCMs because the week itself is one long filled-out liturgy, such as that which used to happen in preparation for and through ancient water baptism, including deliverances, healings, and teachings pertaining to it.[17] For the first time, folk understand what baptism is, and some who have not been baptized before request that they may be. Our pastors and priests grant that request. Those who request baptism are fully prepared to enter into the waters and die fully to the old man and rise in the new. They know they reenact this dying and rising with Christ every time they receive Communion. There they take their place in Christ's death and resurrection once again. In this way the practice of baptism itself is taught, experienced, and lived out.

All I've described in the above is predicated on and emerges out of an orthodox view and experience of the Holy Spirit, one that is in large part compromised or missing in the church today. No one makes this point better than Fr. Schmemann:

> Theology defines the Holy Spirit as the Third Person of the Trinity; in the creed we confess Him as proceeding from the Father; from the Gospel we learn that He is sent by Christ to be the Comforter, to "guide us into all truth" (John 16:13) and to unite us with Christ and the Father. We begin each liturgical service with a prayer to the Holy Spirit, invoking Him as "the Heavenly King, the Comforter, the Spirit of truth, Who is everywhere and fills all things, the Treasury of Blessings and the Giver of life."
>
> . . . Truly the Holy Spirit is at the very heart of Divine Revelation and of Christian life. Yet in speaking of Him, it is extremely difficult to find proper words—so difficult indeed that for many Christians the church's teaching about Him as *person* has lost all concrete, existential significance, and they see Him as divine power, not as *He* or *Thou*, but rather as a divine *It*. Even theology, while maintaining of course the classical doctrine of the Three Divine Persons when speaking of God, prefers—when dealing with the church and Christian life—to speak of *grace*, and not of a *personal* knowledge and experience of the Holy Spirit.[18]

This lack of understanding of the Holy Spirit and His work in our midst has long been a grief and an amazement to me; it has weakened even our awe and understanding of God's abounding grace. We can't make grace stand for the Holy Spirit without in great part losing understanding of both. The Holy Spirit is not just a divine Force, an "It," and we are not to behave as though He were almost the member of the Holy Trinity we are not to talk about or adore.

Although many leaders who wonder about their failure to see healing largely agree with the orthodox view of the Holy Spirit, yet they are conditioned by our modern age or even through their theological training to be in reaction to the *spirituals* (thinking that the charismatic gifts are not for today) and to mystery and therefore Sacrament (for some, as being too Roman Catholic). At present many of these dear ones are awaking to their deficits in worship and, indeed, in prayer. Surely once that hunger is set in, acknowledgment of God's empowering presence will once again be fully part of their spiritual lives.

Healings have to do with faith-filled adoration and reverence for God the Father, Son, and Holy Spirit. A vital worship brings the holy and thereby the power of the Holy Spirit into our midst. It also often brings us to our knees. The ancients knew and practiced this prerequisite to vital worship. Most Christians today, however, attend churches where there is no invitation to repent and where there are no kneelers or even the opportunity to kneel around an old-fashioned altar. There are instead lots of opportunities to visit with neighbors and relate horizontally. The sacramental churches where people can kneel and experience a full liturgy still exist, but all too often these churches are coldly formalistic or immersed in unbelief. There faith and obedience in the presence of a holy God is but a dim memory.

Church should be a space reserved for prayer and worship, where people arrive seeking only to look up and meet Christ in Word and Sacrament, and thereby be cleansed, made new again, and prepared for truly meaningful horizontal relationships once the worship service ends. In such a place, the sense of the holy becomes palpable.

This is what happens in the PCMs even though we often do not have kneelers. However, we do have large crosses before which the faithful can come up and kneel. We ask the folk to get alone with God and thereby sit apart from their spouses, family, and friends. Even when the groups are very large (800–1000), many letters come saying, "It was as if I were the only one there, and God gave me individual attention!"

Many folk come to PCMs repeatedly (even from overseas) because they cannot find such worship in their home churches. Created in the image of God, we arrive in this world with an inborn hunger for the transcendent, even for heaven. Something in us is born *knowing*. We yearn for beauty—transcendence in the midst of the dread darkness in our culture.

In such a time as this, when the Western world finds itself in the horrors of a spiritual and moral freefall, many come out of this culture to our conferences trapped in the ugliest of sinful compulsions, having forgotten this inborn holy craving. And it is in the presence of the Holy One, the very coming into space made sacred by true worship, that these dread bonds begin to break and fall away from them. The true self that yearns for the good, the beautiful, the true, and the noble then begins its heroic journey up and out of the false self, with its layers and layers of sordid and perverted behavior, and breaks through into God's light with His pathway in sight.

As I close my story, the subtitle of which is "A Memoir of One Soul's Steep Ascent," we are celebrating Christ's Ascension into glory, a time when—if we are especially blessed and incredibly fortunate—we will hear some of the greatest of the ancient organ and choral anthems and sing with them the awesome hymns.[19] I come near to ascending myself, just hearing the great choral arrangements of, for example, "God has ascended in Jubilation" (taken from Psalm 47), or "He is the Great King over all the earth," or the arrangement of "The Head of Christ that once was crowned with thorns/Is crowned in glory now" by Jeremiah Clark (1709).

I think it is quite wonderful that I am hearing this music just as I'm ending this memoir about my own personal steep ascent, one that would never have occurred had I not learned to hear God's call, and listening, step-by-step in obedience, undertake. And I am reminded of how, in all things, we imitate Him. Christ shows the way; He goes before us, and we follow in His tread. The marvel, even now in our worship, is that "we join our voices in jubilation with the angels on high."[20]

Acknowledgments

Writing my life story has spanned more than a decade, and as I come to the end of the writing, I am conscious of the many who have strongly encouraged and prayed for me in this venture. As I start to write them out—my prayer partners though the years and at present, the PCM team, and all those stalwart souls who have stood with me from the beginning—I realize the list is far too long to put to paper. To each and every one of you, know that I am humbled by your love and help, and deeply grateful to all of you.

Across the Atlantic in London, Amy Boucher Pye has acted as my editor. She is, believe me, a most stimulating young woman, and had she not gotten in behind me with the strongest encouragement and skillful propelling, I am not at all sure this book would ever have been completed. I am deeply grateful to her, and also to the expert assistance and help of Lila Bishop. Both these women are not only skillful editors, but are intercessors, and their prayer support has meant far more than they know.

I would like as well to mention all those, in America as well as overseas, who are so gifted and tirelessly dedicated in passing this ministry of healing prayer on to the nations, but here again the list is simply too long. I will, however, mention three extraordinary ones who not only comprise the PCM Board but are chief among my advisers and confidants: Jean Holt and the Reverends Conlee Bodishbaugh and Norman Arnold. Once this memoir is completed, I hope to be stepping up my intercessions for you and the harvest fields the Lord has so wonderfully entrusted to you, who now number so many. I thank my God for you, each and every one.

Notes

Preface

1. William Barclay, *The Letter to the He-brews*, rev. ed. (Philadelphia: Westminster Press, 1976), 28, commentary on Hebrews 3:1.

Chapter 1 Hard Times

1. Mary Nancy Williamson (née Townsend).

Chapter 2 God, Our Source and Being

1. Jewish Christians, in their translations, seem freer to more literally express this matter; for example, Hebrews 2:11 from the *Jewish New Testament*, translated by David H. Stern (Clarksville, MD: JNT Publications, 1991): "For both Jesus, who sets people apart for God and the ones being set apart, have a *common origin*—this is why He is not ashamed to call them brothers" (italics mine).

2. By this I do not mean our bodies. In the Judeo-Christian understanding, we do not hate the body but revere and care for it. We celebrate all creation as good, and this is antithetical to the gnostic understanding that spawns doctrines that celebrate *spirit* or the immaterial as only good (there are evil spirits) and the material world as only evil (this is to hate and despise *matter*, all that God has created and called good).

3. William Wordsworth, "Ode: Intimations of Immortality from Recollections of Early Childhood," in *Norton Anthology of English Literature*, vol. 2, rev. ed. (New York: W. W. Norton, 1962), 15.

4. The discovery of Josef Pieper's writings have for me been one of those rare kind of blessings that instantly rejoice the mind and heart and keep on doing so. For at least thirty years I searched for a Christian philosopher who, like C. S. Lewis, truly and in depth understood the great minds (pagan and Christian), and who at the same time understood *incarnational reality*, the infusion of God's Holy Spirit into our lives, and then, as a philosopher, majored on the virtues and vices, the very motions of the human heart.

5. Josef Pieper, *"Divine Madness": Plato's Case against Secular Humanism* (San Francisco: Ignatius Press, 1989), 42.

6. A. W. Tozer, *The Knowledge of the Holy* (New York: Harper and Row, 1961), 17.

7. Josef Pieper, *On Hope* (San Francisco: Ignatius, 1986), 14.

8. Leanne Payne, *Listening Prayer* (Grand Rapids: Baker, 1994), 84.

9. P. T. Forsyth, *The Soul of Prayer* (London: Independent Press, 1916, 1960), 20.

Chapter 3 My All-Time Heroine, Mother

1. C. S. Lewis, *Surprised by Joy: The Shape of My Early Life* (New York: Harcourt, Brace and World, 1955), 21.

2. Forsyth, *The Soul of Prayer*, 19.

3. For the Word of God as creative power, see for starters, Psalms 33:6; 107:20; Isaiah 55:11. Please note how what is written here about the spoken word in teaching and in ordinary communication differs from certain practices and teachings prevalent today that have an unbalanced and/or outright erroneous stress on *speaking* out *in prayer* a word that "names and claims" what one might be asking or demanding of God. This extreme "Faith Formula Theology," derived from E. W. Kenyon, misses the all-important fact that, as Charles Spurgeon writes, "Words are not the essence but the garments of prayer." Here the emphasis is in the right place, on the *spirit* of prayer in contrast to any and all ways in which it is uttered.

4. I'm sorry that I've lost the reference to this; I believe it was a quote cited by F. B. Meyer.

5. Forsyth, *Soul of Prayer*, 11–12.

Chapter 4 A Home Brings Us Together Again

1. If I had not grown up in my particular situation, I would never have written *Crisis in Masculinity* (Grand Rapids: Baker, 1985, 1995), and possibly not *The Broken Image* (Grand Rapids: Baker, 1981, 1996) either. Our God turns the negatives in our lives to something fruitful and good for us and others when we allow Him to do so.

2. Some of these paragraphs have been adapted from *Crisis in Masculinity,* chapter 5.

Chapter 5 Grandma

The epigraph to this chapter is taken from F. B. Meyer, *Paul: A Servant of Jesus Christ* (New York: Revell, 1897), 12.

1. Viktor Frankl, *Man's Search for Meaning* (New York: Washington Square Press, 1959, 1962, 1984). Frankl's insight here comes to us with the greatest possible force, for he came to this insight and lived it out in the midst of the worst life could deal out. He was interned in a Nazi prison camp and lost all of his family there.

2. Catherine Marshall, *Meeting God at Every Turn* (Grand Rapids: Chosen, 1980), 18.

3. I first wrote about these things in the appendix of *The Broken Image*, titled "Listening to Our Dreams."

Chapter 6 The Influence of My Extended Family

The epigraph to this chapter is taken from F. B. Meyer, *Our Daily Walk* (Grand Rapids: Zondervan, 1951), 91.

1. Gradually, even those were lost to new buildings, but the remarkable house stood until about twenty years ago.

2. I am grateful for this memory and that I had such a clear picture on which to hang certain emotions and feelings of loss in regard to my father.

3. A cousin of my father, Cletis R. Ellinghouse, has written a history of the Mabrey family from early America down through the Revolutionary War. Titled *America: The Mabr(e)y Experience*, the book is interesting as a historical account, revealing especially how these families influenced education and law in early Missouri. Their Christian lives and missions reflect courage and vitality.

4. Besides Mr. Ellinghouse's history showing the effects of the resistance, Revolution, and Civil War on the Mabrey family in America, another of my father's cousins, Rose Fulton Cramer, wrote a history of Wayne County, Missouri, and it has a substantial amount of historical data on the family.

Chapter 7 The Fateful Move

The epigraph to this chapter is taken from William Barclay, *The Gospel of Matthew*, vol. 1 (Philadelphia: Westminster Press, 1975), 201.

1. Lewis, *Surprised by Joy*, 51. Of the many things I've treasured about Lewis's writings, one that has meant much to me personally has been his understanding of the teen years. His description of those years in his spiritual autobiography, *Surprised by Joy*, are the closest to mine I've ever seen in print, as well as to a multitude of other souls I've since taught and ministered to.

2. I've written about this at some length in *The Healing Presence* (Grand Rapids: Baker, 1989, 1995), chapter 12; and in my other books as well.

3. Had I been in a church with regular Eucharistic liturgy where I had access to the real presence through the Sacraments, this would have been taken care of.

4. From a letter written on May 15, 1952, in W. H. Lewis, ed., *Letters of C. S. Lewis* (New York: Harcourt, Brace and World, 1966), 241.

5. Lewis, *Surprised by Joy*, 71.

6. This condition is common to adolescence, but if one is affirmed, the tendency would be corrected and left behind as puberty ends.

7. These attempts can lead to what I call the Disease of Introspection, a pathological looking inward that amounts to a practice of the presence of the "old man," the old self in isolation from God and all else that is objectively real. For more on this, see *The Healing Presence*, chapter 12.

8. Openness of communication with the young was not deemed important during days when everyone, the young included, bent every effort toward just getting food on the table.

9. Later, of course, I found sociologists and psychologists worthy of the name, but their teachings and influence were not to be found in the public school texts.

10. C. S. Lewis, "Is English Doomed?" in *Present Concerns: A Compelling Collection of Timely, Journalistic Essays* (Orlando: Harcourt, 1944, 1986), 27–31.

11. C. S. Lewis, *An Experiment in Criticism* (Cambridge: Cambridge University Press, 1961, 1969), 140, 141.

Chapter 8 The Remedial Path

1. Psalm 25:7, translation by Fr. Patrick Henry Reardon in *Christ in the Psalms* (Ben Lomond, CA: Conciliar Press, 2000), 49.

2. The immune difficulties I've had in later life began with that carbon monoxide poisoning of my environment. Encountering industrial pollutants has meant the symptoms mentioned as well as disorientation, an inability to think clearly, hearing loss, and a lack of physical balance.

3. Oswald Chambers, *My Utmost for His Highest* (New York: Dodd, Mead, 1959), August 2.

4. "The scale of marital breakdown in the West since 1960 has no historical precedent and seems unique. There has been nothing like it for the past 2,000 years, and probably much longer" (Lawrence Stone, historian, as quoted by William J. Bennett, *Wall Street Journal*, May 19, 2000).

5. I write at length about this in *The Healing Presence* on pages 101–3 and in *Restoring the Christian Soul through Healing Prayer* (Grand Rapids: Baker, 1991, 1997), 84–85, and I refer to it again in chapter 11.

6. See Leanne Payne, *Real Presence* (Grand Rapids: Baker, 1988, 1995), foreword by John R. Sheets, S.J., and chapters 10 and 11.

7. It should be no cause for wonder that eventually I wrote *Listening Prayer*, and have never taught or written anything that didn't feature the act of listening and receiving from God His commands and guidance as being true obedience.

8. Charles Wesley, "And Can It Be That I Should Gain?"

Part 2

The John Donne epigraph to part 2 is taken from a sermon by John Donne, Dean of St. Paul's Cathedral, cited in Elizabeth Goudge, *White Witch* (New York: Best Sellers Book Club, 1958), 292–93.

Chapter 9 Home to the Father

The epigraph to this chapter is taken from C. S. Lewis, *The Pilgrim's Regress* (1933; reprint, Grand Rapids: Eerdmans, 1994), 166.

1. See Luke 16:16 KJV: "The law and the prophets were until John: since that time the kingdom of God is preached, and every man presseth into it." The NIV says, "everyone forces his way into it." See also Matthew 11:12 KJV: "the violent take it by force."

2. St. Augustine, *Confessions*, as quoted by Elizabeth Powers in "The Self in Full," *First Things*, November 1999.

3. Ibid.

4. See Josef Pieper's classic on this matter, *Happiness and Contemplation* (South Bend, IN: St. Augustine Press, 1998).

5. George MacDonald, *The Princess and Curdie*, (Harmondsworth, England: Penguin Books, 1882, 1966), 66.

6. From C. S. Lewis, *Transposition and Other Addresses*, which was first published in the United States as *The Weight of Glory*. See C. S. Lewis, *The Weight of Glory* (Grand Rapids: Eerdmans, 1949).

7. Chambers, *My Utmost for His Highest*, October 10.

8. I would not have known at that time to call this a "practice of the presence." That descriptive phrase came later on finding Brother Lawrence's wonderful testimony, *Practicing His Presence* (Portland, ME: Christian Books, 1973).

9. For more on this important action of "putting on Christ," see *Listening Prayer*, 46–52. Scriptural references are found in Romans 13:14; Ephesians 4:22–24; and Colossians 3:12–14.

10. Chambers, *My Utmost for His Highest*, September 14.

11. Hom. VIII in Cant., p. 44, 941c. Quoted in Yves Congar, *I Believe in the Holy Spirit* (New York: The Seabury Press, 1983), 2:77.

12. See Romans 2:6–10. The classic work on this, outside the Scriptures, is C. S. Lewis's essay "Weight of Glory," published in *The Weight of Glory*. See also Fr. John Sheets's introduction to my book on C. S. Lewis, *Real Presence*, in which he explicates this matter of the *weight* of divine glory.

13. Chambers, *My Utmost for His Highest*, April 4.

14. Reardon, *Christ in the Psalms*, 69.

15. Greville MacDonald, M.D., *George MacDonald and His Wife* (New York: Dial Press, 1924), 551. It would be years before I would discover the works of MacDonald (or C. S. Lewis or Oswald Chambers or others), but early on I learned many of the same lessons they so wonderfully point out, and one of them is the extraordinary importance of fatherhood.

16. It is interesting that in obedience I came to faith, and that was before there was any understanding and healing of those infantile wounds. Later I shall speak of the "healing of memories" session when I heard the Lord say, "Forgive your father for dying."

17. C. S. Lewis, *George MacDonald, An Anthology* (Garden City, NY: Doubleday, 1947, 1962), on cover.

18. Ibid., Preface.

19. A classic work on baptism and all that we have lost in the meaning and practice of this vital Sacrament of the church is Alexander Schmemann's *Of Water and the Spirit* (Crestwood, NY: St. Vladimir's Seminary Press, 2000).

Chapter 10 The Lighted Path

The epigraph to this chapter is taken from Forsyth, *The Soul of Prayer*, 30, 22.

1. Ibid., 2.

2. Fr. Patrick Reardon, *Christ in His Saints* (Ben Lomond, CA: Conciliar Press, 2000), 13. For an excellent précis on this topic, see 13–14.

3. Biblical "fear of the Lord," which is the beginning of biblical wisdom, is not a psychological state marked by terror or timidity. Perhaps the correct idea is better conveyed by the word "reverence." Still, the fear of the Lord is far more than the cultivated sentiment of reverence. It is, rather, a resolved dedication

of oneself to the accomplishing of God's will through the industry of obedience. As the Psalm (111:10) says, it is something to be practiced (see Reardon, *Christ in the Psalms*, 221).

4. See especially Romans 12:4–8; 1 Corinthians 12; and Ephesians 4:1–17.

5. These words or impressions are always to be (1) received in great humility knowing our fallibility, and (2) *discerned*, as there are always the voices of the world, the flesh, and the devil to contend with.

6. That would be akin to the occult imitations of God's gifts: the striving and carnal ways of attempting to divine the future (the sin of divination) by looking into glass balls, using tarot cards, and so on.

7. Spiritual lust for power and the spectacular reveals great deficits of meaning in an individual life, in which case one's soul lacks the proper knowledge of truth and reality, the *meaning* to pass on to others.

Chapter 11 Learning Lessons through Spiritual Battle

1. I tell of this experience in *The Healing Presence*, chapter 7.

2. I found the answer with the discovery of *The Secret of Guidance* and *Meet for the Master's Use*.

3. Actually, the healing ministry is simply what the Lord sent the Twelve out to do, and then the seventy-two (see Luke 10). It is what the apostolic Epistles teach and is never to be severed from the ministries of preaching and teaching.

Chapter 12 Foundational Lessons

The epigraph to this chapter is taken from Forsyth, *The Soul of Prayer*, 23.

1. Ibid.

2. See Isaiah 3:7: "In that day he will speak out, saying: 'I will not be a healer.'" The ESV note on this verse says that in the Hebrew, the word *healer* means "binder of wounds."

3. I first wrote about the dire effects of Jung's gnostic psychology in *Real Presence: The Christian Worldview of C. S. Lewis as Incarnational Reality*. I was compelled to write it to show the Christian worldview as C. S. Lewis reveals it, and thereby counter the effects of both Freud's and Jung's psychologies on the church's soul care (i.e., its psychology and ministries of healing, counseling, and Christian formation

classes). See chapter 22, footnote 8, for a full list of my writings about Jung and gnosticism.

4. Translated by Gordon Fee in *God's Empowering Presence: The Holy Spirit in the Letters of Paul* (Peabody, MA: Hendrickson Publishers, 1994), 55.

5. Fee, *God's Empowering Presence*, 170.

6. In church history we see these same things repeated: cults arising when the church has grown lax and, neglecting the full gospel, have withheld from the people the true knowledge and workings of the Holy Spirit.

7. See Reardon, *Christ in His Saints*, 35. See all of chapters 1 and 2: "Repentant Saints" and "Saints in Need of Improvement."

8. For more on this, see Payne, *Restoring the Christian Soul through Healing Prayer,* chapter 9, the section entitled "The Need to Acknowledge the 'Bad Guy' Within," 143–46. See also Reardon, *Christ in His Saints*, chapters 1 and 2: "Repentant Saints" and "Saints in Need of Improvement."

9. For more on this, see *The Healing Presence*, chapter 12, "Introspection versus True Imagination." See also *Restoring the Christian Soul through Healing Prayer*, 38, 58, 136, 146, 156, 196.

10. When we use holy water in the exorcism prayers, we say, "Let this put you in mind of your baptism."

11. See Schmemann, *Of Water and the Spirit*. This is the finest in-depth study of baptism that I've seen.

Chapter 13 The Unthinkable Looms

1. Meyer, *The Secret of Guidance*, 17.

2. I think that Oswald Chambers would laud him as a key figure in his life, for he was impacted by him; and in our time, I believe Dr. Dallas Willard would say something of the same.

Chapter 14 Life at Wheaton Academy

The epigraph to this chapter is taken from Forsyth, *Soul of Prayer,* 19.

1. For a fuller account see *Restoring the Christian Soul through Healing Prayer*, 166–69.

2. Payne, *The Broken Image*, 109–15.

3. See Papers of Reuben Archer Torrey III, collection 331, Billy Graham Center, Wheaton College. See http://www.wheaton.edu/bgc/archives/GUIDES/331.htm.

4. At the time of this writing, Wayne Kraiss is president of Vanguard University in Costa Mesa, California.

5. I first wrote of this in chapter 6 of *Restoring the Christian Soul through Healing Prayer.*

Chapter 15 The Birthplace of Renewal

1. I have written previously about Fr. Winkler and the prayer circle in my book *Listening Prayer*. The paragraphs that follow are adapted from that book, chapter 12.

2. Reardon, *Christ in the Psalms*, 7.

3. McCandlish Phillips was a dedicated Christian and a grateful recipient of the Lord's blessings through the very renewal he described. Later he wrote the insightful book, *The Bible, the Supernatural, and the Jews.*

4. This paragraph was adapted from *Listening Prayer*, 190.

Chapter 16 Choosing a Goal

1. Out of attempting to help these students and verbalize my concerns to some of my teachers came the impetus behind the writing of *Real Presence: The Holy Spirit in the Works of C. S. Lewis.*

2. And when it was finally broken, it was gone in a day! I remember the day, and the very sermon that broke the power of that cynicism.

3. Alexander Pope, *Essay on Criticism*, 1711, part ii, line 15.

Chapter 17 The Joy of Academe

1. See *The Healing Presence*, chapter 7 "Incarnational Reality," for the way I symbolized this knowledge to keep it always before my eyes, 89–99, especially 99.

2. In philosophical terms, Josef Pieper, the great interpreter of Thomas Aquinas, explains superbly these ways of apprehending the unseen realities: "Contemplation is a form of knowing arrived at not by thinking but by seeing, intuition. It is not co-ordinate with the *ratio*, with the power of discursive thinking, but with the *intellectus*, with the capacity for 'simple intuition.' Intuition is without doubt the perfect form of knowing. For intuition is knowledge of what is actually present; the parallel to seeing with the senses is exact. Thinking, on the other hand, is knowledge of what is absent, or may be merely the effort to achieve

such knowledge. . . ." (Josef Pieper, *Happiness and Contemplation*, trans. Richard and Clara Winston [South Bend, IN: St. Augustine's Press, 1998], 74.)

3. He eventually became president of Gordon-Conwell Seminary.

4. When a city would fall, the inhabitants would build over the rubble so that a new city would rise on this mound or Tel.

5. Qumran is where the Dead Sea Scrolls were found.

6. The library facilities were the American Schools of Oriental Research, Palestine Archaeological Museum, Hebrew University, and Ecole Biblique.

7. The Ta'amari were the discoverers of the Dead Sea Scrolls, and this improved their economic conditions.

8. Also with us were others from outside the group, including priest archaeologists from Ecole Biblique, a priest from Ceylon, and teachers from both the American School of Oriental Research and the American School of Holy Land Studies.

9. There is much to be found on the Internet, which we had studied before coming, about the extraordinary history of the place.

10. The stone was moved to Edinburgh Castle in 1996, where it is kept when not needed for coronations.

11. I write of this in chapter 6 of *Restoring the Christian Soul*, 74–76.

Chapter 18 Modern Myth with Professor Kilby

The epigraph to this chapter is quoted from a 1970 class handout.

1. For more understanding on myth as a literary genre, see C. S. Lewis, "Myth Became Fact," chapter 5 in *God in the Dock: Essays on Theology and Ethics* (Grand Rapids: Eerdmans, 1970). See as well Lewis's preface to *George MacDonald: An Anthology*; Clyde Kilby, *The Christian World of C. S. Lewis* (Grand Rapids: Eerdmans, 1964); and Edmund Fuller, Clyde S. Kilby, Russell Kirk et al., *Myth, Allegory and Gospel: An Interpretation of J. R. R. Tolkien, C. S. Lewis, G. K. Chesterton, Charles Williams*, ed. John Warwick Montgomery (Minneapolis: Bethany Fellowship, 1974).

2. Mercia Eliade, *Myth of the Eternal Return: Cosmos and History* (Princeton, NJ: Princeton University Press, 1971). My two profound experiences with time were something

that C. S. Lewis and the great thinkers of old understood and even wrote about.

3. Chad Walsh, *C. S. Lewis: Apostle to the Skeptics* (New York: Macmillan, 1949).

4. Clyde S. Kilby, *The Christian World of C. S. Lewis*, 5.

5. For more on the true imagination, see Payne, *The Healing Presence*, part 3, "Imagery and Symbol," and especially chapter 11, "The True Imagination."

6. For much more on this, see the appendix to my book *Real Presence*, a book about the Holy Spirit and incarnational reality in the works of C. S. Lewis.

7. I write at some length about this theological problem and its results in chapter 13 of *The Healing Presence*, "Incarnational Reality and What It Means to Carry the Cross."

8. For more written by Dr. Montgomery see Fuller, Kilby, Kirk et al., *Myth, Allegory and Gospel*.

9. In chapter 11 of *The Healing Presence*, I tell of this experience under the section "Religious and Poetic Awe." There I also warn that this, as with all true experience, has its unfortunate counterpart in the world of darkness. In chapter 12 of *Listening Prayer*, I write on the various ways God speaks to His children and mention this under number 5: "Angels." I recommend that you read number 8: "Dreams and Visions," as well as the section under simply "Vision."

Chapter 19 Revival!

1. Many who read these pages will know them as Fr. Conlee and Signa Bodishbaugh, through Conlee's pastorate and his and Signa's "Journeys into Wholeness," as well as their faithful and extraordinary ministry with our Pastoral Care Ministry schools. Signa, in her book, *The Journey to Wholeness in Christ* (Grand Rapids: Chosen Books, div. of Baker, 1997) describes this first meeting as she experienced it.

2. In cases such as hers, we often find that the woman has experienced sexual abuse in her childhood, and a demon entered at that point, later causing physical problems, such as severe pain or barrenness.

3. For a good overview of the Phoenix as the symbol of Christ, see Louis Charbonneau-Lassay, *The Bestiary of Christ*, translated and abridged by D. M. Dooling (NY: Parabola Books, 1991), 441–52.

Chapter 20 "In the Night My Heart Instructs Me"

The epigraph to this chapter is taken from *Letters of C. S. Lewis*, ed. W. H. Lewis (New York: Harcourt Brace & World, 1966), (21 December 1941), par. 3, p. 197.

1. It was later named the Marion E. Wade Center.

2. These papers are part of "The Leanne Payne Papers," Wheaton College Library Archives.

3. The subtitle was later changed to "The Christian Worldview of C. S. Lewis as Incarnational Reality" and so it is subtitled today.

4. For more on this, see "Listening to Our Dreams," the appendix of *The Broken Image* in which I write about resolving the writer's block.

5. Fr. Martin d'Arcy, *New York Times Book Review*, July 31, 1960; quoted from George Sayer, *Jack: C. S. Lewis and His Times* (London: Macmillan, 1988), 237.

6. Much of the above paragraphs is adapted from "Listening to our Dreams," the appendix of *The Broken Image*, where I write at some length of this experience.

7. Agnes Sanford writes about the healing of memories throughout her books and so do I. See a lengthy discussion in *Restoring the Christian Soul*.

8. This is always the way it has been: no sooner is a book being finished, than a new one is birthed in me, and the creative urge is such that I never quite learned to rest in between!

Part 4

This epigraph is taken from Franz Peter Schubert, *Deutsche Messe*. For a recording of it: *Rediscovered Masterpieces*, vol. II, by the Cathedral Singers and Chamber Orchestra, Richard Proulx, conductor.

Chapter 21 The Search for Home

1. See Agnes Sanford, *Oh Watchman* (Philadelphia: J. B. Lippincott, 1951).

2. Elizabeth was from Church of the Savior in Washington, DC, and wrote about Christian community and service to the poor. A part of the Faith at Work movement, she lived in poverty and died on October 17, 1998.

3. A special charism of love surely characterized Archbishop Camara. I was heartened to see that his theology is *not* to be identified with what later emerged as "liberation theology."

Chapter 22 Beauty and Truth in the Midst of Spiritual Battle

1. See my book, *Listening Prayer*, chapter 12, for the differing supernatural ways God speaks.

2. See chapter 12, "The Gift of Battle," in *Restoring the Christian Soul*. Through the years, I've received many letters from folk set free after learning to pray for a close family member who has irrationally become their most implacable enemy. The prayer that the Lord gave me I named the "Painting the Dragon Red" prayer, one that many now have learned to pray.

3. Morton Kelsey, *The Other Side of Silence: A Guide to Christian Meditation* (New York: Paulist Press, 1976), 111.

4. See chapters 8–12 of *The Healing Presence* for the lectures on these matters. They are titled: "Perceiving God Aright," "Imagery and Symbol: The Imagery Really Matters," "The Terrible Schism in the Heart of Man," "The True Imagination,"and "Introspection versus True Imagination."

5. Many valid ministries do not persevere through these testings, and that is why I write of it here, hoping some will be helped and encouraged in reading this.

6. See Hebrews 5:8: "Although he [Christ] was a son, he learned obedience through what he suffered"; and Hebrews 5:14: "But solid food is for the mature, for those who have their powers of discernment trained by constant practice to distinguish good from evil."

7. See Leanne Payne and Kevin Perotta, "The Unconscious Confusions of Christian Jungianism," *Pastoral Renewal*, May 1988.

8. See *Real Presence: The Christian Worldview of C. S. Lewis as Incarnational Reality* and especially the appendix, "The Great Divorce" (between good and evil), 159, on Lewis's brilliant orthodoxy in contrast to any and all attempts to marry good and evil. His position is the biblical one, stated poetically below in *The Pilgrim's Regress* (177), that we must become:

. . . as glass
To let the white light without flame, the Father pass
Unstained.

In a later book, *The Healing Presence*, chapter 14, "Renouncing False Gods and

Appropriating the Holy," I treat Jung's thought most fully as the gnosticism that it is and write about the "phallic" (Baal) worship that it leads to. I show how his doctrines, from their very inception, are predicated on an actual insinuation of the obscene into the holy, a kind of black mass played out on the plane of the soul.

In *The Broken Image*, see especially "The Appendix: Listening to our Dreams." In *Crisis in Masculinity*, I wrote of the true masculine and the true feminine, and in the appendix, the psychiatrist, Dr. Jeffrey Satinover, a Jungian scholar and past president of the Jungian Society, shows the major problems with Jung's formulation of the *anima* and the *animus*, the masculine and the feminine within man and woman.

In *Restoring the Christian Soul*, the critical need we have for the affirmation of ourselves as persons, as men and women, is set over and against Jung's self-actualization.

Listening Prayer is a book on the ways God speaks to His people and the differing ways His people hear the word He is always speaking. In contrast, I warn of *gnostic listening*, listening to words that come, not from God but from the world, the flesh, and the devil. These are the words that not only delude but are the stuff out of which false prophets and occultists arise. By just such "listening" and interpretation of his own dreams, Jung deemed God to be both good and evil.

As I write, two valuable books are on the market, one showing how C. S. Lewis, the great voice of Christian orthodoxy in our time, answers Freud: Dr. Armand M. Nicholi Jr., *The Question of God: C. S. Lewis and Sigmund Freud Debate God, Love, Sex, and the Meaning of Life* (New York: Free Press, 2002). The other is Michael D. Aeschliman, *The Restitution of Man: C. S. Lewis and the Case against Scientism* (1983: reprint, Grand Rapids: Eerdmans).

9. Charles Coffin, 1736, see verse 4.

Chapter 23 An Abundance of Seeds to Sow

1. I tell of this incident in *The Healing Presence*, 33.

2. See *The Broken Image*, 142.

3. See Agnes Sanford, *Creation Waits* (Plainfield, NJ: Logos International, n.d.), 1–3.

4. The Eternal Child, "the child of the pure unclouded brow, and dreaming eyes of wonder." See *The Healing Presence*, chapter 12, the

section "Being and Creation," where I write of both Dr. Kilby and Agnes, 188–92.

5. Sanford, *Creation Waits*, 1.

6. Ibid.

7. "I am the bread of life; whoever comes to me shall not hunger, and whoever believes in me shall never thirst" (John 6:35).

Chapter 24 The Year at Yale

1. Søren Kierkegaard (1813–55), Danish philosopher and theologian.

2. Ludwig J. Wittgenstein (1889–1951), Austrian philosopher.

3. Henri Nouwen, "Silence, the Portable Cell," *Sojourners*, July 1980.

4. Dom Gregory Dix, *The Shape of the Liturgy* (London: Dacre Press, 1945, 1978), xii.

5. A fellowship group for Christian professional artists that no longer exists.

6. Francis McNutt, a leader in the Schools of Pastoral Care, left the Roman Catholic priesthood to marry. It was a grief to many, whether Catholic or Protestant, in that his impact for good on Catholic clergy and bishops had been worldwide before that.

7. See Bob Slosser, *Miracle in Darien* (Plainfield, NJ: Logos, 1979) for the story of St. Paul's.

8. C. S. Lewis's understanding of this comes out briefly but wonderfully in his novel *That Hideous Strength*.

9. See William L. Vaswig, *I Prayed, He Answered* (Minneapolis: Augsburg Fortress, 1977).

Chapter 25 Interlude

The epigraph to this chapter is taken from Michael O'Laughlin, *God's Beloved: A Spiritual Biography of Henri Nouwen* (Maryknoll, NY: Orbis Books, 2004), 2.

1. Michael Ford, *Wounded Prophet: A Portrait of Henri J. M. Nouwen* (New York: Random House, 2002).

2. I am especially sensitive to people who wrongly (narcissistically) draw attention to themselves when teaching or preaching, or to actors on stage who have a poor stage presence. In fact the embarrassment that I feel for them is so keen that I make sure of the quality of stage presentations before I go. I never heard anyone else speak of Henri's physical movements as he communicated to his audience in any other way than to compliment them highly.

3. The unborn infant is aware of the fears and emotions of the mother, and in prayer for healing of memories, these are uncovered and brought into the healing light of Christ's presence.

Chapter 26 Joy in the Midst of Incorporation

1. Most of this has so stood the test of time that I still use it today. Ivy Upton's generosity paid not only for the home but for the furniture as well.

2. From that time forward, however, I have been unable to do anything but light housework or lifting. With good massage and chiropractic therapy, I very gradually, over two decades, regained the ability to raise my arms normally.

3. This is why it seems so miraculous that I could continue in ministry, now far, far past retirement age.

4. Lucy is as determined and remarkable a soul as I've ever known: once she knows what to search for, she finds it, and everyone around her benefits. At this writing, she is eighty-six years of age and yet continues in her ministry of intercessory and healing prayer. Ted is now bedridden, but his face shines with the light of God; his skin is remarkably smooth and young, his blue eyes full of joy! He goes in and out of sleep and often awakens singing joyfully to the Lord. He is slowly moving toward that day when the holy angels will come for him. In the meantime, Lucy runs a veritable hospital in her home, planning and overseeing all his care—a class act if ever I saw one.

5. Many people will immediately know the names Patsy Casey and Connie Boerner, who were our treasured music leaders in PCM for many years, and who still attend with us on the team all these years later.

6. The convent is now a Lutheran college.

7. The conversation was taped, and Connie's statement neatly tied together much of what Patsy and Lucy had said earlier.

8. Forsyth, *The Soul of Prayer*, 35.

9. One of these, John Fawcett, later led the music ministry in PCM and never fails to rise up and call her blessed.

10. *The Flight from Woman* (New York: The Noonday Press, div. of Farrar, Straus, and Giroux, 1965). He also wrote *The Pillar of Fire*, and *The Third Revolution: A Study of Psychiatry and Religion*.

11. This gift from Fr. Sheets parallels the gift I received from the young woman who gave me the copy of Dr. Frank Lake's book when I was writing *The Broken Image* (see chapter 22).

12. I've written about gender in all of my books, but here are some references to start with: Besides the whole of *Crisis in Masculinity*, see *The Healing Presence*, chapter 9, "Imagery and Symbol," the section "As Persons the Imagery Really Matters," p. 150 in the Baker edition. See as well *The Healing Presence*, p. 256ff, for more on Karl Stern's book *The Third Revolution: A Study of Psychiatry and Religion*.

Chapter 27 "For Such a Time as This"

The epigraph to this chapter is taken from *Book of Common Prayer*, Collect for October 18, adapted version by Phyllis Tickle, *The Divine Hours: Prayers for Autumn and Wintertime* (New York: Doubleday, 2000), 42–43.

1. One understands the true feminine only in its relation to the true masculine, and for a quick basic understanding of gender, I recommend *Crisis in Masculinity*, chapter 4, "What Is Masculinity?", chapter 5, "The Polarity and Complementarity of the Sexes," and chapter 6, "Women in Crisis."

2. Fr. Patrick Reardon, "Pastoral Ponderings," May 6, 2007, "Sunday of the Samaritan Woman."

3. Of course for good father figures there is a heightened ministry to those needing a father's affirmation, but there is bane in it as well. The more successful a man is in symbolizing the true masculine, the more inevitably he will attract the psychological transferences we are exploring in this chapter.

4. Mordecai said this to Esther in Esther 4:14 NIV.

5. The "false masculine" can be characterized as a drive toward personal power, one where man's (or woman's) powers of initiation are not under the lordship of Christ.

6. I can say this same thing of men.

7. "The gift of eternity" as Franz Rosenzweig phrases it, quoted by Spengler in "Christian, Muslim, Jew," *First Things*, October 2007, 29.

8. David G. Benner, ed., *Baker Encyclopedia of Psychology* (Grand Rapids: Baker, 1985), 1173. Read on in this section for more understanding.

9. To understand these transferences, and to see the havoc these transferences create in Christian groups, see Valerie McIntyre's fine

book, *Sheep in Wolves' Clothing* (Grand Rapids: Baker, 1999).

10. Dr. Vaccaro wrote this to me in a letter.

11. Frank Lake, *Clinical Theology* (1966; reprint, London: Darton Longman and Todd, 1973), xx.

12. See *The Broken Image*, 108ff, especially in regard to homosexual and lesbian behavior related to the failure of the infant to achieve an adequate sense of being; and *Restoring the Christian Soul through Healing Prayer*, chapter 8, "Prolonged Healing of Memories: Abandonment Issues and the Repression of Painful Emotions."

13. Lake, *Clinical Theology*, 405.

14. Hudson Taylor, *A Passion for the Impossible: The Continuing Story of the Mission Hudson Taylor Began* (London: OMF Books, 1965), 5.

15. Chambers, *My Utmost for His Highest*, October 16, 17.

Chapter 28 Jubilation!

The epigraph for this chapter is taken from Forsyth, *The Soul of Prayer*, 35 and the "Te Deum Laudamus," with language modernized by Phyllis Tickle, *The Night Offices* (Oxford University Press, 2006), 268.

1. Reardon, *Christ in the Psalms*, 9–10.

2. "The Leanne Payne Papers," Wheaton College Library Archives.

3. What I do at all times, and especially at such times of weariness, is play CDs of the greatest hymns and sung liturgies from throughout Christian history. When without the strength to raise our voices in praise, we can worship quietly with the great hymn writers, poets, and musicians of all times, e.g., J. S. Bach, Handel, Schubert, Luther, and the Wesleys.

4. Ignaz Franz (1719–1790), "Holy God, We Praise Thy Name," para. of "Te Deum," trans. Clarence Walworth.

5. Michelangelo Buonarroti "To the Supreme Being," trans. William Wordsworth, in *Poems in Two Volumes*, vol. 1, infomotions

.com/etexts/gutenberg/dirs/etext05/pwdw110.htm.

6. Richard Mant (1786–1848), "God My King, Thy Might Confessing," para. of Psalm 145.

7. Eddie Ensley, *Sounds of Wonder: Speaking in Tongues in the Catholic Tradition* (New York: Paulist Press, 1977).

8. Such as we see after prayer for healing of memories in a large group.

9. Ensley, *Sounds of Wonder*, 7–8.

10. Ibid., 10.

11. Ibid., 6, 7, emphasis mine, for before knowing the earlier history, we saw the same in PCM Eucharistic liturgies.

12. Lines from "A Mighty Fortress Is Our God."

13. As Jesus says in John 3:3, "Truly, truly, I say to you, unless one is born again he cannot see the kingdom of God."

14. The Lord's people made holy through Christ's sacrifice and our separation unto Him.

15. Alexander Schmemann, *For the Life of the World* (Crestwood, NY: SVS Press, 1973).

16. See Payne, *Restoring the Christian Soul*, 163–68.

17. This fullness of teaching should make up the content of confirmation classes for children baptized as infants.

18. Schmemann, *Of Water and the Spirit*, 104.

19. I stress this, for much of the church today seems to have forgotten and/or failed to rightly comprehend the importance of this truly great feast day of the church, and the depth on depth of teaching that is to go with it. As an organist long ago, those hymns settled deeply into my soul, and I've long wondered why such a feast often does not call forth the greatest of hymns and sermons.

20. Reardon, *Christ in the Psalms*, 91. For more understanding of the Scriptures on Christ's Ascension, see Fr. Reardon's explications of Psalms 24 and 47; 45–46; 91–92.

Index

Achilles' heel (Leanne's). *See* impulsiveness
activism 97, 107, 114, 258, 288, 294–95
adolescence 59–60, 62–64, 66, 70–73, 80,
    86–87, 133–34, 135–37, 274, 317n6
    (chap. 7)
Alexander, Stella Woolfenden 172–73, 196,
    197, 208, 215
angels 106, 110, 183–84, 190, 196–97, 209,
    218, 290, 299, 301, 306–7, 311, 320n9
    (chap. 18), 323n4 (chap. 26)
Aquinas, St. Thomas 82, 171, 242, 255, 302,
    319n2 (chap. 17)
Aristotle 171
Atkins, Henry 227
Augustine, St. 77, 80, 120, 271, 302, 304

Baal 162, 184, 244, 247, 322n8 (chap. 22)
Bach, J. S. 259, 306, 324n3
baptism 9, 87–89, 117–23, 136, 144, 150, 212,
    252, 309, 318n19, 319n10–11. *See also*
    Holy Spirit, baptism of
Barclay, William 5, 10, 57, 105
Barfield, Owen 190, 191, 211
Beasley, William 265, 275–78
Bennett, Dennis 111, 144
bentness 274–75
Berendsen, Lynn and Paul 279–80, 282, 284
Blanchard, John 128–29, 138, 140
Blanchard, Jonathan 150
Bodishbaugh, Conlee 202, 210, 313, 320n1
    (chap. 19)
Bodishbaugh, Signa 202, 205, 210, 214,
    320n1 (chap. 19)

Boerner, Connie 282–84, 287, 323n5 (chap.
    26), 323n7 (chap. 26)
Broken Image, The (Leanne Payne) 136, 217,
    239–41, 252, 258–60, 266, 269, 271,
    280, 287, 316n1 (chap. 4), 316n3 (chap.
    5), 321n4 (chap. 20), 321n6 (chap. 20),
    322n8 (chap. 22)
Brother Lawrence 95, 104, 317n8 (chap. 9)
Bultmann, Rudolph 161

Cain, Paul 114
Callies, E. W. 92, 118
Camara, Helder 227–28, 321n3 (chap. 21)
cannibal compulsion 252–53
Casey, Mike 286
Casey, Patsy 282–84, 287, 323n5 (chap. 26)
Cather, Willa 37
Chambers, Oswald 72, 82, 84, 86, 130, 298,
    319n2 (chap. 13)
charisms. See Holy Spirit, gifts of
Civil War 47, 48, 50, 51, 52, 55, 59, 316n4
    (chap. 6)
Clarke, Adam 28, 92
Coggan, Donald 241, 264
Cold War 65
Communion, Holy. *See* Eucharist
confession of sin 92–93, 104, 117–20, 216,
    233, 239, 241, 275, 297, 300–301, 308.
    See also repentance
Cooley, Robert E. 175, 267
Cowper, William 142
Crisis in Masculinity, The (Leanne Payne)
    217, 230, 269, 285, 288, 289, 316n1–2

(chap. 4), 322n8 (chap. 22), 323n12
(chap. 26), 323n1 (chap. 27)

deliverance (from demons) 96, 97, 100,
102–4, 107, 112–13, 121, 136, 144, 154,
164, 173, 203, 206, 250, 308–9
demons 101–4, 112, 115, 144–45, 162,
163–64, 172–73, 194–95, 206, 218, 227,
244–45, 266, 320n2 (chap. 19)
Depression, Great 13, 14, 16, 25, 31, 33, 48,
55
Dewey, John 65
Diffee, Agnes White 45
discernment, gift of 48, 91, 95–96, 104,
112–13, 115, 117, 130, 152, 163–64, 218,
242, 244–45, 252, 284, 318n5 (chap. 10),
321n6 (chap. 22)
disease of introspection 317n7 (chap. 7)
Donne, John 10, 77
Dostoyevsky, Fyodor 238
Douglas, Lloyd C. 65
Drury, Edith 225–26, 228–29, 231–32, 247,
256–57

Eliade, Mercia 189, 190
Ensley, Eddie 304
eternal life 28, 33, 82, 85, 250, 276
Eucharist 85, 92, 120–22, 143, 148, 153–55,
201, 204, 213, 221, 227, 252, 260, 263,
265, 309, 316n3 (chap. 17), 324n11
Evil One. See Satan
exhortation 112, 145–46
experience orientation 60–63, 73, 80–81,
86–87, 94, 115, 306. See also subjectivity

Fall, the 21
father (Leanne's). See Mabrey, Robert Hugh
fatherhood, importance of 36, 41, 59, 87,
88–89, 274–75, 318n15
Faub, Robert 304–5
Fawcett, John 323n9 (chap. 26)
Fee, Gordon 114, 267
feminine, true 217, 245, 270–71, 275, 284,
285, 288–89, 292–95, 322n8 (chap. 22),
323n1 (chap. 27)
forgiveness 70, 72, 86, 88, 92–93, 100, 104,
118–19, 120, 139–40, 154, 201, 216–17,
240–41, 253, 258, 287, 308, 318n16
Forsyth, P. T. 23, 27, 29–30, 91, 92, 109, 133,
249, 283–84, 299
Frankl, Viktor 35

Freud, Sigmund 103, 110–11, 120–21, 139,
187, 296, 318n3 (chap. 12), 322n8 (chap.
22)
Frey, William C. 203–5
Fullam, Terry 266

Galloway, Helen 145–46, 153
gender 32, 39, 163, 217, 240, 270–71, 274,
276, 285, 288–89, 292–96, 323n12,
323n1 (chap. 27). See also feminine,
true; masculine, true
Gilbert, Ruth 199–200, 202
glossolalia. See prayer language
gnosticism 111, 115, 187, 194, 225, 241–47,
315n2, 318n3 (chap. 12), 319n3 (chap.
12), 322n8 (chap. 22)
God
call of 9, 10, 20, 21–23, 28, 62, 66, 77,
83–85, 88, 105, 130, 133, 138, 144,
146–47, 160, 187, 217, 220, 224, 230–32,
245, 250, 283, 293–94, 298, 311
presence of 23, 28, 29, 30, 49, 60–62, 80,
85, 87, 91, 94, 95, 97, 103, 104, 112,
114, 117, 122, 145, 146, 154–55, 159–61,
163–64, 172, 174, 193, 202, 204, 210,
213, 217, 218, 227–28, 247, 253, 258,
265, 279, 282, 284, 295, 298, 300, 303,
305–8, 310–11, 316n3 (chap. 7)
obedience to 23, 66–67, 75, 80–87, 91,
95, 97, 119, 121, 138, 146, 159, 166–67,
174, 233, 277–78, 292–95, 298, 310–11,
317n7 (chap. 8), 318n16, 318n3 (chap.
10), 321n6 (chap. 22)
our source 19–22, 270, 285
union with 22, 65, 81–82, 85, 86, 88,
94–95, 97–98
Goudge, Elizabeth 53, 303
grandfather (Leanne's maternal). See
Williamson, James Monroe
grandfather (Leanne's paternal). See Mabrey,
William Thomas
grandmother (Leanne's maternal). See Williamson, Mary Nancy
grandmother (Leanne's paternal). See Mabrey, Rose Fulton
Gray, James 150
Gregory of Nyssa 5, 9, 84

healing 36, 49, 52, 66, 75, 83–85, 87–89, 92,
94–97, 105–7, 109–112, 115, 118–23,
134, 140–41, 143–46, 148–49, 151–55,
163, 166–67, 173–74, 185, 191, 194–95,
200, 203–8, 212–217, 223, 225, 231, 238,

239, 240–43, 244, 247, 250, 252, 254–55, 258, 260, 264–65, 266, 267, 270, 274, 276–78, 280, 290, 291, 293–98, 301, 303, 304–5, 306–10, 318n3 (chap. 11), 321n3 (chap. 12), 321n7 (chap. 20), 323n3 (chap. 25), 323n4 (chap. 26), 324n8. *See also* prayer healing
  of memories 121, 139–40, 185, 215–17, 240, 243, 276, 295, 318n16, 321n7 (chap. 20), 323n3 (chap. 25), 324n12 (chap. 26), 324n8
Healing Presence, The (Leanne Payne) 239, 258, 263, 265, 267, 269–70, 316n2 (chap. 7), 317n7 (chap. 7), 317n5 (chap. 8), 318n1 (chap. 11), 319n9, 319n1 (chap. 17), 320n5 (chap. 18), 320n7 (chap. 18), 320n8 (chap. 18), 321n4 (chap 22), 322n8 (chap 22), 322n1 (chap. 23), 322n4 (chap. 23), 323n12
Hemingway Man, the 72, 127
Hession, Roy 95
hiddenness 153–54, 245, 293–94
Holmer, Paul 259, 263, 270
Holy Spirit 30, 44–45, 49, 60–62, 84, 85–86, 91, 94–97, 99, 101, 104, 105–7, 111–18, 120–21, 128, 135, 138, 140, 143–50, 152, 155, 159, 161–62, 164, 166, 167, 173, 174, 202, 203–4, 207–9, 212, 216, 218, 223, 225, 232, 242, 245, 250, 252, 257, 259, 264, 265, 281–82, 291, 294–95, 299, 301, 302–10, 315n4, 319n6, 320n6 (chap. 18)
  baptism of 30, 60–62, 95, 99, 121, 145–46, 150, 207
  gifts of 30, 49, 60–61, 94–97, 99, 105–7, 111–17, 122–23, 138, 140, 143, 145–50, 155, 161, 164, 166, 167, 173, 203–4, 207–9, 223, 225, 232, 252, 259, 282, 303, 305–6, 310
holy water 121, 135–36, 308, 319n10
homosexuality 114, 163, 239–40, 246, 260, 266, 274, 278, 280, 286–87, 297, 324n12 (chap. 27)
Howard, Thomas 267
Hunt, Holman 61, 80, 86, 185

idolatry 81
imagination, true 62–63, 66, 74, 83, 84, 192, 205, 212, 243, 288–89, 319n9, 319n2 (chap. 17), 320n5 (chap. 18), 321n4 (chap. 21)
Imago Dei 20

impulsiveness 17, 22–23, 34–35, 53, 64, 66–67, 69–74, 75, 80, 82, 84, 130, 171
Incarnation, the 21
incarnational reality 86–88, 95, 97–98, 99–104, 109, 117, 120, 121–22, 164, 213, 226, 243, 253, 307, 315n4, 319n1 (chap. 17), 320nn6–7 (chap. 18)

Jesus Christ 5, 9–10, 21, 22, 25, 26, 27, 29, 30, 39, 49, 60, 61–62, 66, 75, 80, 81–83, 85–89, 92, 94–95, 97, 99–102, 103–7, 110, 116, 117, 118–22, 133, 134, 139, 145, 146, 151, 155, 159, 160–61, 163–64, 168, 177, 185, 195, 209, 221, 231, 240, 242, 245, 250–52, 259, 265, 267, 271, 274–78, 280, 282–84, 290, 291, 293, 302, 305, 306, 307, 309, 310, 311, 315n1 (chap. 2), 317n9 (chap. 9), 320n3 (chap. 19), 321n6 (chap. 22), 323n3 (chap. 25), 323n5 (chap. 27), 324nn13–14, 324n20 (chap. 28).
Jesus Prayer, the 146
jubilation 300–7
Jung, Carl 111, 187, 225, 227, 231, 241–47, 318n3 (chap. 12), 319n3 (chap. 12), 322n8 (chap. 12). *See* gnosticism
Jungstinker, Sigmund 226

Kelsey, Morton 225, 243–47
Kempis, Thomas à 95, 245
Kenyon, E. W., 316n3 (chap. 3)
Kierkegaard, Søren 263, 322n1 (chap. 24)
Kilby, Clyde S. 175, 184, 186–87, 189–97, 201, 205, 210, 212, 214, 215, 219, 231, 259, 261, 267
King, Martin Luther 173
Klamecki, Bernie 282
Kraft, Carol 289
Kraiss, Wayne 137–38, 141, 319n4 (chap. 14)
Kundsin, Karl 161

Lake, Frank 240–41, 256, 278, 297–98, 323n11
Laubach, Frank C. 95, 104
Lewis collection (Marion E. Wade Center at Wheaton College) 186–87, 191, 195–97, 210, 211–12, 214, 219
Lewis, C. S. 25, 27, 58, 60–63, 65, 74, 79, 82, 88–89, 138, 152, 159, 175, 184, 186–87, 189–95, 197, 201–2, 205, 206, 210, 211–14, 216, 219, 235, 263, 270, 285, 289, 294, 310n4, 316n1 (chap. 7), 318n3 (chap. 12), 320n2, 320n6 (chap.

18), 321n3 (chap. 20), 321n8 (chap. 22), 322n8 (chap. 22), 322n8 (chap. 24)
listening prayer. *See* prayer, listening
Listening Prayer (Leanne Payne) 22, 317n7 (chap. 8), 317n9 (chap. 9), 319n1, 319n4 (chap. 15), 320n9 (chap. 18), 321n1 (chap. 22), 322n8 (chap. 22)
Little Rock 13, 31, 47, 51, 52, 57, 102, 109, 111, 116, 122, 126, 127, 137, 143, 165, 167, 170, 205, 224, 234, 259
liturgy 45, 74, 85, 92–93, 117–18, 120–22, 144, 150, 153, 185, 221, 252, 264, 304–5, 309–10, 316n3 (chap. 7), 324n3, 324n11
Luther, Martin 136, 161, 306, 324n3

Mabrey, Forrest Irene Williamson (Leanne's mother) 10, 13–17, 19, 20, 22–23, 24, 25–30, 31–34, 36–42, 43–51, 53, 55, 57–59, 64, 67, 69–70, 86, 99–100, 120, 128, 131, 165–67, 183–84, 239
    conversion 16, 25–26, 36, 43–44, 48
    prayer life 28–30
Mabrey, Robert Hugh (Leanne's father) 13–16, 19, 49–53, 55
    death of 13, 15–16, 17, 25, 36, 41–42, 52, 76, 87, 89, 216–17, 316n3 (chap. 6), 318n16
Mabrey, Rose Fulton (Leanne's paternal grandmother) 50–55
Mabrey, William Thomas (Leanne's paternal grandfather) 51–53
MacDonald, George 82, 87, 88–89, 190, 192, 318n15
Marshall, Catherine 37, 137
Mary (mother of Jesus) 21, 116, 164, 277, 284, 288, 292–93
masculine, true 101, 128, 217, 220, 230, 270–71, 275, 285, 288–89, 292–96, 322n8 (chap. 22), 323n1 (chap. 27), 323n3 (chap. 27)
Masons 45
materialism 43, 48–49, 63, 111, 115, 161, 174, 187, 200, 212, 238, 242
McCarthy, Michael 275–76, 278
McIntyre, Valerie 323n9 (chap. 27)
McNutt, Francis 266, 322n6
Meyer, F. B. 35, 43, 84, 94, 103, 128–30, 150
Michelangelo 301
Minns, Martyn 266
Montgomery, John Warwick 195, 250, 320n8 (chap. 18)
Montgomery, L. M. 38
Moody, Dwight L. 129, 150, 161

Moorman, Carolyn Westerfield 93
mother (Leanne's). *See* Mabrey, Forrest Irene Williamson
Murray, Andrew 29

Nelson, Ted 285
Norton, Will 195, 212, 213, 218
Nouwen, Henri 227, 259, 260, 263–66, 269, 273–78, 286, 322n2 (chap. 25)

obedience to God. *See* God, obedience to
O'Connor, Elizabeth 227, 321n2 (chap. 21)
old self, dying to 26, 79–83, 87, 92–93, 117, 119, 121, 246, 308–9, 317n7 (chap. 7). *See also* repentance

Pastoral Care Ministries (PCM) 92, 97, 118, 122, 134, 141, 147–48, 167, 194–95, 251, 252, 259, 265, 271, 280–84, 289–90, 291, 294–95, 296, 298, 300, 303, 304–310, 313, 320n1 (chap. 19), 323n5 (chap. 26)
Payne, J. Barton 175, 176–80, 182–83
Phillips, McCandlish 152–53, 319n3 (chap. 15)
Pieper, Josef 21, 315n4, 317n4 (chap. 9), 317n2 (chap. 17)
Pope, Alexander 165
practice of the presence of God (Jesus) 83–84, 95, 104, 159–60, 164, 174, 252, 264, 283, 307, 317n8 (chap. 9), 322n3 (chap. 25)
prayer 9–10, 16, 20, 22–23, 27, 28–30, 32, 33, 36, 39, 42, 43, 58, 61, 63, 70, 73, 75, 80–81, 84, 85, 86, 88, 91–97, 100–1, 103–4, 105, 107, 109, 111, 112–14, 115–16, 118–20, 126, 127–29, 131, 133–34, 135, 137, 139–40, 141–42, 143–49, 151–54, 160–69, 171–74, 183, 184–87, 194, 195–96, 201, 203, 204–7, 209, 210, 212, 214–19, 223, 225, 226, 227, 229–31, 233–35, 237, 239, 240–41, 244–47, 249–52, 254–61, 264, 265–66, 269, 271–72, 274, 275–78, 279–89, 291–95, 297, 298, 299, 301, 302–3, 306–10, 313, 316n3 (chap. 3), 319n10, 319n1 (chap. 15), 321n2 (chap. 22), 322n8, 323n3 (chap. 25), 323n4 (chap. 26), 324n8. *See also* practice of the presence of God (Jesus)
    healing 42, 84, 88, 106–7, 111, 115, 137, 140, 144–46, 152–53, 166, 194, 206, 212, 223, 231, 233, 241, 244, 252, 264, 265,

266, 271, 280–81, 288, 292, 293–96, 307, 313
intercessory 22, 28–30, 39, 92, 105, 138, 145, 147, 172–73, 194, 201, 203, 271, 283, 286, 313, 323n4 (chap. 26)
listening 9, 20, 23, 62, 75, 81, 85–86, 91, 95, 107, 109, 128, 130, 144–45, 148–49, 153, 159–60, 164, 167, 174, 190, 217, 230, 234, 239, 264, 293, 298, 311, 316n7 (chap. 8), 322n8 (chap. 22)
prayer language 30, 145–48, 152–53, 196–97, 301–2, 303, 304–6
prayer partners 26, 33, 45, 91–92, 94, 100, 104, 130, 136–37, 141, 149, 168, 196, 201, 212, 218, 219, 233, 235, 239, 259, 271–72, 275, 279–80, 282–83, 286, 313
Prince, Derek 285
prophets, false 111, 112–16, 252, 323n8 (chap. 22)
Purdie, Sandy and Gwen 301–2

Real Presence (Leanne Payne) 152, 212–13, 216, 219, 247, 258, 266, 288, 318n12, 318n3 (chap. 12), 319n1 (chap. 16), 320n6 (chap. 18), 321n8 (chap. 22)
Reardon, Patrick Henry 86, 92, 117, 148, 292, 300
Rembrandt 275
renewal. *See* revival
repentance 75–76, 80–83, 89, 92–93, 104, 116, 118–19, 122, 139, 173, 212, 241, 294. *See also* confession of sin; old self, dying to
Restoring the Christian Soul (Leanne Payne) 241, 317n5 (chap. 8), 319nn8–9, 319n1 (chap. 14), 319n5 (chap. 14), 320n11, 321n7 (chap. 20), 321n2 (chap. 22), 322n8 (chap. 22), 324n12 (chap. 27), 324n16 (chap. 28)
revival 26, 45, 60, 85–86, 111–12, 115, 129–137, 143–44, 151, 152–53, 159, 162, 199, 202–5, 206, 208, 209, 212, 213, 216, 223, 225, 232, 241–42, 246, 266, 282, 285, 319n3 (chap. 15)
Rhys, Howard 225, 226, 261
Riffle, Herman and Lillie 216, 217, 233
rift between head and heart 54, 65

Sampson, Gayle 279, 289
Sanford, Agnes 137, 151–52, 215, 216, 217, 224–26, 228–29, 231, 244, 246–47, 250, 252–57, 259, 260–61, 271, 321n7 (chap. 20), 322n4 (chap. 23)

Satan 98, 101, 104, 112, 113, 135, 163–64, 239, 240, 245, 281
Sayer, George 190, 214
Sayers, Dorothy 211
Schlemon, Barbara 216
Schmemann, Alexander 122, 150, 265, 306–7, 309, 318n19
School of Pastoral Care (SPC) 215, 225, 228, 244–45, 257, 259–60
Schrodt, Alvin D. 141
Scofield, C. I. 150
secularism 49, 200. *See also* materialism
self–acceptance 46, 106–7, 274–75
sentimentalism 27, 30
Sheets, John 288, 318n12, 323n11
Shekinah glory. *See* God, His presence
Sheldon, Charles M. 65
Smith, L. B. (Ted) 272, 279, 281–82, 323n4 (chap. 26)
Smith, Lucy 281–84, 287, 323n4 (chap. 26)
Solzhenitsyn, Alexander 237, 238
spiritual warfare 98, 99–107, 111, 115, 148, 159–60, 163–64, 197, 203, 223–24, 237–48, 259–60, 297, 300, 321n2 (chap. 22)
spirituals. See Holy Spirit, gifts of
Stern, Karl 288–89, 294, 323n12
subjectivity 9, 45, 60, 62–63, 66, 73, 74, 80–81, 87, 115, 242. *See also* experience orientation
substitution 194–95, 205–6, 277
symbol of the Holy 45, 73–74, 120, 122, 154, 196, 209, 243

Taylor, Hudson 298
Tolkien, J. R. R. 189–92, 197, 206, 211
tongues, speaking in. *See* prayer language
Torrey, R. A. 94–95, 129, 149–51, 161, 174
Torrey, R. A. III 111, 137, 149–51, 319n3 (chap. 14)
Tozer, A. W. 21
transference, psychological 292, 296–98, 323n3 (chap. 27), 323n9 (chap. 27)
Tyson, Tommy 287

union with God. *See* God, union with
Upton, Ivy 267–69, 280, 283, 286–87, 323n1 (chap. 26)

Vaccaro, Gino 296–97
Vaswig, William 271, 323n1 (chap. 26)

Welsh, Evan 174, 212

Wheaton Academy 128–30, 133–41, 144, 150, 160, 169, 185

Wheaton College 128–29, 138–42, 159–63, 167–70, 171–75, 178–79, 180, 184–86, 189–98, 205, 206–7, 210, 211, 214, 218, 224, 259, 261, 265, 267, 289, 300

Wilkerson, Ralph 250

Williams, Charles 190, 191, 192, 194–95, 205, 206, 211

Williams, J. Rodman 250

Williamson, James Monroe (Leanne's maternal grandfather) 38, 44, 47

Williamson, Mary Nancy (Leanne's maternal grandmother) 15–17, 23, 25, 31–34, 35–42, 44, 46, 47–48, 50, 51, 57–58, 60, 216, 217

Wimber, John 114

Winkler, Richard 137, 143–55, 204, 205, 206, 210, 216, 224, 233, 253–54, 319n1 (chap. 15)

Wittgenstein, Ludwig 263, 270, 322n2 (chap. 24)

word of knowledge 95, 95–96, 166

Wordsworth, William 11, 20

World War I 172

World War II 40, 48, 59, 65, 72, 127, 134

writer's block 39, 210, 213, 216–17, 219, 321n4 (chap. 20)

Yale Divinity School 228, 241, 259–60, 261, 263–269, 271, 277

ALSO AVAILABLE FROM
LEANNE PAYNE

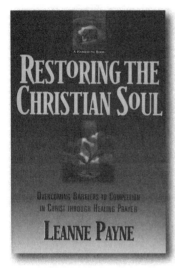

Restoring the Christian Soul

The Healing Presence

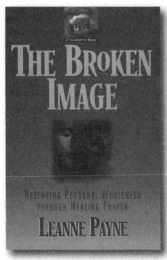

The Broken Image

Listening Prayer

BakerBooks
a division of Baker Publishing Group
www.BakerBooks.com